AF370491

Feminist Philosophy

Feminist Philosophy
Time, History and the Transformation of Thought

Edited by
Synne Myrebøe, Valgerður Pálmadóttir & Johanna Sjöstedt

Södertörns högskola

(CC BY 3.0)
Published under Creative Commons Attribution
3.0 Unported License

© the Authors

Södertörn University
Library
SE-141 89 Huddinge
www.sh.se/publications

The Nordic Summer University
Cover image: Miniatur aus der »Cité des Dames« der
Christine de Pisan, (Master of the City of Ladies, fl. from
1400 until 1415, Public domain,
via Wikimedia Commons).
Cover layout: Jonathan Robson
Graphic form: Per Lindblom & Jonathan Robson

Stockholm 2023

Södertörn Studies in Intellectual and Cultural History 10
Södertörn Academic Studies 94
ISSN 1650-433X

ISBN 978-91-89504-36-3 (print)
ISBN 978-91-89504-37-0 (digital)

Contents

Introduction

Synne Myrebøe, Valgerður Pálmadóttir & Johanna Sjöstedt

Although feminist philosophy is now a recognized field in the institution of philosophy, a tension between the two terms feminism and philosophy persists. Compared to the status of feminism in other disciplines in the humanities and the social sciences, feminist philosophy is generally marginalized in philosophy departments. Similarly, women comprise a smaller portion of the student body and faculty in philosophy in comparison to other disciplines.[1] A great deal of work in feminist philosophy is undertaken in other disciplines, such as literary studies, the history of ideas, gender studies, and sociology.[2] This collection of texts bears witness to the trans-disciplinarity of feminist philosophy or feminist *theory* as some prefer. The anthology is an interdisciplinary initiative at the intersection of philosophy, the history of ideas, and feminist theory where philosophy is scrutinized from a feminist perspective and further asks questions about what philosophy has to offer feminism.

[1] Schwitzgebel, Eric and Dicey Jennings, Carolyn, "Women in Philosophy: Quantitative analysis of specialization, prevalence, visibility, and generational change" in *Public Affairs Quarterly*, Vol. 31, No. 2 April, 2017; Reuter, Martina, "Varf.r s. f. kvinnor? Könsfördelningen inom den akademiska filosofin" in *Tidskrift för politisk filosofi*, Vol. 19, No. 3 (2015).

[2] This can be seen as an indicator that people who are interested in feminist philosophy pursue their philosophical scholarly endeavors in fields other than academic philosophy. Interestingly, in her critique of the male dominated philosophical canon, Mary Ellen Waithe has argued that throughout history, women's philosophical works have been classified as belonging to disciplines other than philosophy and they have thus been omitted from what we understand as the Western philosophical tradition i.e. the philosophical canon. Mary Ellen Waithe, "Sex, Lies, and Bigotry: The Canon of Philosophy" in Sigridur Thorgeirsdottir and Ruth E. Hagengruber (eds.), *Methodological Reflections on Women's Contribution and Influence in the History of Philosophy* (Springer, 2020).

Concepts, Contexts, Critique

Philosophy can be described as a tradition of texts, questions, and concepts. It is a discipline with a long history and it has a rich tradition of dialogue with historical thinkers. As philosopher Andrea Nye has pointed out: "thinking necessarily uses concepts with roots in the past. Always in language, thinking is a reshaping, never an original creation."[3] This simple observation highlights the connection between thinking and language and the importance of taking into consideration the historical context of both the production and the reception of thinking. Critique, finally, refers to feminist scholarship as a transformative practice aimed at change and emancipation. In bringing these notions together, the anthology creates a space for dialogues on feminist practices of reading. Following a feminist tradition, reading is to be considered as a political act with close connections to feminist activism.

According to Nye, there are three main strands in the works and methods of feminist philosophy, the first of which is a critical examination of the exclusion of women from the ranks of philosophers as well as outright misogyny and racism in canonical texts. The second has to do with a revision of the canon with respect to gender; a vast body of literature now exists in which historical women philosophers have been acknowledged as thinkers in their own right.[4] The third strand concerns questions about the possibility of problematizing the very conceptual foundations of modern philosophy in light of critical readings of standard texts and contemporary feminist perspectives. In addition to these three strategies discussed by Nye, there is a growing interest in a productive re-reading and actualization of the history of philosophy for new and creative feminist applications.[5]

Feminist theory understood as an interdisciplinary tradition of texts that interrogates gender, sexuality, and other similar

[3] Andrea Nye, *Feminism and Modern Philosophy. An Introduction,* (New York: Routledge, 2004), p. ix.
[4] See for example Mary Ellen Waithe, *A history of women philosophers* (Vol. 4), (Dordrecht, Boston, Lancaster: Martinus Nijhoff Publishers, 1987–1994).
[5] Nye, 2004. p. x.

categories in critical perspectives, has a rather paradoxical relationship to time and history. If philosophy, as Finnish feminist philosopher and historian of ideas Tuija Pulkkinen points out in the first chapter of this anthology, generally takes an omnipresent ahistorical point of view, feminist theory rather tends to stress what Donna Haraway calls "situated knowledges": the historical, the local, which are first and foremost concerned with questions of transformation.[6] However, the emphasis of historical situatedness is not necessarily matched by an awareness of or interest in the historicity of the concepts that are employed in making such claims. Rather, with the aim of changing oppressive conditions, feminist theory runs the risk of overemphasizing the present and the future at the expense of the past. A similar point is made by Ingeborg W. Owesen who maintains that "contemporary feminist theory is largely oriented towards the present" and that the philosophical history of modern feminism has not received much scholarly attention. This intellectual history of feminist theory, Owesen concludes, "might reveal itself as a valuable source for contemporary feminism in as much as there are several parallels between the arguments of the past and those of the present."[7] We tend to agree with Owesen on this matter, and we also want to emphasize our view that feminist theory needs the modes of reflection developed in the humanities in general and in disciplines such as philosophy, the history of ideas and literary studies specifically. This anthology provides both empirical and theoretical interrogation in this domain.

The chapters in this volume are divided into five thematic parts. Arguing that the tensions between feminism and philosophy should be considered productive conditions for thinking, this anthology demonstrates the transformative potential of feminist philosophy in history, art and in knowledge regimes. The multiple angles, perspectives, interrogations, and applications of feminist philosophy invites openings of understanding

---

[6] Donna Haraway, "Situated Knowledges. The Science Question in Feminism and the Privilege of Partial Perspective" in *Feminist Studies*, (Vol. 14, No. 3, Fall 1988).

[7] Ingeborg W. Owesen, *The Genealogy of Modern Feminist Thinking: Feminist Thought as Historical Present*, (London and New York: Routledge, 2021), p. 1.

and further elaborations for future inquiry. The multiple angles, perspectives, interrogations, and applications of feminist philosophy invites openings of understanding and further elaborations for future inquiry.

Part 1
Feminist Philosophy in the Present Tense

In the opening chapter **Tuija Pulkkinen** reflects on the relationship between philosophy and feminist scholarship with respect to time. Philosophy is underpinned by *omnitemporality,* the notion that thinking is atemporal in nature, engaging with a 2500-year-old history and tradition of texts without necessarily taking into consideration the circumstances in which the texts were written. Feminism, on the other hand, emerged as an academic endeavour in the 1970s and is permeated by an acute awareness of the situatedness of the claims made in its name. Omnitemporality is rarely seen; its very rationale is political, and because of that "feminist research is crucially dependent on the idea of historical change". Moreover, the disciplines are situated differently in relation to truth. While philosophy aims for ahistorical truth, Pulkkinen argues, the project of feminism is rather to undermine (false) claims to universal truth and to demonstrate how patriarchal beliefs have excluded women and others from being considered as subjects of knowledge. However, Pulkkinen also traces points of convergence; by virtue of its claim to being beyond politics, philosophy in some circumstances attains a particular critical force to take a stand in political issues.

A central concern for feminist philosophy is historiographical and philosophical conceptions of time and temporality. In her chapter, "Desiring Difference and the Hierarchies of Time", **Kristina Fjelkestam** addresses the problems with conceptualizations of time and history that have their origins in Western modernity. Without approaching history through binary positions of similarity or difference, Fjelkestam highlights these positions as desirable narratives that need to be challenged.

Departing from discussions of power and politics in critical temporality studies, and in dialogue with queer temporality studies and political theories on affects, Fjelkestam emphasizes the affective and somatic aspects of historiography. Thus, understandings of temporality not only constitute conceptions of the past, but also how difference is conceptualized in the present within a hierarchical structure. Through an exposition of different theoretical perspectives on affect and temporality, the last decades' discussions on chrononormativity, erotohistoriography and anachronism, positions of interpretive precedence are un-tied in favor of pluralistic temporalities that show "a multidimensional model of the desire for the past".

In her chapter, "The Demands of the Historical Unconscious – the psychopathology of history", **Sara Edenheim** challenges the "liberal humanist orientation in [most] versions of historical research," which postulates 'historical consciousness' as its main objective. Edenheim specifically targets a perspective that was introduced by German historians of didactics in the 1970s, which, according to her, conflates *historical* consciousness with *human consciousness*. According to Edenheim, this perspective entails that "the aim of historical consciousness is to fill [the past, present and future] with recognizable contents, coherency, and common sense that all make a claim on reality". Edenheim makes the point that in Germanic languages 'common sense' literally means sane- or healthy sense and that our search for progressive narratives and coherence between past, presence and future is a pathological holding on to "sameness" i.e., "identity". In Edenheim's account, this pathological search for historical meaning forecloses other ways of approaching the past. She argues instead that we should approach the present as the emergency that it is, with all the dangers that this implies.

Naomi Scheman traces the questions posed in modern philosophy back to the historical conditions that produced them. In her chapter "The problems with the problems of philosophy: Challenging Euro-Modernity", she finds that philosophy's questions are the expression of changing power structures and are marked by the emerging democratic efforts to reconceive political coexistence. Tearing philosophical authority from institutions, and placing it within the idea of a generic individual, the individual of modern philosophy was marked by an idea of sameness, equated to a white European, bourgeois male, producing women, queers, indigenous, and colonial subjects as its others. While rooted in specific historical and political conditions, the problems of philosophy have in contemporary academic philosophy lost their historical specificity and are considered timeless problems. As such, they can neither be "solved" – whatever a solution means – nor are they put to the side. The result, Scheman writes, is that we are left with "zombie problems: the life sucked out of them, they stalk the halls of academe, undead unkillable". In contrast to the image of philosophy as the pursuer of eternal truth beyond the various historical and political entanglements, according to Scheman, philosophy ought to reflect on precisely those empirical conditions, if it is to be relevant in today's world. Scheman suggests that philosophers, whether they choose to acknowledge it or not, are "always already engaged". Black Power, queer activism, indigenous cultures, have "emphasized the depth of difference and the resources of differences for knowing and acting", and Scheman argues that we should embrace "diversity as an epistemic and political resource, not a problem to be surmounted".

Part 2
Transformations in Time

The second theme concerns different aspects of women as thinkers, as philosophers, and as producers of texts and ideas: What kind of thinking becomes canonized and integrated into tradition, what kind of ideas deserve the epithet philosophy? How and in what way have women's scholarly and literary work been interpreted, categorized, and archived? These questions are related to the historical, social, and material conditions of thought and of thinking.

In her chapter "Suppose a man be in a deep contemplative study: Margaret Cavendish, Descartes' cogito and the freedom of thought", **Cecilia Rosengren** discusses the thought of early modern British philosopher Margaret Cavendish (1623–1673) and asks whether she should be counted among the society of feminist philosophers. Writing in a period when the personae of the philosopher, the scientist, and the public speaker were coded masculine, yet being reconfigured by the emergence of the idea of the layman philosopher, the printing press, and the public sphere, Rosengren demonstrates how Cavendish through rhetorical strategies navigated the conventions connected to gender and speaking and arrogated to herself the right to a philosophical voice. Cavendish's thought is situated in relation to influential intellectual currents in her time and Rosengren demonstrates how she enters the debate both with Descartes' rationalism and the empiricism of the Royal Society. Cavendish was critical of the Cartesian mechanistic worldview yet proposed a modified version of rationalism that also incorporated the senses. She also criticized what she saw as the unfounded optimist belief in the senses and scientific experiments of the empiricists and emphasized that reason had to evaluate the experience. Rosengren suggests that Cavendish produced an early critique of the "view from nowhere" and that her natural philosophy articulates a feminist ethos.

In **Helgard Mahrdt's** chapter "Hannah Arendt: To think 'without banisters'", thinking as a political act is in question. For can there be – as Mahrdt asks with Arendt – "a thinking without being tyrannical"? Departing from this dilemma of political theory, the chapter explores how Arendt approaches the difficult task of thinking after the experience of WWII. Through Mahrdt's work, we are introduced to a range of the practical events in which Arendt laid out her trains of thought. Inspired by Walter Benjamin's "Concepts of History", Arendt argues that the past can be nothing but fragmented in the present imagery, whereby what is needed is "a thinking that is poetical". Practicing this performative *poiesis*, Marhrdt explains how Arendt, in her rejection of the history of ideas and political philosophy, turns to experience, storytelling, and imagination as the site of political plurality. Here, Mahrdt makes a distinction between a liberal notion of plurality and Arendt's emphasis on pluralism as intersubjective experiences. Thinking without banisters is a fragile act of orientation but also what Arendt has presented as *relating* without subordination.

In her article "Reflections on the Feminist Archive The case of the Bibliothèque Marguerite Durand", **Marta-Laura Cenedese** discusses the conditions for the production of feminist knowledge and history using an archive as a case in point. Built by French actress, journalist, and collector Marguerite Durand (1864–1936), who founded the feminist daily newspaper *La Fronde*, the archive is the only one of its kind in the French context. Collecting material dating back to the 17th century, it consists of 60 000 documents that relate to women and the fight for women's rights: for example, letters by Colette and Mme de Staël. The chapter accounts for how the library was threatened to be closed and moved to become a part of the regular library system of Paris; thereby assimilating to the patriarchal norms of knowledge that had made it necessary in the first place. It also discusses the ultimately successful campaign to restore it and the politics of knowledge involved. Cenedese emphasizes the library as a physical, affective space that makes possible a connection between the past, the present, and the future and between generations of women. She argues that the library could be an example of what Griselda Pollock calls "contexts populated by many women", where each woman might develop her singularity in a shared space.

Part 3
Transformations in Artistic Representations

A central concern for feminist philosophy is to trace thoughts that have been excluded from the *ratio* constituting the philosophical canon. For this, questions of art come to the fore. In "Possessing the Past. Revisiting (a feminist) Swedish 19th Century in Contemporary Fiction", **Claudia Lindén** discuss how fiction plays a central role in the formation of historical consciousness and how the historical novel can facilitate a deconstructive stance to History that highlights its narrative structure. Hence, referring to William Godwin, Lindén shows that the idea that historical novels have a potential for critical historiography is part of a British tradition that long precedes late 20th century's theories on deconstruction. In her article, Lindén sets Derrida's concept of hauntology in dialogue with Godwin's remarks on fiction as history. Following this, Lindén invites her readers to see "how the past is not only stuck in the past but continues to live on and affect us in the present". Thus, what is at stake in the play between fiction and history is not only conceptions of the past, but also of our own contemporality. Lindén gives examples on how the fictional narrative of progress and modernization becomes part of a national identity in Sweden. But contrary to mainstream history writing, the historical novel has been at the forefront of highlighting the importance of women and minorities. Lindén shows how historical novels have functioned as a critical historiography that distributes knowledge on women's role in history to a wider audience. As such, fiction exposes a feminist consciousness and a re-writing of a gendered historical narrative that haunts the present.

The Sophoclean figure Antigone has been actualized in various situations as an omnitemporal image of political resistance. In her chapter "Fantastic Antigones: The Tragic Legacy of Trans Grief", **Fanny Söderbäck** sheds light on the denial of grief as experienced by trans women and exposed in Sebastián Lelio's 2017 film *A Fantastic Woman* (*Una mujer fantástica*). Here, the character of Antigone defies the death that is imposed on her by those who refuse to recognize her as a woman in grief. At the same time, Söderbäck opens for a transgression of a cis-interpretation of Antigone and thus offers queer imagery of Antigone as a temporal yet omnitemporal figure of ethico-political concern.

In the chapter "Haunting Histories: Regarding the political unconscious in the television series *Stranger Things* and the film *Ghostbusters*," **Erik Poulsen** analyzes and contrasts two works of popular culture produced in 2017 and 1984 respectively. Basing his analysis on psychoanalytic theory, Poulsen highlights the unconscious desires at work in both productions. In a comparison of the two works, Poulsen argues that feminism has had considerable influence on film production in the 21st century. For example, while Ghostbusters (1984) is filled with heteronormative anxiety concerning gender expressions and women's excessive sexual desire, *Stranger Things'* (2017) seemingly apolitical and nostalgic outlook (the series takes place in 1984) nevertheless expresses a desire to correct the past in terms of how "we *wish* that it would have been" according to contemporary ideas about gender, sexuality, and representation.

Part 4
Transforming Knowledge Regimes

A growing literature on feminist epistemologies has challenged hegemonic preconditions for knowledge and truth. Questions on epistemic structures have been a recurrent theme in feminist philosophy. In understanding the social, historical, temporal, and spatial aspects of knowledge production, epistemic normativity is challenged from several perspectives. In the following sequence, the chapters are in different ways concerned with the ways in which feminist critique has been, and can be a part of, academic practice broadly speaking. This includes both discussions about and within feminist theory, as well as feminist philosophical engagements with current socio-cultural issues.

In her chapter "Paradox of stubbornness: The epistemology of stereotypes regarding women", **Sagy Watemberg Izraeli** appropriates American analytic philosopher Willard Quine's classical essay "Two dogmas of empiricism" to present an epistemology of stereotypes. Izraeli's point of departure is the fact that stereotypes persist in the face of contrary evidence. What are the epistemic mechanisms which enable conflict between the stereotype and the evidence, and between the stereotype and other knowledge? What is the epistemic source of stereotypes? Quine has proved useful because, although an empiricist, he shifts the question of verification of knowledge from adequacy between knowledge and reality, to internal coherence within the body of knowledge. This opens a space for other influences as to how knowledge is constituted. It is this space in which the chapter situates itself. Izraeli argues that stereotypes are both social and individual and that they "do not originate from empirical evidence but are rather a socially constructed mechanism for the processing and use of empirical evidence". Izraeli also discusses what it would take to change the conceptual schemes that underpin stereotypes, suggesting that a collective effort might produce a critical mass of pressure that could reach a tipping point, thereby exposing the stereotypes as false and forcing a readjustment.

In the chapter "The Child as the Other: Some Epistemological Considerations" **Zlatana Knezevic** brings together perspectives from critical childhood studies and postcolonial feminism to challenge the idea of a universal childhood and simplistic notions of otherness. With a reference to Claudia Castañeda's analysis of figures of childhood in poststructuralist and feminist philosophy, Knezevic argues that "the pre-subjectial generic infant" is a persistent theme in representations of human ontology and alternative ways of being. However, this figure of the child remains empty of subjectivity since, according to Knezevic, it is both dehumanized and decontextualized. In the chapter, she presents both advantages and dangers involved in conceptualizing otherness in terms of children and childhoods and suggests making an analytical distinction between "the child as the other" and "othered childhoods." The former can, according to Knezevic, be used to critically address axes of power related to age, while the second refers to the silencing of childhoods that do not fit the category of the decontextualized image of the child.

In the chapter "The emotionalization of burnout in the health care sector," **Ylva Gustafsson** discusses the implications of applications of New Public Management in the health care sector during the 1990s. NPM's rationalization of health care was accompanied by an increased workload for health professionals with less time dedicated for each patient, which resulted in burnouts among nurses. Gustafsson then connects these effects of NPM to literature about the supposed role of "emotional intelligence" in work-life – and identifies a gendered discourse about work-related stress. While men's coping with stress is described in terms of endurance to be rewarded with "health and wealth", women are expected to be resilient and cope without reward – and their failure to do so is defined as a character issue, described in terms of a lack of emotional intelligence. Furthermore, nurses' narratives of work-related stress are often interpreted as expressing "emotional distress" or "emotional dissonance" while Gustafsson reads them as expressions of ethical distress, related to a lack of time and resources to provide adequate care.

In the chapter "Emancipatory Engagement with Oppression: The Perils of Identity in Feminist and Anti-Racist Politics" **Oda Davanger** argues against basing emancipatory struggles on identity categories. According to Davanger, conceptualizing oppression in terms of different axes, i.e. identity categories, can be harmful to feminist philosophy and ideology since it contributes to upholding whiteness and maleness as norms and therefore fails to "dismantle the system of domination". In opposition to different versions of identity politics and the analytical and political concept of intersectionality, Davanger complements bell hooks' notion of *imperialist white supremacist capitalist patriarchy* with a post-structuralist perspective. Davanger's answer to feminist and anti-racist struggles based on identity categories is a politics that is built around an "abstract and alienated desire" that makes possible engaging in the struggle for a world without oppression based on identity, regardless of individuals' own experience of oppression.

Part 5
Openings of Understanding

Andrea Nye's reminder of the basic premise of thinking as something which "necessarily uses concepts with roots in the past" is, as we have seen, not to be understood as an ingrained cementation of meaning. Within feminist philosophy there is also a desire to break with tradition and open up for novel ways of conceptualizing and connecting the seemingly unrelated. In this last sequence of texts, three chapters will expose some of the ways in which feminist philosophy offers trains of thought with an ambition of grafting the roots of the past.

Feminist attention to the division of the private and the public as an ahistorical exclusionary practice is called into question by **Jorunn Økland** in her chapter "Private, Public, Sacred Space: Why Gender Studies, in Particular, should consider Sacred Space a Third Spatial Category". Here, Økland follows Joan Scott, in exposing the ways in which the connection between secularization and gender equality has underpinned the idea of the uniqueness of white Western culture. In focusing on the public space as the space for free speech and emancipation, historical roles of women in religious spheres are recurrently ignored. In her chapter, Økland explores various examples from Ancient Greece to 19th century English poetry and shows how the distinction of the private and the public leads to misunderstandings about women's roles in sacred- or religious space.

In the chapter "The Inner Landscape of the Body: Phenomenology of Thinking" **Guðbjörg R. Jóhannesdóttir** begins by making a series of conceptual and metaphorical connections between body parts and names for features of the landscape. Jóhannesdóttir pays particular attention to the Icelandic word "leg" (which means a place where something lies; for example, a uterus and a final resting place) and its connection to the Icelandic word for landscape "landslag," which in many older sources is written as "lands*leg*." Starting from these linguistic connections, Jóhannesdóttir continues by phenomenologically exploring "the feeling of situatedness" in an environment and its role in the creation of knowledge. While feminist philosophies of situated knowledge have primarily focused on socio-political conditions of knowledge, Jóhannesdóttir's approach is rooted in feminist phenomenologies of embodiment.

How is it possible to approach truth without violence? In her chapter "Philosophical Compassion and Active Hesitation: A Non-Critical Approach to Understanding", **Nicole des Bouvrie** explores different paths of understanding as a philosophical task. Engaging with Bracha Ettinger, Anne Dufourmantelle, and others, des Bouvrie develops an ethical approach that takes hold of the radical openness of a matrixial borderspace as the topos of truth. The practice within this spatiality is what Des Bouvrie calls philosophical compassion and active hesitation.

Afterword

Feminist philosophy: Time, history, and the transformation of thought is the result of the eponymous network hosted by the Nordic Summer University (NSU) from 2016– 2019. Founded in 1950, the NSU is an independent, nomadic and non-profit academic institution that fosters intellectual and cultural exchange between the Nordic and the Baltic countries – although open for participation irrespective of one's location. Committed to egalitarian and interdisciplinary modes of learning, the NSU is open for senior scholars, doctoral and master students as well as artists and professionals with relevant backgrounds.

During a four-year period, the NSU network *Feminist Philosophy* organized two symposia per year, four of which have been in collaboration with the University of Umeå and Södertörn University in Sweden, Oslo University in Norway and the University of Iceland. These symposia have gathered around 200 scholars and students from around the world to discuss feminist philosophy in relation to questions of history and time from various angles. The aims of the network were inter alia: to explore the borders, connections, and tensions between feminism and philosophy from critical perspectives; to emphasize the importance of time and history for contemporary feminist theory, and to create a generous transdisciplinary platform to philosophize about feminism. The chapters in the book are all written by participants in the network and include young and senior scholars from various fields within the humanities and social sciences, as well as invited keynote speakers who mostly come from the discipline of philosophy.

The closing Afterword, "Configurations of Feminist Philosophy: Time, History, and the Transformation of Thought within the Context of Nordic Summer University", gives a brief understanding of the institutional structure and history of The Nordic Summer University in general and the circle *Feminist philosophy* in particular. As coordinators of the study circle *Feminist Philosophy*, we, Synne Myrebøe, Valgerður Pálmadóttir and Johanna Sjöstedt, provide an overview of the questions and themes of the symposia organized. As part of this, we reflect on feminist pedagogy and philosophize about feminist intellectual spaces, with the NSU network and the organized symposia as case studies.

PART 1
Feminist Philosophy in the Present Tense

Chapter 1
Feminism and Philosophy
– A Matter of History and Politics

Tuija Pulkkinen

In this essay I will address the relation between feminism and philosophy and will highlight two aspects that I see as being relevant to it. First, the aspect of history: both the history of feminism as a social movement and the history of philosophy as a particular type of textual tradition. And second, the aspect of politics: politics that I believe is inextricably intertwined with feminism, and politics which ideally remains outside of philosophy as a tradition of pure thought. I will discuss these two aspects of the relation between feminism and philosophy, but I will start and end with something that had caught my interest in the call for papers for the Feminist philosophy event for which I originally gave this talk. What caught my attention was the word 'tension' in the following sentence: "although feminist philosophy is now a recognized field, a tension between the two terms seem to persist." It is this tension between the two terms, feminism, and philosophy, that I will be focusing on here.

For inspiration, and following in the footsteps of Jacques Derrida, I looked up the word 'tension' in some online dictionaries. 'Tension' is a word used in physics, in electricity, and in psychology. It is, for example, a "Condition of being held in a state between two or more forces, which are acting in opposition to each other", as well as being "a psychological state of being tense."[1] Pictures of tension on the internet include lots of stretched ropes and pictures of people with headaches.

I realized that as a word in English, tension has quite a negative connotation, apart from electricity where high or low tension in terms of voltage are fairly neutral expressions. Tension is connected with opposition, and with being psychologically

---

[1] HS Sanakirja.org. https://www.sanakirja.org/search.php?q=tension&l=3&l2=15.

tense. I also realized that in Finnish and in Swedish the equivalent word carries with it slightly less negative associations: in Finnish *jännite, jännitys, jännittävä*, and in Swedish *spänning, spännande* can also have a positive meaning. *Jännitys* and *jännittävä* as well as *spänning* and *spännande* not only mean opposition and headache, but they also mean exciting, interesting, and even fun.

In this essay, I would like to invoke some of that feeling of fun and excitement – that electric tension – which is also very productive, and which I believe is at work in between feminism and philosophy. Or, perhaps not between femin*ism* and philoso*phy* as abstract entities, but rather, which is present in the work of those people who do both feminist and philosophical scholarship: that is, those who take part in both academic traditions.

My own current work consists of looking at the tensions related to philosophy in between some known contemporary feminist theorists, such as Rosi Braidotti, Judith Butler, Elizabeth Grosz, Adriana Cavarero, and Luce Irigaray, among others. Primarily I work on tensions in between their respective texts and their use of concepts. I call this project 'the politics of philosophy in contemporary feminist theory'.[2] Simultaneously, of course, I am working with the tension between philosophy and feminism in these authors' texts. While I will provide some specific examples from contemporary feminist theory, my primary focus here is at a more general level, concerning the tension between feminism and philosophy as academic traditions. In what does this tension consist? Why is there a tension? I argue here that the tension between philosophy and feminism has two dimensions. It is a matter of history, on the one hand, and a matter of politics on the other. I will concentrate on each of these two dimensions of the tension in turn.

First, the dimension of history. This is related to what I call the 'trace of omnitemporality' within the philosophical tradi-

---

[2] The phrase has appeared over a decade in various forms in my Academy of Finland funded research projects, in talk titles and in publications. https://researchportal.helsinki.fi/en/persons/tuija-pulkkinen

tion, in contradistinction to feminist scholarship, where the emphasis is on change in time. Second, the dimension of politics. In feminist scholarship, this is related to the role of conflict, contestation and, most of all, to what I call 'intervention'. This contrasts significantly with the role of these same aspects in philosophy. By way of a conclusion, I will return to tension in general, and reflect on what to do with the tension. I argue that the tradition of philosophy needs the perspectives of both history and of politics in order to serve feminist thought well, and that with the combination of philosophy, history and politics, a positive tension is achieved, and feminist philosophy will thrive. Alternatively, and in order to add more tension, I suggest that rather than talk of 'feminist philosophy' it would be more radical instead to use the phrase 'feminist theorizing.'

History

Why is there tension between philosophy and feminist scholarship in relation to history and time?

Philosophy is a very peculiar discipline in terms of time and tradition: both within the analytical and the phenomenological traditions of philosophy, a philosopher can start thinking about or analyzing an object of thought as if that thought happened only right here and now. It is as if nothing had happened before, and as if the thinking started with a completely clean slate. In multidisciplinary settings, this quite often amazes scholars who come from other traditions within the social sciences and humanities, traditions in which beginnings are generally less self-secure. As a philosopher, one can just simply pose a question: What is money? What is justice? What is gender?

Simultaneously, within the discipline of philosophy – and this is also unlike most other disciplines – discussions constantly refer to texts which stretch over a period of more than 2000 years. Some of the oldest texts are quite often considered to be just as valid as contemporary ones, or even more significant. With respect to argumentation, they are often deemed to be better than many contemporary texts. Basically, there is a strong trace within philosophy which states that so far as the content and value of ideas and thoughts are concerned, it is irrelevant whether they were formulated in Athens in 300 BC, around 1800 in Germany, or in present-day United States. It is also irrelevant in which language they were formulated. This level of universal validity and abstraction from context is exactly the point, as much as we can say it is, say, in geometry.

I call the above a 'trace of omnitemporality', again improvising from Derrida.[3] This trace, as we know, is not an explicit road and rule to be followed, and it is not all that is done, or done in all philosophy, but it is a strong feature in the textual tradition and practice of philosophy. It is followed, although also sometimes lost, but it persists, and like footsteps in a forest, it is created by those who went before. It is also a stronger trace than just a feature of one kind of philosophy, the Platonist type. Derrida, for example, comes up with the term 'omnitemporality' in his *Politics of Friendship* in the section in which he discusses Aristotle and certainty, stability, and fidelity with respect to philosophical knowledge, instead of discussing Plato and eternal ideas. With respect to stable, reliable, certain, stability, reliability, certainty, *bébaios,* Derrida writes:

> In a state of immense philosophical concentration, we have here the whole story of *eidos* all the way up to the Husserlian interpretation of the idealization or production of ideal objects as the production of omnitemporality, of intemporality *qua* omnitemporality.[4]

This is the same theme that Derrida worked on in his *Writing and Difference,* where he writes about "[...] absolute, infinite omni-temporality and universality, without limits of any kind.

---

[3] Derrida has used the phrase 'omnitemporality,' although more or less in passing, and it is not one of his regularly cited phrases.

[4] Jacques Derrida, *Politics of Friendship*, transl. George Collins (London: Verso, 2005), pp. 16–17.

The Idea of truth, [….][5] Of course, we know that in reality, doing philosophy means not only focusing on pure truth, but it is instead much more like doing research in other disciplines. Those who do philosophy follow particular conventions in terms of constructing a paper, an argument, a chapter, or a book, as is done in other disciplines which follow their own conventions. Quite often this happens in a determined setting with particular discussants at a particular point in time: in order to qualify as part of a discussion, a set of people and texts, as well as repetitions and new ideas, must be included. It is like this in philosophy as it is in other disciplines, but I have the sense that philosophers are regularly in denial about that. Quite often the discussion is posed in philosophy as if it started from a new beginning around a table which could be in any place and at any time, a table at which the present writer sits alongside Aristotle and/or Kant, Dewey and/or Wittgenstein, Heidegger and/or Deleuze, or Parfit and/or Rawls, perhaps, or some other past or contemporary leading figures within the discipline. When and where they wrote their contribution is not very often referred to at all. This is what I refer to here as the omnitemporal setting.

How is feminist scholarship constructed in terms of time? There is a completely different trace in feminist scholarship, which has to do with the history of feminist studies arriving in university settings along with the feminist movement in the course of the second wave of feminism in the 1970s. It is rarely the case that you encounter omnitemporality in feminist-inclined scholarship – although, again, there are exceptions. Quite often in discussions of theory, and after more than fifty years of feminist argumentation in academic settings, time and place are attached to arguments.

I argue that this is because through its history of becoming an academic field, feminist scholarship has become thoroughly and acutely aware of the time-and-place relatedness of thoughts, and also aware of how thoughts change the world. That the

---

[5] Jacques Derrida, *Writing and Difference*, transl. Alan Bass. (London: Routledge, 2001), p. 200.

world changes, that new thoughts and new conceptions are born – this, which is not the area of strength of philosophy – is *the* area of strength of feminist studies: feminist research is crucially dependent on the idea of historical change, it is indeed, the whole point of study within feminist movements.

By being aware of the time and place of study, I do not mean only the idea of situated knowledges, which is in itself an important theme in feminist scholarship. I mean more profoundly and in a more general sense the heightened consciousness of the time-relation of truths. There is the strong memory of all that knowledge, which was claimed to be universal, and not time- and place-specific, and which was questioned in the course of feminist consciousness-raising and in the wake of academic feminism. These truths proved to be the production of very time- and place specific gender hierarchies, gender orders, and gendered oppressions. This knowledge included various ideas on and about gender and sexuality, which after all were not at all eternal, even if strongly claimed to be so.

This realization, precisely, that the status of a truth changes, and that academic authority can be on the side of change, rather than on the side of stability and reliability of knowledge and ideas, is foundational for all feminist scholarship.[6]

In sum, given that the dominant trace in the philosophical tradition is omnitemporality, and in feminist scholarship it is change, it is not hard to see that this creates a certain tension for those who take part in both academic traditions, the feminist and the philosophical. The profound impulse for change, on the one hand, and the ideal of omnitemporality, on the other; high history-consciousness, on the one hand, and an imperative to

---

[6] I have elaborated more on the specificity of feminist scholarship in Tuija Pulkkinen, "Identity and Intervention: Transdisciplinarity and Disciplinarity in Gender Studies" in Special Issue Transdisciplinary Peter Osborne, Stella Sandford, and Eric Alliez (Eds.). *Theory, Culture & Society*, 32 (5–6) September–November 2015, pp. 183–205; and in Tuija Pulkkinen, "Feelings of Injustice: The Institutionalization of Gender Studies and the Pluralization of Feminism" in special issue Transatlantic Gender Crossings eds. Anne-Emmanuelle Berger and Éric Fassin. *differences. A Journal of Feminist Cultural Studies* 27 (2), (2016), pp. 103–124.

universalize and maximize stability, on the other. Unsurprisingly, the two orientations often clash.

I think this same tension between omnitemporality and time-and-place boundedness is present in the work of Derrida, though perhaps for other reasons, and this is also, perhaps, why he appears in this essay. Derrida constantly returns to the canon of the philosophical tradition, and even to a certain degree formulates omnitemporal statements, that is, non-time and place specific statements. He calls them 'structures,' but always with a 'perhaps' attached. Yet he never fails to attach a 'here' and 'now' to whatever he says, as if to ward off the thought of this being said in an omnitemporal manner, in order to underline the place and the time.[7] The simultaneity of the two approaches, the play with the tradition of omnitemporality combined with a constant deconstruction of it, produces a different type of text than would result from a focus solely on time-bound phenomena. Perhaps it is a play between the two registers that makes the text more exciting.

What do the contemporary feminist theorists whom I study – such as Luce Irigaray, Rosi Braidotti, Judith Butler, Elizabeth Grosz, Adriana Cavarero – do with this tension? I would argue that the tension between philosophy and feminism is productive in all of their work. None of them have a simple or uncomplicated, or a simply positive relation to the textual tradition of philosophy, but rather, all have a tense, and many a highly charged relationship with it.

The philosophy they relate to most intimately is contemporary philosophy from the second half of the 20th century, and in particular, contemporary French philosophy. This is philosophy based in the phenomenological tradition of Husserl, and therefore relates to the omnitemporal subject of thought – that is, consciousness. From the beginning to the current moment, Rosi Braidotti's work, for example, circulates around the issues

---

[7] I discuss this also in Tuija Pulkkinen "Tradition, Gender and Democracy to Come – Derrida on Fraternity" in *Redescriptions. Yearbook of Political Thought, Conceptual Change and Feminist Theory*, Vol. 13, (2009), pp. 103–124.

of the philosophical subject, and subject-philosophy in general.[8] Cavarero's work circulates around the singularity of the subject within the same tradition, but in a more Heideggerian mode,[9] and Irigaray focuses on the oneness of the subject.[10] They all have an intense relationship with the subject of philosophy, yet also an intensively troubled or negative relation. This is a fascination that is simultaneously a denunciation. It is a very interesting and indeed, tense relationship.

Braidotti is a good example. If you look through her entire published work, from beginning to the end, she emphasizes constantly that she was trained in philosophy, yet what she most intensively struggles against is subject-philosophy. She says that this tradition is what she works to undo, if philosophy is perceived as "the rational discourse of (the) dominant masculine, Eurocentric subject."[11] Yet in her self-presentations she writes that she wants to connect to the tradition,[12] and she often emphasizes her own formation as a philosopher: "As a first-generation poststructuralist who was initiated into these philosophies by those who founded them, I shall not even attempt to deny that I am approaching feminist theory as a philosopher trained in Paris in the late seventies by Deleuze, Lyotard, Fou-

---

[8] Some indication of this are: that the phrase 'the death of the subject' appears as a subtitle frequently in Braidotti's books, from her earliest to her latest; that one of her book-titles is *Nomadic Subjects*, and that she writes of herself as looking for "building blocks for a posthuman theory of subjectivity." Rosi Braidotti, *The Posthuman* (Cambridge: Polity 2013), p. 56.

[9] I have discussed this more in Tuija Pulkkinen, "Judith Butler's Politics of Philosophy in Notes Toward a Performative Theory of Assembly: Arendt, Cavarero, and Human 'Appearing' and 'Plurality'" *Redescriptions. Political Thought, Conceptual History and Feminist Theory* Vol 21:2, (Autumn 2018), pp. 128–147.

[10] Tina Chanter, *Ethics of Eros. Irigaray's Rewriting of the Philosophers* (New York: Routledge, 1995); Sara Heinämaa, "On Luce Irigaray's Phenomenology of Intersubjectivity" in Maria C. Cimitile & Elaine P. Miller (eds.) *Returning to Irigaray* (Albany: SUNY Press, 2007) pp. 243–265; Tuija Pulkkinen, "The Role of Darwin in Elizabeth Grosz's Deleuzian Feminist Theory – Sexual Difference, Ontology, and Intervention." *Hypatia. A Journal of Feminist Philosophy* Vol 32: 2, (Spring 2017), pp. 279–295.

[11] Rosi Braidotti, *Nomadic Subjects: Embodiment and Sexual Difference in Contemporary Feminist Theory*. Second Edition (New York: Columbia University Press, 2011), p. 14.

[12] Braidotti, *Nomadic Subjects*, p. 14.

cault, and Irigaray."[13] What the negative charge towards philosophy mostly consists of in Braidotti's work is quite often its status as the discourse of mastery and domination, yet it is also directed against its purported universality and omnitemporality.

Within the phenomenological tradition, there always is a pull toward the universal. Some feminist theorists are closer to that than others. In my view Irigaray, for example, is closer to suggesting omnitemporal structures, to the extent that she engages with the philosophical subject, which in her work merges with the psychoanalytical subject. She proposes that instead of being one, the subject is two or more. In other words, sexual difference is to a degree an omnitemporal claim. Cavarero also makes the claim of sexual difference, – which is evident in the body and also in the voice –, in an omnitemporal manner although she does it in a more Heideggerian mode, in terms of the singularity of the finite subject.

Sexual difference is, to a degree, an omnitemporal claim, yet posing it within the tradition of oneness of the omnitemporal subject expresses a heightened sense of historical change. More than anything, there is an appeal to change in both Irigaray's and Cavarero's work: they aim to change something with their omnitemporal claims concerning unveiling of the difference that has been forgotten. The content of the philosophizing slips from omnitemporality, and the tone slips occasionally too, because the context of the philosophizing is done in the context of claims for change.

Most feminist thinkers, philosophers, and theorists struggle with this tension. For example, consider Elizabeth Grosz: there is a pull towards the universal from within the philosophical tradition. In her case, it manifests itself in terms of a Deleuzian philosophical ontology. Grosz combines an interest in Deleuze, and Bergson in the background of Deleuze, with Irigaray's sexual difference, and proceeds to make some omnitemporal claims of her own. This is all philosophy, and yet, the entire

---

[13] Braidotti, *Nomadic Subjects*, p. 69.

purpose of Grosz's complicated maneuvering is to convince the reader of the possibility of change.[14]

Judith Butler has been quite consistent in her resistance to omnitemporality. She is very careful to avoid both proposing truths and working as a philosopher, by consistently avoiding omnitemporal claims. So, although she is often referred to as having proposed a 'theory of gender,' I would argue that it is hard to find an explicit proposition of a theory in her work. Instead of presenting a theory, she presents an act of theorizing; mostly, this happens in relation to some other work of theory and in the form of constant interventions into whatever is moving in time. She does not primarily pose an omnitemporal question such as, 'what is gender?'

In a peculiar way, which deserves study, Butler draws from the resources of the textual tradition of philosophy in a very serious and engaging fashion, yet at the same time, she absolutely does not do this in the tradition of a philosopher.[15] The same holds for Braidotti, in fact. In many respects they are very different, but in this regard there is resonance. Both the work of Braidotti and Butler is in constant motion with whatever is here and now. Both of them, as well as the others I have mentioned – perhaps with the exception of Cavarero – also clearly state that they work not as philosophers, while constantly referring to philosophy. This is a difficult balance to achieve: building on philosophical challenges, yet completely living within time.

I argue that we should not underestimate this quality of feminist scholarship, it may well be its strength: the philosophical pull of omnitemporality, while simultaneously challenging that with a profound reluctance towards it. This tension is very productive. In my view, the most interesting work in contemporary feminist thought is informed by the philosophical

---

[14] I have argued this more extensively in Pulkkinen, "The Role of Darwin in Elizabeth Grosz's Deleuzian Feminist Theory – Sexual Difference, Ontology, and Intervention."

[15] I have analyzed the ways Butler does this through 'discharging' some philosophically charged concepts used by Hannah Arendt and Adriana Cavarero in Pulkkinen, "Judith Butler's Politics of Philosophy in Notes Toward a Performative Theory of Assembly: Arendt, Cavarero, and Human 'Appearing' and 'Plurality'".

tradition and various traditions within the philosophical tradition, and yet it does not engage in doing philosophy.

This is why it could be said that feminist philosophy is always at the edge of philosophy. It cannot wholeheartedly take part in the omnitemporal or universal human project. The feminist tradition is, so to say, too conscious of historical change and its stakes. But it can work along its borders, changing perspective constantly from the universal to its challenge, and in this manner, it can profit from, and take part in, the strengths of the academic tradition of philosophy.

I will end my reflection on the dimension of history here, and take up the second dimension, namely politics. This is another angle that is very much part of the same or similar tension between philosophy and feminism.

Politics

Interestingly, politics is in itself related to an opposition which is present in the word 'tension.' Politics is always about opposition, at least if we believe Chantal Mouffe, for whom politics is about agonism. In that sense, politics is related to the very topic of tension. I If we are to believe Chantal Mouffe, for whom politics is about agonism, politics is always about opposition.[16] This way construed, politics is related to the very topic of tension. The tension between the tradition of philosophy and feminist scholarship in terms of politics is based on a fundamentally different attitude toward politics in each of them.

In terms of the relationship between philosophy and politics, no one has been clearer than Hannah Arendt in expressing an opposition or tension between them. Much has been written on Arendt's views on philosophy.[17] Famously for Arendt, instead of being a rational animal, the human is a political animal. Instead

---

[16] Chantal Mouffe, *Agonistics: Thinking of the World Politically* (London: Verso, 2013).
[17] Dana Villa, *Arendt and Heidegger. The Fate of the Political* (Princeton: Princeton University Press, 1996); Jacques Taminiaux, *The Thracian Maid and the Professional Thinker, Arendt, and Heidegger.* Trans. Michael Gendre. (Albany: State University of New York Press, 1997); Linda M. G. Zerilli, *Feminism and the Abyss of Freedom.* (Chicago: University of Chicago Press, 2005).

of being regarded as a subject or consciousness, the human should, according to her, be conceived as being in a condition of plurality. By virtue of speech, humans, in Arendt's view, constantly act vis-à-vis each other in a state of plurality, and this is more distinctive of humanity than solitary thought, which the tradition of philosophy has always emphasized.[18]

The philosophical tradition, which Arendt is critical of here, carries a strong trace of respect for thinking that is carried out in a solitary mode. It is as if it is beyond politics, beyond multiplicity, plurality, beyond conflict and tension. Ideally, philosophical truth is calm. Yet, we all know – at least those working at philosophy departments and also those who study the history of philosophers and their ideas – that there are plenty of tensions and oppositions lurking within the discipline, and also that there exist plenty of political struggles between different schools of philosophy. This does not disturb the self-image of philosophy as calm: no politics, no opposition, just strict and rigorous reasoning.

In the self-image of philosophy, calm reason rules. Although thinking itself consists of critique, opposition, and challenge, the ultimate measure of reasoning is still supposed to be evident and the best argument wins. There is a strong ethics of argumentation here involved within philosophy. There is no reason to mock or to underestimate the power of this ethical code in the field: it produces a more rigorous way of arguing than is prevalent in many other fields, and there is much good in it. It also produces its own space for doing politics within the argumentation. Nevertheless, politics as a state of permanent disagreement can never be declared to be a desired end state within philosophy. Philosophical truth is not supposed to be a matter of politics, it is opposed to politics.

---

[18] Hannah Arendt, "Philosophy and Politics", *Social Research*, Vol. 57 (1) Spring 1990, 73–103; Villa, *Arendt, and Heidegger. The Fate of the Political*; Taminiaux, *The Thracian Maid and the Professional Thinker. Arendt and Heidegger*; Pulkkinen, "Judith Butler's Politics of Philosophy in Notes Toward a Performative Theory of Assembly: Arendt, Cavarero, and Human 'Appearing' and 'Plurality'".

How is feminist scholarship different? Unlike philosophy, in feminist scholarship awareness of conflict and politics is – again because of the history of the field – extremely acute. It has been argued by bell hooks,[19] for example, and in an interesting dissertation in my own department by Anna Elomäki,[20] that feminist awareness grows through conflicts, that feminist political togetherness is strongly bound to conflict. As a movement feminism is all about conflict with, and contesting of, what is presently believed to be true. Historically, this is at the heart of feminism.

It is unsurprising then, that within academic study which has developed as a result of the feminist movement, the contestation of established truths is a central element. As an academic discipline feminist scholarship is primarily designed to make interventions. I have argued elsewhere that as an academic discipline, gender studies is different precisely because it does not aim to establish truths, but to contest established truths. Unlike many other disciplines, gender studies, which is based in feminist scholarship, is not primarily aimed at knowledge production, as it were, but rather at challenging established conceptions, that is, at making interventions.[21]

More precisely, what I mean is that there are many disciplines within academia in which gender and sexuality are studied with the intention of producing knowledge about gender and sexuality: medicine; sociology; sexology; anthropology, and ethnology, etc. But within feminist studies, at gender studies departments, there is a distinctly different tone. That difference in tone consists of the relationship to politics and to the political dimension of academic study. That relationship is extremely in-tense, and in-tensively positive in feminist studies.

The special relationship to politics in feminist scholarship is present in everyday work at gender studies departments. You do

---

[19] bell hooks, *Talking Back: Thinking Feminist, Thinking Black.* (Boston, MA: South End Press, 1989).

[20] Anna Elomäki, *Feminist Political Togetherness: Rethinking the Collective Dimension of Feminist Politics* (University of Helsinki, 2012), pp. 113–119.

[21] More extensively in Pulkkinen, "Identity and Intervention: Transdisciplinarity and Disciplinarity in Gender Studies."

not apologize for having an agenda, as you would in a philosophy or social science setting. For example, at the University of Helsinki, where I teach, I recently had a discussion with some of the MA students who are also trans-activists. Having written their BA theses in another discipline, and now working on a thesis in our MA program, they were worried about 'objectivity' and about the tone of their theses. Is it okay to indicate that you also wish some change in these matters? I found myself explaining that yes, in Gender studies it is actually very common for researchers to be involved in the very political processes of change that constitute the objects of their studies. A fact that one should not be ashamed of. On the contrary, the kind of wide (or deeply ethnographic, if you wish) knowledge of the field is very good. And also, you can, yes, be openly in favor of certain change, and dispense with the need to dress your views into a seemingly neutral, objective, scientific point of view jargon. You just need to argue well, and with good grounds and references.

This is not completely foreign within philosophy departments, either. As an academic tradition, perhaps, philosophy also sometimes differs from many other fields which more pronouncedly 'produce knowledge.' In philosophy people are, perhaps, more critically minded in inquiry. Yet, the difference from gender studies is notable. There is a crucial difference between the transformative intervening principle of feminist scholarship in its entirety, and the intervening character of some philosophical scholarship. Most importantly, intervention is not the goal in philosophical scholarship, as it is in feminist scholarship; in philosophy the goal is truth, the non-political truth.

With that truth, the most general and the most abstract of truths, as the posited end of philosophical contemplation or philosophical analysis, analysis, the discipline of philosophy often also places itself above other disciplines which aim to simply produce knowledge to organize those disciplines. What it arrogates for itself is the task of organizing those disciplines. In the philosophy of science, it is common to talk of 'specialist sciences' versus philosophy as the general science; and to talk about 'folk' science as opposed to the sciences proper, amongst which philosophy is furthest away from the 'people'. There is, both in analytical and in phenomenological modes of doing philosophy, a particular certainty of being above the other disciplines. Philosophy never seems to be just a perspective, not even for those who do Nietzschean perspectivism; it is *the* perspective. The mode of doing philosophy is just this; it is a tradition, even if philosophy does not acknowledge itself as a tradition, constantly claiming instead the authoritative voice of pure thought.

As an attitude, this is very different from the one prevalent in feminist studies, which not only entertains politics, disagreement – and with that a constant state of disagreement – as its horizon but it is also constantly aware of the open nature of what is considered to be true and real. Feminist academia is therefore often busy in actually producing new concepts that transform what we can see and feel as reality.

Again, the experience of second wave feminist activists is crucial here: there was a huge amount of academic knowledge that seemed to address 'the truth' while systematically ignoring, torturing, mistreating, twisting, misinforming, and bullying women and purposefully misunderstanding gender in order to maintain certain orders and hierarchies. This academic knowledge could only be understood as being political through and through and confronted as such. As this is the 'founding act' of the discipline, it results in a very different attitude from that of the tradition of philosophy. The calm is not the horizon, neither is its goal to establish the most general possible truth on the matter; instead the horizon is change, the possibilities of openings for politics within the stability of truth. You cannot imagine feminist scholarship without a horizon of change and politics.

Concerning those contemporary feminist thinkers whom I study, there are differences, of course, depending on the philosophical attachments of the thinker concerned, in terms of how they relate both to the production of 'truth' and the task of intervention. However, in a manner very similar to their relationships with history and change, their relationship with politics and openings for change, only vary in degree. Of course, all of them are interventionist in the sense that all feminist scholarship is interventionist. But they have various degrees of a sense of politics – whether in terms of openings, or in terms of conflict – in their approaches.

Irigaray, even with her omnitemporal arguments concerning sexual difference, is very hopeful, since her horizon is change; Grosz, whom I would criticize for having as her goal a scientific form of explanation, one that closes down the space for politics, nevertheless constructs such scientific explanations in order to explain that change can happen.[22] And Braidotti and Butler entirely refuse a non-political stance, as far as I can see. Their work is driven by intervening politically, and it is precisely this drive that accounts for the fact that they constantly change their fields and topics of interest. While these traits are common to both authors, it would be a matter for other investigations to go deeper into their specific differences and similarities.

Conclusion

Philosophy and feminism: there is indeed a tension between these terms. So much tension in fact that for quite a long time, I myself have verbally rejected the combination. I have refused to speak of 'feminist philosophy', instead choosing to speak of 'feminist theory' or 'feminist theorizing'. As a by-product of that position, I have also acknowledged other intellectual traditions comprising theoretical discussions in feminist studies, such as psychoanalysis, literary theory, semiotics, etc.

While avoiding the term 'feminist philosophy' I was for a long time a board member of the International Association of Women Philosophers (IAPh). This board usually includes people who work in philosophy departments and those in gender studies departments. I have mostly talked of 'feminist theory,' even if I deal principally with the tradition of philosophy, and truly enjoy it, and even if moreover I have a particular research interest in how philosophy as a tradition works within feminist scholarship. If I reflect on why I would have

---

[22] My criticism is published in Pulkkinen, "The Role of Darwin in Elizabeth Grosz's Deleuzian Feminist Theory – Sexual Difference, Ontology, and Intervention."

avoided using 'feminist philosophy,' I think it has been, more than anything, in response to the attitude that sometimes seems to creep in with this phrase: it brings in omnitemporality and the horizon of truth, instead of highlighting the horizon of politics.

I think philosophy needs history and politics in order to serve feminist thought properly; simultaneously, I think the philosophical tradition is essential to make feminist theory the exciting intellectual journey that it is. My own recipe for doing feminist research is constantly trying to challenge the three traditions of philosophy, history, and politics, with each other.

Yet I also fully engage with the philosophical tradition within feminist scholarship. I enjoy Elizabeth Grosz's ambitious developments in the area of ontology, Luce Irigaray's incredible work, and Adriana Cavarero's ideas of voice as unique.[23] I probably enjoy them precisely because they are all overambitious in generalizing and universalizing. And I think that even those who more consistently battle against the trace of omnitemporality in contemporary feminist theory, as I see both Braidotti and Butler do, would not really be so intriguing if their work was not set against that tradition of omnitemporality and truth, and constantly referring to it. This means I am not against philosophy; it is just that philosophy needs a constant reminder, a constant pulling back and forth, and it needs to be taken a little less seriously. I suppose this is quite a Derridean position: even without proper faith in 'real philosophy,' it makes sense to act 'as if' there was one. Philosophy is an incredible tradition which needs exercise to be kept alive, meaningful, and in motion. And this is what feminist theorizing today is also doing, in its way.

For feminist theorizing, the tradition of philosophy, I believe, brings with it that tension, that exciting tension, that we can express with the words *jännittävä and spännande*. The most interesting work in contemporary feminist thought, I think, is informed by the philosophical tradition and, what is even more *jännittävää /spännande*, it is inspired by different and contra-

---

[23] Adriana Cavarero, *For More than One Voice: Toward a Philosophy of Vocal Expression*, transl. Paul Kottman (California: Stanford University Press, 2005).

dictory traditions within the philosophical tradition, and therefore creates interesting tensions in the field. It is a productive tension.

In conclusion, indeed the tension between the two terms philosophy and feminism persists – and so it should, as far as I am concerned. Tension is not necessarily a bad thing, and as I have noted, it may be exactly the thing that keeps thinking alive; it is productive, and it is *spännande, jännittävää,* interesting!

Chapter 2
Desiring Difference and the Hierarchies of Time

Kristina Fjelkestam

When do we claim to have seen better days, look forward to a brighter future, or strive to be more present in the actual moment? Whose time is considered valuable and whose is considered worthless?

In this essay I want to critique hierarchical valuations of time through the lens of queer temporality, focusing on "difference". We are still under the influence of a conception of time indicative of sharp distinctions between then, now, and later, in which temporality is continually valued and assessed. This time paradigm of Western modernity, shaped by European Enlightenment and its idea of progress in the form of the linear and irreversible sequence, "forces us to emphasise change, development and replacement and to ignore the contemporary in the non-contemporary", as the literary scholar and cultural historian Aleida Assmann points out.[1] The past thus turns into what no longer happens, and such a construct makes us define time as something in which the present can only exist in relation to what it is not, i.e. the non-contemporary. Contemporaneity then becomes the norm for our understanding of the world, and in which the past, but also the future, are assigned only the role of the Other.

Sure, our perception of the past always contains a measure of contemporaneity, but problems arise when present perspectives include hierarchical evaluations. These ratings can have various discriminating consequences and be sexist (as in a classic interpretation of Goethe's *Faust* in which Faust is named "modern"

---

[1] Aleida Assmann, *Zeit und Tradition: Kulturelle Strategien de Dauer* (Köln: Böhlau Verlag, 1999), p. 50: "zwingt dazu, Wandel, Entwicklung und Ersetzung zu betonen und die Gleichzeitigkeit des Ungleichzeitigkeiten des Ungleichzeitigkeiten zu übersehen" (my translation).

and Gretchen "outdated"), ageist (children as a stretch of "not-yets" and the elderly as a pile of rattling "has-beens"), hetero-normative (when the heterosexual life curve is deemed normal), or xenophobic (non-Western cultures depicted as "primitive").[2] In the end, strategies of temporal difference are all about power and the precedence of certain interpretations.

Practices such as history writing take place in the present and are thus limited by knowledge and ideas of its time. We are then forced to revise history at regular intervals based on new facts and changed values, something which may sound reasonable in an epistemological sense. But this conception on the other hand ontologically implies that the past is static, frozen in time, and supposed to be something we can return to again and again with ever sharpened analytical tools. This means that the idea of the past as a kind of fixed essence, as constantly "the same" waiting to be continually visited, might be just as problematic as the concept of "difference".[3] Critique of a conception of time based on "similarity" is here put into words by new historicist scholar Catherine Belsey:

> Time travel is a fantasy. We cannot reproduce the conditions – the economy, the diseases, the manners, the language and the corresponding subjectivity – of another century. To do so would be, in any case, to eliminate the difference which makes the fantasy pleasurable [...] Reading the past depends on this difference. The real anachronism, then, is of another kind. Here history as time travel gives way to history as costume drama, the reconstruction of the past as the present in fancy dress. The project is to explain away the surface strangeness

---

[2] Marshall Berman, *All That is Solid Melts Into Air: The Experience of Modernity* (New York: Simon&Chuster, 1982); Clary Krekula & Barbro Johansson (Ed.), *Introduktion till kritiska åldersstudier* (Lund: Studentlitteratur, 2017); Elizabeth Freeman, *Time Binds: Queer Temporalities, Queer Histories* (Durham: Duke University Press, 2010); Johannes Fabian, *Time and the Other; How Anthropology Makes Its Subject* (New York: Columbia University Press, 2002).

[3] Ethan Kleinberg, *Haunting History: For a Deconstructive Approach to the Past* (Stanford: Stanford University Press, 2017).

> of another century in order to release its profound continuity
> with the present.[4]

The conception of ontological "similarity" between past and present creates the figure of the "time traveller" in which differences are erased. The time traveler strives to experience the past in terms of temporal location, which generates a historical perspective in which similarity and continuity are emphasized in a static and ahistorical fashion. The possibility of change and the emancipatory potential are then ignored.

When the relation between past, present, and future is defined in terms of similarity, people are considered to have the same driving forces throughout history and also in what is to come. We are, amongst other things, presumed to love our children and to feel pain in the same way as both our ancestors and our future generations. The conception of similarity erases the sharp distinction between then, now, and later which is otherwise characteristic of modernity's chronologically sequential temporality governed by notions of development and progress. History or futurity as similes and parables transgress the conception of a one-way movement of time, and also diffuse conceptions such as anachronism as non-chronological, unsynchronized, what is misplaced. As such, similarity embodies an effort to compensate for the loss of what no longer exists, or the want of what may never exist.

So, to regard history as something which is "similar" to the present obviously presents problems, but I claim that it is just as questionable to emphasize "difference" even though Belsey in the quote above seems to prefer it. The concept of difference on the one hand certainly makes our historical fantasies enjoyable since they then can contain exoticizing aspects of both threat and allure in our longing for something else. But on the other hand distinct boundaries between various time dimensions tend to function hierarchically by emphasizing either the now of the

---

[4] Catherine Belsey, *The Subject of Tragedy: Identity and Difference in Renaissance Drama* (London: Methuen, 1985), p. 2.

present or the then of the past as something superior – either we talk about the good old days, or of the past as something we should count ourselves lucky to have missed out on.

I will here argue that a pivotal driving force in Western hierarchical historiography consists of a desire for the past which implicates a desire for difference. In the following I will try to unnaturalize this driving force without ending up in locked binaries where difference is set against similarity, linear time is set against cyclical, the timeless against the time-bound, etc. I am not alone in doing so, however. Several interesting contributions have appeared in the growing research field of critical temporality studies. Sure, mainstream historiographical research has also had a renaissance of late, for instance proposing an ongoing "time crisis" in Western historical consciousness, but I find the discussions of power and politics in critical temporality studies more innovative.[5] The political implications of the Western time paradigm have first and foremost been observed in the feminist critique of linear progression, queer theory's questioning of chrononormativity, and in postcolonial analyses of the continuous impact of history.[6] Temporality has in this context been defined as "power relations as they play out in time".[7]

My contribution to this field involves establishing a multidimensional model of the desire for the past which complicates the hierarchical time paradigm of difference. In this mission I will also relate to findings of the so-called affective turn in which affects and emotions in political, economic, social, and cultural power structures are actualized. History scholars, for example, write up various kinds of histories of emotion, media scholars

---

[5] Cf. François Hartog, *Regimes of Historicity: Presentism and Experiences of Time* (New York: Columbia University Press, 2015).

[6] Cf. Clare Hemmings, *Why Stories Matter: The Political Grammar of Feminist Theory* (Durham: Duke University Press, 2011); Freeman, *Time Binds*; Dipesh Chakrabarty, *Provincializing Europe: Postcolonial Thought and Historical Difference* (Princeton: Princeton University Press, 2000).

[7] Sarah Sharma, *In the Meantime: Temporality and Cultural Politics* (Durham: Duke University Press, 2014), p. 4.

talk about popular culture trends of "affective history", while queer theorists discuss "erotohistoriography".[8] This kind of research on embodied emotional reaction to realizations of the past is something which will be of interest to me here.

Diffusing Desire

The desire for the past is a multidimensional and complex driving force for historiographical expressions which in various ways represent a strive to replace what no longer exists – or, rather, what may never even have existed. These close to erotically charged desires contain also cognitive, emotional, and political aspects. That is, the desire for the past includes a quest to achieve not only knowledge but an emotion-laden sensual relationship to the past. It can also be driven by the political longing for recognition and restoration or an effort to recapture what is perceived of as past phenomena such as "the nation" or "the welfare state". I regard this multidimensional desire for the past as the driving force through which the past is actualized by the queries and questions of the present, thus turning into what we call "history".

In postcolonial and queer theory of history, the binary division of either "difference" or "similarity" between the past and the present has been deconstructed through a focus on asynchronous temporalities that intersect each other. Instead of being similar or different to the present, the past can be regarded in Derridean terms as an absent presence and a haunting spectre.[9] In the United States, for example, the history of slavery still has implications for African-American citizens, and in various ways the colonial legacy lives on in previously colonized countries. This has been described by Achille Mbembe as a

---

[8] Cf. Jan Plamper, *The History of Emotions: An Introduction* (Oxford: Oxford University Press, 2017); Alison Landsberg, *Engaging the Past: Mass Culture and the Production of Historical Knowledge* (New York: Columbia University Press, 2015); Freeman, *Time Binds.*

[9] Jacques Derrida, *Spectres de Marx: l'état de la dette, le travail du deuil et la nouvelle Internationale* (Paris: Galilée, 1993).

temporal "entanglement", something which "encloses multiple durées made up of discontinuities, reversals, inertias, and swings that overlay one another, interpenetrate one another, and envelope one another".[10] History is not considered as made up of diachronic linear seriality, but rather as a synchronous "interlocking of presents, pasts and futures that retain their depths of other presents, pasts and futures, each age bearing, altering, and maintaining the previous ones."[11]

Queer theorists, such as Carolyn Dinshaw, for their part speak of "a touch across time" in which emotional connections are forged through the epochs and create context and even political solidarity over time, or as Elizabeth Freeman who uses the term "erotohistoriography" based on the idea of temporal hybridization creating bodily affect.[12] Freeman, perhaps the most well-known scholar of queer temporality studies, is also the editor of the GLQ issue in which this new research field was presented in 2007. The focus on body and emotion characteristic of queer temporality studies becomes obvious already in her introduction, for instance in her interpretation of the Hamlet quote most often cited by scholars of the theory of history – "time is out of joint." The familiar words are uttered by Hamlet as he speaks to his father, the ghost, who informs his son that he has been murdered. Since the publication of Derrida's *Spectres of Marx* in 1993, the quote has been used as pretext for the postcolonial conception of the past as something still haunting the present. This conception has prompted several important and interesting interpretations, but instead Freeman significantly chooses to shed light on the somatic aspects of the quote. "Time is out of joint" turns into an image representing something felt on the bare skin and bones, even the actual skeleton being dislodged: "In this metaphor, time has, indeed is,

<hr>

[10] Achille Mbembe, *On the Postcolony* (Berkeley: University of California Press, 2001), p. 14.

[11] Mbembe, *On the Postcolony*, p. 16.

[12] Carolyn Dinshaw, *Getting Medieval: Sexualities and Communities, Pre- and Postmodern* (Durham: Duke University Press, 1999), p. 21; Freeman, *Time Binds*, p. 95.

a body."[13] The asynchronous, the queer, in this sense becomes a purely bodily experience. In relation to sexuality, time has also previously been a central marker – Freeman highlights Freud who based his theories on normative sexuality on temporal terms such as *Nachträglichkeit* (deferred action), and considered deviation either as "a sign of being stuck in a developmental phase or as an endless return to the past in a kind of psychic atavism."[14] Normative aspects of time in relation to sexuality can of course still be found today, also in queer theory, but queering temporality contains more than just observing feelings of timelessness, lateness, failure and delay. It can also be about political visions of the future and queer utopias.[15]

Indeed, perceptions and conceptions of time have somatic as well as political consequence; "temporality itself raises the question of embodiment and subjectivity", as queer theorist and medieval historian Carolyn Dinshaw points out.[16] An important aspect highlighted in queer temporality studies is the problem of "chrononormativity", i.e. the chronological norm of the heterosexual life curve which constitutes "a technique by which institutional forces come to seem like somatic facts", both shaping and being shaped by our actual bodies.[17] Childhood and puberty must in the right order be followed by adulthood's marriage and childbirth, which in older age leads to grandchildren – life's "dessert". The concept of chrononormativity, as coined by Elizabeth Freeman, reveals how naturalized this pattern is and how self-evidently individuals, society and politics relate to this norm for the supposedly ultimate distribution of reproduction and production.

In the end, the values that are critically highlighted by chrononormativity are about succession, maturity and development,

<hr>

[13] Freeman, "Introduction", GLQ 13:2–3 2007, p. 159.

[14] Freeman, "Introduction", p. 162.

[15] José Esteban Muñoz, *Cruising Utopia: The Then and There of Queer Futurity* (New York: New York University Press, 2009).

[16] Carolyn Dinshaw, "Temporalities", in Paul Strohm (Ed.), *Oxford Twenty-First-Century Approaches to Literature: Middle English* (Oxford: Oxford University Press, 2007), p. 109.

[17] Freeman, *Time Binds*, p. 3.

and if you oppose them, you risk appearing immature, outdated and out of joint with time. However, violations of normative conceptions of time also make possible a multiplication or dissemination of time. Alternate and queer violations of time norms can consist of "asynchrony, anachronism, anastrophe, belatedness, compression, delay, ellipsis, flashback, hysterone-proteron, pause, prolepsis, repetition, reversal, surprise", as Elizabeth Freeman puts it.[18] These kinds of terms and concepts describing time ruptures flourish also within Western modernity. For example, the concept of "anachronism" is an invention that was established in the 18th century.[19] In pre-modernity "syncretic chronology", a kind of timelessness, reigned instead.[20] A medieval painting could quite obviously depict soldiers at Jesus' tomb in contemporary 14th century armor, which created a temporal unity between the past and the now where Jesus is "not of a distant, foreign past, but of an eternal present".[21] Carolyn Dinshaw gives another example when she highlights the medieval mystic Margareta Kempe who falls into inconsolable tears in front of the altar's Jesus figure, exhibiting feelings of him just having died.[22] A syncretic chronology forms a temporal unity between past and present into an eternal now, the past turning constantly present instead of being "different".

Today, the worst anachronistic sin is to apply contemporary theories and concepts to the past – to talk about "homosexuality" when discussing pre-modernity, for instance. On the other hand, it becomes necessary to commit a certain amount of interpretive violence against the past in order to be able to con-

---

[18] Freeman, *Time Binds*, p. xxii.

[19] Cf. Margreta De Grazia, "Anachronism", in Brian Cummings & James Simpson (Eds.), *Cultural Reformations: Medieval and Renaissance in Literary History* (Oxford: Oxford University Press, 2010); Peter Burke, "The Sense of Anachronism from Petrarch to Poussin", in Chris Humphrey & W. M. Ormrod, *Time in the Medieval World* (York: York Medieval Press, 2001.

[20] Anthony Kemp, *The Estrangement of the Past: A Study in the Origins of Modern Historical Consciousness* (Oxford: Oxford University Press, 1991), p. 47.

[21] Kemp, *The Estrangement of the Past*, p. 50.

[22] Dinshaw, "Temporalities".

ceptualize it at all in the present; if it is to be possible to approach the past, a "necessary anachronism" is required (at least according to G. W. F. Hegel's claim in his *Ästhetik*). In classical historical materialist terms à la Walter Benjamin it is rather a matter of actualizing history, i.e. to constantly put the past in dialogue with the present perception of it in order to achieve political change.[23] New historicists point out that actualization in this sense actually constitutes an approach that can be compared to that of anachronism, which means that an interpretation – as well as objects, people, events or ideas – is placed in a time where it does not belong. Catherine Belsey emphasizes in the previously cited quotation that it is precisely this concept of difference between now and then that makes our imagination about the past enjoyable, while a figure like the time traveler, who strives to experience the past in its temporal location, instead creates a time conception in which similarity and continuity are stressed at the expense of possibilities of change.

Thus, anachronism in the sense of awareness of difference displays productive aspects too. It does not have to equal accusations of mistakes and wrongdoings but can infer contemporaneous political commitment. The real mistake, according to Belsey, is to try to reconstruct the past on the premise of similarity and its implied strive to bridge the time gap between now and then. To smooth out difference instead of affirming it and believing that the past and the present "resemble" each other, is according to Belsey in fact the properly pejorative anachronism. A conscious use of anachronism in the sense of clashing differences also implies that one takes responsibility for one's political and ideological positions, according to Swedish historian Sara Edenheim.[24] Rather, according to both Belsey and Edenheim, it ought to be a matter of alienating the past instead of identifying with it. In this way our questions of the past can be nothing but anachronistic. But precisely because of this can

[23] Walter Benjamin, "Eduard Fuchs, der Sammler und der Historiker", *Gesammelte Schriften II:2* (Frankfurt am Main: Suhrkamp, 1977), p. 468.
[24] Sara Edenheim, *Anakronismen: Mot den historiska manin* (Gothenburg: Glänta, 2011), p. 75.

our contemporary questions become interesting, important even, and a measure of "untimeliness" can hold emancipatory potential.

To dictatorially place the Other into a homogenizing temporality can be likened to abusive behavior, resulting in a loss of meaning: "History cannot represent, except through a process of translation and a consequent loss of status and significance for the translated, the heterotemporality of that world", writes postcolonial theorist Dipesh Chakrabarty.[25] Although temporality indeed requires some rewriting and translation – time requires metaphor according to Lynn Hunt[26], but to emphasize Otherness is not only a spatial marker but also a temporal one. The colonial heritage makes it obvious that space instead holds "a plurality of times existing together".[27]

Conclusion

Crucial ideas concerning asynchronous temporality have been presented by postcolonial and queer theorists in the last decade, but oddly enough they have left no mark whatsoever in mainstream history of theory.[28] Beside norm-critical aspects of temporality, which are key, queer- and postcolonial theory also pay attention to the somatising effects of temporality norms. Bodily affect, interwoven with sensory sensations and cognitive reactions, turns into emotions. They can entail feeling immature, to feel ahead of your time, passé, or even timeless. Emotions are not about chronology. Various emotions and emotional structures can exist in parallel at the same time, in the same place and in the same person. Mainstream history of emotions is more interested in studying diachronic perspectives, while a post-

---

[25] Chakrabarty, *Provincializing Europe*, p. 95.

[26] Lynn Hunt, *Measuring Time: Making History* (Budapest: Central European University Press, 2008), p. 3.

[27] Chakrabarty, *Provincializing Europe*, p. 109.

[28] Cf. *Breaking Up Time: Negotiating Border Between Present, Past and Future*, Berber Bevernage & Chris Lorenz (Eds.) (Göttingen: Vandehoeck & Rupprecht, 2013), a mainstream anthology discussing historiographical issues similar to this essay but without any reference to queer theorists and with only one reference to a postcolonial theorist.

colonial theorist like Achille Mbembe instead studies synchronic "entanglements" and its intersecting and clashing dimensions of time and emotion, and a queer theorist like Carolyn Dinshaw talks about a "touch across time" in which emotional connections are forged through the epochs creating coherence and political solidarity across temporal dimensions.

So, what kind of time conception ultimately takes shape – who speaks to whom, how and why? If the historical past in the universalizing sense of the Enlightenment signifies *all* pasts since it is assumed to be the *only* past, then the number of histories has certainly multiplied by now. Queer temporalities are critiquing linearity and causality, but not by opposing them and thus getting stuck in binaries such as linearity versus cyclicity, timeless versus time bound, contemporary versus non-contemporary, and so on. Instead of alteritism's static difference in the singular between present and past, it is all about differences in the plural. Time has several histories, evoked by multidimensional desires in which the past does not have to be assigned to the role of the excluded Other. Assuming the relevance of the body and its sensory experiences in relation to temporality, alternate non-hierarchical ways of conceiving connections between past, present, and future present themselves.

Chapter 3
The Demands of the Historical Unconscious
– the Psychopathology of History

Sara Edenheim[1]

> History is a deferred, symbolic substitution for the traumatic loss the past represents, an imaginary compensation for the temporality of existence, the projection of the desire for a redemptive significance in human behaviour. Consciousness needs this symbolic dimension since it cannot cope adequately, immediately, with the predicaments human behaviour occasions. The historical predicament is psychopathological.[2]

The liberal humanist orientation in most versions of historical research assumes that a historical consciousness is essential for human beings – often to such a high degree that *human* consciousness in itself has become synonymous with this *historical* consciousness. If history is the "common sense" of a society, then our "sense" is historical. As "common sense" in Swedish and other Germanic languages literally translates to "sane sense" (*sunt förnuft, sunt* meaning "healthy", "sound", "sane"), there is indeed a direct link to claims on knowledge of history and saneness, which are now lost in translation.

"Consciousness" often refers to cognition or understanding and it is possible to find historians also using concepts such as "historical understanding" or "historical awareness". The specific term consciousness (*medvetande/Bewusstsein/conscience*), however, dominates within the specific field and perspective introduced by German historians of didactics in the 1970s and

---

[1] This is a longer and translated version of an article entitled "Historiens psykopatologi" published in *Glänta*, Vol. 2 (2016).
[2] Martin L. Davies, *Historics – Why History Dominates Contemporary Society* (New York: Routledge, 2005), p. 236.

specifically developed by Jörn Rüsen and others. Even though the concept obviously can be found within many other different fields such as philosophy, psychology, phenomenology, neuro-sciences, psycho-analytical theory, etc., it is not evident from which of these fields historians of didactics have picked it up. Rüsen occasionally refers to the cognitive sciences, mainly in relation to different types of learning, but otherwise there are few definitions of the concept "consciousness" itself in his-torians' writing on historical consciousness. Rather focus is on the "historical" part, i.e., what it is that makes (the undefined) consciousness specifically *historical*:

> Rüsen's premise is that we comprehend the past in the form of narratives. Through 'narrative competence', Rüsen postu-lates, historical consciousness informs moral deliberation by connecting past, present, and future into a perceived actuality. Narrative competence brings this actuality into focus along with concomitant moral obligations. By creating a typology of possible narrative interpretations of the past, as his work seeks to do, empirical researchers may ask questions such as 'What role does historical consciousness play in everyday life, in politics, and in other spheres of life? Are there laws governing its development that are analogous to the laws that govern the development of logical, moral, and other cognitive skills [...]?'[3]

There are exceptions. In an interview with Rüsen and historian Roger Simon, Simon argues that focusing on identity, recogni-tion, and narrative are insufficient to understand historical consciousness. Simon wants to draw attention to other forces organizing memory and temporality (such as social perform-ance, fragments/trace, or fantasies of wholeness).[4] Their discre-pancies are defined by the interviewer in the following way:

---

[3] Roger Simon and Jörn Rüsen, "A dialogue on narrative and historical consciousness", in K. D. Heyer (Ed.) *Theorizing Historical Consciousness* (Toronto: University of Toronto Press, 2004), p. 203.
[4] Simon Rüsen, "A dialogue on narrative and historical consciousness".

> For Simon, a historical consciousness is a moral awareness that traces of the past arrive 'demanding something of us.' Rüsen too recognizes that the past demands something of us, but that something is cognitive coherence and moral action formed through narrative interpretations by the subject [...].[5]

This demand, issued from the past in the cases of both Simon and Rüsen, takes a very different form depending on how the past is perceived: as traces or as coherent narratives. For Rüsen, the demand is a clear moral imperative: only by knowing your past will you know yourself and know which action is right and which is wrong. The past is here filled with agency, and the consciousness is pre-filled with the capability to handle the demands of the past: it is a consciousness that already knows that by making a narrative interpretation it will manage to translate the demand into a comprehensible message, where only that which is comprehensible is moral. Consciousness hence seems to overlap with the historical: they are one and the same, making "historical consciousness" a tautology that embraces all human thinking and action. This is not specific to historians using the concept, but rather a signifying trait of all historical research that ex-historian Martin L. Davies describes as "organic": "[t]he organic conception of history has thus a distinct, pragmatic force. It underpins a self-authenticating, holistic view of history 'as everything" [...]".[6]

The historical consciousness is imagined as sovereign and all-inclusive, and therefore there would be no point in going 'behind' it, to understand its causes and its constitutive limits. However, this organic history, Davies argues, is a late creation, modern and Western, where we are all assumed to be constituted through historical thinking ("historic sense as natural sense"). In its place, Davies proposes a splitting of the tautology, by showing how consciousness precedes the historical and hence is independent of the historical. His is neither a decon-

---

[5] Rüsen, "A dialogue on narrative and historical consciousness", p. 203.

[6] Davies, *Historics – Why History Dominates Contemporary Society,* p. 38.

structive nor a psychoanalytical approach, but I think this splitting of the historical from consciousness is helpful to start an investigation into the important difference between history and temporality. When Derrida, e.g., states that *time* is the origin of difference, and hence for subjectification, he meant time and not *history*. Historical consciousness is rather based on the assumption of history as the origin of *sameness*; historical consciousness requires recognition and identification over time, not alienation and difference. Even though the differentiation between the past, the present, and the future is intrinsic to historical consciousness (as well as to many other versions of consciousness), the aim of the historical consciousness is to fill these entities with recognizable contents, coherency, and common sense that all make a claim on reality. This is what makes history legitimate in relation to, for example, myths, bad memory, anachronisms, fantasies, and gossip. History hence uses a certain perception of the past to stabilize not only the present, but also the future, by filling these temporal states with coherency and meaning, i.e. what is recognizable as *the same*. To not only be constituted by this historical consciousness, but also to accept it and not interrogate it, are the prerequisites of organic historical research. This consciousness is usually presented as the only resource we have to understand ourselves and our world. Because it demands sameness, Davies claims that the historical consciousness is not only a conservative impulse, but also instigates an unethical approach by foreclosing other alternatives of human action and responsibility. It also, interestingly, produces quite dogmatic and inferior forms of representation:

> The 'organic' conception of history is, then, the most comprehensive, coercive version form of knowledge. It explains why history perpetuates 'the same old thing', is regarded as society's 'default knowledge', and inevitably affirmative. It also explains why history is essentially conservative, why it activates archaic, regressive tendencies. Though it imposes itself metaphorically, e.g., as (a) 'an everlasting animal' or as an 'inexorable chain', history proves to be (b) secondary to the

immediate sense of personal purpose or self-possession [*aesthesis, Eigensinn*], and (c) a subordinate genre of aesthetic representation.[7]

Within psychoanalytic theory there are many ways to relate to temporality and especially the relationship between the past, present, and future. As metaphor, of course, the *Id* could be seen as the past – uncontrollable, incomprehensible drives that constitute us but that are difficult, usually impossible to acknowledge and handle without enormous psychological dangers, just as immutable as the acts of the past that cannot be changed because they have already been committed. Still they are our responsibility since we are dependent on them for who we are. The *Ego*, that present state we always find ourselves in, that we can influence and alter, orient ourselves in, feel at home or lost in, that which we think we know. And then the *Super-ego*, the future, for whom we do everything for, for whom we act and adapt ourselves for, for this is where the verdict will come from, where we will be held responsible for our acts and desires. A very simplified metaphor, but still one example of a relation to past, present, future that is not dependent on coherent narratives for ethical orientation and knowledge.

It is also an approach that takes in account all events and experiences from the past, not only those we remember or have taken notice of and hence have ended up in an archive of sorts. As Djuna Barnes once wrote: "Those long remembered can alone claim to be long forgotten".[8] Rather, it is by assuming that most things happening to us are forgotten or foreclosed, and that all we will be able to know about them is that they (forever undefined and unknown) are part of that which constitutes us and our present state, that the unknown, the incomprehensible, the non-colonizable – that which escapes us – is not going away no matter how hard we try. They are there as our memento mori. They are so many and vast, these events and experiences,

---

[7] Davies, *Historics – Why History dominates Contemporary Society*, p. 39.
[8] Djuna Barnes, *Nightwood* (New York: A New Direction 2006; 1937).

forever lost and not recoupable, and what they can teach us is 'only' how to handle and live with lost events and experiences, without dreaming of their redemption.[9]

Why are some events treated as more historical than others? Are they remembered for no particular reason? Of course, all events – also the most well-known ones – are forever lost, but we keep reproducing narratives of them for specific reasons, reasons that have more to do with us than with the events themselves. Arbitrariness and coincidences are part of everything, but the unconscious tries to make sense even of that and hence, retroactively, even the random fluke is accorded meaning. What we have then are unnarratable events (as all events are) that haunt us – sometimes because they are traumatic and sometimes it is just their general unnarratability that haunts us – and then we have the efforts to make sense of some of these events: that we call history. And this history is therefore always contingent.

Now, the institutionalization of historical research and methods has made history 'less' arbitrary and more predictable (one could even say more boring): the national archives organize history in accordance with state laws and state interests, and the archives of social movements organize history in accordance with a specific group's interests. Desire, then, seems to organize history, no matter if it is a nation's desire or that of an individual. *This* could make history interesting and useful, but only if it stops reproducing 'the same old thing'.

Lacan, too, wanted to understand how we perceive temporality. Just as in the case of Derrida, time is not about history or even narratives. Even though language is the cause of the temporal experience, it is language in the form of sentences, words, phonemes, that interest Lacan – not the specific and contextual content of language – as is the case of the historian that has to fill 'the past' with a specific content to be able to write anything historical to constitute the historical consciousness (no

---

[9] See also Sara Edenheim, *Anakronismen – mot den historiska manin* (Gothenburg: Glänta, 2011).

wonder this consciousness always ends up belonging to a modernist, liberal subject). A syllable must be placed in front of another to become a word; when I speak, I am dependent on the ability (or rather the limitation) to make a temporal difference between the first and the next syllable, and when I write, I am equally dependent on the spatial difference between letters or signs. This is a physical dependency; we cannot place the syllables and letters on top of each other or utter them all at once even if we wanted to. It is this that Davies refers to as the *real* organic consciousness – as opposed to the historical one that only tries to become organic. The ability to make temporal differences – gaps in time that create a before and an after – is necessary for any language. As we all know, though we often forget it, language is something we all must learn – it is not there from the beginning and, hence, our sense of temporality is not there from the beginning either. More importantly though, the kind of temporality that language requires and that is required of all of us, is not the same temporality which is produced by a historical consciousness. The necessary temporality of language is a source of frustration – every time we say something we are forced to subject ourselves to this temporality that tears up all emotions and thoughts into systematically organized syllables, while simultaneously having to deal with the fact that it is only through this tearing up that we become intelligible subjects before others and ourselves, that it is only through this constant destruction of any imaginary wholeness that our emotions and thoughts can not only be expressed but even constituted (the unconscious is, as Lacan remarks, structured like a language). The temporality of language uncovers our lack and impotence, our inability to communicate freely and autonomously without limitations. This is why we continue to speak, hoping that the continuous flow of words will somehow fill the gaps, make them less noticeable, and maybe even reach a stage of completeness, of a successful transmission, a final concluding remark where nothing more has to be added.

Historical temporality, on the other hand, is a source of enjoyment – not despair – where the petty fantasy scenarios of the Ego all fall in place, the gaps are filled and the content pointing towards the present (i.e. us), explaining our existence, our origin and our objective. This is why the end of history – famously declared by Fukuyama after the fall of the Berlin wall – created a hysteric reaction in the field of history. Not because the field was critical of the liberal capitalist positioning of Fukuyama, but because the statement itself threatened to uncover the underlying fundament of history as a field: that historians always consider themselves to be at the end of history (what Walter Benjamin called "empty time"). At the same time, seemingly paradoxical, the statement also threatened the very idea that historians could become redundant if there were no more history. "The end of history", hence, worked on two levels: the representative and the literal. The representative was too close to the truth and hence dangerous; the literal was too close to the fantasy scenario of historians: of having filled all the gaps and reached the final concluding remark, and that afterward, all that would remain is the death of the field, the death of the historian. That which in one sense is the force of history – to fill the gaps – is hence simultaneously the most dreaded aim *if* fulfilled. The possible fulfillment of this aim therefore must be foreclosed for the enjoyment to go on – forever into the future. The field of history is founded on this foreclosing of the death drive and the continuation of the imaginary omnipotence of the present/Ego. Davies describes this as follows:

> Historians may well claim to revive the past. In reality the past keeps historians alive; through history death directs present life. If the past really were over and done with, history would be redundant, historians superfluous. Were it not so self-absorbed, present historical consciousness would realize that, to identify with the past at all, it must first have produced itself as a historical object, become petrified in historical form. That is ultimately why historical interests are not existential interests, why history is an anaesthetic [an-aesthesis], nothing vital. As a 'pure culture of the death drive', the already historicized world is a typically melancholic formation (Freud

1982: 203). The historicization process conceals a morbid psychopathology.[10]

The field of history is founded on this foreclosing of the death drive and the reproduction of an imaginary omnipotent "present/Ego" that this foreclosure enables. There are many reasons why it is important to identify this psychopathology of history: one reason is that this pathology demands a historical consciousness of us all, not least those marginalized groups that can only reach recognition and rights by demonstrating a historical continuity, an inborn identity, and a common experience over time (not to mention those groups that cannot demonstrate such a narrative and hence are left without recognition and rights). As Benjamin wrote, we live in a constant state of emergency, but the demand of a historical consciousness permits us to call this state *progress*:

> The tradition of the oppressed teaches us that the 'state of emergency' in which we live is not the exception but the rule. We must attain to a conception of history that is in keeping with this insight. Then we shall clearly realize that it is our task to bring about a real state of emergency, and this will improve our position in the struggle against Fascism. One reason why Fascism has a chance is that in the name of progress its opponents treat it as a historical norm. The current amazement that the things we are experiencing are 'still' possible in the twentieth century is not philosophical. This amazement is not the beginning of knowledge – unless it is the knowledge that the view of history which gives rise to it is untenable.[11]

Is it not quite remarkable how Benjamin's words, written in 1940, also portray Europe in 2023? His own text has become such a monad, a snapshot, that he claimed we need to shatter the idea of history as inexorable progression. If the unconscious is conditioned by temporality, it is a temporality without any

[10] Davies, *Historics – Why History Dominates Contemporary Society*, pp. 243–235.
[11] Walter Benjamin, *On the Concepts of History* (1940) Thesis VIII.

demands on continuity; it is rather discontinuity, disruption, and the silence in between words, that constitute it. The conscious, too, is structured like a language, but with a demand on continuity between the past, the present, and the future, at least when it is forced to be historical. The conscious consists of what the unconscious has condensed, that is, of that which the subject can handle without risking a total dissolving of the self (psychosis), of that which is picked out to build consistent and comprehensible identities (images) of this self. Today there is an effort to build such selves and as in all efforts, a certain pleasure is involved. A pleasure to replace that which hurts – here and now. Through this flight from pain, from the real, history becomes synonymous with consciousness; as a condensation of the past, a corrected comprehension of acts and desires already carried out and experienced by others. This is why history is both conservative *and* pleasurable: it shelters the subject from all that demands change and hence prevents the eradication of the self as it is known by itself. Instead, organic history promises more of the same. If the present is an emergency, which it is, we must look at the past and its relation to our time in another way than the one that is presently mass-produced in an almost hysterical effort to deny us the responsibility of this emergency.

Chapter 4
The Problem with the Problems of Philosophy
– Challenging European Modernity

Naomi Scheman[1]

> The sickness of a time is cured by an alteration in the mode of
> life of human beings, and it was possible for the sickness of
> philosophical problems to get cured only through a changed
> mode of thought and of life, not through a medicine invented
> by an individual.[2]

Three-year-olds (in many, though perhaps not all times, and places) are given to asking "why?", persistently repeating the query long after grown-ups take themselves to have adequately responded to it. As proto-scientists, children are trying to figure out the world around them, and they have not yet been disciplined into distinguishing between proper and improper questions – the "proper" ones being those that lend themselves to being answered, either by someone who already knows the answer or by some form of investigation likely to produce one. "Improper" questions are often the residue, what's left over after experts have been consulted and investigations carried out. There will always be residue – in particular, the unexamined assumptions that form the ground on which we stand and that

[1] An earlier version of this paper was written for, and presented at, a conference on Feminist Utopias: Transforming the Present of Philosophy: Historical and Contemporary Perspectives, which met in Reykjavík and Skálholt, Iceland, 30 March–2 April 2017, co-hosted by Feminist Philosophy Transforming Philosophy at the University of Iceland and the Nordic Summer University Study Circle on "Feminist Philosophy: Time, History, and the Transformation of Thought". My thanks to my fellow participants for lively discussions and, especially, to the organizers Eyja Brynjarsdóttir, Synne Myrebøe, Valgerður Pálmadóttir, Johanna Sjöstedt, and Sigríður Þorgeirsdóttir.
[2] Ludwig Wittgenstein, *Remarks on the Foundations of Mathematics*, (Ed.) G. H. von Wright, R. Rhees, & G. E. M. Anscombe, trans. G. E. M. Anscombe, 3rd ed. (Oxford: Blackwell, 1978), p. 132.

cannot be excavated down to bedrock. The demand for such absolute excavation was at the heart of Descartes's agenda-setting for modern European philosophy, and the impossibility of carrying it out is at the heart of Wittgenstein's revolutionary attempt to wean us from what he saw as the problematic problems of philosophy.

Descartes' method of doubt was his response to the crises facing Europe as it attempted to democratically overturn structures that had been grounded in stable religious, social, economic, and political hierarchies, at the same time as voyages of "discovery" led to encounters with people who thought and acted in radically different ways. The challenge was to empower ordinary people without unleashing a cacophony of different, conflicting voices; and the solution was to posit that, underneath merely superficial differences, people (those who mattered: see below) were fundamentally the same, and could be counted on to reach the same conclusions, whether concerning (to take the paradigm example) mathematics, or science, or even how to organize society. Descartes's method was an attempt to find that common ground, that core of rational selfhood that could yield unassailable knowledge, the bedrock on which science and, ultimately, ethics, could rest. As I will suggest below, this project generated what we have come to identify as the central problems of philosophy, the problems Wittgenstein works not to solve but to dissolve.

The problem with philosophical problems, however, is not with our tendency to ask them, but rather with our demand that they be properly, finally, answered. Unlike most three-year-olds, who grow out of what they are taught to see as pointless querying, philosophers persist in being preoccupied with what's left over to worry about after the serious grown-ups have gotten on with whatever it is that serious grown-ups do, including asking only proper questions. This disciplining of inquiry is especially evident in the training of scientists and other credentialed grown-up inquirers. Those who raise questions unsanctioned by the relevant disciplinary methods often find those questions characterized as "philosophical", and some of those undisciplined inquirers discover that the term is not just a slur but rather an actual discipline of its own, and they sometimes find their way to our classrooms and offices. Unfortunately, however, what they too often find there is, precisely, a discipline, committed to framing answerable questions, even if those questions continue to look odd to outsiders. Academic, especially analytic, philosophy has, I want to suggest, succumbed to the prestige structures that reward inquiry that looks "scientific". I want to make a case for undisciplining philosophy, for keeping open the space for improper questions, and for thinking critically about what those questions ought to be, and about why – despite not lending themselves to proper answers – it is nonetheless important to ask them.

Modern Philosophy and Euro-Modernity

Modern (Western) philosophy emerged in explicit engagement with the political, economic, and social transformations that shaped modern Europe, including Europe's interactions with the rest of the world. The philosophical subject – the bearer of the problems of philosophy, the philosophical "we" – was the (allegedly) generically human modern European, heterosexual, able-bodied, Christian, bourgeois man (*sic*); and he needed to be articulated, theorized, and empowered, alongside the "external" world that complemented him. This practical, political philosophical task was explicit in the work of early modern philosophers, even when they were doing what we would now characterize as epistemology or metaphysics (i.e., what in many European universities explicitly, and problematically, contrasts with "practical" philosophy). The problems that have defined modern Western philosophy are the residue of the specific project of becoming this sort of person, that is, of acquiring the forms of distinctively modern privilege that allow one to count as an exemplar of generic humanness. I follow Stanley Cavell in placing skepticisms of various sorts at the heart of these problems – not surprisingly, I have argued, when the projects of self-crafting demand that one push away anything that threatens the autonomy and rationality of the self. Small wonder that everything – one's own body, including one's senses, the "external" world, other people – on the other side of this carefully crafted chasm should seem problematic, and that admitting all of that, however tenuously, into the sphere of what one knows should require exercizing control over it.[3]

These are not "pseudo-problems"; they are poignantly real, and it is not the need to ask them that Wittgenstein finds problematic. They do genuinely trouble the projects of constructing privileged (as generic) modern European subjectivity. And they haunt all those who have, over the centuries, succeeded, however tenuously and incompletely, in being included in the ranks of those who are taken, however grudgingly, to be relevantly the same as European heterosexual, able-bodied, Christian, bourgeois men. But over the centuries the project of constructing this character – of articulating his possibility and enthroning his status as generic – has receded from explicit attention, no longer needing to be fought for.

Along with the normalization of modern European subjectivity – that is, the hegemonic status of that way of being human – we have seen the institutionalizing of philosophy as an academic discipline, increasingly specialized as other disciplines broke off from it, going their own ways at the point at which their problems became methodologically tractable. The combination of these two processes has led to the hollowing out of philosophical problems, which have become increasingly abstract, scholasticized, needing to be "motivated". Thus, for example, we try to convince our students that the ground on which they uncritically stand when judging both what is and what ought to be the case is, strictly speaking (we say, speaking strictly) mere quicksand, however firm it may feel beneath their feet. We may take this unsettling to be heroic, disrupting the

---

[3] I have made this argument in a number of papers, most explicitly in "Othello's Doubt/Desdemona's Death: The Engendering of Skepticism" in Judith Genova (Ed.), *Power, Gender, Values* (Edmonta, Alberta: Academic Printing and Publishing, 1987), reprinted in Scheman, Naomi, *Engenderings: Constructions of Knowledge, Authority, and Privilege* (New York: Routledge, 1993).

complacency of unexamined assumptions, challenging entrenched ideologies. But a wholly general, unfocused demand to "question everything" is ill-suited to genuine critique, not so much because it is a demand that cannot be met as because it cannot coherently be undertaken: we are always of necessity making choices about just what to call into question, and those choices are guided by the projects in which we are engaged. Academic philosophy's questions have been framed by the project of grounding the authority of the privileged modern European subject, and while those questions may reveal the ground under his feet to be unstable, it has been far too easy to dismiss that instability as both inevitable and, for serious grown-ups, ignorable. The instability seems inevitable so long as the project that rests on that particular ground is seen as the achievement of generically human rationality, while the demonstrable successes of that project (the achievements of Euro-modernity, science not least among them) license ignoring the instability, shunting the problem off onto philosophers and taking neither it nor them seriously. What doesn't get called into question is precisely the project itself. What we are left with are what I call "zombie problems": with life sucked out of them, they stalk the halls of academe, undead and unkillable.

Might the solution be to breathe life back into those problems – to reconnect with the political projects that originally animated them? After all, the achievement of privileged-as-generic subjectivity is an on-going project, both for those individuals expected to engage in it and for those who have fought for the right to be included, not to mention that this fight for inclusion is far from won. Maybe, that is, the core philosophical problems of Euro-modernity are the problems we ought to have, and what we need to do is to recognize them for what they are – not the free-floating scholastic zombies they have become, but the flesh and blood anxieties that haunt the achievement of subjectivity. The work of Stanley Cavell can be seen as engaging in this sort of resuscitation, uncovering the anxieties that pulse beneath the tamed and trivialized problems that exercise academic philosophy.[4]

Looking back on how I became a feminist philosopher (specifically, a feminist epistemologist), I am struck by the major role played by Cavell's work. I was immensely moved by his grounding philosophical problems – notably those of skepticism – in the human condition, but I was unable to place myself, as a woman philosopher, within the story. His central example was Othello, whose gender is hardly irrelevant to the story; nor, of course, is Desdemona's.[5] If a woman philosopher is to take on the problems emblematized by Othello's inability to live with or without Desdemona's separate, independent subjectivity, she needs to regard her own gendered experience as irrelevant to her philosophizing. For many women – even many feminists – such irrelevance is more a promise than a threat, a liberation from sexist constraints rather than a deprivation of a liberatory standpoint.[6] But such a move requires our accepting the generic status of the markers of masculine privilege, making the feminist project one of extending that status and that privilege to women. Such, of course, is the unfulfilled promise of liberalism, including liberal feminism, along with analogous (also unfulfilled) promises made with respect to the other sorts of privilege (race, class, etc.) that mark the subject of Euro-modernity.

[4] See especially Stanley Cavell, *Must We Mean What We Say*, updated edition (Cambridge: Cambridge University Press, 2001); and *The Claim of Reason: Wittgenstein, Skepticism, Morality, and Tragedy*, new edition (Oxford: Oxford University Press, 1999).

[5] It was grappling with Cavell that framed "Othello's Doubt/Desdemona's Death: The Engendering of Skepticism", my first paper on the ways in which the "human condition" is in fact gendered. For a fuller discussion of the dilemmas of finding one's voice as a woman philosopher, see Naomi Scheman, "A Storied World: On Meeting and Being Met" in Richard Eldridge & Bernie Rhie (Eds.), *Stanley Cavell & Literary Studies* (New York: Continuum Press, 2011).

[6] See, for example, Louise Antony, "Sisters, Please, I'd Rather Do It Myself", *Philosophical Topics* (1995) 23: 59–94.

Philosophy Beyond Euro-Modernity

The struggles for inclusion in the ranks of those who count as essentially the same as privileged European men are on-going, but especially since the mid-20th century those struggles have lost their grip on liberatory imaginations. Movements such as anti-colonial nationalisms, Black Power, queer activism, indigenous politics and culture, and some strains of feminism have all emphasized the depth of difference and the resources of differences for knowing and acting. While some of these movements have embraced essentialisms of various forms, many have not: differences are often seen as historical, multiple, intersecting, and shifting – but all the same neither superficial nor ignorable, and, importantly, they are sources of insight, passion, resistance, and imagination. Versions of standpoint epistemologies have emphasized the ways in which marginalized perspectives can yield (with intellectual and activist effort) knowledge less available to those who see the world through the distorting lenses of privilege. And resistant imaginations have expanded the repertoire of the possible, "queering" the presumptively normal and desirable. As diverse as these new (and some not-so-new) visions are, there are many points of striking congruence across great distances of time, space, and social location, a congruence that can seem puzzling until one understands it as revealing the specific peculiarity of Euro-modernity.[7]

Central to that peculiarity is the figure of the autonomous individual, crucially articulated through a focus on epistemic independence. The central figures of early modern European philosophy were arguably more attentive than they are often portrayed to the necessities of relying on the testimony of others for much of what we know (or at least, on their view, justifiably believe).[8] And certainly the growth of modern science would have been impossible without the ability to rely on the observa-

---

[7] See, for example, Sandra Harding, *Science and Social Inequality: Feminist and Postcolonial Issues* (Urbana/Chicago: University of Illinois Press, 2006).
[8] See Joseph Shieber, "Locke on Testimony: A Reexamination", *History of Philosophy Quarterly* (2009) 26: 21–41.

tions and experimental results of others. But the rationality of such reliance rested in large measure on the essential interchangeability of those dependent on one another: it was a mere accident that placed you but not me in a position to acquire a particular piece of knowledge – presuming, of course, that both you and I are among those whose observational and rational capacities are deemed worthy of respect. In other words, the modern European individual is fundamentally generic; individualism in practice rested on a denial of the deep significance of individuality. We may be dependent, but those on whom we properly depend are in all important respects indistinguishable from us. And the progress of liberalism has in large measure been a matter of the expansion of the ranks of the "we" who count as essentially the same.

Thus, for example, recent analytic epistemology has explicitly recognized the fact of massive doxastic dependency (albeit primarily in the marked subfield of "social epistemology", leaving the individualist conception at the unmarked center). While people were always dependent on others for much of what they believed, when it came to the sorts of systematized knowledge with which the philosophers were most concerned, a large degree of independence made a certain amount of sense – as today it obviously does not.[9] This recognition centrally includes taking on the problem of testimony, meaning the acquisition of beliefs based on what others tell us. But in most discussions of the problem, both the testifiers and those who are dependent on them are generic, "zombifying" the problem by writing out of its conceptualization social locations and relations, importantly those that involve the discrepancies and inequities of power and privilege that crucially inflect questions of whom and when and why to trust what we are given to believe. It is within feminist epistemology – and allied fields committed, often explicitly intersectionally, to addressing issues from post-

---

[9] For the classic statement of this situation – even among people who are experts in aspects of the relevant field – see John Hardwig, "Epistemic Dependence", *The Journal of Philosophy* (1985) 82: 335–49.

and de-colonial, anti-racist, indigenous, queer, and anti-ableist perspectives – that these important questions are transforming epistemology, breathing life back into it through engagement with the problems distinctive of the 21st century.[10]

If we take seriously the historical specificity of the philosophical subject and of the problems of philosophy, the meta-question becomes: What are the tasks of philosophy in a world in which the allegedly generic status of the modern European bourgeois (etc.) man is increasingly challenged by a diverse range of "others"? What residues of the diverse projects of the acquisition of subjectivity in today's world shape the philosophical problems we *ought* to have – not in order to answer them, but rather to critically trouble those projects, to have a sense of when and how and why we (different ones of us) need to unsettle the ground on which we stand? Distinctively feminist – along with anti-colonial, indigenous, critical race theoretic, queer, and disability-centered – philosophy grapples with this question about philosophy's questions. However, to date the challenge has had little impact, especially in analytic epistemology and metaphysics, where the core problems are still seen, zombie-like, as ahistorical, and universal.

---

[10] Much of this attention has been prompted by Miranda Fricker's *Epistemic Injustice: Power and the Ethics of Knowing* (Oxford: Oxford University Press, 2007) but a great deal of related work both precedes and critically responds to that important book, including work in standpoint epistemology and in epistemologies of ignorance. See, for example, Partricia Hill Collins, *Black Feminist Thought: Knowledge, Consciousness and the Politics of Empowerment*, 2nd ed. (New York: Routledge, 2000); Charles Mills, *Black Rights/White Wrongs: The Critique of Racial Liberalism* (Oxford: Oxford University Press, 2017); and José Medina, *The Epistemology of Resistance: Gender and Racial Oppression, Epistemic Injustice, and Resistant Imaginations* (Oxford: Oxford University Press, 2013). For overviews of the field, see, for example, Kristie Dotson (Ed.), *Interstices: Inheriting Women of Color Feminist Philosophy*, Special issue of *Hypatia* 29 (2014); and Ian James Kidd, Gaile Pohlhaus, & José Médina (Eds.), *The Routledge Handbook of Epistemic Injustice* (New York: Routledge, 2017). I drew on the trope of breathing life back into a moribund subject in Naomi Scheman, "Epistemology Resuscitated: Objectivity as Trustworthiness" in Sandra Morgen & Nancy Tuana (Eds.), *(En)Gendering Rationalities* (New York: SUNY Press, 2001); reprinted in Scheman, *Shifting Ground: Knowledge & Reality, Transgression & Trustworthiness* (Oxford: Oxford University Press, 2011).

Among the very few things these days about which I am optimistic is that the discipline of philosophy is changing. Here feminist philosophy has played and will continue to play a major role in those changes – so long as it is deeply committed to intersectionality and to solidarity with other, intertwined liberatory struggles. Thus, we need to start by asking, not whether philosophy ought to engage with the larger society, as though that were one option some of us some of the time might pursue, but, rather, how philosophers (all of us) ought to grapple with our various personal and institutional entanglements (of dependence, complicity, vulnerability, resistance) in political, economic, and social structures. We (meaning here philosophers, even those who take their work to have no political ramifications whatsoever) are, whether we choose to acknowledge it or not, always already engaged; and those engagements and entanglements are part of who we are, parts of the subjectivities whose problems it is our disciplinary mission to take on. As María Lugones has argued, we "animate", independently of our own intentions, the figures whose social locations we occupy, and the meanings of our words are (not determined but) shaped by that animation.[11] If, to use a Cavellian turn of phrase, we don't *want* to mean what we say, if we want to mean differently, we need to struggle to change the social structures within which we, and what we mean, take shape.

Some questions we need to be asking: What will become of philosophy when those who practice it engage *explicitly and critically* with the fraught complexities of saying "we"? What would it mean for philosophy to play as germinal a role in the struggles around diverse emerging alternative (post)modernities as it did in the emergence of European modernity? In order to play that role philosophers will need to be variously engaged with those struggles – to learn from them as much as to contribute to them – and that argues for the importance not only of

---

[11] Maria Lugones, "Playfulness, 'World'-Travelling, and Loving Perception", *Hypatia* (1987) 2: 3–19; reprinted in Lugones, *Pilgrimages/Peregrinajes* (Lanham MD: Rowman and Littlefield, 2003).

increasing diversity in the professoriate but equally for confronting the zombies and moving "from margin to center" approaches to core philosophical problems that take such diversity seriously.

Increasing diversity in academic philosophy is not just a matter of justice, of remedying histories of unjust exclusion: it is equally a matter of challenging the nature of philosophy itself. While people from under-represented groups have diverse philosophical interests and should not be expected to choose their fields of interest based on their membership in those groups, it is nonetheless true that a great deal of philosophical work is emerging from the perspectives of those who, for a wide range of reasons, do not see themselves as generic subjects and whose philosophizing is inflected by that sense of alienation. They are, in José Medina's words, "speaking from elsewhere", in (in Lugones's terms) new and emerging "worlds of sense", in which they and their words mean differently.[12] From such perspectives, saying "we" is a consciously political move, one that is grounded not in demographic commonality but rather in political solidarity. As such, it calls for acknowledgment – not agreement, but respectful, thoughtful engagement.[13] Such engagement, as an intentional activity, needs to start with acknowledgment of the multifarious ways in which we are always already engaged, specifically as philosophers, especially those of us who are institutionally embedded and supported, but more broadly as the people we are, located in a landscape shaped by a range of entangled inequities – engaged in what the Chicana theorist Cherríe Moraga has called "theories in the flesh" and the trans philosopher Talia Bettcher has called "ground-bound philosophy".[14] What – we need to ask – are we doing when we speak,

---

[12] José Medina, *Speaking from Elsewhere* (Albany NY: SUNY Press, 2006); Maria Lugones, "On the Logic of Pluralist Feminism" in Card, Claudia (Ed.), *Feminist Ethics* (Lawrence KS: University Press of Kansas, 1991), reprinted in Lugones, *Pilgrimages/ Peregrinajes*, where "worlds of sense" are further theorized in many of the chapters.

[13] See Naomi Scheman, "A Storied World: On Meeting and Being Met".

[14] Cherrie Moraga & Gloria Anzaldúa (Eds.), *This Bridge Called My Back: Writings by Radical Women of Color* (San Francisco: Aunt Lute Press, 1981), p. 23; Talia Mae Bettcher, "What Is Trans Philosophy", *Hypatia* (2019) 34: 644–667.

write, and teach? To whom do we hold ourselves accountable? To whom do we listen; from whom do we learn; whose critical responses do we take seriously?

One place to start is with a slogan with a long history but nowadays most associated with the disability rights movement: "Nothing about us without us". As many have pointed out, while much philosophy and other theorizing have gone on as though everyone (or, anyway, everyone who mattered) were able-body-minded, heterosexual, affluent, Christian, European cis-men, it has hardly been uncommon for there to be treatises aimed at accounting for one or another sort of deviation from that norm. Being "other", that is, has frequently meant being a particularly fascinating or problematic object of knowledge, never being either a knowing subject or a credible critic of the knowledge claims being made about one. Talia Mae Bettcher has aptly characterized this state of affairs in a paper entitled, "When Tables Speak", in which she takes on those who theorize trans identities from an unproblematized stance of gender conformity, seemingly oblivious to the fact that there are trans women and men (along with variously other gender non-conforming people) among one's readers, actual people struggling with the stigmatization that comes from having one's identity subject to legitimacy tests set by privileged outsiders.[15]

The field of epistemologies of ignorance also addresses this problem. Starting with Charles Mills' work on white ignorance,[16] the field focuses on the ways in which privilege creates, sustains, and rewards ignorance: white people, for example, are both enabled and motivated not to know the extent and depth of racism and derive tangible benefits not just from the operations of white supremacy but also from their ignorance of those operations. And the flip side of the epistemology of ignorance is

---

[15] Talia Mae Bettcher, "When Tables Speak: On the Existence of Trans Philosophy", Guest post on the *Daily Nous* blog, 30 May 2018. https://dailynous.com/2018/05/30/tables-speak-existence-trans-philosophy-guest-talia-mae-bettcher/, accessed 26 October 2021.

[16] Charles Mills, "White Ignorance" in Shannon Sullivan & Nancy Tuana (Eds.), *Race and Epistemologies of Ignorance* (Albany NY: SUNY Press, 2007).

standpoint epistemology, going back to Marx's account of how and why the proletariat is better positioned – given the development of class consciousness – to understand the workings of capitalism than are the capitalists. It is not just that those in subordinated locations have the right to theorize their own situation, not even that they are better placed than are privileged outsiders to do so, but also that those in such locations are in a better position to understand the structures that subordinate them and, even, to provide insight into those who oppress them – as Lugones urges white women to regard women of color as "credible mirrors". "Nothing about us without us", that is, is not a blanket shield against the perspectives of others but rather a set of power-inflected demands for credible subjectivities on the part of those relegated to the status of objects.

The achievement of those subjectivities requires political struggle – as did the achievement of the normative generic subjectivity of Euro-modernity. One distinctive feature of the shift away from Euro-modernity is relinquishing the demand for the generic, in favor of the embracing of diversity as an epistemic and political resource, not a problem to be surmounted. Consequently, the political struggles will need to be coalitional, and the theories that help make sense of them will need to be intersectional. Such coalitional praxis calls for what María Lugones has called "complex communication", which relinquishes the demand that others make themselves intelligible to me before I can engage with them:

> Complex communication thrives on recognition of opacity and on reading opacity, not through assimilating the texts of others to our own. Rather, it is enacted through a change in one's own vocabulary, one's sense of self, one's way of living, in the extension of one's collective memory, through developing forms of communication that signal disruption of the reduction attempted by the oppressor.[17]

[17] Maria Lugones, "On Complex Communication", *Hypatia* (2006) 21: 75–85, p. 84.

We will, that is, need to learn to move in other worlds of sense, to grapple with disorientation,[18] to acknowledge that we are in part the people others see us as and to take responsibility for how we animate those beings, to live on shifting ground, recognizing that the ground is not bedrock and that that makes it more, not less, worthy of our respect, as it is in need of our care.

This paper, like almost everything I write, is deeply indebted to María's work and the inspiration of her life.

[18] On the moral value of disorientation, see Ami Harbin, *Disorientation and Moral Life* (Oxford: Oxford University Press, 2016).

PART 2
Transformations in History

Chapter 5
"Suppose a man be in a deep contemplative study"
Margaret Cavendish, Descartes' Cogito and the Freedom of Thought

Cecilia Rosengren

Opinion is Free

Should Margaret Cavendish (1623–1673) be included in the society of feminist philosophers? For she did not elaborate on the rights of women in general, neither did she actively defend changes to the legal system that would favor women's autonomy, nor explicitly propose an education system for girls.[1] However, she was a philosopher who wrote and published extensively at a time when women were generally considered less capable of intellectual work. She also developed an original natural philosophy and sent her books to university libraries and to other scholars hoping for a response and the prospect of being part of the republic of letters and learning of her age. Meaning that she did not let her opinions remain in private circulation, under a pseudonym nor anonymously, as many other early modern women preferred, but licensed herself to be a public thinker. As she declared in *Philosophical Letters* (1664):

---

[1] Scholars have been puzzled by Cavendish's contradictory opinions on gender. See for instance the chapter "Cavendish, a Feminist?" in Londa Schiebinger, *The Mind has no Sex? Women in the Origins of Modern Science* (London/Cambridge Massachusetts: Harvard University Press, 1991), pp. 54–59. For a critical reading of Cavendish as a feminist (or proto-feminist) see Deborah Boyle, "Margaret Cavendish on Gender, Nature, and Freedom" in *Hypatia*, Vol. 28, No. 3 (Summer 2013) and "Margaret Cavendish's Non-feminist Natural Philosophy" in *Configurations*, Vol. 12, No. 2 (Spring 2004). For an affirmative view see for instance, John Rogers, *The Matter of Revolution: Science, Poetry and Politics in the Age of Milton* (Ithaca, New York: Cornell University Press, 1996) who maintains that the metaphysical writings of Cavendish aimed at "the liberation of women from the constraints of patriarchy", p. 181.

> [B]y reason Opinion is free, and may pass without passport, I
> took the liberty to declare my own opinions as other Philoso-
> phers do [...] I am willing to have my opinions contradicted,
> as I do contradict others: for I love Reason so well, that who-
> soever can bring most rational and probable argument, shall
> have my vote, although against my own opinion.[2]

Her œuvre consists of fourteen published volumes between 1653
and 1668, including essays on natural philosophy as well as fictitious correspondence, a biography on her husband, plays,
novellas, poems, and orations.[3] Despite being a prolific writer,
the immediate impact of her intellectual endeavors was negli-
gible and the public attitude toward her philosophy was overall
negative. The reaction of the Cambridge philosopher Henry
More is telling. After browsing through one of Cavendish's
books, he condescendingly rejected her critical opinions of his
work and remarked in a private letter:

> This great Philosopher. She is affrayed some man should quitt
> his breeches and putt on a petticoat to answer her in that
> disguize, [...] but I believe she may be secure from anyone
> giving her the trouble of a reply.[4]

[2] Margaret Cavendish, *Philosophical letters* (London, 1664) "A Preface to the Reader",
p.(b). In *Philosophical Letters* Cavendish develops a critical assessment of the major
natural philosophers of her time – Thomas Hobbes, René Descartes, Henry More and
others – in the form of fictitious correspondences.

[3] Margaret Cavendish's works, all printed in London, no second editions included here:
Poems and Fancies (1653), *Philosophical Fancies* (1653), *Philosophical and Physical
Opinions* (1655), *The World's Olio* (1655), *Nature's Pictures Drawn by Fancie's Pencil to
Life* (1655/56), *Playes* (1662), *Orations of Divers sorts, Accommodated to Divers Places*
(1662/63), *CCXI Sociable Letters* (1664), *Philosophical Letters: Or Modest Reflections
Upon some Opinions in Natural Philosophy* (1664), *Observations upon Experimental
Philosophy. To which is added, The Description of a New Blazing World* (1666), *The Life
of the Thrice Noble, High and Puissant Prince William Cavendishe* (1667), *Plays, never
before printed* (1668), *Grounds of Natural Philosophy* (1668).

[4] Henry More, letter to Lady Conway, 15 May 1665, in Marjorie Hope Nicolson (Ed.) &
Sarah Hutton (Rev. Ed.), *The Conway Letters. The Correspondence of Anne, Viscountess
Conway, Henry More, and their Friends. 1642–1684* (Cambridge: Cambridge University

In More's eyes, therefore, Cavendish was "no competition" – to use the phrase from Siri Hustvedt's essay on male dismissal of women as fellow competitors in the literary field.[5]

Cavendish was well aware of the misogynist circumstances of her times, and she anticipated the great amnesia that she (and other contemporary women philosophers) would suffer. Still, she remained hopeful that, as she wrote in the preface to *Observations upon Experimental Philosophy* (1666), "if she [her philosophy] be slighted now and buried in silence, she may perhaps rise more gloriously here after; for her ground being sense and reason, she may meet with an age where she will be more regarded, than she is in this".[6] Cavendish's foresight turned out to be right. Since the late twentieth century she has emerged from oblivion with her work attracting growing scholarly attention, both within philosophy and across the wider humanities.[7] There are, of course, various reasons why this recuperation has occurred, including the establishment of women's history in academia, the appraisal of women intellectuals in history by feminist philosophers, and growing availability of sources from

Press, 1992 [1930]), p. 237.

[5] Siri Hustvedt, "No competition" in *A Woman Looking at Men Looking at Women. Essays on Art, Sex, and the Mind* (London: Hodder & Stoughton Ltd/Sceptre books, 2017), p. 83f.

[6] Margaret Cavendish, *Observations upon Experimental Philosophy*, Eileen O'Neill (Ed.) (Cambridge: Cambridge University Press, 2001 [1666/1668]), "To the Reader", p. 12f. All quotes from *Observations* are from this edition.

[7] For a recent historiography on this interest in early modern women philosophers (including Margaret Cavendish), see Sarah Hutton, "Women, philosophy and the history of philosophy" in *British Journal for the History of Philosophy* (2019), Vol. 27, No. 4, pp. 684–701. For a substantial bibliography on secondary literature concerning the philosophy of Margaret Cavendish, see the article by David Cunning, "Margaret Lucas Cavendish" in Edward N. Zalta (Ed.), The Stanford Encyclopedia of Philosophy (Summer 2017 Edition), https://plato.stanford.edu/archives/sum2017/entries/margaret-cavendish/ [accessed 2020-10-29]. To Cunning's list I would like to add Lisa T. Sarasohn, *The Natural Philosophy of Margaret Cavendish. Reason and Fancy during the Scientific Revolution* (Baltimore: The John Hopkins University Press, 2010); Emma L. E. Rees, *Margaret Cavendish. Gender, Genre, Exile* (Manchester and New York: Manchester University Press, 2003); Deborah Boyle, *The Well-Ordered Universe: The Philosophy of Margaret Cavendish* (Oxford: Oxford University Press, 2017). For ongoing digital work on Margaret Cavendish see: http://digitalcavendish.org

the digitalization of early modern texts. Beyond this, however, it is worth underscoring the topicality of Cavendish's philosophical ideas to contested issues in modern times and their resonance concerning the concepts of nature, body and mind, knowledge and perception, technology, and communication, as well as the private and public spheres.[8] In particular, Cavendish was deeply critical of the Cartesian dualistic worldview that presupposed a clear distinction between free thinking and mechanistic matter. Accounting for Cavendish's non-dualistic understanding of nature, I aim to show in this article how she, in relation to her public presence as a woman and intellectual, negotiated the question of Cartesian free thinking through her natural philosophy. In what way did Cavendish consider herself a free thinker?

Cavendish was in many respects a typical philosopher of the seventeenth century. Her intellectual life was partly made possible by growing protections for intellectual pluralism that many, as Sarah Hutton argued, considered a way to fight an outdated and dogmatic variant of Aristotelian philosophy.[9] As Cavendish commented: "In this present age those are thought the greatest wits that rail most against the ancient philosophers, especially Aristotle, who is beaten by all".[10] Cavendish did not join in the bashing, but she agreed on the fact that the Aristotelian paradigm had reached a dead-end in European knowledge production. It could no longer function as the overarching explanation of nature and an alternative system of knowledge was opening. One of "the greatest wits" Cavendish

---

[8] Jacqueline Broad, "Is Margaret Cavendish worthy of study today" in *Studies in History and Philosophy of Science* (2011), Vol. 42, pp. 457–461, is a thorough review essay of Sarasohn's book *The Natural Philosophy of Margaret Cavendish*, and of the topicality of Cavendish's philosophy, focusing on its originality, quality of argument, influence, and enduring relevance.

[9] Sarah Hutton, "Liberty of Mind. Women Philosophers and the Freedom to Philosophize", in Jacqueline Broad & Karen Detlefsen (Eds.), *Women and Liberty, 1600–1800. Philosophical essays* (Oxford: Oxford University Press, 2017), pp. 123–137.

[10] Cavendish, *Observations*, "Ancient Learning Ought Not to be Exploded, nor the Experimental Part of Philosophy Preferred Before the Speculative", p. 195.

had in mind, René Descartes, famously wrote in his *Discours de la Methode* (1637) that every human being has the capacity to challenge Aristotle to think, because:

> [...] the power to judge correctly and to distinguish the true from the false – which is, strictly speaking, what we mean by common sense or reason – is naturally equal in all men. Hence the diversity of our opinions arises, not because some of us are more reasonable than others, but only because we direct our thoughts along different paths, and consider different things.[11]

The time was ripe for Descartes' message. It spread to a wider public and encouraged the emergence of "a new kind of *philosopher* – the philosophical 'layman'", who was associated with intellectual pluralism and skepticism, and for whom the printing press and public sphere constituted a space for different outlooks and new modes of philosophizing.[12] Indeed, Descartes' views on intellectual pluralism echo in Cavendish's writings, for instance when she is claiming that "[...] it is impossible for one Person to be of every one's Opinion, if their opinions be different, and that my Opinion in Philosophy, being new, and never thought of, at least not divulged by any, but myself, are quite different from others".[13] Epistemological skepticism of a Cartesian kind was, for sure, as Lisa Sarasohn rightly states, "particularly congenial to a woman who wanted to write natural philosophy. [Cavendish's] work shows that the new philosophy had radical implications far beyond the purview of science. It became a self-fashioning tool for a woman trying to define a new

---

[11] René Descartes, *Discourse on Method, Optics, Geometry, and Meteorology*, translation and introduction by Olscamp, Paul J., (Indianapolis/Cambridge: Hackett Publishing Company 2001), p. 4; *Discours de la Méthode,* (Paris: Librairie philosophique J. Vrin, 1989), p. 44: "[...] la puissance de bien juger, et distinguer le vrai d'avec le faux, qui est proprement ce qu'on nomme le bon sens ou la raison, est naturellement égale en tous les hommes; et ainsi que la diversité de nos opinions ne vient pas de ce que les uns sont plus raisonnables que les autres, mais seulement de ce que nous conduisons nos pensées par diverses voies, et ne considérons pas les mêmes choses."

[12] Hutton, "Liberty of Mind", p. 125.

[13] Cavendish, *Philosophical Letters*, p. (a).

construct: a woman natural philosopher".[14] Cavendish had in fact met Descartes several times during the scientific gatherings arranged by her husband and brother-in-law during their exile in Paris in the 1640s.[15] He appears to have made no great impression on her on these occasions – neither seems to have been talkative. All the same, the quote that inspired the title of this article – "suppose a man be in a deep contemplative study" – denotes a Cartesian starting point for Cavendish's philosophical practice and its anticipated result.[16] For one thing, free thinking demands certain conditions, such as privacy and rest, as Descartes himself stresses in his *Méditations métaphysiques* (1641):

> Accordingly, I have today suitably freed my mind of all cares, secured for myself a period of leisurely tranquillity, and am withdrawing into solitude. At last I will apply myself earnestly and unreservedly to this general demolition of my opinions.[17]

Even if Cavendish did not agree with Descartes that it was possible to rid oneself of all opinions, she shared his trust in the necessity of privately engaged reason and freedom of mind. She said: "I will not eagerly affirm what I do not certainly know; I only endeavour to deliver my judgement as reason directs me."[18] Following this rationalist impulse, she criticized those of her contemporaries (the experimental philosophers at the Royal Society) for relying on the senses rather than reason in their search for knowledge. In her opinion, the senses were not a

---

[14] Sarasohn, *The Natural Philosophy of Margaret Cavendish*, p. 17.

[15] Margaret Rees, *Cavendish. Gender, Genre, Exile*, p. 35.

[16] Cavendish, *Observations,* "Of the Different Perceptions of Sense and Reason", p. 150.

[17] René Descartes, *Discourse on the Method and Meditations on First Philosophy*, translation Donald A. Cress, (Indianapolis/Cambridge: Hackett Publishing Company, 1998), ("Meditation One" in Meditations on First Philosophy [1641]) p. 59; *Méditations métaphysiques* (Paris: Quadrige/Presses Universitaires de France, 1996), p. 26: "Maintenant donc que mon esprit est libre de tous soins, et que je me suis procuré un repos assuré dans une paisible solitude, je m'appliquerai sérieusement et avec liberté à détruire généralement toutes mes anciennes opinions.

[18] Cavendish, *Observations,* "Of Telescopes", p. 136.

reliable basis for knowledge, for "how shall a man practise, if he does not know what or which way to practice? Reason must direct first how sense ought to work".[19]

Already in her first publications in exile, *Poems and Fancies* (1653) and *Philosophicall Fancies* (1653), natural philosophy was the focus of Cavendish's intellectual attention. Her interest grew upon returning to England in 1660, which allowed her the opportunity to deepen her study of major philosophical works in her mother tongue. As a result, Cavendish's mature natural philosophy appears in publications from the 1660s onwards: *Philosophical Letters, or, Modest reflections upon some opinions in natural philosophy maintained by several famous and learned authors of this age, expressed by way of letters* (1664), *Observations upon Experimental Philosophy, to which is added the Description of a New Blazing World* (1666), and *Grounds of Natural Philosophy* (1668). Considering Cavendish's mode of philosophizing, letting opinions meet opinions with repetitive variations, it would be conceivable to discuss Cavendish as a free thinker through all these books. My examples, however, focus on *Observations upon Experimental Philosophy* (1666) due to its central position in Cavendish's work on natural philosophy. It provides, on the one hand, the most comprehensive account of her alternative to a Cartesian mechanistic worldview; on the other hand, the text offers an important critique of the experimental philosophical method favored by the newly established Royal Society.

Speaking in public

The transformation of the private and the public spheres in early modern times, which for long has been regarded as one of the decisive aspects in the shaping of modern scientific, political, and social institutions, was crucial to the development of Margaret Cavendish as a free thinker.[20] New distinctions

---

[19] Cavendish, *Observations*, "Ancient Learning Ought Not to be Exploded, nor the Experimental Part of Philosophy Preferred Before the Speculative", p. 196.

[20] Jürgen Habermas, *Strukturwandel der Öffentlichkeit. Untersuchungen zu einer*

between the private and public realms implied a gender divide, which excluded women's intellectual agency from public visibility. The situation was nevertheless often muddled in reality and the private thinking individual – woman or man – was, as Martine van Elk interestingly suggests, "paradoxically produced in the imagination by being *published*".[21] As a private thinker Cavendish could thus insist on her presence, agency and right to engage in public philosophical disputes. However, as mentioned, she lived at a time when a woman intellectual was generally considered a contradiction in terms, regardless of the fact that societal changes and advancements in communication technologies since the Renaissance had made it possible for a growing number of women to participate in the creation of culture and science.[22] A woman who wanted to publicize her

Kategorie der bürgerlichen Gesellschaft (Frankfurt am Main: Suhrkamp, 1962) is of course the groundbreaking analysis in this regard, a very influential and still thought-provoking study.

[21] For inspiring reflections on theoretical, historical as well as gender perspectives on the private and public distinction, see the chapter "Public and Private" in Michael Warner, *Publics and Counterpublics* (New York: Zone Books, 2005), pp. 21–63; Michael McKeon, *The Secret History of Domesticity. Public, Private, and the Division of Knowledge* (Baltimore: The John Hopkins University Press, 2005). In relation to Cavendish's own historical context, see Peter Lake & Steven Pincus (Eds.), *The politics of the public sphere in early modern England* (Manchester and New York: Manchester University Press, 2012). For the theme in this chapter, I am also very much in debt to the studies by Martine van Elk, *Early Modern Women's Writing. Domesticity, Privacy, and the Public Sphere in England and the Dutch Republic* (London: Palgrave Macmillan, 2017), citation p. 6; David Norbrook, "Women, the Republic of Letters, and the Public Sphere in the Mid-Seventeenth Century" in *Criticism*, Vol. 46, No. 2, Spring 2004, pp. 223–240; Marta Straznicky, *Privacy, Playreading, and Women's Closet Drama 1550–1700* (Cambridge: Cambridge University Press, 2004), "Margaret Cavendish: the closing of the theaters and the politics of playreading", pp. 67–90; Sylvia Brown, "Margaret Cavendish: Strategies Rhetorical and Philosophical Against the Charge of Wantonness, Or Her Excuses for Writing So Much" in *Critical Matrix*, Vol. 6, No. 1 (1991).

[22] Merry E. Wiesner-Hanks, *Women and Gender in Early Modern Europe* (Cambridge: Cambridge University Press, 2008 [third edition]), "Part II: Mind", pp. 141–204, gives a good overview, including further reading of the situation for early modern women concerning learning and participation in cultural and scientific production. The developments in media and society were connected to the burgeoning public sphere, for which court-supported academies, salons, learned societies, public lectures, the printing press, journals, and other institutions played a part. Londa Schiebinger's

intellectual endeavors was almost always alarming, as the well-known quote by Cavendish's contemporary, the author and teacher Bathsua Makin, indicated: "A Learned Woman is thought to be a Comet, that bodes Mischief, whenever it appears."[23]

Certainly, the public sphere offered women different spaces and possibilities within which to make themselves heard.[24] But, the formation of a distinct private sphere in contrast to this public realm also "strengthened the long-standing prohibition on the female public speech."[25] Indeed, the silencing of women's voices from public spaces has a long history, which the classicist Mary Beard illustrates in her manifesto, *Women & Power* (2017).[26] She points to the fact that public speech has been an attribute of masculinity since antiquity: "Or, to quote a well-known Roman slogan, the elite male citizen could be summoned up as *vir bonus dicendi peritus,* 'a good man, skilled in speaking.' A woman speaking in public was, in most circumstances, by definition not a woman."[27] Nonetheless, Beard mentions two exceptions to this rule, which can be applicable to Cavendish's public performance. Firstly, a woman could be tolerated to raise her voice in public in the defense of her family in need; or, secondly, she could do so to tell her personal story of sacrifice and martyrdom (as in the face of a death sentence).

In line with this thinking, it has been suggested that Margaret Cavendish's writings can be interpreted as a reappraisal and defense of the wealth and social status that her husband William

seminal work *The Mind Has No Sex? Women in the Origin of Modern Science* (Cambridge MA: Harvard University Press, 1991) discusses the (partial) inclusion of early modern intellectual women in these settings, pp. 10–65.

[23] Quote from Eileen O'Neill, "Disappearing Ink: Early Modern Women Philosophers and Their Fate in History" in Janet Kourany (Ed.), *Philosophy in a Feminist Voice* (Princeton: Princeton University Press, 1998), p. 36.

[24] Norbrook writes "[s]ome women in the seventeenth century did indeed assume that certain spheres of discourse were universal, rather than specifically masculine, and hence vigorously claimed inclusion", in "Women, the Republic of Letters", p. 224.

[25] van Elk, *Early Modern Women's Writing,* p. 2.

[26] Mary Beard, *Women & Power. A Manifesto* (London: Profile Books, 2017).

[27] Beard, *Women & Power,* p. 17.

Cavendish, and exiled British royalists more broadly, lost during the English civil war. Her writings can be seen as an effort to memorialize their aristocratic way of life.[28] Alternatively, one can argue that she raised her voice in public to expose her lived experience as a woman banished from her home-country for sixteen years, suffering difficult and uncertain circumstances – even if her testimony came from a place of considerable privilege. Such confessional accounts reflect a form of "public femininity", which Martine van Elk argues is comprised of three components: "deliberative performativity, a public voice that is the product of retirement, and a reputation that includes only occasional display and visibility."[29] Indeed, the third, visual dimension was especially problematic for female public speech, since it was most often associated with disreputable sexuality and lower social status. Thus, this made it hard for learned women to play a part in discussions that were taking place on the male domain. A woman speaking from a general point of view, promoting her own opinions with a universal audience in mind, was disturbing.

Moreover, the idea that a woman's voice in public had a harmful effect on society at large was common in the seventeenth century – it was certainly believed to seduce and confuse men as Eve had lured Adam into sin by her speech. This explains why women were normally advised to shut their mouths in public in early modern handbooks on rhetoric and social con-

---

[28] Modern readers might react against Cavendish's insistence and straightforward wish for her writings to bring her posthumous fame, but in the seventeenth century this was a conventional desire. See Keith Thomas, Keith, *The Ends of Life. Roads to Fulfilment in Early Modern England* (Oxford: Oxford University Press, 2008), "Fame and afterlife", pp. 236–267. Thomas writes that in the literary and scientific culture of early modern England it was commonplace to fear oblivion and to regard posthumous remembrance as the ultimate fulfillment of human life: "Many of the central social practices of the early modern period, from publishing books to commissioning portraits, become more intelligible when they are seen as the product of this concern with posthumous fame", p. 240. John Milton wrote that "the desire for immortal fame was 'seated in the breast of every true scholar.' The learned knew that if they did not publish, their learning would perish with them", p. 239.

[29] van Elk, *Early Modern Women's Writing*, p. 168.

duct. An example: Richard Brathwait, author of the popular book *The English Gentlewoman, drawne out of the full Body* (1631), claimed that "without Speech can no Society subsist" but since women's voices were intrinsically treacherous they must hold their tongues and "in publike consorts to *observe* rather than *discourse*".[30] Indeed, Brathwait admitted that he had met women who discoursed rather than observed, but from his point of view these prattling women, these "She-Clarkes [...] broach strange opinions" that no one understands, not least the speaker herself.[31] Cavendish was equally, perhaps unfairly, judgemental towards what she saw as women's fondness for idle gossip and trivialities, but she would have refuted Brathwait's sexist statement. She wrote that as a woman of learning – a "she-clarke" – she did not publicize her thoughts "out of an ambitious humour, to fill the world with useless books [equivalent to useless speech], but to explain and illustrate my own opinions. For, what benefit would it be to me, if I should put forth a work, which by reason of its obscure and hard notions, could not be understood?"[32] Furthermore, she assured readers that she did not seek a "pedantical kind of quarrelling", but to see the philosophical venture "united for the good and benefit for the whole Common-Wealth, nay, the whole World".[33]

Unsurprisingly, all of Cavendish's works comment in some way or another on the situation of being a woman in a field dominated by men. These views are often presented in a satirical tone, as in the introduction to *Observations*:

> It is probable, some will say, that my much writing is a disease; but what disease they will judge it to be, I cannot tell [---] if

---

[30] Richard Brathwait, *The English Gentlewoman Drawne out of the Full Body* (London, 1631), p. 88ff.

[31] The word 'clarke' was, according to the Oxford *English Dictionary*, used in early modern times for "a man (or woman) of book learning, one able to read and write; a scholar. (Now a *historical archaism*.)", "clerk, n.". OED Online. September 2020. Oxford University Press [accessed 2020-10-29].

[32] Cavendish, *Observations*, "To the Reader", p. 11.

[33] Cavendish, *Philosophical Letters*, p. (a2).

> much writing be a disease, then the best philosophers, both moral and natural, as also the best divines, lawyers, physicians, poets, historians, orators, mathematicians, chemists, and many more have been grievously sick: and Seneca, Pliny, Aristotle, Cicero, Tacitus, Plutarch, Euclid, Homer, Virgil, Ovid, St. Augustine, St. Ambrose, Scotus, Hippocrates, Galen, Paracelsus, and hundreds more, have been at death's door with the disease of writing.[34]

For Cavendish, a woman's lack of learning said nothing of her potential to learn. She acknowledged that "many of our sex may have as much wit, and be capable of learning as well as men; but since they want instructions, it is not possible they should attain to it."[35] And yet, a lack of schooling was not necessarily the most important impediment for someone, woman or man, who aspired for true philosophical thinking. Thus, in line with Descartes' opinion, Cavendish thought it far better not to trouble the "conscience by being a mountebank in learning, but [...] rather prove naturally wise than artificially foolish."[36] The difficult question was how and where a woman might practice this natural wisdom.

In the Company of Philosophers

Cavendish described herself as bashful and taciturn in company, and therefore as a woman who – true to Brathwait's pleasing – observed rather than discoursed in public settings. To efface her intellectual persona, she often used the so-called "the plea of incapacity."[37] This humble and unassuming voice in public was probably a rhetorical gesture. Cavendish was a savvy orator and performed her expected femininity when circumstances re-

---

[34] Cavendish, *Observations*, "The Preface to the Ensuing Treatise", p. 7.

[35] Cavendish, *Observations*, "To the Reader", p. 11.

[36] Cavendish, *Observations*, "To the Reader", p. 12.

[37] Gérard Genette, *Paratexts. Thresholds of Interpretation* (Cambridge: Cambridge University Press, 1997), p. 208. Genette writes that the plea of incapacity is "above all the surest way [...] for an author to ward off critics, that is, to neutralize them – and indeed, to forestall criticism by taking the initiative".

quired, but always reluctantly. There is no doubt she preferred her privacy where she could act in accordance with the philosophical persona Descartes imagined: "I had rather sit at home and write, or walk [...] in my chamber and contemplate."[38] Cavendish chose the company of her own inner life rather than attending social gatherings for "the effeminate Sex" or public recreations where she would be marginalized as philosopher.

Her famous visit to the Royal Society in May 1667 is a case in point. The Society, as a new scientific institution in London, had a demonstratively public profile. Yet, although the Society described itself as a novel public space for knowledge production, its members were unwilling to include women, since "the prospect of a woman attending the meeting led members of the Royal Society to fear the tarnishing of their reputation as 'serious' scientists."[39] Jo Wallwork has convincingly shown that Cavendish must have realized that she had not been invited to the society as a participant in the scientific enterprise, nor even as a spectator, but as the spectacle herself. Her bleak and oft-cited words that she was "full of admiration" of the performed experiments, reveal that she really had nothing to say while there.[40] All the same, Cavendish was remarkably eager to communicate her ideas in public: "I hope my Book may set a worke every Tongue" she wrote in her first publication *Poems and Fancies* (1653).[41] This sense of urgency was strong throughout

---

[38] Margaret Cavendish, *Natures Pictures, drawn by Fancies Pencil to the Life* (London, 1656), "A True Relation of my Birth, Breeding, and Life", p. 386.

[39] Jo Wallwork, "Disruptive Behaviour in the Making of Science: Cavendish and the Community of Seventeenth-Century Science" in Salzman, Paul and Wallwork, Jo (Eds.), *Early Modern Englishwomen Testing Ideas* (Farnham/Burlington: Ashgate Publishing Limited, 2011), p. 43. For a nuanced interpretation of Cavendish's hostility toward the programme of Royal Society, see Emma Wilkins, "Margaret Cavendish and The Royal Society" in *Notes & Records. The Royal Society Journal of the History of Science* (2014), 68, pp. 245–360.

[40] Samuel Pepys, who was very negative toward Margaret Cavendish in his diary, had been at the Royal Society and heard her comments on the performed experiments. See Wallwork, "Disruptive Behaviour in the Making of Science", p. 44.

[41] Margaret Cavendish, *Poems and Fancies* (London, 1653), "To all Noble, and Worthy Ladies", p. (A3).

her career, always "confident and resolute", she wrote in *Orations of divers sorts* (1662), "to put them [her ideas] to the Press, and so to the Publik view, in despite of these Critical times and Censorious age, which is apt to find fault with every Action."[42]

Hence, when circumstances made it possible, she did not hesitate, but sent her manuscripts to the press in haste. How could she be so daring? One explanation is that Cavendish had a strong commitment to her natural philosophy, which she considered to be more in line with common sense and reason than her counterparts – Descartes, Hobbes, More, Boyle, among others. After reading Thomas Stanley's three-volume *History of Philosophy* (1655/1656/1661), covering ancient philosophy from Thales to Sextus Empiricus, she was also certain that her philosophy was original. She was convinced, referring to Stanley's book in *Observations*, that were it not for her gender it might have been possible to found her own philosophical school:

> [...] were it allowable or usual for our sex, I might set up a sect or a school for myself, without any prejudice to them: But I, being a woman, do fear they would soon cast me out of their schools; for, though the muses, graces and sciences are all of female gender, yet they were more esteemed in the former ages, than they are now; nay, could it be done handsomely, they would now turn them all from females into males: So great is grown the self-conceit of the masculine, and the disregard of the female sex.[43]

[42] Margaret Cavendish, *Orations of Divers Sorts, Accommodated to Divers Places* (London, 1662), p. (a). Quote from the dedication to her supportive husband, "To his Excellency the Lord Marquis of Newcastle".

[43] Cavendish, *Observations*, "Observations upon the Opinions of Some Ancient Philosophers", p. 249. The sole woman philosopher mentioned with a paragraph in Stanley's extensive book of male voices – the cynic Hipparchia. Cavendish does not comment upon it, but she probably read the story of Hipparchia standing up for her choice of life, how she was harassed by Theodorus the atheist, and how she answered when he said: "*Her Web and Loom/She left at home,* I did, saith she, *Theodorus,* and I think have not erred in choosing to bestow that time which I should have spent in

Cavendish questioned why her fellow male philosophers did not acknowledge the roots of their own thinking: in feigning the novelty of their ideas and ignoring the influence of the ancient philosophers, they were nothing but intellectual "botchers and brokers".[44] Though she did not mention anyone by name, her criticism clearly applied to the rationalists and empiricists of her time. Her words were consciously chosen: Botcher, rarely used in modern English, was a common expression in early modern times.[45] It referred to a person who made a living by mending and repairing things, but not creating anything new. The result was often unskillful and clumsy work. There was a difference between a botcher and a tailor, a cobbler, and a shoemaker. A broker referred to both a second-hand dealer and an intermediary of a dubious kind. Cavendish therefore questioned the authority of her fellow philosophers. In a paragraph entitled "Ancient Learning Ought Not to be Exploded, nor the Experimental Part of Philosophy Preferred Before the Speculative" she called for greater analytical reflexivity:

> I perceive the knowledge of several ages and times, is like the increase and decrease of the moon; for in some ages 'art and learning' flourishes better than in others, and therefore it is not only an injury, but a sign of ill nature, to exclaim against ancient learning, and call it pedantry; for if the ancients had not been, I question whether we should have arrived to that knowledge we boast of at this present.[46]

Furthermore, Cavendish doubted it was possible to establish facts by putting artificial effects on par with natural effects, as the experimental philosophers of Royal Society had done. To her

weaving, on Philosophy." Stanley, Thomas, *The History of Philosophy: Containing the Lives, Opinions, Actions and Discourses of the Philosophers of every Sect*, second edition, (London, 1687), p. 420.

[44] Cavendish, *Observations*, "Observations upon the Opinions", p. 250.

[45] The words 'botcher' and 'broker', *Oxford English Dictionary*, OED Online. September 2020. Oxford University Press [accessed 2020-10-29].

[46] Cavendish, *Observations*, "Ancient Learning Ought not to be Exploded", p. 196.

mind, experimental philosophers naïvely trusted what they saw – i.e. privileging the eye as a witness to experience and truth – as it brought "ignorance, instead of advancing knowledge; for when the light of reason begins to be eclipsed, darkness of understanding must needs follow."[47] All the same, the critique did not make her less motivated to proceed with scientific investigations. Cavendish was not, as Emma Wilkins writes, "arguing *against* scientific inquiry *per se*; rather, she was deeply troubled by the uncritical enthusiasm for inquiry based on artifice."[48]

In hindsight, the Royal Society proved to be very productive in a way Cavendish could not predict. Nevertheless, she may have recognized the exploitative practices of the new science that reinforced the idea of human superiority and the objectification of nature. A rationalistic-inclined philosopher, Cavendish could not support its scientific program, since:

> [...] the variety of nature, is a stumbling block to most men, at which they break their heads of understanding, like blind men, that run against several posts or walls [...] For, they [the experimental philosophers] consider not so much the interior natures of several creatures, as their exterior figures and phenomena [...] supposing that sense and art can only lead them to the knowledge of truth; whereas they rather delude their judgement, instead of informing them. But nature has placed sense and reason together, so there is not a part or particle of nature, which has not its share of reason, as well as of sense: for, every part having self-motion, has also knowledge, which is sense and reason; and therefore it is fit we should not only employ our senses, but chiefly our reason, in the search of the causes of natural effects [...] leaving to our moderns, their experimental, or mode philosophy, built upon deluding art, I shall addict myself to the study of contemplative philosophy, and reason shall be my guide.[49]

[47] Cavendish, *Observations*, "Ancient Learning Ought not to be Exploded", p. 197.
[48] Wilkins, "Margaret Cavendish and The Royal Society", p. 250.
[49] Cavendish, *Observations*, "Of the Motions of Heat and Cold", p. 99.

Though, by putting "sense and reason together" Cavendish comes out as an unorthodox rationalist. She is not averse to sensory knowledge, but is aware of how our senses can mislead us and thus how artificial devices, such as scientific instruments, telescopes and microscopes, can magnify the error. So:

> […] that particular sensitive knowledge in man, which is built merely upon artificial experiments, will never make him a good philosopher [---] The truth is, our exterior senses can go no further than the exterior figures of creatures, and their exterior actions: but our reason may pierce deeper, and consider their inherent natures, and interior actions. And although it does sometimes err, (for there can be no perfect or universal knowledge in a finite part, concerning the infinite actions of nature) yet it may also probably guess at them, and may chance to hit the truth.[50]

These statements clearly show that Cavendish considered the epistemological "view from nowhere" nonsensical, and strictly deductive modes of thinking as artificial as the search for nature's essence through a microscope. This constant play of opinions demands a degree of skepticism, and therefore the sharp Cartesian distinction between *scientia* (what is true and certain) and *opiniones* (the shifting and changeable) must be considered invalid.[51] Cavendish's own "rational inquisition" manifests itself through various intimate deliberations of contrasting opinions – pro et contra, questions, and answers, then and now, natural and artificial, particular and general, and so on. This recurring, open interrogation of opinions, her own and others, lead up to the most probable, rational argument con-

---

[50] Cavendish, *Observations,* "Of the Motions of Heat and Cold", p. 100.

[51] For Cavendish as a modest skeptic, see Deborah Boyle, "Margaret Cavendish on Perception, Self-Knowledge, and Probable Opinion" in *Philosophical Compass* 10/7 (2015), pp. 447. On the concept of probability in Cavendish's reasoning, see Boyle, "Margaret Cavendish on perception", p. 447; Stephen Clucas, "Variation, Irregularity and Probabilism: Margaret Cavendish and Natural Philosophy as Rhetoric", in *A Princely Brave Woman: Essays on Margaret Cavendish, Duchess of Newcastle*, Stephen Clucas, (Ed.), (Aldershot: Ashgate, 2003), pp. 199–209.

cerning the philosophical problem under debate. Doing so, she defends repetition as a philosophical method of writing:

> I am not ignorant, that endless questions and objections may be raised upon one subject; and, to answer them, would be an infinite labour. But since I desire to be perspicuous in delivering my opinions, and to remove all those scruples which seem to obstruct the sense thereof, I have chosen to rather to be guilty of prolixity and repetitions, than to be obscure by too much brevity.[52]

Cavendish's Philosophical Opinions

A good illustration of Cavendish's way of reasoning, and how she uses natural philosophy to establish herself as a free thinker, is found in her discussion of what *cold* is.[53] Cavendish scrutinized the problem over several chapters in *Observations*, with questions like: What is the origin of cold? What kind of qualities does cold exhibit? Are these primary or secondary characteristics? Is it possible to measure coldness? The issue of cold was of considerable interest not only to Cavendish, but many contemporary rationalists and experimentalists alike during the period we now often call "the little ice age".[54] It was a sign of the times, but also closely connected to new theories on matter and criticism toward Aristotelian knowledge about nature. The experimental philosopher Robert Boyle, for example, designed a number of experiments to solve the mystery.[55] Descartes

---

[52] Cavendish, *Observations*, "Several Questions and Answers Concerning Knowledge and Perception", p. 155.

[53] Cavendish, *Observations*, "Of the Motions of Heat and Cold", pp. 95–100; "Of the Measures, Degrees, and Different Sorts of Heat and Cold", pp. 101–106; "Of Congelation and Freezing", pp. 106–117; "Of Thawing or Dissolving of Frozen Bodies", pp. 117–119; "Several Questions Resolved Concerning Cold, and Frozen Bodies", pp. 120–124.

[54] Geoffrey Parker, *Global Crisis. War, Climate Change & Catastrophe in the Seventeenth Century* (New Haven and London: Yale University Press, 2013), "The Little Ice Age", pp. 15–25.

[55] Robert Boyle, *New Experiments and Observations touching Cold, or an Experimental History of Cold, begun* (London, 1665). Many of the experiments relate to everyday

deduced truths about coldness from his own personal experience of extreme winters in Amsterdam.[56] For her part, Cavendish approached the problem by activating her own senses and reasoning to judge different opinions about the motions and measures of hot and cold, the freezing, thawing and dissolving of frozen bodies, and finally to present the most credible opinion. Her observations were taken from everyday life – in a way the same kind of experiences as Descartes used in his observations on cold matter – so as to invite readers to add their own opinions about the different sensations of coldness, "shaking, freezing, chilly, windy, numb, stiff, rare, dense, moist, dry, contracting, dilating, ascending, descending, and other numerous sorts of cold."[57] She asks the reader why the cold retreats into cellars during the summer heat, if the cold preserves bodies from corruption, if wood is apt to freeze, what produces floating icebergs, if there is a difference between natural and artificial snow, which animal is most sensible of cold, etc.

Though, these were exterior observations. To really understand the ontology of the cold, Cavendish lets her reason pierce deeper into the causes of natural effects. She argues that the most probable and rational opinion is connected to the fact that nature in its totality consists of rational matter, sensitive matter, and inanimate matter. Thus: "Matter, self-motion, and self-knowledge, are inseparable from each other, and make nature one material self-moving, and self-knowing body."[58] Matter moves in various ways, but it is never mechanically determined as Descartes claimed. Rather, nature has the freedom to move as she pleases, though not beyond her own nature. Since matter by definition is divisible, nature is bound to divide and compose

experiences, such as the "Preservation and Destruction of (Eggs, Apples, and other) Bodies by Cold". Compare Cavendish, *Observations*, p. 118.

[56] René Descartes, *Discours de la méthode, plus la dioptrique, les météores et la géométrie* (Paris: Librairie Arthème Fayard, 1987 [1637]), Les météores, sixth discourse "de la neige, de la pluie, et de la gresle", pp. 268–279.

[57] Cavendish, *Observations*, "Of the Measures, Degrees, and Different Sorts of Heat and Cold", p. 102.

[58] Cavendish, *Observations*, "Of Knowledge and Perception in General", p. 137.

her several parts into several particular figures, and dissolve and change those figures again in infinite ways, which explains the multitude of forms and actions in the world. Leibniz's philosophy comes to mind when Cavendish asserts that this variety is so great, "that even in one and the same species, none of the particulars resemble one another so much, as not to be discerned from each other."[59] Since matter is a commixture of rational and sensitive parts, the fundamental actions of nature are knowledge and perception. Nature's self-movement is thus self-regulating, it keeps nature in order, and all actions "whatsoever in nature, [such] as respiration, digestion, sympathy, antipathy, division, composition, pressure, reaction, etc. are all particular perceptive and knowing actions."[60] Consequently, the idea of passive matter, like the Cartesian *res extensa*, is not probable. All of nature's constituent parts are perceptive and this perception consists of ordering – or, in Cavendish's words "patterning" – exterior objects. This constant preceptive activity implies that in different ways nature is self-knowing. The consequences are thrilling. She writes:

> [...] it is absurd to confine all perceptions of nature, either to pressure and reaction, or to the animal kind of perception; since even in one and the same animal sense, (as for example seeing) there are numerous perceptions: for, every motion of the eye, were it no more than a hairsbreadth, causes several perceptions: besides, it is not only the five organs in an animal, but every part and particle of his body, that has a peculiar knowledge and perception, because it consists of self-moving matter [and] a piece of wood, stone, or metal, may have a perceptive knowledge of man, yet it hath not a man's perception |...| no more than the eye patterning out a tree or stone, can be said to have a vegetable or mineral perception.[61]

---

[59] Cavendish, *Observations*, "Of Knowledge and Perception in General", p. 139.
[60] Cavendish, *Observations*, "Of Knowledge and Perception in General", p. 139.
[61] Cavendish, *Observations*, "Of Knowledge and Perception in General", p. 140f.

Cavendish is thus challenging prevailing notions of human superiority and the objectification of the natural world by refusing to accept that knowledge about nature can be derived from a fundamental, privileged position. It is a radical critique of the Cartesian *cogito*, and the distinct separation between body and soul, mechanistic necessity and free thinking: "Some learned conceive, that all knowledge is in the mind, and none in the senses: For the senses, say they, present only exterior objects to the mind; which sits as a judge in the kernel, or fourth ventricle of the brain [...] which in my apprehension, is a very odd opinion."[62] Meaning, she cannot understand how the senses can inform the mind of things they do not know themselves. Since knowledge and perception are the fundamental actions of matter, thought is active in all parts of nature.

Secondly, Cavendish's statement implies that the perceiver is also perceived and patterned: A man perceives the trunk he is leaning on to rest, but the trunk also perceives the man. Every perception entails a new perspective, and therefore a new possibility for knowledge. This implies a certain amount of agency in every part of nature. But is this thinking *per se*? Cavendish does not talk about laws of nature, but she emphasizes regularities and stabilities. She compares nature to a wise and provident lady, a good housewife that keeps her home in good and orderly shape.[63] So, the world does not move randomly, nor mechanically either. Every part of it has both rational and sensitive forms of perception – and thereby forms of knowledge – which must cooperate in order to function.

Opinions are Free

It is worth noting that *Observations upon experimental philosophy* (1666) was published as a companion piece to a fantastic story of a kidnapped young woman who ends up becoming an

---

[62] Cavendish, *Observations*, "Of the Different Perceptions of Sense and Reason", p. 153.
[63] Cavendish, *Observations*, "Of the Measures, Degrees, and Different Sorts of Heat and Cold", p. 105. For an argument that order is an overarching motif in the philosophy of Cavendish, see Boyle, *The Well-Ordered Universe*.

empress in a utopian world inhabited by strange talking creatures (*A Description of a New World, Called the Blazing World,*
1666). In the preface to this book, Cavendish writes:

> If you wonder, that I join a work of fancy to my serious phi-
> losophical contemplations; think not that it is out of a dis-
> paragement to philosophy [...] The end of reason, is truth; the
> end of fancy, is fiction; but mistake me not, when I distinguish
> fancy from reason; I mean not as if fancy were not made by
> the rational parts of matter; but by reason I understand a
> rational search and enquiry into the causes of natural effects;
> and by fancy a voluntary creation or production of the mind,
> both being effects, or rather actions of the rational parts of
> matter.[64]

While human beings are a commixture of rational, sensitive and
inanimate matter, they are also fundamentally creative beings,
with the capacity to imagine, to fancy, to figure, and to set their
opinions free.[65] The rational parts of human nature are "more
free and at liberty than the sensitive, which are more encum-
bered with working on, and with inanimate parts of matter; and
therefore it may very well be, that a man in a deep contemplative
study, doth not always feel when he is pinched or touched;
because all the rational motions of his body concur or join to the
conception of his musing thoughts."[66] Is this voluntary creation
of the mind like a quasi-divine power that can create and
transform worlds? Lisa Walters has argued for this radical
dimension in Cavendish's thought, not least in relation to *The
Blazing World*, which she sees as advancing an anti-hierarchical
view of humanity.[67] Jay Stevenson, however, claims that Caven-

---

[64] Margaret Cavendish, *The Description of a New World, Called the Blazing World*
(1666), in *Margaret Cavendish, Political Writings*, James, Susan (Ed.), (Cambridge:
Cambridge University Press, 2003), "To the Reader", p. 5f.
[65] Cavendish, *Observations*, "Of the Different Perceptions of Sense and Reason", p. 150.
[66] Cavendish, *Observations*, "Of the Different Perceptions of Sense and Reason", p. 152.
[67] Lisa Walters, *Margaret Cavendish. Gender, Science and Politics* (Cambridge: Cambridge University Press, 2014), p. 168.

dish's philosophy "offers little reassurance to those who wish to believe in a stable and permanent cosmic order."[68] Meaning, Cavendish can be interpreted in both a conservative *and* radical direction. Different perceptions of matter shape the order of things, but ideas in the mind can also take the form of external objects irrespective of the influence of sensory organs, as conceptions. What can be conceived is also something created, something new.

Cavendish's philosophy supposedly did not openly aim at "the liberation of women from the constraints of patriarchy", instead in many ways she paradoxically benefited from the patriarchal order.[69] But her published opinions on the material mind and mindful matter nevertheless prove the idea that, following Sarah Hutton, to "be free to philosophize meant overcoming deep-seated customs and prejudices about female mental capacities and social destiny."[70] The frequent play between different registers in her work makes it hard to pin down a consistent voice. Further attention to aspects such as the uses of satirical elements, various genres and rhetorical techniques would allow for a more coherent understanding of her contradictory views on gender. Regardless of these differences, my contention has been that Cavendish's natural philosophy articulates a feminist ethos. In making public her philosophical presence, she served as an example for other women. She thus

---

[68] Jay Stevenson, "The Mechanist-Vitalist Soul of Margaret Cavendish", *Studies in English Literature*, 36:3 (1996), p. 537.

[69] Rogers, *The Matter of Revolution*, p. 181. Martine van Elk, *Early Modern Women's Writing*, convincingly shows how women philosophers in the seventeenth century, regardless of their social, cultural, and religious background, frequently represented themselves and other women writers along the lines of a traditional model of absolutist power and publicity. This model authorized women to write and counter the new bourgeois ideals of the household, which did not allow for female agency in the public realm.

[70] Hutton, "Liberty of Mind", p. 126; See also David Cunning, "Margaret Cavendish on Metaphysic of Imagination and the Dramatic Force of the Imaginary World", in Emily Thomas (Ed.), *Early Modern Women on Metaphysics* (Cambridge: Cambridge University Press, 2018), for an argument about Cavendish's works provide a vision of "how things could be different", p. 210.

represents an important figure in the history and development of feminist philosophy today.

Chapter 6
Hannah Arendt
– To Think "Without Banisters"

Helgard Mahrdt

Hannah Arendt insisted repeatedly on the novelty of the phenomenon of totalitarianism, its unprecedentedness. She thought, "Few guides [are] left through the labyrinth of inarticulate facts if opinions are discarded and tradition is no longer accepted as unquestionable".[1] If there can be no return to tradition, if we have permanently lost "the Ariadne thread of common sense," "we can no longer rely on traditional categories, concepts and standards to comprehend what has happened", is there then nevertheless a way for thinking to illuminate the darkness of our times? Can we reconcile ourselves to the past? If we are to follow Arendt, then "we have to learn 'to think without banisters' (Denken ohne Geländer).

Favoring storytelling over theories is one of the conclusions Arendt draws from the loss of tradition. Storytelling is a non-Hegelian way of reconciling with reality. It also is an adequate way of taking human plurality seriously. The openness inherent in the notion of plurality is relevant for a conception of history that differs from the tradition. In this article, I will address the question whether there is a way of thinking without being tyrannical. To try to answer this question I will first sketch the conditions of the activity of thought after 1945 that Arendt describes by turning to literature. I will then ask whether there is a way to face reality and to reconcile us with the past. I conclude that non-tyrannical thinking remains related to experience, is expressed in 'concrete' words, it uses metaphors, and allows for thinking the particular without subordinating it. Arendt's way of writing opens possibilities in the search for non-

---

[1] Hannah Arendt, *The Origins of Totalitarianism* New Edition with Added Prefaces (San Diego/New York/London: Harcourt, Inc., 1994), p. 9.

tyrannical thought, and it is worth considering for feminist philosophy.

Navigating Without an Anchored Tradition

Arendt viewed being "unburdened and unguided by any tradition" as our chance "to dispose of a tremendous wealth of raw experiences without being bound by any prescriptions as to how to deal with these treasures".[2] In 1974, she gave a lecture course on "Thinking" at the Graduate Faculty of the New School for Social Research in New York. She told her listeners that she "wish(ed) to stress only one thing, namely, that this course of lectures will be organized by a question concerning the nature and experience of *thinking*. […] What are we doing when we are *thinking*, that is, when we are *active* without *doing* anything at all?"[3] She thought when one raises such questions, "it would be reckless to rely only on one's own experience and fail to consult those whom Kant called *Denker von Gewerbe*, 'professional thinkers'."[4] She did not only consult 'professional thinkers', but "poets and scientists as well as philosophers".[5] In addition, "she felt entirely free of Tradition and chronological order, and also liberated from any so-called field of expertise."[6] She told her students that "she put the books 'in alphabetical order, instead of chronological, to indicate that we shall leap freely over the centuries, without paying attention to the suspicions of the historians of ideas who assume that ideas, handed down from generation to generation, develop according to their own intrinsic nature."[7]

---

[2] Hannah Arendt, *The Life of the Mind*, One-volume Edition, M. McCarthy (Ed.) (New York: Harcourt Brace Jovanovich, 1981), p. 12.

[3] Hannah Arendt, "Preliminary Remarks about the Life of the Mind", in *Thinking Without A Banister. Essays in Understanding 1953–1975 – Hannah Arendt*, Jerome Kohn (Ed.) (New York: Schocken Books, 2018), p. 515.

[4] Arendt, "Preliminary Remarks about the Life of the Mind".

[5] Arendt, "Preliminary Remarks about the Life of the Mind".

[6] Arendt, "Preliminary Remarks about the Life of the Mind".

[7] Arendt, "Preliminary Remarks about the Life of the Mind", p. 514.

After 1945, thought found itself in a situation that she wished to describe in exact terms. To do this, she turned to literature with Franz Kafka.[8] "Kafka", she argues, "by sheer force of intelligence and spiritual imagination, created out of a bare, 'abstract' minimum of experience a kind of thought-landscape which, without losing precision, harbors all the riches, varieties, and dramatic elements characteristic of 'real' life".[9] "The story", she refers to, "records a mental phenomenon, something which one may call a thought-event. The scene is a battleground on which the forces of past and future clash with each other; between them, we find the man whom Kafka calls 'he,' who, if he wants to stand his ground at all, must give battle to both forces. Hence, there are two or even three fights going on simultaneously: the fight between 'his' antagonists and the fight of the man in between each of them".[10] Arendt emphasizes that the "forces of the past and the future clash with each other",[11] because "he" is already there. "'His' standpoint is not the present as we usually understand it but rather a gap in time, which 'his' constant fighting, 'his' making a stand against past and future, keeps in existence."[12]

For Arendt Kafka's "he" on the battlefield between past and future is "the perfect metaphor for the activity of thought." Accordingly, "the path paved by thinking, this small track of non-time which the activity of thought beats within the time-space of mortal men and into which the trains of thought, of remembrance and anticipation, save whatever they touch from the ruin of historical and biographical time, [...] cannot be inherited and handed down from the past".[13] Instead, "each new generation, indeed every new human being as he inserts himself between an infinite past and an infinite future, must discover

[8] Edle, "Dis/Placing Thought: Franz Kafka and Hannah Arendt".

[9] Hannah Arendt, "Preface", in *Between Past and Future, Eight Exercises in Political Thought* (New York: Penguin Books, 1968), p. 10.

[10] Arendt, "Preface", in *Between Past and Future*.

[11] Arendt, "Preface", in *Between Past and Future*.

[12] Arendt, "Preface", in *Between Past and Future*, p. 11.

[13] Arendt, "Preface", in *Between Past and Future*, p. 13.

and ploddingly pave it anew".[14] Roger Berkowitz emphasizes this permanent struggle to think and understand the world. He writes, "Thinking today […] demands that we continually recommit ourselves to the loss of a knowable and hospitable world and instead commit ourselves to the struggle of thinking and acting in a world without banisters."[15] If we cannot mend the broken thread of tradition, can we nevertheless comprehend what has happened?

Relating to the Past – But a Fragmented Past

In 1971, Arendt gave a seminar entitled "The History of the Will". After she had spoken about Nietzsche and Heidegger, she drew the attention of her listeners to the fact that these "thinkers […] had set it as their main task not to destroy […], but to dismantle metaphysics and philosophy with all its categories, as we have known it from the pre-Socratics to today. This dismantling was possible only after the past, or rather the tradition of the past, had lost its authority." What is important is that "the dismantling process does not destroy the past, it only draws the consequences of this loss, which is a fact, and it destroys the continuity of the past which consisted in its being handed down in its own consistency". "What we then are being left with", she goes on, "is still the past but a *fragmented* past."[16]

How, then, do we relate to a *fragmented* past, which has lost its certainty of evaluation? We may find an answer in Walter Benjamin's "Concept of History" which supplied a frame for Arendt's work. Benjamin's answer to the irreparable loss of tradition was to salvage a fragmented past. He believed that the

---

[14] Arendt, "Preface", in *Between Past and Future*.

[15] Roger Berkowitz, "Reconciling Oneself to the Impossibility of Reconciliation: Judgment and Worldliness in Hannah Arendt's Politics", Roger Berkowitz & Ian Storey (Eds.), *Artifacts of Thinking. Reading Hannah Arendt's Denktagebuch* (New York: Fordham University Press, 2017), p. 27.

[16] Image 26 and 27 of Hannah Arendt Papers: Addition I, 1966–67; Speeches and Writings; Essays and Lectures; "The History of the Will", Seminar, New School for Social Research, New York, N.Y., 1971,. For Arendt's treating of tradition as a kind of collage see Eva von Redecker, *Gravitation zum Guten. Hannah Arendts Moralphilosophie* (Berlin: Lukas Verlag 2013), p. 73ff.

historian had to break fragments out of the fossilized past to put them together in a new way, so as to testify to the subterranean stream of history.

In the prefix to the first edition of *The Origins of Totalitarianism* Arendt precisely uses this language: "The subterranean stream of Western history has finally come to the surface and usurped the dignity of our tradition. This is the reality in which we live. And therefore all efforts to escape from the grimness of the present into nostalgia for a still intact past, or into the anticipated oblivion of a better future, are in vain".[17] As Peg Birmingham notes, "For both Benjamin and Arendt, the site of history is the site of the present, the moment of discontinuity that requires the activity of collecting and assembling".[18]

For Arendt relating to the past despite its fragmentation aims at comprehending what has happened. The importance of comprehension is beautifully expressed in a passage of the prefix to the first edition of *The Origins of Totalitarianism*:

> Comprehension does not mean denying the outrages, deducing the unprecedented from precedents, or explaining phenomena by such analogies and generalities that the impact of reality and the shock of experience are no longer felt. It means, rather, examining and bearing consciously the burden, which our century has placed on us – neither denying its existence nor submitting meekly to its weight. Comprehension, in short, means the unpremeditated, attentive facing up to, and resisting of, reality – whatever it may be.[19]

Arendt's request of attentively "facing up to and resisting reality" is not at all an easy task. It requires a way of thinking that remains related to experience and avoids losing one's connection to reality.

---

[17] Hannah Arendt, *The Origins of Totalitarianism*, "Preface to the first Edition", ix.
[18] Peg Birmingham, "Why Are We So Matter of Fact about the Facts?" in *HA–The Journal of the Arendt Center for Politics and Humanities at Bard College*, 2012, p. 77.
[19] Arendt, "Preface to the First Edition", in *The Origins of Totalitarianism*, viii.

The Relevance of Experience and the Tyranny of Reason

According to Arendt, "the philosophers [are] in love with Being (thaumadzein), the natural scientists [...] in love with the universe, the philologist [...] in love with the printed word, [and] the political scientist: in love with the world, mundus [kosmos], something the Greeks called polis, what men do. This includes: Worry for the world, we are afraid something may happen to the mundus hominum".[20]

Something happened to the world, totalitarianism broke the continuity of Occidental history. However, despite this new situation, political philosophy, Arendt argues, "so far as [it] still exists, it is being taught by traditionalists – Voegelin, a Platonist, Strauss an Aristotelian, Kojève a Hegelian. Each of them, believes that tradition is valid (…)".[21] Contrary to them, Arendt believed that a return to tradition is no longer possible because "we have lost the thread which safely guided us through the vast realms of the past".[22] The loss means a challenge since "History [...] is the sine qua non for political sciences". She argues, "Without historical knowledge we don't know what we do and what we are talking about. [Consequently], Political theory between History and Philosophy: Its experiences are all historical, but its terms are all terms, which at one time have been coined by philosophy".[23]

---

[20] Image 6 of Hannah Arendt Papers: Subject File, 1949–1975; Courses; University of California, Berkeley, Calif.; "History of Political Theory", lectures 1955; Introduction; The Hannah Arendt Papers, Library of Congress, Washington D.C.

[21] Image 6 of Hannah Arendt Papers: Subject File, 1949–1975; Courses; New School for Social Research, New York, N.Y.; "Philosophy and Politics: What Is Political Philosophy?" Lectures and Seminars, 1969 (1 of 2 folders) Blatt 024420; The Hannah Arendt Papers, Library of Congress, Washington, D.C.; see also Wolfgang Heuer, *Citizen. Persönliche Integrität und politisches Handeln Eine Rekonstruktion des politischen Humanismus Hannah Arendts*, Berlin Akademie Verlag 1992, p. 240.

[22] Hannah Arendt, "What is Authority?", in *Between Past and Future*, p. 94.

[23] Image 5 of Hannah Arendt Papers: Subject File, 1949–1975; Courses; University of California, Berkeley, Calif.; History of Political Theory", Lectures 195; The Hannah Arendt Papers, Library of Congress, Washington, D.C.

The crucial point Arendt makes is that "the end of a tradition does not necessarily mean that traditional concepts have lost their power over the minds of men. On the contrary, it sometimes seems that this power of well-worn notions and categories becomes more tyrannical as the tradition loses its living force and as the memory of its beginning recedes; it may even reveal its full coercive force only after its end has come and men no longer even rebel against it".[24] How, then, can the human mind properly understand events and things in the realm of human affairs?

Here, Arendt insists that thinking must take over tradition's former task of finding the meaning of the past. However, to be able to do this, thinking must differ from the tradition of political and philosophical thought. "[T]his kind of thinking", she writes, "is different from such mental processes as deducing, inducing, and drawing conclusions whose logical rules of non-contradiction and inner consistency can be learned once and for all and then need only to be applied".[25] It is also different from "the tradition of political thought [that] degrades political action into the category of means and ends".[26] The tradition "began when the death of Socrates made Plato despair of polis life".[27] "After Socrates' death", Arendt writes, "Plato began to discount persuasion as insufficient for the guidance of man and to seek for something liable to compel them without using external means of violence".[28] He discovered "that truth, namely the truths we call self-evident, compels the mind, and that this coercion, though it needs no violence to be effective, is stronger than persuasion and argument. [...] This is the central predicament of Plato's political philosophy and has remained a predicament of all attempts to establish a tyranny of reason".[29] Additionally,

---

[24] Hannah Arendt, "Tradition and the Modern Age", in *Between Past and Future*, p. 26.

[25] Hannah Arendt, "Preface", in *Between Past and Future*, p. 14.

[26] Jerome Kohn, "Introduction" in Jerome Kohn (Ed.), *The Promise of Politics. Hannah Arendt* (New York: Schocken Books 2005), xxxvii.

[27] Hannah Arendt, "Socrates", in *The Promise of Politics*, 6f.

[28] Arendt, "What is Authority?", 107.

[29] Arendt, "What is Authority?", 107f.

it "matters for the tradition [...] that Plato introduced the concept of rulership into the political realm, despite the fact that it originated in the thoroughly apolitical rule over household slaves".[30]

The tradition saw "action as the means *necessary* to achieve an end higher than itself".[31] It subjugated reality to thought and it ended with Marx, who "made possible the kind of process-thinking so characteristic of nineteenth-century ideologies, ending in the devastating logic of those totalitarian regimes whose apparatus of violence is subject to no constraints of reality".[32] It is well known that Arendt rejected the idea that Nazism could be explained by reference to German and European traditions. In March 1951, she wrote to Karl Jaspers that "[o]ne compelling reason why I took such trouble to isolate the elements of totalitarian governments was to show that Western tradition from Plato up to and including Nietzsche is above any such suspicion."[33] Yet, she "suspects(s) that philosophy is not altogether innocent".[34] Consequently, Arendt sets out on a journey to discover a way of thinking that does not subordinate reality to thought, to discover a way of thinking that is non-traditional and not tyrannical.

Arendt emphasizes that "[a]ll thought arises out of experience".[35] This means that "understanding, as distinguished from having correct information and scientific knowledge",[36] grasps the sense and meaning of experience. Arendt does not deny that the sciences can illuminate our preliminary understanding, but they can "neither prove nor disprove [that] from which they

[30] Kohn, "Introduction" in Jerome Kohn (Ed.), *The Promise of Politics*, p. xxvi.

[31] Kohn, "Introduction" in Jerome Kohn (Ed.), *The Promise of Politics*, p. xxvii.

[32] Arendt, "Socrates", in *The Promise of Politics*, 74.

[33] Hannah Arendt to Karl Jaspers, March 4, 1951, in Lotte Kohler and Hans Saner (Eds.), *Hannah Arendt – Karl Jaspers Correspondence 1926–1969*, San Diego/New York/London: Harcourt Brace & Company 1992, 166.

[34] Hannah Arendt to Karl Jaspers, March 4, 1951.

[35] Hannah Arendt, *The Life of the Mind*, p. 87.

[36] Hannah Arendt, "Understanding and Politics", in *Essays in Understanding 1930–1954*, p. 307.

start".[37] The complete sentence from *The Life of the Mind* reads, "All thought arises of experience, but no experience yields any meaning or even coherence without undergoing the operation of imagination and thinking".[38]

In a spring and summer 1968 seminar at the New School, entitled "Political Experience in the Twentieth Century", Arendt wished for her students "to experience for [them] selves experiences that were not [their] own, to experience them not immediately but […] mediated through works [they] would be reading […], fiction as well as nonfiction".[39] Jerome Kohn, Arendt's former assistant, writes that she "might also have called the seminar 'Exercises in Imagination', indicating that [the students'] success in this common enterprise would depend on the most mysterious of [their] mental faculties".[40] How, then, are we to understand the faculty of imagination? Jerome Kohn explains, "by exercising imagination she did not mean remembering what [the students had] seen with [their] own eyes or heard with [their] ears, nor recognizing what [they had] touched, tasted, or smelled – in all of which […] the imagination also plays a role. She meant, firstly, the ability of human beings to form images of things never given to their senses and, secondly, their submission of those images to the process of thought".[41] For her, "the activity of thinking issues not in truths of any kind but in a plurality of meanings, and *that* distinction was essential for her in comprehending experience […]".[42] Consequently, she favors storytelling as a form that allows reflecting experiences properly. This entails encounters with the poetics of narrative.

---

[37] Arendt, "Understanding and Politics", p. 311.

[38] Hannah Arendt, *The Life of the Mind*, p. 87; see also the Preface of *Between Past and Future*: "[…] thought itself arises out of incidents of living experience and must remain bound to them as the only guideposts by which to take its bearings". Hannah Arendt, "Preface" in: *Between Past and Future*, p. 14.

[39] Elisabeth Young-Bruehl & Jerome Kohn, "Truth, Lies, and Politics: A Conversation", in *Social Research*, Vol. 74, No. 4, Winter 2007, p. 1047.

[40] Young-Bruehl & Kohn, "Truth, Lies, and Politics: A Conversation", p. 1048.

[41] Young-Bruehl & Kohn, "Truth, Lies, and Politics: A Conversation".

[42] Young-Bruehl & Kohn, "Truth, Lies, and Politics: A Conversation".

Storytelling: reconciliation with reality

Arendt was convinced that "we can no more master the past then we can undo it", and "narration [...] solves no problems and assuages no suffering".[43] But she believed, "even in the darkest of times we have the right to expect some illumination, and that such illumination may well come less from theories and concepts than from the uncertain, flickering, and often weak light that some men and women, in their lives and their works, will kindle under almost all circumstances and shed over the time span that was given to them on earth".[44]

To return to my opening question: is there a way of thinking that enables us to reconcile with the past? Arendt suggests, not turning to theories but to storytelling. Storytelling is not a naïve exercise. The storyteller does not rely on theories or concepts, but on imagination; with the help of imagination he brings particular experiences to light, thus providing examples for our consideration. Stories may help to find a reasonable attitude to what has happened. "The best that can be achieved," Arendt writes, "is to know precisely what it was, and to endure this knowledge, and then to wait and see what comes of knowing and enduring".[45] Arendt shares William Faulkner's understanding that "the past is never dead, it's not even past". The simple reason for this is that "the world we live in at any moment *is* the world of the past." In other words, "the facts [of the world] are always what has *become*." In this sense, Arendt remarks, "it is true that the past *haunts* us."

Stories are "the results of action and speech," "every individual life between birth and death can eventually be told as a story with beginning and end."[46] "Each human life," Arendt writes, "tells its story and [...] history ultimately becomes the

---

[43] Hannah Arendt, "On Humanity in Dark Times: Thoughts about Lessing", in *Men in Dark Times* (New York: Harcourt, Brace & World, Inc.), p. 21.

[44] Hannah Arendt, "Preface", in *Men in Dark Times*, p. ix.

[45] Hannah Arendt, "On Humanity in Dark Times: Thoughts about Lessing", in *Men in Dark Times*, p. 20.

[46] Hannah Arendt, *The Human Condition*, p. 184.

storybook of mankind, with many actors and speakers and yet without any tangible authors".[47] Both, stories and history are the outcome of action. Since action takes place in "an already existing web of human relationships, with its innumerable conflicting wills and intentions," it "almost never achieves its purpose".[48] Moreover, action is unpredictable; it has a start but no end. Therefore, nobody can ever know "with certainty the outcome" of one's actions. Arendt emphasizes this aspect in *The Human Condition* and writes, "The process of a single deed can quite literally endure throughout time until mankind itself has come to an end".[49] Therefore, it can sometimes take a long time before action becomes "a story susceptible to narration", and the meaning of a committed act is revealed. In other words, "a clear perception of experience requires the passage of time".[50]

In the case of the First World War, "nearly thirty years were to pass before a work of art appeared which so transparently displayed the inner truth of the event that it became possible to say: Yes, this is how it was".[51] William Faulkner's novel *A Fable* is for Arendt such a work of art. "Very little is described, still less explained and nothing at all 'mastered'; its end is tears, which the reader also weeps, and what remains beyond that is the 'tragic effect' or the 'tragic pleasure,' the shattering emotion which makes one able to accept the fact that something like this war could have happened at all".[52]

The process of reconciling with the past is represented in the literary form of tragedy. The tragic hero re-experiences "what has been done in the way of suffering and in this *pathos*, in re-suffering the past, the network of individual acts is transformed

---

[47] Hannah Arendt, *The Human Condition*, p. 184.

[48] Hannah Arendt, *The Human Condition*, p. 184.

[49] Hannah Arendt, *The Human Condition*, p. 233.

[50] Ari Hyvönen, "The Janus Face of Political Experience", in *Arendt Studies*, Vol. 2, 2018, p. 138.

[51] Hannah Arendt, "On Humanity in Dark Times: Thoughts about Lessing", *Men in Dark Times*, p. 20.

[52] Arendt, "On Humanity in Dark Times".

into an event, a significant whole".[53] The tragedy has a dramatic climax, and this climax "occurs when the actor turns into a sufferer; therein lies its peripeteia".[54] Whether the plots are tragic or non-tragic, they "become genuine events only [...] [when] memory operates retrospectively and perceptively. Such memory can speak only when indignation and just anger, which impel us to action, have been silenced – and that needs time".[55] What then is established is the meaning of committed acts. However, this does not mean that "any 'mastering' of the past is possible", but by such narration we can reconcile ourselves to it. The form for it is the lament".[56] Arendt illustrates this by quoting Goethe in the dedication to *Faust*

> Der Schmerz wird neu, es wiederholt die Klage
> *Des Lebens labyrinthisch irren Lauf.*
> *(Pain arises anew, lament repeats*
> *Life's labyrinthine, erring course.)*

To Arendt, who was convinced of the relevance of philosophy, it was characteristic that philosophers had refused to analyze in philosophical terms the background of the horrible experiences of her own time. She therefore concluded, "crucial for a new political philosophy will be an inquiry into the political significance of thought; that is, into the meaningfulness and the conditions of thinking for a being that never exists in the singular".[57]

Of course, tradition has several meanings. In Hegel's philosophy of history the contingency of all action is replaced by predetermined necessity.[58] According to him, it is possible to

---

[53] Arendt, "On Humanity in Dark Times".

[54] Arendt, "On Humanity in Dark Times".

[55] Arendt, "On Humanity in Dark Times", pp. 20–21.

[56] Arendt, "On Humanity in Dark Times", p. 21.

[57] Hannah Arendt, "Concern with Politics in Recent European Philosophical Thought", p. 445.

[58] Jerome Kohn, "Tradition", in Wolfgang Heuer, Bernd Heiter & Stefanie Rosenmüller (Eds.), *Arendt Handbuch. Leben – Werk-Wirkung* (Stuttgart: Metzler 2011), pp. 320–

select events that correspond to the process of progress. For Arendt, history is not one progressive process but a multitude of independent events.[59] To gain access, to name and reflect on them, we need a way of thinking that is able to make distinctions instead of subsuming things and events under one concept. In other words, we would need a way of thinking that is non-traditional, which is to say, not tyrannical.

Following Arendt, language and thought are interconnected, but "no language has a ready-made vocabulary for the needs of mental activity".[60] Therefore, I turn to language, in particular to the metaphor, which is language's greatest gift for thinking.

Thinking, poetry, and 'concrete' thoughts

Best known is a way of thinking that is "the solitary and sound-less dialogue between me and myself, the inner 'two-in-one'." Arendt links this way of thinking especially to Socrates who "engaged into friendly dialogues on the essence of concepts like justice, courage etc."[61] What also comes into our mind is an activity of thinking which she calls "representative thinking", i.e., a mode of thinking that is linked to Kant and his notion of "enlarged mentality" (*erweiterte Denkungsart*). In this activity of thinking a "plurality of perspectives is present in and constitute the public realm, in order to prepare the formation of opinions and judgments future projects and past events".[62]

What interests me particularly is a third form of thinking which Arendt relates to Walter Benjamin. Benjamin, I said earlier, was important for Arendt's effort to understand a past that is fragmented. He is also important for a thinking that is poetical. In her essay on Benjamin (1968), she writes, "[w]hat is so hard to understand about Benjamin, is that without being a

21.

[59] Kohn, "Tradition".

[60] Hannah Arendt, *The Life of the Mind*, p. 102.

[61] Wout Cornelissen, "Thinking in Metaphors" in Roger Berkowitz & Ian Storey (Eds.), *Artifacts of Thinking. Reading Hannah Arendt's Denktagebuch* (Fordham: Fordham University 2017), p. 76.

[62] Cornelissen, "Thinking in Metaphors".

poet he *thought poetically* and therefore was bound to regard the metaphor as the greatest gift of language".[63] In the *Thought Notebook (Denktagebuch)* from April 1970, an entry titled "On the difficulties I have with my English Readers", Arendt defends Benjamin's (and, I might add, her own way) against the Anglo-linguistic philosophy or what she characterizes as "Thesaurus philosophy". When she raises "the question of what is a meta-phor … and what does a metaphor achieve […], [then] these considerations, according to our English friend, have nothing to do with a profile of Benjamin".[64] Instead the "*Times Literary Supplement* reviewer complains of [her] 'ideology'". She ima-gines, "what he means is my <u>thinking</u> that transcends mere des-cription. Or similes and metaphors", and she concludes, "What this adds up to is that the whole notion of thinking a matter <u>through</u> is alien to English 'philosophy'".[65]

Arendt explicitly speaks of a correspondence between the use of concepts and of metaphors, "what connects thinking and poetry [*Dichtung*] is metaphor. In philosophy one calls concept what in poetry [*Dichtkunst*] is called metaphor. Thinking creates its 'concepts' out of the visible, in order to designate the invi-sible" (D XXVI.30.728).[66] Metaphors are the greatest gift of language because they are "securing the access of humans to and their relationship with the world".[67] Arendt states that "no lan-guage has a ready-made vocabulary for the needs of mental

---

[63] Arendt, *Men in Dark Times*, p. 166.

[64] U. Ludz & I. Nordmann (Eds.), *Hannah Arendt, Denktagebuch II, 1950 bis 1973* (München/ Zürich: Piper 2002), XXVII: 45, p. 771.

[65] Ludz & Nordmann (Eds.), *Hannah Arendt, Denktagebuch II*, see Martin Blumenthal-Barby, "The Odium of Doubtfulness": Or, the Vicissitudes of Metaphorical Thinking", in *New German Critique*, no. 106, winter 2009, p. 64.

[66] Quoted from Wout Cornelissen, "Thinking in Metaphors", in *Artifacts of Thinking. Reading Hannah Arendt's Denktagebuch*, p. 84. Similarly Sigrid Weigel, "For Arendt thinking […] maintains a proximity to poetry, to the language of metaphor, to per-ception in analogies and to experience". Sigrid Weigel, "Poetics as a Presupposition of Philosophy: Hannah Arendt's Denktagebuch", in *Telos* 146, 2009, p. 98.

[67] Hannes Bajohr, "The Unity of the World: Arendt and Blumenberg on the Anthro-pology of Metaphor", in *The Germanic Review: Literature, Culture, Theory*, Vol. 90, No. 1, 2015, p. 56.

activity; they all borrow their vocabulary from words originally meant to correspond either to sense experience or to other experiences of ordinary life".[68]

At this point Arendt makes an important distinction; she distinguishes "common-sense reasoning" from thinking and remarks, "what we need for common-sense thinking are *examples* to illustrate our concepts". It is quite clear to Arendt, however, that "if reason's need transcends the boundaries of the given world and leads us on to the uncertain sea of speculation," then "it is altogether different." Then we do not need examples but metaphors. "The metaphor," she explains, "achieves the carrying over' – *metapherein* – of a genuine and seemingly impossible *metabasis eis allo genos*, the transition from one existential state, that of thinking, to another, that of being an appearance among other appearances, and this can be done only by *analogies*."[69] "Analogies, metaphors, and emblems," she adds, "are the threads by which the mind holds on to the world even when, absent-mindedly, it has lost direct contact with it, and they guarantee the unity of human experience."[70]

To recall my earlier question if there is a way of thinking that enables us to face the "shock of reality" and to reconcile with the past, what Thomas Wild describes as "to face and to come to terms with what really happened"[71], Arendt started all her think-

---

[68] Arendt, The Life of the Mind, p. 102. "According to Kant", she writes, "speaking in analogies, in metaphorical language [...] is the only way through which speculative reason, which we here call thinking, can manifest itself. The metaphor," she goes on, "provides the 'abstract', imageless thought with an intuition drawn from the world of appearances whose function it is 'to establish the reality of our concepts', and thus, undo, as it were, the withdrawal from the world of appearances that is the precondition of mental activities".

[69] Arendt, The Life of the Mind.

[70] Arendt, *The Life of the Mind*, p. 109; see also Cornelissen, "… Arendt praises the capability of metaphor to turn a phrase back into a word again, and thus to (re)establish a 'correspondence' between our inner mind and the outer world", in: "Thinking in Metaphors", p. 85; see Martin Blumenthal-Barby, "The Odium of Doubtfulness": Or, the Vicissitudes of Metaphorical Thinking", in *New German Critique*, Vol. 36, No. 106, winter 2009, p. 65.

[71] Thomas Wild, "By Relating It": On Modes of Writing and Judgment in the Denktagebuch" in *Artifacts of Thinking. Reading Hannah Arendt's Denktagebuch*, p. 54.

ing from the fact that God created both Adam and Eve as the original plurality. Already one of the first lines in *The Human Condition* is fascinating in this regard. Here we read the well-known line, "men, not Man, live on the earth and inhabit the world".[72] This leads Arendt to state, "plurality is specifically *the* condition – not only the *conditio sine qua non,* but the *conditio per quam* – of all political life".[73] Plurality becomes a key concept, "radically different from our liberal understanding of plurality".[74] It is a kind of "qualitative pluralism [that] emerges in the course of intersubjectivity, of in between people and [this] is utterly different from the modern age subjectivism so familiar to us".[75]

Thomas Wild supplements this "qualitative pluralism" with a "plurality of languages." These languages "differ in vocabulary and grammar, and therefore in their 'mode of thinking' (*Denk-weise*), and all are learnable".[76] Consequently, "we, who are many and various, and more than simply descendants of one 'animal rationale' or '*zoon logikon*', we are beings gifted not with reason or language, but with languages and with the faculty of speaking to one another".[77]

The Capacity of Judging

I began this article with the question whether we can reconcile ourselves to the past, whether there is a way of thinking that is

---

Thomas Wild points out that Arendt does "not arrange the two activities 'to face' and 'to come to terms with' in a chronological, intentional, or causal order. Instead, *the sentence expresses a mode*: to look reality in the face, to confront what happened and to find words for what one thus discovers, to bring it into language. An oscillating 'and' that joins and creates distance. A break and a space between" (italic added).

[72] Arendt, The Human Condition, p. 7.

[73] Arendt, *The Human Condition* for the notion of plurality see Helgard Mahrdt, "The Joy of Thinking" in *Filosofisk Supplement* (3–4), 2019, pp. 9–11; Sophie Loidolt, *Phenomenology of Plurality. Hannah Arendt on Political Intersubjectivity* (New York: Routledge, 2018).

[74] Wolfgang Heuer, "Plurality", in *Arendt Studies,* Vol. 2, 2018, p. 51.

[75] Heuer, "Plurality", p. 53.

[76] Wild, "By Relating It".

[77] Wild, "By Relating It".

not tyrannical and remains related to reality. If the past is no longer handed down from generation to generation, if we have lost the continuity of the past, if, what we are left with is but a *fragmented* past, and if, nevertheless, we are in need of finding meaning and reconciling with events, how can thinking contribute to understanding the past? This seems particularly difficult since the "path paved by thinking [...] cannot be inherited and handed down by tradition. Each new generation, every new human being, as he becomes conscious of being inserted between an infinite past and an infinite future, must discover and ploddingly pave anew the path of thought".[78]

Here Arendt brings in another faculty of the mind, i.e., judging. Judgment as a capacity for dealing with the past has "its own *modus operandi,* its own way of proceeding".[79] According to Arendt, the life of the human mind is not the life of one faculty, but of three basic mental activities, of "thinking, willing, and judging [...]; they cannot be derived from each other and, though they have certain common characteristics, they cannot be reduced to a common denominator".[80] How, then, does the capacity for judgment, "which one may call with some reason the most political of man's mental abilities",[81] proceed? What is its own *modus operandi*?

Arendt argues that "thinking results in conscience as its by-product," and that "judging, the by-product of the liberating effect of thinking, realizes thinking, makes it manifest in the world of appearances, where I am never alone and always much too busy to be able to think".[82] Thinking and judging are inter-

---

[78] Arendt, The Life of the Mind, p. 210.

[79] Arendt, The Life of the Mind, p. 216.

[80] Arendt, *The Life of the Mind,* p. 69; see also Jerome Kohn: "The ability to judge, [...] is an autonomous faculty of the human mind and by no means a readily applicable 'middle term'." Jerome Kohn, "Hannah Arendt's Jewish Experience. Thinking, Acting, Judging", in Roger Berkowitz, Jeffrey Katz & Thomas Keenan (Eds.), *Thinking in Dark Times. Hannah Arendt on Ethics and Politics* (New York: Fordham University Press 2010), p. 193.

[81] Kohn, "Hannah Arendt's Jewish Experience", p. 192.

[82] Hannah Arendt, "Thinking and Moral Considerations", in Jerome Kohn (Ed.), *Hannah Arendt – Responsibility and Judgment* (New York: Schocken Books, 2003), p.

related. However, we cannot derive "the faculty to judge particulars" from the activity of thinking because "thinking deals with invisibles, with representations of things that are absent; judging always concerns particulars and things close at hand".[83] Arendt claims that it is Kant's third critique, the *Critique of Judgment*, which offers the greatest insight into the process of judgment. In her Kant lectures, she writes, "the chief difficulty in judgment is that it is 'the faculty of thinking the particular'; but to *think* means to generalize, hence it is the faculty of mysteriously combining the particular and the general."[84]

In the Postscript to *Thinking* in *The Life of the Mind*, Arendt writes, "If judgment is our faculty for dealing with the past, the historian is the inquiring man, who by relating it sits in judgment over it."[85] Thomas Wild suggests that "this emphatic 'by relating it' " could be read as the particular capacity of judging, namely "to think the particular *by relating it*".[86] He explains, "The English expression 'by relating it' has a double meaning here: the process of telling, and a way of relating things, of putting them in relation to each other".[87] That is what historians do in their process of telling; they put things in relation to each other.

However, in Arendt's view, the tradition of political thought failed in telling and relating things. To counteract a concept of history as progress, she refers to Herodotus who "never would have doubted that each thing that is or was carries its meaning within itself and needs only the word to make it manifest".[88] She writes in the same passage, "Everything that was done or happened contained and disclosed its share of 'general' meaning within the confines of the individual shape and did not need a

---

189.

[83] Arendt, "Thinking and Moral Considerations".

[84] Ronald Beiner (Ed.), *Hannah Arendt – Lectures on Kant's Political Philosophy* (Chicago: The University Press of Chicago, 1989), p. 76.

[85] Arendt, The Life of the Mind, p. 216.

[86] Wild, "By Relating It", p. 60.

[87] Wild, "By Relating It", p. 60.

[88] Arendt, "On the Concept of History p. 64.

developing process to become significant".[89] Wild reads Arendt's sentence, "[t]he flux of his narrative is sufficiently loose to leave room for many stories, but there is nothing in this flux indicative that the general bestows meaning and significance on the particular",[90] as her answer to a tradition that failed to shed light over the past. "Herodotus' writing style, the *presentation* of his *Histories,* is what makes the difference". It makes the difference in what "an understanding of history as a universal meaning-creating process is".[91] "This way of writing," Wild suggests, "makes distinctions that open possibilities; it creates relationships without subordinating. It is able to think the particular *by relating it*, which characterizes the capacity of judging, according to Arendt and Kant".[92]

Conclusion

So, is there a way of thinking that is not tyrannical? Yes, it is a thinking that remains related to experience, that is expressed in concrete words, that uses metaphors, that carries a non-Hegelian way to reconcile us with the past, and that can think the particular without subordinating it. We realize it in the "attempts to think our ability 'of mysteriously combining the particular and the general' to judge, for example, or to present 'by relating it'".[93] We may now better understand why "illumination may well come less from theories and concepts than from the uncertain, flickering, and often weak light that some men and women, in their lives and their works, will kindle under almost all circumstances and shed over the time span that was given to them on earth."[94]

[89] Arendt, "On the Concept of History.
[90] Arendt, "On the Concept of History, p. 64.
[91] Wild, "By Relating It", p. 62.
[92] Wild, "By Relating It", p. 62f.
[93] Wild, "By Relating It", p. 69.
[94] Hannah Arendt, "Preface", in *Men in Dark Times,* p. ix.

Chapter 7
Reflections on the Feminist Archive
– The Case of the Bibliothèque Marguerite Durand

Marta-Laura Cenedese*

When I was a doctoral student, I spent several months in France conducting archival research. Although I was based in Paris, most of my research material was kept at the IMEC, the Institut Mémoires de l'édition contemporaine, which is located just outside of Caen in Normandy. But one day, as I was browsing the Paris National Library (BnF) catalogue, I found out there were some resources available at the *Bibliothèque Marguerite Durand* (BMD), a specialized city library located in the thirteenth *arrondissement*. I had already lived in Paris years before then, but I had never been to that particular library. My curiosity was piqued when I read that it was the only library in France dedicated to the history of women and feminism, and that it was founded in 1932. The webpage of the City of Paris informs the public that the library, called after the feminist activist Marguerite Durand, keeps a rich documentation on the history of women and feminism, including the quasi-totality of French feminist texts of the 19th and 20th centuries.[1] A few years have gone by since I registered and accessed the documents I needed. Today, the *Bibliothèque Marguerite Durand* is open and fully operational, however, for some time between 2016 and 2019, its existence as an "independent" feminist archive was in peril. Indeed, as the library closed for renovations in 2016, the mayor of Paris, Anne Hidalgo, announced a new project that provoked the public outcry of the academic world, unions, and citizens, both in France and internationally. Eventually, the *mairie*

---

* Many thanks to Giselle Bernard for her gentle (proof)reading of this text.
[1] https://www.paris.fr/equipements/bibliotheque-marguerite-durand-bmd-1756

127

revoked the project and the library reopened to the public in January 2020.[2]

In this contribution I want to address the specific case of this French library, which speaks to us all about time, memory, and the transmission of knowledge. The 'BMD affair' is symptomatic of the place of women and feminism in twenty-first century society, and brings to the fore issues of enduring structural inequalities, power imbalances, and social justice. What happened in the case of the BMD is, in fact, a display of the vulnerable and precarious position of women as political subjects with agency and presence in public life. My intervention approaches these events by considering the notion of the archive within the legacy of feminist history and knowledge – thus addressing its transformations and transmissions in time. I contend that the projected plan for the library foregrounds the logics of domination and the production of certain kinds of episteme at the expense of, or by officially manipulating, others. I then turn to the issue of the BMD's lack of storage space and the impossibility of enlarging its collections, which concerns which 'histories' the BMD keeps and hands down to the future. Building on feminist critical theory, I highlight the importance of embodied and sensory knowledges that are acquired through physical encounters (with both people and objects), and therefore I insist on the necessity of having physical spaces for feminist 'contact zones', such as the *Bibliothèque Marguerite Durand.*

Marguerite Durand and the Birth of the Library

Marguerite Durand (1864–1936) was a woman of extraordinary talents and charisma: a former actress of the *Comédie française,* she was also a journalist, a collector, the founder and owner of

---

[2] Anaïs Moran, "À Paris, la bibliothèque Marguerite Durand restera finalement dans ses locaux", *Libération,* 10/12/2017. https://www.liberation.fr/france/2017/12/10/a-paris-la-bibliotheque-marguerite-durand-restera-finalement-dans-ses-locaux_1615708. See also https://www.archivesdufeminisme.fr/actualites/reouverture-de-la-bibliotheque-marguerite-durand-3/; https://information.tv5monde.com/terriennes/bibliotheque-marguerite-durand-paris-rouverture-d-un-lieu-de-memoire-des-femmes-et-du

the feminist daily newspaper *La Fronde* (1897–1903) and a candidate at the 1910 municipal elections.[3] In 1886, as staff writer at *Le Figaro*, she was asked to cover the International Feminist Congress with the commission to write a humorous piece. Instead, she was seduced by the speeches and convinced by the debates, to the point that not only did she become a convert but an outspoken feminist and front-line activist. She then founded the "major daily newspaper" *La Fronde*, which was "political and literary. Managed, administered, and compiled exclusively BY WOMEN. [...] [T]hey [women] claim the right to be allowed to voice their opinion on all questions affecting society and humanity, of which they are members on a par with men" (from *La Fronde*'s first issue).[4] Durand was an activist of the so-called 'first' feminist wave, for which the pressing matter was to open the public sphere to women, that is, to respond to women's political demands for education, work outside of the house, equal pay, the right to vote and to be elected: in sum, the righteous request to be fully-fledged equal participating citizens. According to Julia Kristeva, this was a political project turned toward "the rejection, when necessary, of the attributes traditionally considered feminine or maternal" as a way of affirming oneself equal to men by likeness, unlike for the second generation of feminists, who will be "interested in the specificity of female psychology and its symbolic realizations."[5]

An example of this 'unessentialising', yet individualistic, approach to women's emancipation is to be found in Madeleine Pelletier, who argued that women needed economic and legal independence from patriarchal control as well as to be liberated from "socially imposed roles" (*La Femme en lutte pour ses droits*,

---

[3] Maggie Allison, "Marguerite Durand and *La Fronde*: Voicing Women of the Belle Époque" in Diana Holmes and Carrie Tarr (Eds.), *A 'Belle Époque'? Women in French Society and Culture 1890–1914* (New York, Oxford: Berghahn Books, 2006), pp. 37–50 (p. 41).

[4] Quoted in Allison, "Marguerite Durand and *La Fronde*", p. 38.

[5] Julia Kristeva (1979), "Women's Time" in Toril Moi (Ed.), *The Kristeva Reader* (New York: Columbia University Press, 1986), pp. 187–213 (p. 193, 194).

1908).[6] However, Pelletier's model was a minority. As shown by historian Karen Offen (1988), well into the twentieth century "sexual dimorphism" and the family were paramount to the French vision of social and political order and, therefore, despite their critique of male/female relationships and patriarchal family structures, most feminist groups insisted on sexual difference, complementarity and interdependence.[7] Indeed, Marguerite Durand's ultra-feminine and charming appearance did not resemble the Pelettier-like image of a first-wave feminist. However, as Mary Louise Roberts has argued (1996) her feminist aesthetics mimicked traditional notions of femininity in a subversive and destabilizing way so that, while she seemed to be reinforcing gender ideologies, she was instead transgressing conventions "without appearing to do so", and therefore "securing both social acceptance and power".[8] Using 'seduction' as 'power', Marguerite Durand was able to challenge a male-constructed feminine identity and to defend the interests of women workers.[9] With *La Fronde*, she gave "unprecedented visibility to the feminist movement and had a cultural impact in all of France".[10] Finally, with her library and feminist archive, Durand was able to to add to the (masculine) linear temporality what Jeffrey Wallen (2009) calls "droplets of time" or, in Arlette Farge's (1989) words, "tear[s] in the fabric of time".[11] For me, talking of archival documents as "droplets of" and "tears in"

[6] Karen Offen, "Defining Feminism: A Comparative Historical Approach" in *Signs*, Vol. 14, No. 1, 1988, pp. 119–157 (pp. 144–145).

[7] Offen, "Defining Feminism", pp. 145–146.

[8] Mary Louise Roberts, "Acting Up: The Feminist Theatrics of Marguerite Durand" in *French Historical Studies* 19 (4), 1996, pp. 1103–1138 (p. 1128). For an early influential study of "womanliness" as something "assumed and worn as a mask", see Joan Riviere (1929), "Womanliness as a Masquerade" in Russell Grigg, Dominique Hecq, Craig Smith (Eds.), *Female Sexuality: The Early Psychoanalytic Controversies* (London and New York: Routledge, 1999), pp. 172–182.

[9] Roberts, "Acting Up", p. 1114.

[10] Roberts, "Acting Up", p. 1131.

[11] Jeffrey Wallen, "Narrative Tensions: The Archive and the Eyewitness" in *Partial Answers: Journal of Literature and the History of Ideas* 7 (2), 2006, pp. 261–278 (p. 261); Arlette Farge, *Allure of the Archives*, transl. Thomas Scott-Railton (New Haven and London: Yale University Press, 2013), p. 6.

time conveys the painstakingly slow and painful process endured by women to access the stage.

The BMD library, originally Marguerite's own, resided at first in the premises of *La Fronde* in rue Saint Georges,[12] and consisted in works that related to women and the fight for women's rights. In 1931 Durand decided to lease her collection to the city of Paris with the promise that it would be kept in a place open to any member of the public, where documents could be easily and freely accessed by anyone who was interested in women's history and in the fight for equality.[13] As a public institution, the library was initially located on the fifth floor of the Town Hall of the fifth *arrondissement*, opposite the Panthéon. Anecdotal history tells us that Marguerite, then volunteering director, died in the library itself in March 1936. Closed between 1940–42, we know very little about its life until the late 1960s, when librarian Yolande Léautey was appointed to classify and update the library, followed in 1983 by curator Simone Blanc, "who managed to obtain more staff and a larger budget."[14] In 1989 the library was moved to a new address at 79 rue Nationale in the thirteenth *arrondissement*, and since then it has shared the building with the *Médiathèque Jean-Pierre Melville*. Caroline Verdier points out how this move, although well intentioned for it was meant to provide the library with more space, could be seen from a political standpoint as a desire to give less prominence to the library: not only did its relocation bring the library from the center to the south-eastern area of Paris, but ironically it also made it share locales with an insti-

---

[12] Allison, "Marguerite Durand and *La Fronde*", pp. 47–48.

[13] The choice to donate her library and archives was taken after having witnessed the disappearance of "another important series of archives on women at the death of [Durand's] close friend Eliska Vincent, and not wanting the same thing to happen to her collection." Caroline Verdier, "Trajectories of Two Women's Libraries: A Comparative Study of the Bibliothèque Léonie La Fontaine and the Bibliothèque Marguerite Durand" in Maggie Allison and Angela Kershaw (Eds.), *Parcours de femmes: Twenty Years of Women in French* (Oxford: Peter Lang, 2011), pp. 23–37 (p. 25).

[14] Verdier, "Trajectories of Two Women's Libraries," p. 28.

tution named after Jean-Pierre Melville, who was well known for his misogyny.[15]

As I previously mentioned, the *Bibliothèque Marguerite Durand* is the only feminist library in France. It contains more than sixty thousand documents, among which one can find: French and foreign books on feminism; feminism and the arts; history; politics and science; militants' biographies; doctoral theses defended by women since the 19th century; periodicals, letters (e.g. by Mme de Staël and Colette); literary works; postcards; posters – the most precious one being a *placard* of Olympe de Gouge dating from 1792. The library's collection goes back to the 17th century.[16] Scholars and the public alike have immediate, free access to the entirety of the collections, which are kept in the small space of the reading room, and mostly in the building's underground storage, where they cover two linear kilometers. Unfortunately, the storage space has been completely full for the past fifteen years and, since then, the library has therefore been unable to accept new donations, save for rare pieces. Since the year 2000, thanks to a co-operation with the BMD, it is the *Centre des archives du féminisme* at the University of Angers that provides this essential archiving service.

The BMD Affair

In 2016 it was announced that the site of the Médiathèque Melville and the BMD would close for renovations from June 2018. On the occasion, the mayor of Paris also announced that the BMD (and its permanent personnel) would be transferred to the *Bibliothèque historique de la ville de Paris* (BHVP) in the fourth *arrondissement*. The project was advertized as the creation of a space solely dedicated to feminist literature and related activities: since "this library manages important archival docu-

---

[15] Verdier, "Trajectories of Two Women's Libraries," p. 29.

[16] For more information on the archival collections see Christine Bard, Annie Metz and Valérie Neveu (Eds.), *Guide des sources de l'histoire du féminisme* (Rennes: Presses Universitaires de Rennes, 2006).

ments […] that, unfortunately, are not clearly identified" the new location would allow them to be better identified and, especially, to have better visibility. Finally, the new planning would allow to "bring the documents to life and to feed contemporary debates on these fundamental issues" (i.e. the history of women and feminism).[17]

This sounds all very good. But then, why did the unions, feminist associations, scholars and private citizens mobilize around the collective *Sauvons la BMD*, sign petitions, organize sit-ins and demonstrations against this project?[18]

The association *Archives du féminisme* wrote a column for the daily newspaper *Libération* on October 5, 2016, in which they expressed their concern for a "dangerously vague project". They suggested that the inclusion in the BHVP might be a covert way to eliminate the BMD, given that the new location would be inadequate in space and conservation resources, both for the current personnel (seven of them to be housed in one room) and for the archival documents themselves. Indeed, these would be allocated only 500 linear meters – compared to the current two kilometers – in an already-saturated library, which implies that the majority of the documents would have to be moved into storage to the outskirts of Paris, which is in stark contrast to the BMD's present-day direct availability. The association is not against a move per se, but they stress that for such a move to occur, there needs to be an ambitious project that would upgrade both the personnel's working conditions and the public's access to the documents.[19] Therefore, in their opinion "the new

[17] "Pour une bibliothèque des femmes et du féminisme". Budget participatif, projet N. 7.
https://budgetparticipatif.paris.fr/bp/jsp/site/Portal.jsp?document_id=2691&portlet_id=158. Unless otherwise stated all translations from French are my own.

[18] For the collective Sauvons la BMD see https://www.facebook.com/CollectifsauvonslaBMD/ and https://www.instagram.com/collectif.sauvonslabmd/?hl=en; "Sauvons la bibliothèque Marguerite Durand!", Archives du féminisme. http://www.archivesdufeminisme.fr/actualites/sauvons-bibliotheque-marguerite-durand/

[19] Historian of feminism Bibia Pavard has also echoed the necessity of a more ambitious project for the BMD. See *La Poudre*, épisode 81 – Le point sur la révolution avec Bibia Pavard, 22/10/2020. https://open.spotify.com/show/1WgrGarkpE3efj57f8uvzo

library must, firstly, keep in a single place in central Paris the staff, the reading rooms and the archival documents. Then, it must be housed in premises larger than those of the current library, in order to permit the enrichment of the collections and to ensure good conditions for conservation. Lastly, in order to continue to better guarantee its mission of research and heritage valorization, it must preserve its autonomy in relation to any other library of the city of Paris".[20]

Militants are not only preoccupied that the library will be swallowed by the BHVP, but that it will also lose its visibility and autonomy because of the out-of-city storage and ensuing access delays. In fact, the lack of space means that the collections will not increase, and therefore, in the future, feminists will not feel encouraged to donate their archives to the library. This is a crucial point because, as historian of feminism Christine Bard says, "we need to think about the safeguard of present-day archives, of today's feminism". In conversations with feminist-activist and journalist Lauren Bastide, Bard and Bibia Pavard affirmed that the issue with the inclusion of the BMD into the BHVP catalogue is the erasure of the library's specificity and the loss of its identity – an identity built on the will to be a lasting place of generational transmission.[21] The fight against this project shows "our attachment to a library that is more than a library, it is a place of history, of memory, a place of culture that is fundamental for the struggles of yesterday, today, and tomor-

[20] Association Archives du féminisme, "Pour un projet ambitieux de bibliothèque d'histoire des femmes et du féminisme à Paris", *Libération*, 5/10/2016. https://www. liberation.fr/debats/2016/10/05/pour-un-projet-ambitieux-de-bibliotheque-d-histoire-des-femmes-et-du-feminisme-a-paris_1519505. See also: Commissaire, Claire, "Féminisme: pourquoi le transfert de la bibliothèque Durand inquiète les syndicats", *Libération*, 3/8/2017.https://www.liberation.fr/france/2017/08/03/feminisme-pourquoi -le-transfert-de-la-bibliotheque-durand-inquiete-les-syndicats_1587909; "La seule bib-liothèque féministe de Paris va-t-elle disparaître?". *Télérama*, 22/08/2017. https://www. telerama.fr/sortir/la-seule-bibliotheque-feministe-de-paris-va-t-elle-disparaitre,n515 2844.php
[21] *La Poudre*, Épisode Bonus – Bibliothèque Marguerite Durand, 2/11/2017 and *La Poudre*, épisode 81 – Le point sur la révolution avec Bibia Pavard, 22/10/2020. Both epi-sodes are available at https://open.spotify.com/show/1WgrGarkpE3efJ57f8uvzo

row".[22] In another interview Bard reiterated that the library is "a site of memory, of culture and citizenship" and that the documents kept at the BMD are "the archives of the future".[23]

All in all, to many activists the proposed new project for the BMD seemed to be an attempt at erasing women's voices, at denying the existence of feminism and its specificity, and a way to keep subsuming women to patriarchal structures that make them inaudible – hence insignificant. Thus, it is not only a technical issue but also, and most importantly, a symbolic one.

The Archive

Having laid out the vicissitudes surrounding the BMD, I would like to turn to the meaning of the presence of a feminist library and feminist archive as a tangible space. I would like to reflect on the role that archives play in preserving and accessing the past of feminism, in decoding the present, and in fostering feminist visions of the future. How do they create the possibility of (and potential for) feminist encounters? What are the limits and possibilities of the archive as a site – both in the physical and symbolic sense – of production of feminist knowledge? My questions echo those raised by Marianne Hirsch (2018) in her fantasy for 2027: "How do feminist archives, and feminist theory archives, in particular, shift our structures of knowledge and intelligibility? […] How do particular archival practices enhance the generation and transmission of this knowledge and the imagining of new feminist theoretical futures?"[24]

The notion of *archive* illuminates the forces at work in the affair in question while it also provides a terrain for highlighting, challenging, and resisting the economies of desire that subtend archival encounters. An archive is, literally speaking, a physical

---

[22] Christine Bard in *La Poudre*, Épisode Bonus – Bibliothèque Marguerite Durand.

[23] Arièle Bonte, "Pourquoi faut-il sauver la bibliothèque Marguerite Durand?", *RTLGirls*, 17/11/2017. https://www.rtl.fr/actu/debats-societe/pourquoi-faut-il-sauver-la-bibliotheque-marguerite-durand-7790978068#

[24] Marianne Hirsch, "Feminist Archives of Possibility" in *differences: A Journal of Feminist Cultural Studies* 29:1, 2018, pp. 173–188 (pp. 174–175).

place that collects material, documents, objects.[25] Jacques Derrida reminds us that "the meaning of 'archive,' it's only meaning, comes to it from the Greek *arkheion*: initially a house, a domicile, an address, the residence of the superior magistrates, the *archons*, those who commanded."[26] For Derrida this *domiciliation* (i.e. the archive) marks a passage from the private to the public, whereby what he calls an "archontic power" is applied – a power that gathers, unifies, identifies and classifies "by virtue of a privileged *topology*."[27] Behind the initial perception of the *archive* as a material site, i.e. an archival institution, the conditions and circumstances that create and preserve the archive emerge: the relations of power that underpin the rules of inclusion and exclusion.[28] Michel Foucault's engagement with the archive as rules of practice underlines the dynamic relation between knowledge production and power.[29] Addressing this process of production – inclusion, exclusion, dispossession, appropriation, regulation – has been fundamental for feminist, queer, and postcolonial studies and theory in order to challenge the technologies of imperial/patriarchal/heteronormative hegemony. In the words of postcolonial philosopher and public intellectual Achille Mbembe, "the archive is primarily the product of a judgment, the result of the exercise of a specific power and authority, which involves placing certain documents in an archive at the same time as others are discarded. The archive,

[25] See e.g. Jens Brockmeier, *Beyond the Archive: Memory, Narrative, and the Autobiographical Process* (Oxford: Oxford University Press, 2015), p. 71; Ernst van Alphen, "The Politics of Exclusion, or Reanimating the Archive" in *The Nordic Journal of Aesthetics* 49–50, 2015, pp. 118–137 (p. 118); Wallen, "Narrative Tensions", pp. 261–262.

[26] Jacques Derrida, *Archive Fever. A Freudian Impression,* transl. Eric Prenowitz (Chicago: University of Chicago Press, 1996), p. 2. See also Carolyn Steedman, *Dust: The Archive and Cultural History* (New Brunswick: Rutgers University Press, 2002).

[27] Derrida, *Archive Fever,* p. 3.

[28] Carolyn Hamilton, Verne Harris and Graeme Reid, "Introduction" in Hamilton, Carolyn et al. (Eds.), *Refiguring the Archive* (Dordrecht, Boston, London: Kluwer Academic Publishers, 2002), pp. 7–18 (p. 9).

[29] Cf. Michel Foucault, *The Archeology of Knowledge,* transl. A. M. Sheridan Smith (London and New York: Routledge Classics, 2002), pp. 89–143.

therefore, is fundamentally a matter of discrimination and selection, which, in the end, results in the granting of a privileged status to certain written documents, and the refusal of the same status to others, thereby judged 'unarchivable'."[30] Through these rules of discrimination and selection, a power legitimates certain memories over others, and thus maintains specific themes, norms and values to be carried on through time.

By overlooking certain practices and enabling a judgment of value that categorizes them as unimportant, the archive can therefore become a site of violence: assembling the archive involves the application of particular forms of censorship and manipulation – the devaluation, repression and rejection of the 'other' within the archive.[31] Against the persistence of patriarchal societies, it is therefore essential to build, nurture and, as is the case with the BMD, maintain archives of women and feminism, which tell the alternative story (or one of the many stories) of that 'other' that has been rejected from the 'official' preservation of time. However, a feminist archive is not without its own logics of power and its own privileged "mechanism for shaping the narratives of history".[32] Indeed, Hamilton, Harris and Reid remind us that marginal archives, those preserving materials "excluded from the mainstream repositories" are "no less constructed than mainstream archives and are likewise the product of processes of both preservation and exclusion". They argue that "Collections compiled in opposition to a particular hegemonic discourse are equally shaped by the kind of material collected, and the way it is arranged and described, as well as by

[30] Achille Mbembe, "The Powers of the Archive and its Limits" in Hamilton, Carolyn et al. (Eds.), *Refiguring the Archive*, pp. 19–26 (p. 20).

[31] See Ariella Azoulay, "Potential History: Thinking through Violence", in *Critical Inquiry* 39:3, 2013, pp. 548–574; Ariella Azoulay, *Potential History: Unlearning Imperialism* (London: Verso, 2019), in particular ch. 3, "Archives: The Commons, Not the Past".

[32] Antoinette Burton, "Introduction: Archive Fever, Archive Stories" in Antoinette Burton (Ed.), *Archive Stories. Facts, Fictions, and the Writing of History* (Durham and London: Duke University Press, 2005), p. 2. See also Hirsch, "Feminist Archives of Possibility".

what is excluded from an alternative recording of history".[33] Within the issue of the logics of power inscribed into the archive – which account for specific "political, cultural, and socio-economic pressures" – some considerations need to be made.[34]

First of all, if we return to the practicalities of the projected move of the Marguerite Durand Library we notice that, were the BMD subsumed under the BHVP, the rules of inclusion and exclusion proper of the latter would: (a) contribute to the erasure of certain feminist memories deemed unimportant by a hegemonic power; and (b) manipulate certain others by including them within a catalogue that follows specific (non-feminist) labels and/or classifying norms that might end up changing or distorting their meaning and epistemic import. As an active producer of content (rather than a passive and uncritical receiver), the archive "gathers together signs" and thus brings together singular objects into a collective that gives them meaning.[35] The cry for help for the BMD is thus justified. If objects are included in function of a whole, then, whether they are integrated into a pre-existing *historical* library or a *feminist* library dramatically changes their semantics (i.e. their meaning-endowing to and -endowed within the collection). Thus, the move implies the inscription within a different episteme – that which "governs the principles according to which archival organizations are structured in such a way that archives can be seen as emblematic examples of the nature of an episteme".[36] Submitting to these other organizational principles will also change the rules selecting what is archivable and what is not archivable, what is deemed important and what irrelevant, what is part of history and what can be silenced. Hence, the result will be a different episteme. This does not even take into account the impossibility of accepting new documents for lack of space, which reveals the (un)conscious desire to relegate women's struggles to a buried past (one that does not need to be revived). On the contrary, the

---

[33] Hamilton et al., *Refiguring the Archive*, pp. 11–12.

[34] Burton, *Archive Stories*, p. 6.

[35] Derrida, *Archive Fever*, p. 3.

[36] van Alphen, "The Politics of Exclusion, or Reanimating the Archive", pp. 75–76.

struggle is ongoing, feminist documents are ever-increasing, and an independent institution that collects and archives women's and feminist memories has not only the power to "shape and produce the identities of those it registers", but also to serve as a place of encounter that shapes and nurtures feminist identities, and that produces, shares, and transforms feminist epistemologies.[37]

Indeed, an alarming consequence of the move of the BMD would be the *de facto* end of any expansion of its archive. As the only institutional library of women and feminism, the BMD plays an important part in how the narrative is told and remembered. Moreover, the fact that it is a closed archive seems to relay the message that the narrative of feminism is finished, accomplished, rather than incomplete, constituted of *stories-(still)-in-the-making*. This means that the current closed archive will stand as the legitimate memorial narrative of feminism, one that is mostly told by white, privileged women – "a formation specifically of [first- and] second-wave feminism".[38] However, the history of oppression recorded by white women is not the same history of oppressions experienced by black women, women of colour, lesbians, and trans-women. The point I am trying to make here is far away from undermining the BMD and its importance; on the contrary, I want to underline the essential value of its material presence. The archive needs to grow and include more and new resources – be they books, letters, photographs, artworks, documents, videos, recordings, podcasts, etc.– that notwithstanding their format (digital/material) will increase the BMD archive and thus add new tassels to the story-in-the-making. Here 'story-in-the-making' means not only the development of feminism as a (her)story that can be told, but also foregrounds the hermeneutic value of the archive, whereby its interpretation is not fixed but instead an ever-evolving narrative in itself: a *story-in-the-making*.[39] But whereas nowa-

---

[37] Wallen, "Narrative Tensions", p. 269.

[38] Hirsch, "Feminist Archives of Possibility", p. 174.

[39] Brian Schiff, "The Hermeneutics of Crisis and the Crisis of Interpretation", Keynote

days and in the future it might be (and will be) easier to create and sustain digital archives of intersectional, decolonial feminism that will counteract (if not erase) symbolic restrictions, the "paradigm shift from a culture of scarcity to a culture of abundance" does not, in my opinion, resolve the issue of the fundamental importance of the library/archive as a physical site for encounter.[40] The archive needs to be a physical space, where human and non-human (textual) bodies can meet and interact. In this sense, I am inspired by theorizations of embodied experience as the basis for knowledge and by "how affective experience can provide the basis for new cultures".[41] I consider here in particular the 'bodily' and 'sensory' contact that happens in a library – interacting with the personnel, holding books, touching documents, entering into material contact with them, breathing their "eternal dust" in.[42]

Christine Bard, who is the founder and director of the *Archives du féminisme* in Angers, evokes the fundamental role of books along the feminist quest: according to her, a feminist conscience often emerges out of the encounter between reading and experiencing. Facilitating this encounter with feminist ideas, the book encourages awareness, situates knowledge, inspires a 'conversion', and stimulates activism, as it happened to be the case with Marguerite Durand herself. Sara Ahmed (2017) also stresses how books make communities: hers is a very "sense'itive" description of the encounter between books and bodies.[43] Reading groups have been historically important for

address "The Psychology of Global Crises: State Surveillance, Solidarity and Everyday Life", American University of Paris, 20 May 2020. Available online: https://www.youtube.com/watch?v=jZ3RD0Q1BuI

[40] Françoise Vergès, *Un féminisme decolonial* (Paris: La Fabrique éditions, 2019); Roy Rosenzweig, "Scarcity or Abundance? Preserving the Past in a Digital Era" in *American Historical Review* 108:3, 2003, pp. 735–62 (p. 739).

[41] Ann Cvetkovich, *An Archive of Feelings: Trauma, Sexuality, and Lesbian Public Cultures* (Durham and London: Duke University Press, 2003), p. 7.

[42] Steedman, *Dust*, p. 157.

[43] I adopt here the term used by Kay Anderson and Susan J. Smith's (2001), which conveys the idea of sensitivity while also giving legitimacy to research and writing attuned to the senses and to corporeal experiences. See Anderson, Kay and Susan J.

women and the articulation of feminist communities, and still play a pivotal role, as Ahmed's experience highlights: "Participating in the group with books made me aware of how feminist community is shaped by passing books around; the sociality of their lives is part of the sociality of ours. There are so many ways that feminist books change hands; in passing between us, they change each of us".[44] The words she employs foreground the sensory, bodily, material encounters afforded by the "fragile archive" of feminism. Indeed, in an earlier book, Ahmed proposed a model of archive as a "contact zone" where, among multiple forms of contact, she also includes "institutional forms of contact", such as, among many others, libraries and books.[45] My understanding of the archive as a contact zone builds on Ahmed's 'personal archive' but also includes the concrete space that fosters close encounters (physical, emotional, intellectual, and political). Therefore, I also read this contact zone as "a site where past and present converge in the architecture of the space itself, whose very materiality is linked to regime changes past, present, and future".[46] The archive is a contact zone between past and present, both symbolically and as a physical space, and as such it can shape the future and the transmission of knowledge.

In such a *lieu de mémoire*, strong affective (and affecting) encounters are able to influence, change, and shape a whole existence. In the encounters between past and present afforded by the feminist library, present-day engagements and future possibilities are envisioned in multidirectional and intersectional perspectives. Going knee-deep into the feminist archive

Smith, "Editorial: Emotional Geographies" in *Transactions of the Institute of British Geographers*, Vol. 26, No. 1, 2001, pp. 7–10 (p. 9). Many thanks to Samira Saramo for sharing this idea with me.

[44] Sara Ahmed, *Living a Feminist Life* (Durham and London: Duke University Press, 2017), p. 17. For a long-term sociological study of women and book clubs, see e.g. Elizabeth Long, *Book Clubs: Women and the Uses of Reading in Everyday Life* (Chicago: University of Chicago Press, 2003).

[45] Sara Ahmed, *The Cultural Politics of Emotion* (Edinburgh: Edinburgh University Press: 2004), p. 14.

[46] Burton, *Archive Stories*, p. 10.

creates for the reader an epistemic and affective map of women––what Griselda Pollock calls "contexts populated by many women".[47] Each one of these many women is "a singular intellect, shaped by her own double axis within generation and geography and hence different in their particularities." Yet, in the archive "the collective history of many women allows to recover the complex created worlds of women engaging critically, aesthetically and politically with the challenges of femininity, modernity and representation."[48] It is on the basis of this context of histories of women and history made by women that I see the empowering strength of the feminist archive as a space of (collective) memory. Thus the archive offers the hope for "the possible encounter not only with the traces of memory" but also with other memories that narrate alternative, non-normative experiences.[49] In this way the archive fosters critical awareness, creates the condition of transformation of the self and of society, shapes new political and ethical models and challenges our historical imagination.

Conclusions

Months of rallying against a short-sighted project have saved the *Bibliothèque Marguerite Durand* from being literally effaced from the geography of France. Its founder's desire to awaken and educate future generations of feminists has prevailed over and against a myopic logic that was about to silence her will. The troubles with the BMD are emblematic of how the cultural memory of women and feminism is still under the rule of patriarchy, and therefore considered readily dismissible. It is for everybody to see on an everyday basis that the agency of women is still under siege, and that their position within our societies is still, to varying degrees depending on geography and context, mostly relegated to the margins and almost to a state of exclu-

[47] Griselda Pollock, *Encounters in the Virtual Feminist Museum: Time, Space, and the Archive* (London: Routledge, 2007), p. 163.

[48] Pollock, *Encounters in the Virtual Feminist Museum*, p. 163.

[49] Wallen, "Narrative Tensions", p. 276.

sion. The decision to keep the library in its current location, however, does not signify that the struggle is over. Indeed, as the collective *Sauvons la BMD* has made apparent, the library should be the object of serious discussions about a move to reorganize its space and collections with the aim of expanding their capacities. The BMD needs more resources – from personnel, to space, to storage for increasing its archives. Indeed, whereas the transmission of the past may seem to be safe, the creation of new memories and knowledges, their evolution and future development depend on unconditionally available and accessible encounters, as well as on the political will to allow and encourage them.

In this chapter, I have addressed the case of the *Bibliothèque Marguerite Durand* through the lens of what it may tell us about the history of feminism, its evolution and transmission to future generations. My approach started from the notion of the archive, which has been amply theorized as enacting forms of systemic violence: this means that the archive functions on the basis of specific, socially-sanctioned power structures. From these premises, my reading of what I called 'the BMD affair' is twofold: on the one hand, I located a form of hegemonic patriarchal power in the project of moving the BMD library under the BHVP, whose system would be responsible for reassembling the archive according to its rules of exclusion and inclusion. On the other hand, I also pointed out how the impossibility for the BMD to enlarge its archive is in itself a form of structural violence, given that the feminist memory contained therein does not (equally) speak for women of different class, race, and generations – among them, white women, black women, women of colour, lesbians, and trans-women. Therefore, I contend that the expansion of the BMD archive is fundamental in fostering an intersectional transmission of the feminist project. Finally, guided by feminist notions of embodied and affective knowledge I have also explored the notion of archive as a physical space for encounters. I have argued that, not only do we need the feminist archive to be a physical space for the sake of upholding its narrative in-the-making as an inclusive (i.e. intersectional) one, but also because it is by leafing books, feeling documents, and liaising with people that we can build a community that can touch us – physically, emotionally, and intellectually – and move us into action.

PART 3
Transformations in Art

Chapter 8
Possessing the Past
– Revisiting (a Feminist) Swedish 19th Century in Contemporary Fiction

Claudia Lindén

What does the historical novel have to do with history? History and fiction – are they not opposites? Today we experience a wave of historical novels, films, and TV series, both internationally and in Sweden. Since these fictions often attract large audiences, they contribute to and shape our contemporary historical consciousness and national self-image. At a time when there is a politically charged struggle over Sweden's history and national identity and museums and institutions are looking for new ways to represent cultural heritage, it is particularly interesting to look at how Swedish history is depicted in contemporary historical fiction.

Our image of nineteenth-century Sweden has in fact been shaped by literature. The impact of Vilhelm Moberg's emigrant epos and Per-Anders Fogelström's Stockholm series cannot be measured.[1] With numerous editions and adaptations in film, a TV series, a musical, and in theater continuing to be made, shaping our historical consciousness, the work of Moberg and Fogelström constitute our cultural memory of that epoch.[2] Nineteenth century Sweden appears as poor, dirty and miser-

---

[1] Vilhelm Moberg, *The Emigrants*, Minnesota Historical Society Press, St. Paul, 1995, the first part in Moberg's tetralogy written between 1949–59, is a story of a group poor peasants leaving starvation and oppression behind for a better life in the U.S. Per Anders Fogelström, *City of my dreams: A Novel*, Penfield Press, Iowa City, Iowa, 2000 is the first of a pentalogy written 1960–68. The series takes place between 1860 and 1968 and is an epic tale of a family's and a city's joint development from poor and miserable to a life with much better circumstances in a modern Stockholm, in the Swedish welfare state.
[2] In 2017 Stadsteatern in Stockholm staged *City of my dreams* as a play spanning over the whole pentology, directed by Linus Tunström, and a new TV-series adaptation of *The Emigrants* started filming in 2020.

able, and the present becomes a positive development away from the past, especially for women. The legacy of Moberg, Fogelström and the project of modernization can be discerned through an ambivalence toward the past in Swedish fictions situated in the nineteenth-century.

How then, does the image of Sweden's history and our relationship to the past appear in contemporary historical fiction with their female protagonists and stories from the margins about unmarried mothers, prostitutes, oppressed Sami or forbidden same-sex desire? In some stories, especially those dealing with prostitution and sexual harassment, the past is not past, but very much alive and haunts the present. Historical fictions provide other models for understanding the past and for criticizing how the past is constructed. Temporality creates a relation to history and therefore shapes historical consciousness, as well as an understanding of the feminist task in the present.

In England, the historical novel is an established genre and a field of research, in its own right. However, in the Nordic countries, there is virtually no research at all on the historical novel as such, despite our long tradition of this genre. I will therefore situate this article in the context of British research. Taking as my starting point William Godwin's defense of fiction, as the best genre for history writing, I will argue that historical fictions, with their ability to transgress the borders between past and present and between fiction and facts, engineer what Ethan Kleinberg has labeled "deconstructive history". Through a reading of a few contemporary historical fictions, especially the TV series *Fröken Frimans krig* (*Miss Friman's War*), I will show how these historical fictions establish a temporality, which transgresses past and present, and which in turn shape our historical consciousness. In this way, these historical fictions serve as both the history of feminism and as critical historiography, creating new knowledge, not only about the women of the past but our ongoing relationship with them.

Women, History, and the Historical Novel

The historical novel's regained influence coincided with theoretical developments within historiography and theory of history after it began to reflect on the relation between history and literature.[3] What could be labeled the 'narrative turn in history' had its equivalent in a 'historical turn in narrative'. New theoretical developments within literary theory, such as Hayden White's metahistory, Linda Hutcheon's 'historiographic metafiction, and Amy Elias 'meta-historical romance' a "postmodernist historical fiction which is obsessed with historiographical questions in a self-reflexive mode", all contributed to the development of the historical novel.[4] Inspired by critical discourses like postcolonialism and feminism the metahistorical fiction was grappling with the meaning of history, in the manner of realist historiography.

According to Alan Robinson, criticism of historical novels is still dominated by a now outdated model of historiographic metafiction: "it is also inadequately narrow in reducing historiography to epistemological issues and in neglecting the crucial importance of temporality in the interplay between *past present* and *past future* and *present past*."[5] The issue of temporality runs as an undercurrent in both history and historical fiction. Derrida has been an important influence on the fields of both history and literature. Inspired by Derrida, a few historians have developed the concept of history as haunting especially when it comes to unresolved political traumas but also as a deconstructive ap-

---

[3] See Frank Ankersmit, *Meaning, truth, and reference in historical representation*, (Cornell University Press, Ithaca, 2012); Michel de Certau, *The writing of history*, (Columbia Univ. Press, New York, 1988); Hayden White, *Metahistory: the historical imagination in nineteenth-century Europe*, [New ed.]., (Johns Hopkins U.P., Baltimore, Md., 1979), and Hayden White, "Introduction: Historical Fiction, Fictional History, and Historical Reality" *Rethinking History*, Vol. 9, No. 2/3 (2005).

[4] Compare Linda Hutcheon, *The Politics of Postmodernism* (London: Routledge, 1989), Ch. 3, and Amy J Elias, "Metahistorical Romance, the Historical Sublime, and Dialogic History", *Rethinking History*, 9:2–3, (2005), p. 159.

[5] Alan Robinson, *Narrating the past: Historiography, Memory and the Contemporary Novel* (New York: Palgrave Macmillan, 2011), p. xiii.

proach, as "haunting history".[6] Another discussion of temporality is rooted in German history and cultural memory studies with, among others, Reinhart Koselleck and Aleida Assman, and post-colonial studies where history's hauntings of the present is described as a kind of "entanglement" of time dimensions.[7]

For centuries, the historical novel has been the only genre of history open to women. Women have been excluded from recorded history both as subjects, writers, and readers before they were admitted to the universities around 1900. A historical setting has frequently been used by women (and male) writers "as a way of writing about subjects which would otherwise be taboo, or of offering a critique of the present through their treatment of the past" as Dina Wallace has pointed out. She continues: "It is not surprising that in women's hands the historical novel has often become a political tool. Perhaps even more important for women writers has been the way that the historical novel has allowed them to invent or 're-imagine' […] the unrecorded lives of marginalized and subordinated people".[8] In historical fiction, the time that separates the present from the past can be transgressed and we, as modern readers, can for a moment situate ourselves in another historical room.

Women's reading and writing of historical fiction have often been regarded as escapism. These two uses of history – escapism and the political – are connected, according to Wallace, since escapism indicates dissatisfaction with what is available. Marginality or exclusion breeds skepticism toward the grand narratives of history and makes women into "resisting readers" as Judith Fetterly once coined it. Wallace continues: "But the understanding that much of history is 'invention' as Austen puts

---

[6] For history as trauma see Berber Bevernage, *History, memory, and state-sponsored violence: time and justice*, Routledge, New York, 2012; For history as haunting history see Ethan Kleinberg, *Haunting history: For a Deconstructive Approach to the Past* (California: Stanford University Press, 2017).

[7] Joseph-Achille Mbembe, *On the postcolony*, (University of California Press, Berkeley, Calif., 2001).

[8] Diana Wallace, *The Woman's Historical Novel: British Women Writers 1900–2000* (Basingstoke: Palgrave Macmillan UK, 2004), p. 2.

it, 'narrative' or 'fiction' as a postmodernist theorist such as Hayden White might argue, may also bring certain freedoms."[9] If history has traditionally excluded women, the historical novel, on the other hand, has "offered women readers the imaginative space to create different, more inclusive versions of 'history'", Wallace concludes.[10]

The contemporary interest in transgressing the borders between history and literature, is often perceived as an exclusively postmodern discourse (White, Ankersmit, Kleinberg etc.) with no historical precedent. But the debate between the historian and the writer of fiction can be traced to the inception of the modern era. Before Walter Scott's immensely popular historical novels and Ranke's criticism of them in 1824, the philosopher and writer William Godwin (1756–1826) argued in "Of History and Romance" that "[t]he writer of romance is to be considered as the writer of real history."[11] According to Godwin, a novel is a superior form of history-writing because it relates human action to character and circumstance. My point is that Godwin from his 18th-century pre-Ranke perspective could express a very similar idea as the contemporary deconstructive historian does. He could do that because he built his argument on romance or the gothic novel, an early form of the historical novel. The genre that Austen's heroine Catherine Morland in *Northanger Abbey* prefers is "history, real solemn history".[12] However, contemporary philosophy of history is not aware that the gothic historical novel theorized the relationship between history writing and literature already at the formation of the science of history. I will start with recapitulating Derrida's reflections on the ghost in *Spectres of Marx*, and then turn to Ethan Kleinberg's idea of haunting history that builds upon Derrida.

[9] Wallace 2004, p. 3.
[10] Wallace 2004, p. 3.
[11] William Godwin "Of History and Romance" 1797, https://web.english.upenn.edu/~mgamer/Etexts/godwin.history.htmln
[12] Jane Austen, *Northanger Abbey* (1803) ch. 14 https://www.gutenberg.org/files/121/121-h/121-h.htm

From there I will move to a closer analysis of Godwin's text, before offering a reading of *Fröken Frimans krig*.

Derrida's Spectres

In his very influential book *Spectres of Marx* (1993), Jacques Derrida develops a theory, or rather a metaphor, for understanding history. Starting from the first sentence of Marx's Manifesto "A spectre is haunting Europe – the spectre of communism", in combination with the famous line from the opening scene where Hamlet speaks with his father's ghost and utters "The time is out of joint: Oh cursed spite/That ever I was born to set it right", Derrida creates the neologism *hauntology*, a word-mix of haunting and ontology. Haunting is repetition and a first time, it is a ghost, something that is both present and absent at the same time. "After the end of history," Derrida writes, "the spirit comes by *coming back* [revenant], it figures both a dead man who comes back and a ghost whose expected return repeats itself, again and again."[13] That which repeats itself is of course something that cannot be confined to a single given space and time.

What is important for Derrida's argument, concerning Marx and Marxism, is how the image of the ghost, the spectre, helps to deconstruct the notion of historical time as an irreversible linear succession of events. To understand the history and legacy of Marxism and how it has haunted not only history and our present but also threatens to haunt the future, it is necessary to talk of both history, something contemporary and a possible future *and* to be able to do so from different historical viewpoints. Derrida emphasizes an idea of history where the relation between past, present, and future are both looser than traditionally understood, and yet are connected at the same time.

Even though Derrida primarily discusses the legacy of Marx and Marxism his ideas have gained relevance for historians interested in another way of understanding and writing history.

[13] Jacques Derrida, *Specters of Marx: The State of Debt, the Work of Mourning and the New International* (London: Routledge, 2006), p. 10.

The notion of history as a ghost that returns to haunt the present, as something not necessarily confined to a given time and place, opens up for seeing how the past is not only stuck in the past but continues to live on and affect us in the present. History of oppression often works in this ghost-like way, as a revenant. Holocaust and antisemitism, slavery and racism as well as centuries of legal and moral differences between men and women are all examples of oppression in history that continue to haunt the present.

Haunting History

In his book *Haunting History*, the American historian Ethan Kleinberg, following Derrida, argues for an understanding of the past as polysemic, conflicting, and as both present and absent at the same time. This understanding sets itself against the current trend toward a fetishization of lived experience, materialism and the "real" (ontological realism). The main reasons why deconstruction never has gained influence on the practice of history, Kleinberg argues, "is a commitment to history as an endeavor concerned with events assigned to a specific location in space and time that are in principle observable and as such are regarded as fixed and immutable."[14] This leads to the wrong assumption that there can be something like a permanently enduring past. Getting the past right becomes a question of historical method.

History, Kleinberg argues, is a replacement where the past event or figure is silently determined by the retelling that replaces it.[15] He embraces Hayden White's emphasis on language and constructivism in the historical endeavor, and he looks to Derrida for a hauntological approach to history that "accounts for the entangled and unstable relation of presence and absence without privileging one over the other."[16] Kleinberg

---

[14] Kleinberg, *Haunting history*, p. 1.
[15] Kleinberg, *Haunting history*, p. 2.
[16] Kleinberg, *Haunting history*, p. 3.

calls this a "past that ~~is~~" to emphasize something that is at the same time both present and absent.[17]

As Derrida did, Kleinberg turns to literature when he tries to map out a deconstructive history. The example he chooses is Washington Irving's gothic novel *The Legend of Sleepy Hollow* (1820) about the headless horseman. The story is set in 1790 where the schoolteacher Ichabod Crane comes to a small, former Dutch, settlement called Sleepy Hollow, a place renowned for its ghosts and the haunting atmosphere that pervades the imaginations of its inhabitants and visitors. To Kleinberg *Sleepy Hollow*:

> is a story of a past that haunts history – a past of American Indian dispossession, of the revolutionary war, of the unspoken atrocity that took place at Major André's tree /.../ Sleepy Hollow is laden with the ghosts of a past half-remembered if remembered at all. This is the latent past beneath the ghosts that haunt the inhabitants. /.../ It is a past that we cannot touch but that nonetheless touches us. The histories, the tales, the haunted spots are all partial configurations, like a headless horseman.[18]

History is, according to Kleinberg, the presence of absence, of things hidden, buried and forgotten. "And when what is latent appears returns, history is haunted, and we are confronted with the possibility that our understanding of the past is polysemic and contradictory."[19] Haunting history is a past that comes again with the possibility to still affect, disturb or even hurt us. Kleinberg argues: "Insofar as history serves *to make the past legible in the present, it should be seen as a writing whose function it is to make present what is absent,* to render legible that which would otherwise be illegible".[20] (my italics).

<hr>

[17] Kleinberg, *Haunting history,* p. 12.
[18] Kleinberg, *Haunting history,* p. 136.
[19] Kleinberg, *Haunting history,* p. 138.
[20] Kleinberg, *Haunting history,* p. 143.

When Kleinberg needed an example of how a haunting history may function, he turned to the gothic – the genre that invented the writing of the haunted, to begin with. Gothic, or romance as it is called in the 18th-century, was not only literature of terror and haunting – it was historical fiction. Not with exact dates and places, as Walter Scott would later practice it, but history with a vague sense of pastness that often hides secrets that affect and haunt the protagonists in their present. As a fiction with multi-layered temporality, it is a genre that already from the beginning destabilized the relation between past and present.

Despite Kleinberg's reference to *Sleepy Hollow* it is just an example or at best a metaphor (the headless horseman) of how a deconstructive history should be understood. Literature, fiction, is never allowed to be a *method*. Even though he notices that Derrida's interest in transgressing the border between "'fiction' and 'fact' as well as between the living and the dead, the past and the present, presence, and absence" Kleinberg never himself crosses that line.[21]

Fiction is – in fact – the ghost that haunts history writing. The historical scholar Michel de Certeau has said that "fiction is the repressed other of historical discourse."[22] In commenting on this quote, Hayden White asks "Why? Because historical discourse wages everything on the true, while fictional discourse is interested in the real – which it approaches by way of an effort to fill out the domain of the possible or imaginable."[23] To think the possible, also opens up for the fictional, for the invented. And, as we have seen from Kleinberg, it is what we are willing to accept as 'past possibilities' that also "conditions what we are willing to accept as possible pasts".[24]

---

[21] Kleinberg, *Haunting history*, p. 8.

[22] Quoted from Hayden White, "Introduction: Historical Fiction, Fictional History, and Historical", *Rethinking History*, Vol. 9, No. 2/3 2005, p. 147.

[23] White "Introduction" 2005, p. 147.

[24] Kleinberg, *Haunting history*, p. 137.

Why the Writer of Novels is the Better Historian

If we now move to William Godwin's 1797 essay "Of history and Romance" we can see that thinking about the relation between past possibilities and possible pasts is a key question for him concerning writing on history. The Godwinian scholar Pamela Clemit has pointed out that Godwin in this essay extends his claims for the educative power of fiction into the realm of history, "arguing that the imaginative study of the past liberates the mind from prescription and prejudice and stimulates ethical enquiry."[25]

Godwin was a leading radical political philosopher, novelist, and social thinker of the British Enlightenment.[26] The same year he wrote "Of History and Romance" his wife Mary Wollstonecraft worked on a gothic novel *Maria: or the Wrongs of Woman* perceived as the sequel to *Vindication of the Rights of Women*.[27] In the same way as Godwin, Wollstonecraft had moved toward a greater reliance on the mainstays of fiction: emotion and imagination. As Deborah Weiss has pointed out, the novel "illustrates how female experience and female feeling can be

[25] Pamela Clemit, The Godwinian Novel: The Rational Fictions of Godwin, Brockden Brown, Mary Shelley (Oxford: Clarendon, 1993), p. 79.

[26] Godwin had written both a famous philosophical book *An Enquiry Concerning Political Justice* (1793) and a novel dealing with the same themes: *Things as They are: or, The Adventures of Caleb Williams* (1794) and had a new book set for press: *The Enquirer. Reflections On Education, Manners, And Literature. In A Series Of Essays* (1797). Godwin had met Mary Wollstonecraft the year before and during 1797 she was expecting their child. A pregnancy that ended in her tragic death in September the same year, and left Godwin alone with Fanny, Wollstonecraft's daughter from her former relationship, and the baby who was to become Mary Shelley, the author of *Frankenstein*.

[27] The Wollstonecraft research differs over how to interpret the unfinished novel. Even though many scholars see *Maria...* as a sequel to *Vindication*, there are others interpreting it more as a betrayal of *Vindication* than a continuation. The latter tradition regards the novel's investigation of Maria's emotions, especially her love for Darnford, as proof that Wollstonecraft did not believe anymore in the development in women's rationality. For a summary of the different traditions see Deborah Weiss, *The Female Philosopher and Her Afterlives Mary Wollstonecraft, the British Novel, and the Transformations of Feminism, 1796–1811*. Palgrave Studies in the Enlightenment, Romanticism and the Cultures of Print. (Cham: Palgrave Macmillan, 2017), p. 81.

used to generate social theory."[28] In this sense *Maria...* was a forerunner to a long tradition, leading up to today's feminist literature.

Wollstonecraft and Godwin both used the novel as a tool for their progressive political agendas and theorized the relationship between history, politics and fiction almost two centuries before the postmodern critique of history writing. Godwin provides an early argument for how historical writing can and should serve the transformation for a different future. But most of all it acknowledges that the border between fact and fiction are always already transgressed when it comes to historical writing.

In "Of history and Romance" Godwin makes a distinction between "two principal branches of history; the study of mankind in a mass, of the progress, the fluctuations, the interests and the vices of society; and the study of the individual."[29] The former looks for facts, but even if that history comes closest to the truth, a mere chronicle of facts, places, and dates is, in reality, no history, writes Godwin. Godwin criticizes a history that only gives bits and pieces of facts but does not talk of individuals and their motives. Those who disdain the records of individuals but find this fact-history the only kind deserving serious attention, they think, Godwin writes: "To interest our passions, or employ our thoughts about personal events, be they of patriots, of authors, of heroes or kinds, they regard as a symptom of effeminacy."[30] What Godwin here points out is that the difference between history and romance is what we today would call gender-coded, where fiction is perceived as feminine. Later in the article, he also highlighted how this genre paradoxically sells well but is assumed to be read only by "women and boys". Diana Wallace has also pointed out how "Godwin summarizes critics' reactions to historical romances in fascinatingly sexualized

---

[28] Weiss, The Female Philosopher and Her Afterlives, p. 77.
[29] Godwin, "Of History and Romance" 1797.
[30] Godwin "Of History and Romance" 1797.

terms" when he writes that history in romance fiction is "debauched and corrupted."[31]

In the same way as Derrida and Kleinberg, Godwin connects the study of the history of individuals to a possible story of power, and above all, that knowledge of the past has implications for the future: "It is thus, and thus only, that we shall be enabled to add, to the knowledge of the past, a sagacity that can penetrate into the depths of futurity", Godwin writes.[32] Godwin takes as his example the study of Antiquity and how we regard those men as intellectual giants. Still, this knowledge is more like a fable. "Let us take it for granted that it is a fable. Are all fables unworthy of regard?"[33] Such fables have, according to Godwin "a moral perfectly adapted to the human heart. I ask not, as a principal point, whether it be true or false? My first inquiry is, '[c]an I derive instruction from it?" If so, he continues, is it not better to be profoundly versed in such a fable, "than in all the genuine histories that ever existed. *It must be admitted indeed that all history bears too near a resemblance to fable. Nothing is more uncertain, more contradictory, more unsatisfactory than the evidence of facts.*"[34] (my Italics) So, all history is like a fable, according to Godwin.

It is remarkable, I think, to find that Godwin, before the advent of conventional history, with its methods, and long before Hayden White, Derrida and Kleinberg, saw that the writing of history always resembles a fable, but foremost that 'facts' can never be mere facts but are also uncertain and contradictory. This leads Godwin to conclude that if "history be little better than romance under a graver name," we might as well enquire into "that species of literature, which bears the express stamp of invention, and calls itself romance or novel."[35]

---

[31] Diana Wallace, "Difficulties, discontinuities and differences: Reading Women's historical fiction", *The Female Figure in Contemporary Historical Fiction*, Katherine Cooper & Emma Short (Eds.) (Basingstoke, Palgrave Macmillan, 2012), p. 208. William Godwin, "Of History and Romance" 1797.

[32] Godwin, "Of History and Romance" 1797.

[33] Godwin, "Of History and Romance" 1797.

[34] Godwin, "Of History and Romance" 1797.

[35] Godwin, "Of History and Romance" 1797.

Romance, or the gothic historical novel, transgress the border between past or present.

> Romance then, strictly considered, may be pronounced to be one of the species of history./…/ The historian is confided to individual incident and individual man, and must hang upon that his invention or conjecture as he can. The writer collects his materials from all sources, experience, report, and the records of human affairs/.../ *The writer of romance is to be considered as the writer of real history;* while he who was formerly called the historian, must be contended to step down into the place of his rival, with the disadvantage, that he is a romance writer, without the arduous, the enthusiastic and the sublime license of imagination, that belong to the species of composition.[36] (my italics)

If we follow Godwin's argument, we can see how he opens up similar questions, pointing to the same problems that Kleinberg identifies: Facts without a story are not really history, they are just facts bound in time and fixed to a certain place. In this, Godwin echoes Aristotle's distinction from the *Poetics* between history and poetry, namely a difference between the particular and the universal, making poetry the more philosophical and elevated form of the two.

Fact, Fiction, and Temporality

Literature can mix fiction and facts in all imaginable constellations and allow for a transgression of past and present. But literature does not offer only examples, or metaphors for a haunting history. *It is a method in itself.* Godwin had deconstructed the demand for ontological realism in history writing even before it was truly invented. Long before Derrida, before the advent of the science of history with Ranke, Godwin showed that fiction can be a better form of history because it not only deals with facts, but also can stage affection and thus be open to moral reflection.

---

[36] Godwin, "Of History and Romance" 1797.

The fact that literature creates affective links between the reader and the protagonist is of course nothing new. So how does this have a bearing on the more philosophical debate about temporality in relation to history, and on feminism? Fiction's ability to awaken emotions, to make the reader feel lust and fear, can make the reader experience the effect of past events or what previous generations may have felt. The difference in reading as, not only about, puts the reader in an affective connection with the past, which also opens for an ethical commitment to the past. Godwin would later use the first-person perspective in his historical novels just as a way to create affective links between the reader and the protagonist in the past. Such an identification with the protagonist allows the modern reader/viewer to identify with a person from another time. It opens up an anachronistic relationship to history in a positive way.

For Kleinberg, the important thing is to get away from ontological realism and its way of regarding people and events as bound up in specific times and places, in order to create a thing of the past that allows for a simultaneous presence and absence. But the question of presence and absence is still bound to the notion of the real. A truly deconstructive history needs to move beyond the absence/presence dichotomy to the question of temporality. A true hauntology must destabilize time as well. In fact, by putting his emphasis on the fact/fiction dichotomy Godwin comes closer to destabilizing the dichotomy between past and present than Kleinberg. That is because the fact/fiction dichotomy opens up to the question of temporality.

"History" creates versions of the past, a textual substitute for something that is not there, which is absent, empty and without content. History is a replacement, a way to put something in place namely the missing absent other – the past. The conditions for the discipline of history are, however, that the past in a fundamental way is cut off from us. The historical novel, on the other hand, perverts history or our perception of the difference between past and present, between fact and fiction, since it lures the reader to take it not as a substitute, but as the thing itself. Jerome de Groot has pointed out that historical fiction "forces the reader into a temporal distortion. The historical fiction requires a changing and fickle relation to time and perhaps most obvious, the temporal otherness."[37] By transgressing the gap between then and now, historical fiction creates alternative temporalities.

Feminist Re-negotiation of Sweden's Past

The ability of historical fiction to cross both the line between fact and fiction, and between then and now, gives it unique opportunities to (re)interpret, (re)discover and (re)write history.[38] As Wallace pointed out, contemporary historical fiction often has politico-critical ambitions. They question established history writing at the same time as they bring previously concealed horrors to light. As Alan Robson claims, "historical fiction resembles historiography in that its interpretive employment constructs a subjective *present past*; this differs from a wholly invented spatiotemporal world, as it is modeled on and anchored in a former actuality."[39]

Renegotiations of the past are important for today's understanding of history and identity, especially in a national context. The established success story of *folkhemmet's* path from "dirt-Sweden" ("lort-Sverige"), as the critic Ludvig Nordström labeled it in a radio program 1938, to the welfare state and a successful industrial nation with equality between men and women, is both problematized and confirmed in the novels by Ola Larsmo, Lena Kallenberg, Anneli Jordahl, or in the TV series *Fröken Frimans krig* (Miss Friman's War). The role of women in the transformation of society, and the relevance of feminism and women's emancipation for the modernization project are still, to a large extent, underground knowledge shared between gender scho-

---

[37] Jerome De Groot, *Remaking history: The Past in Contemporary Historical Fictions* (London: Routledge, 2016), p. 15.

[38] This is Heilmann's and Llewellyn's definition of Neo-Victorianism, but it could be said of most historical fiction. Ann Heilmann & Mark Llewellyn, *Neo-Victorianism: the Victorians in the Twenty First Century, 1999–2009* (Basingstoke: Palgrave Macmillan, 2010), p. 12.

[39] Robinson, *Narrating the past*, p. 28.

lars, but not present in mainstream history writing. In contemporary historical fiction, on the other hand, women are often at the center and the emancipation of women is made part of the modernization project. Women's sexual vulnerability through unwanted pregnancies, death of puerperal fever, syphilis and prostitution, as well as sexual liberation and resistance to the 19th-century gender norms are all central concerns in contemporary historical fictions. Such stories from the margins create alternative stories about the past that allows for multifaceted identities and different versions of history. These fictions thus function as new history writing and at the same time as critical historiography.

(Re-)writings of the Past. Prostitution and Syphilis, the Ghosts that Haunt the Story of Modernity

History becomes a haunting history especially in historical fiction that deals with prostitution because we still have prostitution and dangerous, even lethal, venereal diseases in the same way as in the nineteenth century. Even though we have a variety of laws and women's situation in society is very different, stories of the horrors of prostitution and trafficking are still part of our popular culture, such as Jens Lapidus' books *Snabba Cash* (2006) and *Livet deluxe* (2011), and the movie trilogy based upon them.

Many women were forced into prostitution in the 19th century driven by poverty when the emerging industrialization led to quick urbanization. As a result, this development led to rampant syphilis and other venereal diseases in the cities. There were significantly more men than women who were infected with venereal disease, which was taken as proof that women were the main source of infection. Women were made responsible for the spread of sexually transmitted diseases and regulations of prostituted women were introduced in Sweden, according to the model that already existed in Paris and other European cities. Between 1847 and 1918, women, who the police considered to live an "immoral life", were registered at the Prostitution Bureau or Inspection Bureau, as it was also called. There were about seven thousand women who at some point during the period 1856–1918 had their names printed in the rolls of the inspection office.[40]

The enrolled women were required to follow strict rules in their behavior and to go for health examinations twice a week. If they were found to be sick they were sent to special hospitals, and if they did not show up for the checkup, or in any other way broke the regulations, they were sentenced to a fine or penal servitude up to one year.[41] Stockholm grew explosively as a city during this time, and the work of creating a functioning sewage system was an ongoing project that was referred to on a metaphorical level. As Lennartsson writes: "Through a metaphorical language, the sex trade, and indirectly also the women within it, were equated with sewers and drain pipes".[42]

The women's movement protested intensely at the time against the treatment of prostitutes and regulation. But, when regulation ceased in 1918, and Swedish women finally got the right to vote in 1919, the memory of the state's atrocities against women was forgotten. It would take almost a hundred years before feminist researchers began to examine the deeply problematic regulation and its far-reaching consequences for the view of gender difference and sexuality well into the 20th century. Dissertations by the historian Yvonne Svanström *Policing Public Women: The Regulation of Prostitution in Stockholm 1812–1880* (2000) and the historian of ideas Rebecka Lennartsson's *Malaria Urbana. Om byråflickan Anna Johannesdotter och prostitutionen i Stockholm kring 1900* (2001) paved the way for deeper knowledge about regulation of prostitutes in 19th century Sweden.[43] Lennartsson's book also contains large quotes

---

[40] Rebecka Lennartsson, Malaria Urbana. Om byråflickan Anna Johannesdotter och prostitutionen i Stockholm kring 1900 (Eslöv: Symposion, 2002).

[41] Lennartsson, *Malaria urbana*, pp. 57–59.

[42] Lennartsson, *Malaria urbana*, pp. 58–59 (my transl.)

[43] Yvonne Svanström, *Policing Public Women: The Regulation of Prostitution in Stockholm 1812–1880* (Stockholm: Atlas, 2000). A few years later came a second part: Yvonne Svanström, Offentliga kvinnor. Prostitution i Sverige 1812–1918 (Stockholm: Ordfront,

from the authentic diary of the prostitute, Anna Johannesdotter.[44]

The prostitute, or the issue of prostitution, was definitely present in nineteenth century literature, but usually in the periphery of the plot.[45] A rare exception is Anne Charlotte Leffler's daring, socialist drama *Hur man gör godt* ("How to do good" 1885) where the prostitute actually is one of the main characters. In contemporary historical fiction, on the other hand, both the prostitute herself and the question of prostitution is at the very center of the story. Amy Elias has pointed out that one important feature of the postmodern historical imagination, is that it is a post-traumatic imaginary, that rather confronts than represses the historical knowledge.[46] The Swedish historical fictions testify to this especially in the stories about prostitution.

Lena Kallenberg's *Apelsinflickan* (The Orange-Girl 1997) and the sequel *Stockholmskärlek* (*Stockholm love* 1999) portrays poor women who are driven into prostitution ("Orange-girl" was an epithet for prostitutes). Prostitution is also portrayed from the inside in Henning Mankell's *Minnet av en smutsig ängel* (Memory of a Dirty Angel 2011) in the story of a Swedish woman who becomes the owner of a brothel in East Africa around 1900. In Ola Larsmo's *Jag vill inte tjäna* (I Do Not Want to Serve 2012), the regulation of prostitution is

---

2006). Lennartsson also wrote another book on the same theme going into more detail on the brothels and clients in 19th century Stockholm: Rebecka Lennartsson, *Den sköna synderskan. Sekelskiftets Stockholm: betraktelser från undersidan* (Stockholm: Norstedt, 2007).

[44] Johannesdotter's diary was edited and published by Klara Johansson in 1907. The original is lost, but Johansson claimed that she had only made corrections for spelling errors and such. Johansson, Anna Mathilda Cecilia Johannesdotter, *Den undre världen. En lifshistoria* (Stockholm: Wahlström & Widstrand, 1907).

[45] Arvid, the protagonist in August Strindberg's *The Red Room* (1879) goes to a brothel with his friends. In Gustaf af Geijerstam's *Erik Grane* (1885) as well as Hjalmar Söderberg's *The Serious Game* (1912) and Anne-Charlotte Leffler's *Sanna kvinnor* (True women 1883) the men pick up 'a girl' in the street. In Leffler's drama it is William, Bertha's brother-in-law, who has brought home a prostitute, thereby causing a crisis in his marriage. In Elin Wägner's *Pen Woman* (1910) the protagonist's old friend Klara earns her living by selling sex.

[46] Elias, "Metahistorical Romance..." (2005), p. 165.

depicted from a doctor's perspective through his contact with a young woman who chooses prostitution over life as a maid. Although medical science as an institution of power, is problematized in the novel, the protagonist in Larsmo's novel becomes a representative of the "good" doctors when he performs a forbidden abortion and thereby saves the woman's life. The book can be read not only as a defense of the right to abortion, but a deeper reading of the complex relation between science and women's emancipation. The doctor in the novel has problems with his career and he is assigned the post as a medical examiner of those prostituting women who come in for the required examination. Through his work the reader comes in contact with what seems as authentic excerpts from nineteenth century medical records. Retroactively these quotes from medical records tell us something about the individual women's fates. In this sense, Larsmo's novel is given a double function as fiction and facts about the women that were forced to register at the Inspection Bureau. Syphilis as an effect of prostitution also appears in Annelie Jordahl's *Augustenbad en sommar* (*Augustenbad: A Summer* 2011). In *Fröken Frimans krig* (Miss Friman's War 2016) season 3, the topic is the regulation of prostitution and the women's movement's fight against it.

Our present historical fiction has often taken part of feminist research. Contemporary historical fiction, therefore, functions as a way of spreading this feminist research of historical knowledge to a wider audience. This is especially true in the case of *Fröken Frimans krig* (Miss Friman's War) a mini-TV series inspired by the life of educator and women's rights activist Anna Whitlock, produced by Swedish television in three episode installments across four seasons 2013–2017. The series aired during the Christmas holidays every year and therefore attracted large audiences. To many people this was the first time they encountered the history of feminism and the conditions of women in 19th century Sweden when women did not have the right to vote, and husbands were women's guardians. The series built on a lot of previous feminist research, both the story of

Svenska hem and the women's movement pictured in season two, as well as the story of prostitution and regulation in season three, a fact that was not fully acknowledged.[47] When the producers after the last season made a separate program with the history "behind" Miss Friman's War they were severely criticized for not crediting all the feminist research they had built upon.[48]

In season one, the women's rights activist Dagmar Friman and her friends decide to open the cooperative grocery store in Stockholm *Svenska hem* (Swedish home). They worked with women in all chains of the food production to sell good food at reasonable prices, and where customers received a refund on their purchases. Friman and her friends face a lot of resistance from the established retailers. The cooperative store *Svenska hem* did exist and was very successful in Stockholm for ten years between 1905–1916. In 1915, the number of members was 3,134. In 1916, *Svenska Hem* merged with the then newly started cooperative *Konsum* in Stockholm and was subsequently shut down. All stores then changed their names or were closed. The female managers were replaced by male ones.

In season three of *Fröken Frimans krig*, the sister of Lottie Friman's maid is unwillingly forced into prostitution by a member of parliament. She is just a young, poor, woman from the countryside, who gets seduced by a rich man. While leaving her to sleep in the hotel room, he goes directly to the regulation bureau and reports her as a prostitute, to make her go to the checkups that will mean she is "safe" for him. The police then come and pick her up in the morning. They find money on her and refuse to listen to her protestations about being a prostitute. The result is that Miss Britta becomes registered as a "byrå-flicka", that is, a prostitute. She then faces three months in prison if she does not report herself regularly to the bureau as someone practicing as a prostitute. With the help from Dagmar and Lottie

---

[47] See for example Monika Björk & Eva Kaijser, *Svenska hem. En passionerad affär* (Stockholm: Stockholmia, 2005).

[48] https://www.svd.se/fyra-forslag-efter-froken-friman-debaclet published 170116.

Friman and their friends, and with some unexpected help from the real women of the trade, Miss Britta is finally released from the regulation bureau.

Through the story of Miss Britta, the series manages to give the viewers a glimpse of the history of prostitution in Sweden, regulation and the women's movement's fight against regulation, as well as their ambivalence toward prostitutes. Engaging in the question of prostitution could be a sensitive issue for the women's movement who wanted to be taken seriously in their demand for the vote. In the series, Dagmar is afraid of letting Swedish homes address the issue and its regulation while her more radical friend Kinna disagrees. They argue, and Kinna shouts at her: "Food controls, there you dare to fight, but when women are controlled as goods, then it is not as important".[49] Kinna's words echo the wording in Svanström's book: "There existed two examples of inspection bureaux in the nineteenth century: the inspection bureau for public women, and the inspection bureau for meat. Both usages of the word indicating merchandises, which needed to be inspected and found healthy before being put on the market."[50]

In the following episode one of those critical of regulation is upset by the way prostituted women are described, she mocks the ineffective system and wonders why men stick to defending regulation: "'Infectious material in the population' – as if they were not even human! They know that the system is ineffective, they know that it is wrong to hold women solely responsible, morally, and medically. Why hold on?" Dagmar then responds by connecting the support of regulation to the resistance against women's demands for the right to vote: "Because they can. It benefits them and they can. The right to vote, prostitution, there is no difference. A woman is less worthy, that's just the way it is. Nobody has ever told them anything else."[51] When Dagmar Freeman makes this connection between the demand for the

---

[49] *Fröken Frimans krig*, Episode 1, min. 34.33–34.39.
[50] Svanström, *Policing women* 2000, p. 41.
[51] *Fröken Frimans krig*, Episode 2, min. 01.35–01.49.

vote and the critique of legalized prostitution, she echoes the real nineteenth-century women's movement and again the connection to feminist history. Here, the research about the connection is made explicit. In this way, *Fröken Frimans krig* serves as both a history of feminism and as critical historiography. Since it creates new knowledge of women's conditions in Sweden a hundred years ago for a mainstream audience. It thus serves as a critique of the previous silence about regulation, prostitution and syphilis.

The regulation is a forgotten trauma in the general historical consciousness, in the same way that sterilization was for a long time. It was legislation whose consequences for gender difference and sexuality still affects us. In this respect, historical fictions about prostitution and regulation become a critique of conventional history writing, where the usual history teaching in schools, for example, have not related these facts and events. Contemporary popular historical fictions like *Fröken Frimans krig*, therefore, function as a (feminist) history for a wider audience. It often builds on feminist research but reaches far outside the research community. Since, to a large degree, it is a former unknown history, historical fictions, like *Fröken Frimans krig*, help to shape our historical consciousness.

Fröken Frimans krig's gender-critical perspective on prostitution, different sexual morals for men and women, men who exploit women, sexual harassment and feminism's fight against all this, establish affective links to the women of the past that obliterate the difference between then and now. Stories of a feminist engagement with nineteenth-century misogyny in historical fictions like *Fröken Frimans krig*, establish a temporality where the past is still active, a haunted history. Nineteenth-century misogyny is a spectre that, to paraphrase Derrida, we would like to believe belongs to the past, but which returns and haunts us even today.

Chapter 9
Fantastic Antigones
– The Tragic Legacy of Trans Grief

Fanny Söderbäck

As Trans folks we know there are so many different types of *Grief* that go unrecognized within a cis framework.

For trans people know *Grief*

There is *Grief*   for the people who will never accept us

There is *Grief*   for our chosen family that we may outlive

There is *Grief*   for those we see in newspapers who look like us

There is *Grief*   for the lies told about our bodies

and *Grief*   that is held within our flesh

For trans people who know *Grief,* let this be a moment to breathe out all the grief you are carrying. The *Grief* you did/do not deserve. The *Grief* you are a master at forgetting.

– J Mase III[1]

---

[1] J Mase III, *And Then I Got Fired: One Transqueer's Reflections on Grief, Unemployment & Inappropriate Jokes About Death* (Lulu: 2019), pp. 29–30.

> It is a challenge to one's stamina to follow the traces of this 2,500-year-young Theban princess, who looks younger every day. She is indefatigable, as all the undead seem to be. […] By the nineteenth century, she had made numerous transoceanic voyages to visit places she had never heard of or dreamt of visiting, where she shared the drama of the political theft that had incited her own anger back home. Her geographic range expanded dramatically in the twentieth century, especially after the great European wars, and the invitations she received around the world enticed her to new dialogues, taught her new ideas, offered her new outfits, opened new ways of linking her ancient drama to the modern undead.
>
> – Moira Fradinger, "Nomadic Antigone"[2]

The Timeliness of an Ancient Drama: Resurrected Antigones

The ancient Greek figure of Antigone is stubbornly reborn. Fueling stories and narratives across the globe, she rises from the dead, time and again, and appears in times of oppression and injustice wherever the need arises for dissidence and resistance. In their volume *The Returns of Antigone*, Tina Chanter and Sean D. Kirkland succinctly ask: "What, then, are we to make of the ostensible death of tragedy on the one hand, and Antigone's refusal to attend her own funeral on the other?"[3] They speak of her "persisting capacity to illuminate our world," which has spurred a "continued appeal today for thinkers, poets, and activists of every stripe."[4] As the title of George Steiner's now classic book suggests: there is not one, but many Antigones, and while she may have first appeared on the ancient Greek stage, her journey by no means ends there.[5]

---

[2] Moira Fradinger, "Prologue: Nomadic Antigone," in Fanny Söderbäck (Ed.), *Feminist Readings of Antigone* (Albany: State University of New York Press, 2010), p. 15.

[3] Tina Chanter & Sean D. Kirkland, *The Returns of Antigone: Interdisciplinary Essays* (Albany: State University of New York Press, 2014), p. 1.

[4] Chanter & Kirkland, *The Returns of Antigone*, p. 2.

[5] George Steiner, *Antigones: How the Antigone Legend Has Endured in Western Literature, Art, and* Thought (Newhaven: Yale University Press, 1996).

From Argentina to Turkey, via Australia, Brazil, Colombia, Cuba, Egypt, Ghana, Greece, India, Indonesia, Ireland, Mexico, Nigeria, Palestine, Poland, Puerto Rico, South Africa, Spain, and beyond – is there any country in the world she has not visited in one of her many guises? Whenever and wherever civil liberties are endangered, when the rights or existence of indigenous peoples are threatened, when revolutions are underway, when injustices take place – wherever she is needed, Antigone appears. A shapeshifter of sorts, her name varies depending on where she emerges on the modern stage: Antígona Vélez, Mariana, Antígona Pérez, Akwele, Odale, Clara Luz, Antígona Furiosa, Sofia, Melissa, Anita, Tègònni…

Antigone is, in other words, a figure from the past who helps us grapple with the tragic conditions of our present. Indeed, despite her coming to us from an ancient Greek context marked by misogyny and authoritarian power, she has been viewed, especially by feminist scholars and activists, as someone who can inspire transformation in our own time. Throughout my work – and most systematically in my book *Revolutionary Time* – I have insisted on the need for continuous return to the past to make possible a more dynamic-embodied present as well as a future that avoids both repetition and teleological closure.[6] But it is essential of course that our return to the past – including past figures and texts – not serve to determine the present or the future, but rather open them up to new and unforeseen imaginaries and possibilities. As Catherine A. Holland cautions in an essay that examines the historical legacy of Antigone for feminist thought:

> whenever we mine past texts as resources for evaluating contemporary concerns, the danger is that the 'persistent and contemporaneous influence' of those texts can limit our political vision and thus narrow our political horizons, a danger

---

[6] See Fanny Söderbäck, *Revolutionary Time: On Time and Difference in Kristeva and Irigaray* (Albany: State University of New York Press, 2019).

that the past will overfill the present, shrinking rather than expanding the space of political possibility.[7]

To be sure, if we are to productively engage Antigone in our present, we need to do so by insisting not only on similarities but also on the distance between our times and hers. If Antigone herself has been firmly situated as a European cis woman celebrated by male philosophers and cis feminists alike, her global journey and her shape-shifting capacities demand that we reimagine her story in terms that are irreducible to – indeed that might fundamentally challenge – her original context.

Antigone appeared in 2018 at the Classical Theater in Harlem, in a performance directed by Carl Cofield, where the walls of the stage were chalked with graffiti and covered with placards: "RIP Eteocles," "Say His Name," "Black Lives Matter." In a cultural context where Black lives are marked as ungrievable, and where Black folks are navigating grief (and the anticipation of grief through an acute awareness of imminent death and loss) as the ongoing condition of life, the figure of Antigone offers a cultural imaginary for framing that experience. Consider, for example, the response that the author Claudia Rankine received when asking a friend what it is like being the mother of a Black son: "'The condition of black life is one of mourning', she said bluntly. For her, mourning lived in real time inside her and her son's reality: At any moment she might lose her reason for living."[8] It is easy to see how this experience finds a voice in Antigone, whose demand that she be allowed to publicly mourn her dead brother, Polyneices, is rejected by royal decree, and whose own life is marked by looming death and foreclosed dreams. As Creon buries Antigone alive on stage, we hear echoes

---

[7] Catherine A. Holland, "After Antigone: Women, the Past, and the Future of Feminist Political Thought," in Söderbäck, (Ed.), *Feminist Readings of Antigone*, p. 27. Holland cites Sheldon Wolin's work on theoretical imagination here.

[8] Claudia Rankine, "The Condition of Black Life Is One of Mourning," *The New York Times Magazine*, June 22, 2015. Accessed at https://www.nytimes.com/2015/06/22/magazine/the-condition-of-black-life-is-one-of-mourning.html on July 7, 2020.

of the "I can't breathe" of our own times, the tragic condition of Black life, or what Denise Ferreira da Silva has described as a kind of temporal suspension that haunts our political present: "That moment […] between the release of the trigger and the fall of another black body, of another brown body, and another."[9]

And yet, of course there is also a distance here, an immense distance, between the Black mothers of our own times whose lives are conditioned by perpetual mourning, and the work of grief that marked the life of Antigone, a Theban princess, for whom slavery was a present reality relegated to the subtext of the play, or, as Tina Chanter has argued, for whom the very insistence on burying her brother is symptomatic of the need to make a distinction between free cultured individuals and barbarian non-Athenian slaves. Consequently, Chanter notes, "the Oedipal model, as inflected through Freud and Lacan, cannot be taken up and applied to colonial issues, as if it constituted an adequate hermeneutical tool that operates independently of those very issues its dominance has helped to eclipse."[10]

In an article from *The Atlantic*, Antigone's story was used as a foil to illustrate the practice of separating children from their parents at the U.S.–Mexico border: "In the family separation described by Sophocles, the brother is not just exiled but dead; the king, Creon, has left his body to rot outside the city walls without a burial," Quinta Jurecic notes, and she goes on to suggest that when the Trump administration "justifies pulling migrant parents away from their children at the U.S. border, it is speaking Creon's language."[11] Here, Antigone is called in as a figure whose story speaks volumes to the cruelty of a legal system that – in the name of security and state power – upholds contingent distinctions between 'friend' and 'enemy' (even when this

---

[9] Denise Ferreira da Silva, *Toward a Global Idea of Race* (Minneapolis: The University of Minnesota Press, 2007), p. xi.

[10] Tina Chanter, *Whose Antigone? The Tragic Marginalization of Slavery* (Albany: State University of New York Press, 2011), p. x.

[11] Quinta Jurecic, "A Choice Between Cruelty and Mercy: A 2,500-year-old play illustrates the emptiness of the administration's arguments about enforcing the law," *The Atlantic*, June 18, 2018. Accessed at https://www.theatlantic.com/ideas/archive/2018/06/border-policies-antigone/563126/ on July 7, 2020.

entails tearing families apart) so as to set an example and deter others from trying to cross the borders of the United States. If Creon, by refusing Polyneices' proper burial and by decreeing that he be left to rot outside the city walls, sought to reaffirm "the distinction between whom he wants in his city and whom he doesn't, defining the boundaries of his community," the Trump administration repeated this violent gesture in an attempt to more narrowly restrict who belongs here, and who belongs together. Reading *Antigone* today, Jurecic suggests, might thus serve as "a reminder both of the visceral wrongness of what is happening at the border and of the emptiness of the administration's arguments about law enforcement."[12]

And yet, while Antigone might have served as the constitutive outside of a political order bound to ultimately exclude her, she inevitably also inhabits a vantage point of privilege – she is, after all, King Creon's niece, and he tries his best to make exceptions for her, even as he runs into her stubborn refusal to be saved. Her agency, as much as it is used in the spirit of resistance to the law, is embodied by someone whose kinship ties situate her at the very center of political power (she is, as Sina Kramer puts it, excluded *within*).[13] Her crime is that she ventures outside of the city to bury her brother – not that she desperately tries to make it into a city that refuses her entry.

It nevertheless remains the case that the actions of Antigone, who stubbornly and courageously opposed state law and patriarchal power, come to life in circulating images of contemporary protests and stand-offs between daring women and the male powers that be: Whether in the now famous image of Tess Asplund, who stood up to uniformed demonstrators in a Nazi demonstration in Borlänge, Sweden, in May 2015; or that of Ieshia Evans, protesting the death of Alton Sterling near the headquarters of the Police Department in Baton Rouge, in July

---

[12] Quinta Jurecic, "A Choice Between Cruelty and Mercy."

[13] For a rich analysis of Antigone's situatedness as illustrative of the kind of exclusion that occurs *within* a political body, according to the logic of constitutive exclusion, see Sina Kramer, *Excluded Within: The (Un)Intelligibility of Radical Political Actors* (New York: Oxford University Press, 2017), especially pp. 133–144.

2016 (later detained by law enforcement); or, finally, that of an unnamed young demonstrator facing down a riot policeman during a pro-democracy protest in Santiago, Chile, in September 2016. Notably, these are all women of color standing up not only to patriarchy but to a racist state apparatus and a police force that has rendered Black and Brown lives criminal by decree.

It is to Chile that I want to turn in this essay, and more specifically, to Sebastián Lelio's 2017 film *A Fantastic Woman* (*Una mujer fantástica*), which won an Academy Award for Best Foreign Language Film in 2018. The film tells the story of a trans woman, Marina, grappling with a double loss: that of her lover and that of her right to grieve. It was well received and much celebrated within the queer community for offering a rich account of trans experience, and for casting a trans actress, Daniela Vega, in the role as Marina. In what follows, I want to suggest that we read Marina as echoing the fate of Antigone, as their lives and stories intersect in myriad ways, the most obvious of which is their shared experience of being refused to publicly mourn and partake in the burial of their loved ones. I will offer a reading of the film through the lens of *Antigone*, as I think about the tragic elements of our own culture as well as the specific ways in which trans experience might activate but also complicate themes from the original Sophoclean drama. Through the figure of Marina, I hope to offer a queer imaginary that both returns us to and moves us beyond the one Antigone herself provided.

A Fantastic Woman, A Fantastic Antigone: On Trans Grief

When Marina's partner Orlando suddenly dies from an aneurism, she finds herself rejected by his family and banned from his funeral. The two have just celebrated her birthday, dining and dancing, and their relationship is presented as one of deep and mutual love. When Orlando wakes up not feeling well, Marina rushes him to the hospital, where he dies within hours, and that event sets into motion a series of unpleasant encounters with doctors, police officers, Orlando's ex-wife and adult son, and more broadly a social fabric that, unlike Orlando, fails to see Marina for what she is – a truly fantastic woman.

If Antigone was fighting state power embodied in a patriarchal tyrant (Creon), Marina is instead faced with a cascade of micro aggressions and everyday individual and institutional prejudice that serve to question her very existence. The doctor in the hospital insists on using male pronouns, and casts suspicion on Marina because of the bruises and wounds found on Orlando's dead body (resulting from him falling down the stairs as they rushed to the hospital). A police officer called into the hospital demands that she show her ID and refuses to record her chosen name in the report. Another police officer shows up at the restaurant where she works and wants to know if Orlando was paying her for sex. The officer proceeds to require that she come to the police station the following day, without warning her in advance that the purpose of that visit is an intrusive medical examination, where Marina is forced to undress to be photographed (a scene in which the director, thankfully, resists the temptation to make us into complicit voyeurists, by ensuring that the camera remains on her face when she strips naked). And of course, there is the ongoing abuse directed at her from Orlando's family. His son, Bruno, repeatedly trespasses into her home, steals her dog, compares her to an animal, tells her he does not know *what* she is (while stubbornly failing to get her name right), and ultimately gangs up with two friends to force Marina into their car, taping her face tight, and leaving her in an alley, trembling, as she catches a glimpse of herself in a window that reflects the disfigured monster that *they* have been seeing all along.[14] And then there is Sonia, the ex-wife, whose ice-cold penetrating gaze and sharp tongue are aimed at undoing her very existence.

Taken together, these experiences pile up, and the infamous glass ceiling that has prevented women from taking to the sky is

---

[14] *Una Mujer Fantástica*, directed by Sebastián Lelio (2017), 1.07.15–1.10.20.

here metaphorized through the mighty wind that Marina struggles to tackle as she navigates her way through narrow-minded bigotry and never-ending discrimination.[15] She is simultaneously pathologized and criminalized: her very existence is on trial. And, as Judith Butler remarks about Antigone in the final chapter of *Antigone's Claim*: "She is one for whom open grieving is itself a crime."[16] To be sure, trans folk have a particularly complex relationship with grief, not only because of this societal refusal to acknowledge their relations as legitimate ones, but also because of the manifold ways in which the very process of transitioning tends to be overshadowed by cis-grief (whether it be that of parents 'losing' the child they once had, or partners grieving the 'loss' of the lover they first met).[17] And while important work in trans studies has been undertaken to attend to and complicate our collective response to the loss of trans lives – especially trans of color lives that have been lost to acts of violence – less has been said about what it means to take up the work of grief *as* a trans person.[18]

[15] Lelio, *Una Mujer Fantástica*, 1.00.28–1.01.15.

[16] Judith Butler, *Antigone's Claim: Kinship Between Life and Death* (New York: Columbia University Press, 2002), p. 79.

[17] Sly Sarkisova explains: "Our social spheres online and in real time are deluged with accounts and experiences of parental grief at a transgender child coming out, at a partner's 'loss' of their loved one in the gender they preferred… with accounts of strangers' unsavoury reactions and unsolicited observations that 'so-and-so used to be so…pretty/handsome before…it's such a shame'" (Sly Sarkisova, "On Transgender Grief," November 7, 2014, accessed at https://www.slysarkisovacounselling.com/single-post/2014/11/07/On-Transgender-Grief on July 14, 2020). For an example of a scholarly study of the grief experienced by parents of trans children whose transition is viewed as loss, see Ines Testoni & Manuela Anna Pinducciu, "Grieving those Who Still Live: Loss Experienced by Parents of Transgender Children," *Gender Studies*, Vol. 18, No. 1 (2019), pp. 142–162.

[18] For important discussions of our response to and understanding of the loss of trans lives, with particular emphasis on violence against trans women of color, see, for example, Viviane Namaste, "Undoing Theory: The 'Transgender Question' and the Epistemic Violence of Anglo-American Feminist Theory," in McCann, Carole R. & Kim, Seung-Kyung (Eds.), *Feminist Theory Reader: Local and Global Perspectives* (New York: Routledge: 2017), pp. 608–621; C. Riley Snorton & Jin Haritaworn, "Trans Necropolitics: A Transnational Reflection on Violence, Death, and the Trans of Color Afterlife," in Stryker, Susan & Aizura, Aren Z. (Eds.), *The Transgender Studies Reader 2*

This underscores the need to establish trans spaces for mourning, for engaging the past and the losses one has experienced on one's own terms. The trans social worker Sly Sarkisova speaks to this need:

> We need our own space to mourn our losses. We need to create that space. A space unknown to people with cis privilege. A space individual to our needs and experiences, and collectively respectful of the common experiences of transphobic erasure. [...] For transgender wholeness and realness, maybe we owe it to ourselves to create rituals that honour our grief and uniqueness, that restore and resist and fortify against any other narrative than our own.[19]

Basil Soper echoes these sentiments in a piece on his own grief as a trans person: "Today, I wish for my entire beautiful, resilient trans family throughout the country – and around the world – to be open to the grief we are feeling. Our mourning may well help illuminate the path home, to a place that is safe and peaceful and our own amidst the exhausting work of putting our lives on the line to enact change."[20] The most explicit attempt to offer a

(New York and London: Routledge, 2013), pp. 66–76; and Sarah Lamble, "Retelling Racialized Violence, Remaking White Innocence: The Politics of Interlocking Oppressions in Transgender Day of Remembrance," *Sexuality Research & Social Policy*, Vol. 5, No. 1 (2008), pp. 24–42. For important analysis of collective loss and mourning within the trans community, see Che Gossett, "Silhouettes of Defiance: Memorializing Historical Sites of Queer and Transgender Resistance in an Age of Neoliberal Inclusivity," in *The Transgender Studies Reader 2*, pp. 580–590. Gossett, who draws from Jacques Derrida's work on mourning and the archive for examining our memorialization of events such as the Stonewall Riots in New York City in 1969 and the Compton's Cafeteria Riot in San Francisco in 1966, asks: "What is the relationship between the memorialization of sites of queer and trans resistance and the politics of loss and mourning?" (588). Gossett's worry is that much historiography and memory work has served to erase the trauma and violence that queer and trans folk experience in the present, by relegating it to the past. They appeal to the concept of "impossible mourning" (588) to describe the condition under which we might grieve trans life in the wake of media's and the state's perpetuation of transphobic deaths.

[19] Sarkisova, "On Transgender Grief."

[20] Basil Soper, "I Am Trans, and Today My Grief Is Visible," *The Advocate*, March 31, 2016. Accessed at https://www.advocate.com/commentary/2016/3/31/i-am-trans-and-

space for collective grief is the Transgender Day of Remembrance, which is celebrated every year on November 20 to memorialize all those who have lost their lives to transphobic violence. But *A Fantastic Woman* offers a welcome alternative imaginary that frames grief in trans terms, while exposing the tragic legacy of trans grief – the societal denial of one's right to mourn *as* a trans person.

Butler's interest in the figure of Antigone stems in part from their own reactions to a cultural moment in which the public ungrievability of certain losses – queer losses – became acutely tangible, namely the AIDS epidemic and the kinship crisis that arose in its wake. Butler asks: "which social arrangements can be recognized as legitimate love, and which human losses can be explicitly grieved as real and consequential losses?"[21] Who gets to grieve and bury whom, and under what conditions? What of life-long partners and lovers who in the eyes of society and the blood kin of those who have died – kin who may have never recognized or approved of their bonds of love and desire in the first place – can have no legitimate or even intelligible claim to sorrow?

For Butler, Antigone embodies pressing contemporary concerns about loss and mourning – ones that reverberate through much of their later work: What lives matter? What lives are grievable? What lives count as properly human? As Marina herself notes, after she has attempted to enter the church during Orlando's wake only to be thrown out by his family: "Saying goodbye to a loved one when he dies is a basic human right, isn't it?"[22] And what do the boundaries we draw when responding to these questions tell us about normativity and the frames for intelligibility? Antigone's – and Marina's – "trespass on the norms of kinship and gender" ultimately "exposes the precarious character of those norms, their sudden and disturbing transferability, and their capacity to be reiterated in contexts and

today-my-grief-visible on July 16, 2020.
[21] Butler, *Antigone's Claim*, p. 24.
[22] Lelio, *Una Mujer Fantástica*, 1.06.40–1.06.44.

in ways that are not fully to be anticipated."[23] As Chanter and Kirkland put it, Antigone is "an aberrant, itinerant, queer, queered, and queering figure."[24] And this marks both our heroines as threats to the social order. They represent "not kinship in its ideal form but its deformation and displacement," which in turn puts "the reigning regimes of representation into crisis" and forces upon us questions that for some might be ground shaking: "What new schemas of intelligibility make our loves legitimate and recognizable, our losses true losses?"[25]

In our present, these questions were again activated in the context of those, mostly queer and trans people of color, who lost their loved ones in the mass shooting at Pulse nightclub in Orlando, Florida. Here, the relation between desire and grief – and the capacity of each to both connect us and to displace us – came to the forefront. As Butler, again, reminds us, this time in *Precarious Life*: "We're undone by each other. And if we're not, we're missing something. This seems so clearly the case with grief, but it can be so only because it was already the case with desire."[26] What this means is that "we are not only constituted by our relations but also dispossessed by them."[27] And for queer and trans folk – especially queer and trans folk of color – dispossession is an acutely felt lived reality. In queer communities, the nightclub comes to represent a place where dispossession can be felt in the more positive way that Butler appeals to in their work. As Che Gossett remarks in a 2016 blog post about the Orlando shooting: "Queer and/or trans nightlife has always been about survival and creating temporary autonomous and temporary fabulous zones that are as much affective – a structure of queer and trans feeling – as material in its electric choreography of bodies."[28]

---

[23] Butler, *Antigone's Claim*, p. 24.

[24] Chanter & Kirkland, *The Returns of Antigone*, p. 6.

[25] Butler, *Antigone's Claim*, p. 24.

[26] Judith Butler, *Precarious Life: The Powers of Mourning and Violence* (New York: Verso Books, 2006), p. 23.

[27] Butler, *Precarious Life*, p. 24.

[28] Che Gossett, "Pulse, Beat, Rhythm, Cry: Orlando and the Queer and Trans Necro-

And so, Marina too seeks out the pulsating rhythms on the dance floor, in the most explicitly campy scene of the film. Here, desire and grief overlap, in the shared figure of the pulsating body, and in the figural sharing of pulsating bodies. Amidst glitter, eyelashes, and sweat, there is the fist in the air, the Antigonean defiance, here staged not in the blazing light outside the city walls, but under the strobe lights of a queer nightclub. And on the dance floor Marina reunites with her Orlando, whose ghost-like appearance reminds us that he, like Polyneices, is un-dead – not quite living but nevertheless not yet at peace under-ground. His ghost ultimately helps Marina find his soon-to-be-cremated body, allowing her, at last, to bid her final farewell.

The Tragic Legacy of Sexual Difference: Woman Outsider

It is worth noting that whatever group or interest Antigone is brought in to defend – religious, cultural, or racial minorities; guerilla fighters; spiritual leaders; war-torn people; the economically oppressed – it is always as a *woman* that she appears on stage. Even, as in some contemporary examples (and of course already on the ancient Greek stage), where the cast is all male. In Athol Fugar's *The Island*, set in an unnamed prison based on the one in which Nelson Mandela was held on Robben Island, John and Winston are cellmates who spend their days doing back-breaking labor, and their nights rehearsing Sophocles' *Antigone* to present to their fellow inmates. For Winston, who is cast to play Antigone, the prospect of having to wear female attire (wig and breasts) provokes intense anxiety about his sexual identity, and of having his fellow inmates make him into a laughingstock. "Despite his vociferous protests," Chanter notes, he "ends up playing the role of Antigone after all," and to his relief nobody laughs.[29] While homophobia is rampant in the

politics of Loss and Mourning," Verso Blog (July 5, 2016), Accessed at https://www.versobooks.com/blogs/2747-pulse-beat-rhythm-cry-orlando-and-the-queer-and-trans-necropolitics-of-loss-and-mourning on July 7, 2020.

[29] Chanter, *Whose Antigone?*, p. 92.

prison, Winston and John are ultimately willing to put their heteronormative attachments aside, since they can relate so deeply to Antigone's quest for justice. They, like she, are "being punished for what they know to be right," and so they need Antigone to tell their own story.[30]

Sexual difference stood at the center of the original Sophoclean drama, and sexual difference continues to mark Antigone's story as she is stubbornly resurrected. It is *as a woman* that Antigone has a moral duty to bury her kin, and yet it is also *as a woman* that she is barred from a political landscape that seems unable to make sense of her agency on the public scene. Ismene, her sister, tries to prevent her from breaking Creon's law precisely by appealing to their sexual identity: "You ought to realize we are only women / not meant in nature to fight against men."[31] And Creon reveals his own misogynistic anxieties when it dawns on him that it is a woman who has disobeyed his decree. Like Winston, he fears emasculation, and the subsequent risk of being made into a laughingstock. Antigone's transgression, her courageous act, and the heroic death it anticipates, puts his masculinity into question: "We cannot give victory to a woman," Creon exclaims, and "we must not let people say that a woman beat us."[32]

As Cecilia Sjöholm has argued, Antigone, both through her deed and through her death, challenges our most basic presuppositions about masculinity and femininity. She observes the mutuality of this reversal: "It has often been pointed out that Antigone does not act like a woman. It has less often been observed that Creon does not act like a man."[33] We are reminded that binary gender roles are co-dependent – masculinity needs femininity to uphold its own dominant status of active man-

<hr>

[30] Chanter, *Whose Antigone?*, p. 93.

[31] Sophocles, *Antigone*, in *The Complete Greek Tragedies: Sophocles I*, transl. David Grene and Richmond Lattimore (Chicago: The University of Chicago Press, 1991), ll. 61–62.

[32] Sophocles, *Antigone*, ll. 678 and 680.

[33] Cecilia Sjöholm, *The Antigone Complex: Ethics and the Invention of Feminine Desire* (Palo Alto: Stanford University Press, 2004), p. 44.

hood, and femininity needs masculinity to maintain any of its current meaning of passive submission. In an effort to protect and maintain his masculine identity, Creon thus insists on viewing and treating Antigone *as a woman*, and she is repeatedly reminded that she must respect the limitations imposed on her due to her sex – despite the fact that she herself never evinces it.

Elsewhere, I have suggested that the many scattered comments about sexual difference in the text do not, as has commonly been suggested, simply point to the well-known tension between an old (matriarchal) society and a new (patriarchal) one.[34] They point, rather, to something paradoxical about the political order that is being inaugurated within the text, namely Greek democracy. At its very foundation is a feminine subject who is its condition of possibility, and yet, who ultimately must be excluded in order for it to exist at all. In acting, as one who has no right to act, Antigone, in Butler's words, "speaks within the language of entitlement from which she is excluded."[35] She is, indeed, an "everlasting irony" or an "internal enemy," as Hegel famously suggested.[36] She figures as someone who cannot be contained within the boundaries of the polis. Butler draws attention to "the way in which the boundaries of the public and the political spheres were secured through the production of a constitutive outside."[37] Woman – indeed Antigone – is this outside. But as a constitutive outside she simultaneously finds herself at the very heart of what remains inside. The polis would not exist without her. And yet the polis can only exist without her. For Antigone, the question is not – as for one of our modern tragic heroes – whether she should be or not be. What is at stake, for her, is the possibility of belonging or not belonging – to be one of them or not be one of them. And insofar as she does not belong, insofar as she is not one of them, she cannot be at all.

---

[34] Fanny Söderbäck, "Impossible Mourning: Sophocles Reversed," in *Feminist Readings of Antigone*, pp. 65–82.

[35] Butler, *Antigone's Claim*, p. 82.

[36] G. W. F. Hegel, *Hegel's Phenomenology of Spirit*, transl. A. V. Miller (Oxford: Oxford University Press, 1977), p. 288, §475.

[37] Butler, *Antigone's Claim*, p. 82. See also Kramer, *Excluded Within*.

The Tragic Legacy of Trans Exclusion: On Being Recognized as a Woman

Where then does this leave us in terms of Marina? As the title of the film suggests, she is not just a woman, she is a *fantastic* woman. There is something extraordinary about her persistence, her strength, her grace, and, in the final scene, her voice. She is a force of nature who defies forces of nature, such as in the scene when she leans into the mighty wind. And yet, her predicament is that others fail to recognize her as, precisely, a woman. Aretha Franklin's words on the soundtrack notwithstanding ("You make me feel like a natural woman"), Orlando's family fundamentally fails to recognize her as the woman – the fantastic woman – that she is, and this is the seemingly irreconcilable conflict (the tragic tension) that organizes the film.

It is important to note that the decree that Marina stay away from Orlando's wake and funeral – that she be excluded from the rites of burial like Antigone before her had been banned from burying her brother – is pronounced not by a male tyrant, but by Orlando's ex-wife, Sonia, a cis woman who refuses to recognize Marina as a fellow woman. Meeting in a parking garage, to which Marina has been summoned to return Orlando's car, the two women face each other for the first time. In the only scene in the film where Marina is subjected to deadnaming, Sonia forcefully denies her the right to grieve in public. In fact, she denies her the right to be at all. "When I look at you, I don't know what I'm seeing. A chimera, that's what I see," she notes with disdain in her voice.[38]

We hear echoes here of generations of trans exclusionary feminists who – oftentimes under the pretext of protecting women only spaces – have accused trans women of deception. Janice G. Raymond, whose infamous book *The Transsexual Empire* is paradigmatic (although by no means unique) in this regard, charged trans women with engaging in the constant act of raping women's bodies, "by reducing the female form to an

---

[38] Lelio, *Una Mujer Fantástica*, 0.47.45–0.47.59.

artifact, appropriating the body for themselves" since, she insisted, rape can "be accomplished by deception."[39] The accusation – perhaps most violently articulated by Raymond but still common within and beyond feminist discourse on trans women – tends to be that they have benefited from male privilege prior to their transition, and therefore have no right to claim the category 'woman' (since one's capacity to embody this category authentically, so the argument goes, results from one's particular position within structures of privilege and oppression).[40] This view has been echoed in our own present by women ranging from J. K. Rowling to Chimamanda Ngozi Adichie. When, in an interview, the latter was asked if trans women are women, she insisted on the fact that trans women are *trans* women, offering an explanation:

> I think if you've lived in the world as a man with the privileges the world accords to men and then sort of change, switch, gender, it's difficult for me to accept that then we can equate your experience with the experience of a woman who has lived from the beginning in the world as a woman, and who has not been accorded those privileges that men are.[41]

[39] Janice G. Raymond, *The Transsexual Empire: The Making of the She-Male* (Boston: Beacon Press, 1979), p. 104. In "The *Empire* Strikes Back" (oftentimes described as the founding text of trans theory), Sandy Stone – who was the explicit target of Raymond's attack – rebukes these transphobic claims and describes Raymond's project as premised upon the assumption that "transsexuals are constructs of an evil phallocratic empire and were designed to invade women's spaces and appropriate women's power." See Sandy Stone, "The *Empire* Strikes Back: A Posttranssexual Manifesto," in Paula Treichler, Cartwright, Lisa; & Penley, Constance (Eds.), *The Invisible Woman: Imaging Technologies, Gender and Science* (New York: New York University Press, 1998), p. 288.

[40] Talia Mae Bettcher labels this position "the radical feminist argument" in her historical overview of transgender and intersex theory and politics. See Talia Mae Bettcher, "Intersexuality, Transgender, and Transsexuality," in Disch, Lisa & Hawkesworth, Mary (Eds.), *The Oxford Handbook of Feminist Theory* (New York: Oxford University Press, 2016), p. 411.

[41] Chimamanda Ngozi Adichie in an interview on Britain's Channel 4 News, March 4, 2017. Accessed at https://www.vox.com/identities/2017/3/15/14910900/chimamanda-ngozi-adichie-transgender-women-comments-apology on July 9, 2020.

The view presented here is flawed not only because it is trans exclusionary, but also because it assumes that feminist solidarity is grounded in a monolithically shared experience of womanhood, and therefore fails to account for the complex manner in which each individual woman's experience of oppression must be understood at the intersection between race, class, geographic location, gender presentation, sexuality, and so on. And while trans feminists like Emi Koyama may be right in suggesting that male privilege in this context should not be *entirely* ignored – trans experience, she argues, must be framed in terms of "a dynamic interaction between male privilege and the disadvantage of being trans" – it seems to me obvious, if we take Marina as an example, that the disadvantages of her being trans far outweighs any potential privileges she might have enjoyed by virtue of her sex assigned at birth.[42] Trans actress Laverne Cox articulates the crux of the matter succinctly: "The irony of my life is that prior to transition I was called a girl and after I am often called a man."[43]

Talia Mae Bettcher has offered the perhaps most systematic analysis of the lived reality – and inherent violence – that results from this view of trans folks as engaging in an act of pretense. She describes trans people as being forced to navigate a double bind between make-believe (through masquerading) and deception (through passing), where the two options available only lead to further marginalization and increased vulnerability to violence. Either "disclose 'who one is' and come out as a pretender or masquerader, or refuse to disclose (be a deceiver) and

---

[42] Emi Koyama, "The Transfeminist Manifesto," in McCann, Carole R. & Kim, Seung-Kyung (Eds.), *Feminist Theory Reader: Local and Global Perspectives* (New York: Routledge: 2017), p. 152. Julia Serano introduced the term *trans-misogyny* to describe forms of discrimination aimed specifically at trans women. See Julia Serano, *Whipping Girl: A Transsexual Woman on Sexism and the Scapegoating of Femininity* (Emeryville, CA: Seal Press, 2007), p. 13. She also speaks of the devaluation of feminine males as "effemimania" (129, 287).

[43] Laverne Cox responding to Chimamanda Ngozi Adichie on Twitter, March 12, 2017. Accessed at https://twitter.com/lavernecox/status/840714224183652354?lang=en on July 10, 2020.

run the risk of forced disclosure, the effect of which is exposure as a liar."[44] She is careful to point out that this "deceiver/pretender bind is part of a larger system of oppression" – one that involves sexual violence against women as well as racial oppression.[45]

The charge of deception, articulated by Raymond and others, reverberates through Sonia's observations when she describes Marina as a chimera, and repeats Bruno's dehumanizing statement: "When I look at you, I don't know what I'm seeing." Both of them consciously use "what" rather than "who" to name Marina, robbing her of her uniqueness and reducing her to a non-human object, a chimera, a monstrous illusion.[46] She is at one and the same time too much of a woman and not enough of a woman, and therefore fails to be recognized as, exactly, a woman. In Koyama's formulation, "every time a group of women previously silenced begins to speak out," other women "are challenged to rethink their idea of who they represent and what they stand for."[47] We are reminded of Sojourner Truth's pressing question, articulated already in 1851 from the vantage point of a Black woman: "Ain't I a Woman?"[48]

If women have always been defined by the male gaze – and as Luce Irigaray has forcefully argued, woman as we know it is nothing but an inferior mirror image of man, not a subject in her own right – then it seems evident that this predicament is

[44] Talia Mae Bettcher, "Evil-Deceivers and Make-Believers: On Transphobic Violence and the Politics of Illusion," *Hypatia: A Journal of Feminist Philosophy*, Vol. 22, No. 3 (2007), p. 50.

[45] Bettcher, "Evil-Deceivers and Make-Believers," p. 56.

[46] The distinction I am making here between the 'what' and the 'who' originates in Hannah Arendt's discussion of uniqueness in *The Human Condition* (Chicago: University of Chicago Press, 1998), p. 179. It is developed at length in the work of Adriana Cavarero, for whom concrete singularity is embodied in the 'who' while abstract universality is marked by whatness. See, for example, Adriana Cavarero, *Relating Narratives: Storytelling and Selfhood*, transl. Paul A. Kottman (London and New York: Routledge, 2000), p. 9.

[47] Koyama, "The Transfeminist Manifesto," p. 150.

[48] Sojourner Truth in a speech delivered at the Women's Convention in Akron, Ohio, on May 29, 1851. A transcript of the speech was published in the *Anti-Slavery Bugle* on June 21, 1851.

even more acute for trans women, like Marina, whose being in the world is constantly subjected to scrutiny and examination, from cis women and men who frame them as always already outside the very category of the human. This notion is reflected, literally, through the use of mirrors in the film. Time and again, Marina finds herself framed by a mirror, forced to look at herself through the eyes of those around her. We see this as she walks down the street and encounters two men moving a large mirror. As they pass by Marina her flickering image appears in the frame, only to disappear as they continue on their way, leaving nothing but the wall behind the mirror for us to see.

Remember also the monstrous image of Marina's taped face reflected in a window, bearing witness to the extreme forms of violence that trans folk – and especially trans women of color – are subjected to on a regular basis. Or the fear in her eyes as her body parts are reflected in the lens of a camera meant to document her anatomy, reducing it to a genital schema that can register but two options: 'naturally' male or 'naturally' female. And we know, of course, that the approval (or not) of that medical penetrating gaze – and the gatekeeping that ensues – is far from inconsequential for trans folk who are seeking to transition, whether this entails gender affirming surgeries, a name change, access to public bathrooms, or correct use of pronouns. Dean Spade describes this predicament powerfully: *"Even though I don't believe in real, it matters if other people see me as real. If not, I'm a mutilator, an imitator, and worst of all, I can't access surgery."*[49]

In a scene toward the very end of the film, however, we are presented with a different kind of image, one where, perhaps for the first time, we see Marina, reflected through a mirror, through her own eyes. Lying naked on her bed, a round mirror placed between her legs, Marina lingers on her own reflection. Here the mirror covers over the very body parts that were subject to scrutiny in the medical exam. They no longer matter.

---

[49] Dean Spade, "Resisting Medicine, Re/modeling Gender," *Berkeley Women's Law Journal* 15 (2003), p. 20.

What we see is a woman looking back at us, returning the gaze, and a nudity that signals pleasure and ease rather than objectification and medicalization. The image represents the beginning of another resurrection: Marina refuses to let the gaze of others define her. And she refuses to let others mandate her mourning process.

As we saw earlier, on the dance floor, fist in air, Marina gathers the strength she needs to make her journey to the graveyard, her final journey with and for Orlando before she can move on with her life. Here she comes across his family again, as they are driving home from the cemetery, and her rage is channeled in a forceful stroke of exalted defiance. Marina climbs up on the roof of their car, and proceeds to jump up and down while demanding that Bruno return Diablo – the dog she had shared with Orlando – to her. Hunching inside the car, both Bruno and Sonia begin to crumble, and again we see a glimpse of the final scene in *Antigone*, where Creon stands alone on the battlefield, hunched under the weight of his own hubris, grappling with the losses he has suffered as a result of his failure to recognize Antigone's right to grieve. Except here, in the film, no such moral maturation takes place. While Orlando's family members drive off in fear, the experience has not changed them one bit. They will go on with their prejudiced lives. They will never be able to see Marina as someone worthy of their respect, or as someone Orlando could have actually loved. They will never see her as a woman, as someone whose grief matters. For them, Orlando and Marina's love will always be a perversion, on par with the incestual legacy of Antigone.

But if the Creons of the film fail to accomplish moral emancipation, its Antigone enters upon a more hopeful path than her ancient predecessor. Marina may not be recognized by Orlando's family, but she is not buried alive. She goes on living, in all of her fantasticness. And we are again reminded that, while Antigone might offer a helpful framework for broaching our own political present, she is also at a distance from us, and even more so at a distance from Marina, who is no Theban-European princess but a working-class trans woman in contemporary

Chile. An Antigone-figure of sorts, Marina is also much more than that, and her being trans as well as concretely situated within a Latin-American context renders her irreducible to the legacy of Antigone. The latter, after all, offers only a limited political imaginary, one that can take us only so far as we travel beyond Europe and beyond cis-feminist assumptions about privilege, grief, and what it means to be a "woman." Marina reminds us of the pressing need for queer and trans imaginaries that not only confirm but also resist the Sophoclean political framework, pointing toward a political future where Antigone need not be buried alive but can go on living, despite her transgression.

And if Antigone looks on in silence as her story is reborn, time and again, across the globe, Marina leaves us singing, her voice lifting towards the ceiling, a voice she has worked hard to cultivate in a culture that does all it can to keep her silent. A voice that expresses her singular uniqueness, as a woman, but always also as so much more than just a woman.[50] Creon might say, as he did to Antigone in a famous line from the play: "There is too much of you!"[51] For Creon, Antigone will always be too much woman – a figure of excess. For Sonia, Marina is not woman enough. Perhaps the emphasis on "woman," in both cases, is ultimately misleading. Perhaps what is at stake, in the end, is Marina's capacity to vocalize her singular embodied uniqueness. One inevitably shaped by the mourning process we have witnessed (in all of its complexity and impossibility), but one that is ultimately also irreducible to that process, always in excess of it. Marina, center stage, singing. A voice. A life. A fantastic woman.

---

[50] Cavarero has offered the most systematic examination of the human voice as a vehicle for uniqueness. See Adriana Cavarero, *For More than One Voice: Toward a Philosophy of Vocal Expression*, transl. Paul A. Kottman (Palo Alto: Stanford University Press, 2005).

[51] Sophokles, *Antigone*, l. 573.

Chapter 10
Haunting Histories
– Regarding the Political Unconscious in the Television Series Stranger Things and the Film Ghostbusters

Erik Poulsen

> History is the subject of a construction whose site consists not of homogeneous, empty time, but of time filled by the presence of the now.
>
> Walter Benjamin,
> Theses on the Philosophy of History, XIV[1]

Anyone who has watched the second season of *Stranger Things* can probably recall the scene where Mike, Lucas, Will and Dustin come dressed up to school. The series takes place in the 1980s in a small American town where "nothing ever happens", and the second season – released on Netflix in the fall of 2017 – begins in the middle of the Halloween festivities. To celebrate the approaching holiday, the four boys have decided to dress up for school, wearing the same beige costumes and accompanying technical equipment as the ghost hunters of their favorite movie, the blockbuster film *Ghostbusters*.

However, just as the nerdy gang are about to enter the school building, Mike and Lucas suddenly begin to quarrel. It turns out that both boys have dressed up as the main character in *Ghostbusters*, namely the scientist Dr Venkman. Mike seems used to getting his way and cannot accept that someone has stolen his part. He insists that Lucas should be acting as another ghost hunter from the same film: Winston. However, Lucas is not convinced: "No one wants to be Winston, man." – "What's wrong with Winston?" Mike retorts, whereupon Lucas answers:

---

[1] Walter Benjamin, "Theses on the Philosophy of History", *Illuminations*, trans. Harry Zorn (London: Pimlico, 1999), pp. 252–253.

"What's wrong with Winston? He joined the team super late, he's not funny, he's not even a scientist!" But Mike will not give in that easily, and the quarrel eventually ends with the following exchange of replies:

> Lucas says: "If he [Winston] is cool, then you be Winston."
>
> Mike: "I can't!"
>
> Lucas: "Why not?"
>
> Mike (starts to stammer): "Be… because…"
>
> Lucas (mockingly imitates his stammering): "Be-be-because you are not black?"
>
> Mike: "I didn't say that!"
>
> Lucas: "You thought it."[2]

However interesting this little intermezzo might be since both Lucas and the ghost hunter Winston happen to be black characters in screenplays where basically every other character is white, it adds little to the plot development. It is obvious that the scene is a metacommentary on how people of color are represented on film, but it does not lead to anything. The children do not manage to settle the issue before the bell and the shifting into the next scene – which is perfectly in order in this case. After all, it would be an exaggeration to call *Stranger Things* a political series. The plot does not exactly revolve around expressions of racist discrimination and prejudices in Western culture. Nor are the protagonists struggling with any economic inequality or social injustice, at least not explicitly. Instead, just as one might expect from an American science fiction horror series, the protagonists are busy struggling against supernatural evil creatures from another dimension who want to take over the human world.

However, in this essay I will argue that *Stranger Things* can be interpreted politically and that it is especially fruitful to

[2] See film clip in *Stranger Things*, Season 2, Episode 2, 10:20–12:25.

analyze it from a feminist point of view. Contrary to what the plot seems to suggest, I am suggesting that *Stranger Things* and other aesthetic artifacts offered by online streaming services such as Netflix and HBO, reveal something interesting about the conditions for contemporary film production. In the following text, I will take the issue addressed by Lucas seriously and consider how class, race, gender, and sexuality are represented. I will show that seemingly redundant scenes like the one just mentioned, have a social and political meaning that exceeds the explicit message of the series (that is: entertainment).

Nevertheless, the point is not to say that a certain fictive character is a representation of a certain marginalized group in the real world. I am not claiming that *Stranger Things* is an allegory over the subaltern subject in the 21st century, or that it bears evidence of the impact that social critique and political activism – as for example the MeToo movement – have had on the film industry and its products. Rather, I am proposing that every work of fiction is imbued with ideology which manifests itself in the forms of the aesthetic object per se. In this case, my object of investigation is a film sequence, and since film is a visual medium, it is crucial to be attentive to semblance. As will become evident later, it is only through appearances that the viewer can achieve a deeper understanding of film; by regarding what is allowed to be seen and to be heard.

However, before presenting my analysis, I will be saying a few words about my theoretical inspirations and formulate a thesis. Let me begin by returning to the supposition that aesthetic artifacts can say something of political interest. The idea that works of fiction are conditioned by social relations or modes of production stems from Marxist literary theory. The proposition above – that all artworks are imbued with ideology – has already been argued by the American literary critic and Marxist philosopher Fredric Jameson whose works, as hinted in the title of this essay, will serve as a theoretical frame for this investigation. According to Jameson, a work of fiction is always something more than an utterance by an individual artist. In his view, an artwork is, first and foremost, a product of a historical situation.

The narrative structure found in a novel or a film will inevitably reflect a socio-political context, not in terms of an imitation or *mimesis* of any external reality, but in the form of a paraphrase which, to a certain degree, distorts the represented. The act of writing a novel or creating a film may therefore be regarded as a translation or circumlocution of an ideological subtext. The ideological subtexts that impregnate and organize works of fiction do not exist anywhere in terms of a "pure" text. However, according to Jameson, they can be deciphered or disclosed retroactively in an act of interpretation. This ideological subtext is what Jameson refers to as the *political unconscious*.[3]

Now to return to my object of investigation. As already stressed by way of an introduction, it would be inaccurate to say that *Stranger Things* is a realistic imitation of actual political events, or that certain characters are representatives for specific demographic groups in real society. In line with Jameson, I have suggested that works of fiction are like derivatives of history, and that they may represent reality by distorting and twisting it. However, I have also claimed that it is crucial to be attentive to appearances when interpreting film. Being attentive to appearances means taking note of what the film is trying to imitate realistically and to what it explicitly is referring. In the case of *Stranger Things*, it should be noted that history is not just a subject but also an object. The second season takes place in the 1980s – to be more precise, in the year 1984 – and it is obvious that the filmmakers have made an effort to create an authentic historic environment by infusing attributes, fashion and music usually associated with the late post-war period (arcade video games, backcombed hair, a post-punk aesthetic, etc.). Judging from the series' aesthetics, a historical past has been turned into an object of desire. A suitable description here would be to say that it is *nostalgic*, since it connotes longing for the past, a wish to revive old memories, or to feel what it used to feel like back in the days.

---

[3] Fredric Jameson, *The Political Unconscious: Narrative as a Socially Symbolic Act* (London: Routledge, 1989), p. 80.

However, on a closer look, the nostalgic aesthetics that permeates *Stranger Things* is not concerned with history in general as much as it concerns film history in particular. The explicit reference of the series is not any actual historic event – not the Cold war, not Ronald Reagan, for example. Instead, the series refers to another work of fiction in the history of film, namely *Ghostbusters*. The intertextual conversation that *Stranger Things* is having with *Ghostbusters* is important in my view, not only because it is the subject of the dispute between Mike and Lucas, but also because the influences from *Ghostbusters* concern the science fiction adventure at the most basic level. In both cases, there are portals leading into other dimensions, characters who become possessed by demons, and several four-legged dog-like beasts who haunt and strike terror into their surroundings – just to mention a few examples. In this regard, *Stranger Things* seems to confirm the assumption made by many art historians that modern works of fiction are essentially self-referential; they represent nothing apart from themselves, and they reveal nothing apart from a fascination for their own medium.[4] The conclusion could be that the series refers to the same old-fashioned science fiction adventure, and it amounts to nothing more.

However, if this is the case, then a question immediately arises: If it is true that *Stranger Things* reflects a tendency to fetishize film history, then why would anyone want to look at a reproduction of the desired object rather than the object itself? If actual times are forever lost, the same cannot be said about film history, which, due to new digital technology, is more available than ever. If film nostalgia is symptomatic of a longing for a certain moment in film history, would it not be fair to assume that the original *Ghostbusters* from 1984 is a more authentic representation of that moment than a Netflix production that is trying to imitate its "historic" style? Considering the

---

[4] The notion that modern art is self-referential is typically emphasized in readings of modernist poetry. For an example, see Friedrich Kittler, *Discourse Networks 1800 / 1900*, trans. Michael Metteer & Chris Cullens (Stanford: Stanford University Press, 1990), pp. 212–225.

commercial success of *Stranger Things*, why is it so that the contemporary audience seems to prefer a reference rather than the referred?

My answer to this question is that the ideological subtext of *Stranger Things* is radically different from its equivalent, *Ghostbusters*. The political unconscious structuring the narratives of the series and the film respectively has altered over time, meaning that a film consumer who finds pleasure in watching the former is most likely going to find the aesthetic experience of watching the latter unbearable. In fact, I would like to go further and claim that the discrepancies between *Stranger Things* and *Ghostbusters* are just as significant as their similarities. The ideological subtext of the series is revealed, not in the identities but in the discords between present and past, memory and amnesia, desire and aversion, pleasure and discontent. As I see it, nostalgia is not a major aesthetic feature, it is just a component, and this is where my thesis comes in: *Stranger Things* can be interpreted as a symptom of ambivalence towards a historic past. To explore this, I shall undertake a comparative study between *Stranger Things* and *Ghostbusters* with the intention to investigate the political unconscious structuring each narrative respectively. By contrasting my objects of investigation, I hope to show that the contemporary series is principally a story about present time rather than the 1980s.

Thus far, I have presented my objects of investigation, a theoretical frame, a methodology, and have advanced my central thesis. However, considering that Jameson's work focuses on the history of literature, my use of his theory might still seem vague. Moreover, I have not explained how appearances, desire and pleasure are interrelated with the experience of watching film. The concept of the *unconscious*, of course, does not stem from Marxist theory but psychoanalysis. I will therefore expand on my theory by turning to the British film theorist Laura Mulvey and the French psychoanalyst Jacques Lacan. Hence, the disposition of the investigation is divided into three parts: first, a theoretical part where I explore Jameson's theory of the political unconscious from a psychoanalytical perspective; second, the analysis of *Ghostbusters*; and third, the comparative analysis of *Stranger Things*.

To explain how Jameson's theory of the political unconscious can apply to film, it will be necessary to remind the reader of some basic ideas from psychoanalytic theory and method. Even though the primary aim of psychoanalysis is to interpret symptoms of psychical illness, it has often been defined in terms of a critique of the human subject rather than as a science.[5] Regarding the benefits that psychoanalysis and art criticism have derived from one another during the last hundred years, it is safe to say that film occupies a place apart compared to other art forms. It has often been highlighted that the founder of psychoanalysis Sigmund Freud elaborated *The Interpretation of Dreams* (1900) in the same historical period as the film medium was invented.[6] In the same book, Freud famously asserted that dreams are the royal road to a knowledge of the unconscious. He equated the dream with a *wish fulfillment* (*Wunscherfüllung*), a manifestation of an inner wish, and suggested that interpretations of dreams could give insight into the unconscious desires that structure and govern the actions and speeches of the human subject.

Similarly, film can – and has – been considered a form of wish fulfillment. Film is usually associated with desire and not least with pleasure because it accentuates sight. In the essay *Visual Pleasure and Narrative Cinema* (1975), Laura Mulvey writes, with reference to Freud, that the gaze may constitute a source of pleasure in itself.[7] However, as she also mentions in passing, it is not only the gaze of the actors and the gaze of the audience that is at stake in film. In each and every film, there is always a third eye which mediates and thus controls the gaze,

---

[5] cf. Elizabeth Grosz, *Jacques Lacan. A feminist Introduction* (London: Routledge, 1990), pp. 1–19.

[6] cf. Kittler, pp. 277–278. See also Walter Benjamin, "The Work of Art in the Age of Mechanical Reproduction", *Illuminations*, trans. Harry Zorn (London: Pimlico, 1999), pp. 228–230.

[7] Laura Mulvey, "Visual Pleasure and Narrative Cinema", *Visual and Other Pleasures* (Basingstoke: Palgrave Macmillan, 2009), pp. 16–17.

namely the eye of the camera. What differentiates the camera eye from the eyes of the actors and the audience is that the camera consists of a completely mechanized gaze. The camera has no consciousness; it is a machine which sees. It takes no human subject for a camera to register things – a film can be recorded without anyone being aware of it.

Here it is important to underscore that Mulvey's essay is not actually about the eye of the camera. Her essay has become required reading within feminist film theory and Gender studies because it efficaciously discloses a patriarchal unconscious that organized most films produced in the palmy days of Hollywood. According to Mulvey, the patriarchal unconscious causes a sexual imbalance that has tangible effects on casting. It equates masculinity with narration by constantly portraying men as agents who direct the gaze and make things happen. On the other hand, the feminine does not even play a minor part in his narrative structure; she is just a visual image or a passive object whose sole purpose is to strengthen the ego of the subject – which is always male. If a female character is allowed to appear (which is not always the case in patriarchal film production), it is because the male subject needs an object upon which he can project his desires, fantasies, and anxieties.

Nevertheless, an ego may not only be strengthened through projection; a strengthening may also occur through identification. According to Mulvey, a viewer may occasionally identify with film characters in two different ways: either by mirroring himself or herself in the image of the actor according to the same principles as in Jacques Lacan's theory of subject formation during the mirror stage; or, the viewer may perceive the film entirely through the eyes of the actor and thereby turn the male gaze into his or her own gaze. Mulvey writes that the identification process, which may occur during a visit to the cinema, tends to become so strong that the viewers momentarily lose themselves. The film medium, therefore, seems to be able to establish a paradoxical double movement, an oscillation where the ego of the viewer, on the one hand, is strengthened, while on the other, is dissolved with the result that the cinema audience momentarily forgets who they are and where they came from.[8]

Interestingly, Lacan describes something similar in one of his early seminars. Commenting on Freud's *Interpretation of Dreams*, Lacan notes that since the subject is shaped through mirroring and projections, the ego can be comprehended as the sum of all identifications of the subject. At stake, though, when someone is dreaming is not the ego but the unconscious. Dreams, therefore, seem to establish an inversion of the logic of subject formation, namely a state of dissolution in which the subject is decomposed into minor parts. Lacan claims that if one image could represent Freud's idea of the unconscious, it would be the image of a *headless subject* – a body without ego. The method of dream interpretation is to try to locate the subject's ego, which tends to get lost in the dream.[9]

Now, for a brief moment, I am going to suppose that Lacan was right. Suppose dreams tend to decompose and dissolve the subject. In that case, there seem to be many similarities between dreams and some of the experiences that Mulvey claims that the audience momentarily may have at the cinema. It could then be suggested that both dreams and films are a form of *headless seeing* in the sense that a subject who is dreaming is just as unable to control what appears in the dream as the cinema audience is unable to control the movements of the camera directing our attention in the diegetic world of the film. Metaphorically speaking, one could say that when we are dreaming, a film is playing inside of us. However, this metaphor works equally well when reversed. Mulvey is neither the first nor the last writer who has alluded to the image of the Hollywood industry as one grand factory which manufactures dreams. If dreams are like films and films are like dreams, then it should not be too far-fetched to interpret films the same way Freud interpreted dreams – that is, as manifestations of collective unconscious structures of desire.

[8] Mulvey, p. 18.

[9] Jacques Lacan, *The Seminar of Jacques Lacan, Book II, The Ego in Freud's Theory and the Technique of Psychoanalysis 1954–1955*, trans. Sylvana Tomaselli (Cambridge: Norton & Company, 1988), pp. 167–172.

I hope to have made it clear now how the theory of a political unconscious can apply to film, and why it is crucial to be attentive to appearances when interpreting them.

So far, I have discussed the elementary mechanisms behind film production and the makings of fictive narrative structures. In the following section, I will turn to my first object of investigation, *Ghostbusters*. There are, of course, several different versions of this incredibly popular franchise. Still, it is the very first version from 1984 that interests me here since its original release in the United States is the same year as the second season of *Stranger Things* is set. Let me begin by simply asking: What kinds of collective unconscious structures of desire are put into play in *Ghostbusters*? For starters it should be said that Freud's theory of the unconscious is something more than a possible perspective in this case. Just as history is both a subject and object in *Stranger Things*, the unconscious is both latent and manifest in *Ghostbusters*, meaning that interpretation becomes almost superfluous. In principle, it is not necessary to analyze *Ghostbusters* to understand what it is about. It is perfectly sufficient just to watch and observe everything there is to be seen and to be heard. I will try to explain what I mean by this without going into too intricate details about the film.

In the leading role, starring Bill Murray, the viewer encounters the scientist Dr Peter Venkman. The film begins with Venkman and his two colleagues, Raymond Stantz and Egon Spengler, losing their grant funding because the management at the university has realized that their research project is pure quackery. It is worth mentioning here that their field of research is within *parapsychology* – the study of paranormal or supersensual phenomena. In order to survive economically, the three scientists decide to start their own business that would allow them to combine their research on supersensual phenomena with social protection. The trio's business idea is to offer services to anyone afflicted by supernatural disturbances in the environment. Initially, business is slow, but it is not long until they are inundated with calls; New York City seems to be crawling with ghosts and lost souls. And so, the ghost hunt begins. The scientists eventually become successful enough to hire a fourth collaborator named Winston Zeddemore – the character that none of the nerd boys in *Stranger Things* wants to be. The fact that Winston is not an interesting character in the eyes of the boys is understandable since he is not introduced until about halfway through the film and plays a peripheral role in relation to the other three ghost hunters.

Needless to say, the viewer does not need to be a certified parapsychologist to be able to understand that the ghosts in *Ghostbusters* are not just any ghosts. It is important to underscore that the scientists are not catching the ghosts in order to kill them. They are only interested in locking them up for safe keeping in the business office's cellar, perhaps for future observations. The motif around which the film pivots is, thus, a pseudo-scientific ability to control and master something that conventional science has never been able to explain. Unconscious desire is part and parcel of the film's content as far as ghostbusting is tantamount to achieving a knowledge of the unknown. Dr Venkman and his colleagues are explorers of the latent; their job is to catch and lock up ghosts in the same way as the psychoanalyst's job is to interpret and remedy symptoms whose causes are unexplainable and irrational.

As I suggested initially, distinctions between manifest and latent tend to collapse in *Ghostbusters*. The fact that the film deliberately mediates between the visible and invisible is especially evident in a scene where the scientists are commissioned to catch a ghost which haunts an old hotel. Judging from the interiors, the hotel is a typical upper middle-class environment with cut-glass chandeliers in the ceiling, heavy draperies along with everything else that goes with it. As the scientists enter the hotel lobby, they encounter a rather stiff company from which they receive plenty of looks in askance. It becomes clear that the hotel's prudish guests and staff are not in command of their ghosts. No wonder, then, that a particularly nasty ghost haunts the hotel in the shape of a green, gluttonous slime ball which guzzles down all the food it comes across. The reason why the ghost has been allowed to ravage the hotel for a considerable time is because the hotel manager has suppressed the situation to maintain the hotel's elegant façade instead of dealing with the problem – anything not to lose face.

In other words, the animated ghosts in the film – the transparent slime balls, the strange four-legged creatures, etc. – are metonymies for the middle classes' unconscious desires. The guests and staff at the hotel cannot or do not want to deal with their ghosts which has the reverse effect: The more suppressed a ghost is, the more annoying it becomes. The green slime ball of a ghost teases and haunts the hotel in accordance with the logic of "the return of the repressed". The Ghostbusters team are depicted as heroes in the film because they are the only ones who know how to tackle unconscious desires and meddle with what is latent. In the scene at the hotel, Dr Venkman and his colleagues – literally – break the stiff, upper middle-class façade by shooting down the cut-glass chandeliers in the ceiling and facing the nasty slime ball rather than shying away from it. By taking the slime ball down and catching it, the ghost hunters manage to clean out the hotel's elegant rooms both literally and figuratively. By contrasting the skeptical looks that the Ghostbusters team receive at the beginning of the scene with the astonished looks shown at the end, it becomes obvious that the ghost hunters have faced down and disclosed the hypocrisy with which the walls of the hotel drip. In this regard, the film could be viewed as a sly dig at bourgeois culture.

However, catching a ghost or cleaning out the lurking stench of hypocrisy remains just a motif in the film. The purpose of my analysis, however, is not to identify motifs but to trace out a political unconscious. To catch a glimpse of the political unconscious, the viewer must look closer, and with a closer look, it is obvious that the ghostbusting business is full of contradictions. As I have already stressed, the Ghostbusters team is never after the ghosts in order to kill them; they just want to put a lid on them once and for all. Their aim is not to liberate, rather the opposite: Dr Venkman and his associates want to control the ghosts even more efficaciously than the reactionary bourgeoisie are capable. As clearly as the ghost hunters are aware of the effects of displacement, they are, however, acutely unaware of transference. In fact, I would like to suggest that the scientists' obsession with chasing animated ghosts and exploring the latent realm has made them blind to their own desires and the actual world under their noses.

As an illustrative example, I would like to bring out an incident that takes place during the above-mentioned scene at the hotel. Minutes before they catch the nasty slime ball, the scientists accidentally shoot at a cleaning carriage that suddenly comes out through a door of one of the corridors. After the laser guns have been fired, a cleaning woman cautiously peeps out of the cleaning carriage, wondering what the heck they are doing. If the viewer looks extra carefully at the scene, he or she will realize that this cleaning woman – who is pictured as completely insignificant since she just flickers by very quickly – is, in fact, the only *real* ghost throughout the whole film. The incident is depicted as a witty joke, or a crazy mistake. However, as every true psychoanalyst knows, jokes and slips of the tongue can have special relations to the unconscious. The fact that three men (Winston is not present in the scene) are accidentally shooting at a woman who is – literally speaking – cleaning up the hotel, might seem ironic at first sight, given that the scientists' mission is to clear away the slimy ghost. However, as far as I can see, this "Freudian slip shot" is by no means an accident. On the contrary, the incident with the cleaning woman is a distinctive trait in the narrative structure of the film.

The most obvious contradiction that impregnates the narrative of *Ghostbusters* is that the more ghosts Dr Venkman and his friends manage to catch, the more aggressive the supernatural forces seem to become in the latent sphere. As already stated, the animated ghosts in the film are metonymies for repressed, unconscious desires. Towards the end of the film, dark forces have awoken and take the shape of a dangerous, unrestrained desire threatening not only the city of New York but the whole of Western civilisation. In this case, the film makers have not bothered to spare the effects and tone down a sense of doom with biblical connotations and references to "judgment day". Interestingly, the dangerous uncontrolled desire often takes the expression of a dangerous sexuality, to be more precise, the sexuality of women and LGBTQ people. To give an example: one of the first customers assisted by Dr Venkman – who also happens to be one of the few female characters in the film – is Miss Dana Barret who has a problem with some strange creatures who seem to have occupied the refrigerator in the kitchen of her apartment. During the film, the viewer gets to know that the strange creatures in miss Barret's refrigerator are guardians who protect a portal which leads into another dimension governed by an evil Sumerian god from ancient Mesopotamia. These creatures – who incidentally, are very similar to the creatures in *Stranger Things* – eventually break out of the kitchen and attack Miss Barret by possessing her body. As possessed, Miss Barret is transformed into an "exotic seducer" who does not want anything else but to get laid with "the key master" – for whom she mistakes Dr Venkman.

As the film gradually reaches its climax, the portal into the other dimension is opened wide. The oriental evil god steps forward and appears in the shape of something apparently meant to represent a being in-between a man and a woman; an androgynous or non-binary person (incidentally, suspiciously similar to David Bowie). Thus, the most terrifying monster the makers of the 1984 *Ghostbusters* film could conjure up is a being that transgresses the male–female binary. The androgynous person untethers on the Ghostbusters team one last ghost that goes by the name of "The Stay Puft Marshmallow Man"; a white, giant marshmallow figure which crushes yellow taxi cabs under its feet like another Godzilla. However, the dudes in the Ghostbuster team manage to save the world by crossing the streams from their laser guns and thereby turning them into one super strong stream, which they then direct against the portal. Finally, in the moment of dramatic closure, everything explodes, including the marshmallow-Godzilla, resulting in a white sticky stuff literally raining over the whole of New York City. The threat from the unconscious desire is defeated, the dangerous sexuality is once more under control, and order is restored.

Needless to say, the film ends with Dr Venkman and Miss Barret kissing and then driving away together in the Ghostbuster car to live happily ever after. It is, in other words, hard to tell whether *Ghostbusters* from 1984 is a comedy or a thriller. I am not sure whether I should laugh or cry out loud.

With all that said, the interpretation of my first object of investigation is complete. I have interpreted *Ghostbusters* with respect to the theory of a political unconscious and reached the conclusion that its narrative structure pleases a stereotypical white male heterosexual desire. Interestingly, representations of class, race, gender, and sexuality in the film are conflated with a psychoanalytic history of reproducing sexism, racism, homophobia, and transphobia. Although there is no explicit reference to Freud or any other psychoanalytic theoretician in the film, I have suggested that the ghost hunting enterprise amounts to a psychoanalytical conception of achieving a knowledge of unconscious desire. The fact that oppositions between the latent and the manifest are interwoven with the film's motifs makes interpretation challenging, but not impossible. I am aware that it might seem contradictory to scrutinize and criticize *Ghostbusters* by using the same theoretical and methodological tool as I am criticizing. Considering that I have charged Dr Venkman and his associates with being ignorant of transference, how can I know for sure that I am not repeating the same analytical fallacy in my interpretation and that I am not disregarding my own unconscious desires?

To avoid the pitfall of transference, I have tried to focus on the manifest realm instead of the latent. I have tried to look at the aesthetic object just like Oscar Wilde's novel character Lord Henry looked at Dorian Gray: "It is only shallow people who do not judge by appearances. The true mystery of the world is the visible, not the invisible."[10] In other words, the biggest mystery is not what *Ghostbusters* "really" is about but rather why one of the most popular Netflix productions of the 21st century is trying to reproduce it, which brings me back to my initial question: What

---

[10] Oscar Wilde, *The Picture of Dorian Gray* (London: Penguin, 2003), p. 24.

exactly does the reference to *Ghostbusters* in *Stranger Things* entail?

I have now reached the third and last part of my investigation where I intend to contrast the film with the series. It is noteworthy that my first object of investigation is an analogous film while my second object is a digital television series. As already noted in the theoretical part of my discussion, the technological medium itself can have effects on the message of the aesthetic object. It is interesting to keep that in mind when considering how television series as an artform has evolved in the 21st century. When the first television series started to appear in the post-war era, they were mostly viewed as a kind of schlock or pulp fiction for housewives and second-rate actors. However, in recent years, due to new digital technology and the commercial success of online streaming services, the television series as a specific genre has transformed and achieved a completely different cultural status. Not only has the digital medium affected the film content; it has also changed the way the cinema audience consumes film.

I am now going to look at my second object of investigation. Despite all the similarities and intertexture, some of the motifs in *Stranger Things* seem to be inversions of those in *Ghostbusters*. In the television series, it is the scientists who have lost control over the evil forces and the androgynous character Eleven who, thanks to her supernatural powers, manages to close the portal leading to the other dimension and thereby saves the world. The four nerdy boys mentioned in the introduction are not the only ones who know how to meddle with the latent. They are surrounded by several female characters who often are depicted as bolder than most of the male heroes. For example, Lucas has a little sister named Erica who not only is intelligent, she also has the coolest and bitchiest attitude in the whole series. Then there is Mike's big sister Nancy, a high school student who at first sight appears to be a typical "good girl" who does her homework on time. However, as the series proceeds, it turns out that Nancy not only knows how to study; she also knows perfectly well how to swing a baseball bat and aim with a shotgun.

These female characters are allowed to be seen and heard; they have their own agencies in ways that would have been unthinkable in the Hollywood film productions scrutinized by Laura Mulvey in her essay. As I see it, the presence of these new characters has nothing to do with film nostalgia, it is not a resurrection of a historic past that has been lost with the passing of time. On the contrary, the presence of strong feminine characters seems to me rather like a historical revenge.

As I have argued initially, history reveals itself in the discrepancies between past and present. In the case of *Stranger Things*, a historic past has turned into an object of desire. If the series pleases contemporary viewers, it does so not by realistically imitating film history as it actually was, but by retelling and modifying the past as the viewer *wish* it would have been. The same can be said about many contemporary television series that tend to fetishize different historical moments in the 20th century. *Mad Men* is another striking example of film aesthetics that is pervaded with nostalgia. In a series such as *Mad Men*, the secretaries, the cleaners, and the homosexuals are for sure still as oppressed as they actually were in the 1960s, but with an essential difference: the camera has become more moveable, more mobile, so to speak. The camera has started to show things through the eyes of the oppressed and not exclusively from the perspectives of white heterosexual middle-class men.

Television series as an art form is especially sufficient for these kinds of shifts of perspectives. Since the duration time is so much longer compared to a single film, the camera is allowed to roam the settings and therefore has the time to delineate more characters and more life stories within the frame of the same narrative. And precisely this is exactly what the quarrel mentioned initially between Mike and Lucas is all about: Who is to play the most important role? Whose perspective is most important in the stories of our time? It is obvious that many contemporary remakes of older film productions reveal a demand for other perspectives and voices that have been silenced earlier in history. It is not for nothing that a contemporary remake of Ghostbusters (from 2016) starred three female actors as the scientists, just to mention one example. However, in many television series, the question of perspective is even more intricate compared to most long feature films, since it is not always obvious who plays the main character anyway.

The fact that the camera eye is prone to see more than it used to is in my opinion a positive outcome of technological development. However, in the case of *Stranger Things*, the positive sides of the development come at a price. Since such fundamental parts of the film narrative in *Ghostbusters* have been repressed, the past has now returned and manifested itself in the shape of the evil forces from the other side of the portal, in the so-called "upside-down world". The uncanny, indefinable creatures from the other dimension are condensations of the dark parts of history – all those memories that most viewers most likely want to forget.

To support my suggestion that the evil forces in the series are metaphors for the past, I would like to dwell on a scene in the third episode of the second season which involves one of the nerd boys, Will. Just like Miss Barrett in *Ghostbusters*, Will's body is possessed by the visitors from the "upside-down word". The scientists try to explain his unpleasant experiences of being possessed by saying that Will is probably suffering from post-traumatic stress. In the scene in the third episode, Will is accidentally trapped in the "upside down world" and tries to escape in a panic. He runs over a schoolyard, but then, all of a sudden, he stops, as if thinking that the scientists might be right. Maybe he is just imagining things, maybe he is just hallucinating. He turns around and sees a dark cloud towering up in the shape of a terrifying spider-like evil demon. He tries to shout, "Go away, GO AWAY", but that will certainly not do any good since the heritage of film history is no figment of imagination – it is real. The dark side of the historical past is a force that produces the monsters of our time. Alternatively, to quote a famous line from James Joyce's *Ulysses*: "History is a nightmare from which I am trying to awake".

PART 4
Transforming Knowledge Regimes

Chapter 11
Paradox of Stubbornness
– The Epistemology of Stereotypes Regarding Women

Sagy Watemberg Izraeli[1]

1. The Paradox of Stubbornness

"Women are too empathetic to be engineers"[2]
"[W]omen aren't up to the job of running an airline"[3]
"Women are less spatial and logical thinkers than men"[4]
"[T]he complicated whirlwind of politics is not the arena for the female role"[5]

The above statements are but a few of the numerous stereotypes regarding women. They are generalized traits attributed as intrinsic to the group of women as a whole. Indeed, many women fulfill at least some stereotypic claims ascribed to their group. Yet, no woman fulfills them all. The discrepancy between individual women and the stereotypes ascribed to the group has become progressively greater and more explicit over the course

---

[1] Foremost, I would like to thank Dr. Michal Gleitman, whose guidance encouragingly and relentlessly pushed forward the work and insights that see light in this article. Gratitude is owed to Dr. Ittay Nissan-Rozen for welcoming me through the doors of epistemology, and for his prophetic claim that in the future I will return to Quine's "Two Dogmas".

[2] Vicki May, "Are Women Too Empathetic to Be Engineers?", *The Huffington Post*, 24 June 2014 updated 24 August 2014, https://www.huffpost.com/entry/are-women-too-empathetic-_b_5522153

[3] David Koenig, "In airline-business rarity, Air France picks a woman CEO", *The Associated Press*, 13 December 2018, https://apnews.com/article/b56ea6cb019c44d6 b2bda75b9eaa35ec

[4] Michelle G. '18, "Picture Yourself as a Stereotypical Male", *MIT Admissions*, 3 September 2015, https://mitadmissions.org/blogs/entry/picture-yourself-as-a-stereotypical-male/

[5] Tamar Beeri, "Responding to rabbi's sexist remarks, Shaked says women can do anything", *The Jerusalem Post*, 6 July 2019, https://www.jpost.com/israel-news/ayelet-shaked-women-can-be-heads-of-state-594699

of history in alignment with changes in women's social and political situations. For, despite the developments in the traits women have opportunity to express, stereotypes regarding women remain the same age-old allegations. Furthermore, constituting 50% of society, women are encountered on a regular basis. Thus, evidence which refutes stereotypical knowledge[6] is rendered inevitable – deeming stereotypes regarding women a valuable edge-case for the epistemic inquiry of stereotypes in general. For, despite the contrary evidence, it appears that society and individuals within it continue to hold these stereotypes as true. This conflict between evidence and stereotypes constitutes an epistemic paradox.

The epistemic paradox following from the conflict between evidence and stereotypes is the retention of the stereotypical knowledge despite contrary evidence. Ordinarily, when a person encounters evidence conflicting with previously attained knowledge, that knowledge is updated in light of the evidence so that one's knowledge will be true. However, it seems that stereotypes negate such revision. Even numerous encounters with contrary evidence do not cause one to abandon the stereotype nor to replace it with knowledge better correlated with the empirical evidence arising from experience.

Such a lack of revision of stereotypical knowledge in light of new evidence causes two epistemic sub-conflicts. One is the conflict between knowledge and the empirical evidence with which it comes in contact. Second is the conflict that emerges within the body of knowledge itself. For, experience generates the creation of a new knowledge in one's body of knowledge. In the case of evidence contrary to stereotypes, the new knowledge formed is one contrary to the previously existing stereotypical knowledge. Hence, the abstention of stereotypes from revision in light of new contrary evidence is a cause for conflict between

---

[6] Knowledge is referred to in this paper as that which is believed to be a justifiable true belief. Therefore, even if a stereotype may be false empirically, it constitutes knowledge in as much as it is believed to be justifiably true.

knowledges[7] within the aggregate body of knowledge itself. The latter is thus rendered incoherent, consisting of two contrary knowledges both held to be true. These two conflicts – between the stereotype and the evidence, and between the stereotype and other knowledges – give rise to the epistemic paradox of the retention of the stereotype despite contrary evidence. This paradox will be termed here the *paradox of stubbornness*.

The epistemic distortion entailed in the paradox of stubbornness, though, is revealed to be more severe than only stereotypes' lack of revision. The latter could be the sole epistemic difficulty if initial experience of women would produce evidence in line with such stereotypical deductions, to be challenged only by later contrary evidence. Yet, encounters with women provide diverse evidence from the outset, not the generalized and simplified version entailed in stereotypes. It is found, then, that stereotypical knowledge does not stem from empirical evidence, as previously assumed. For, if knowledges regarding women as a group were founded upon experience, more diverse and complex knowledges would have formed – in correlation with the empirical evidence. Therefore, it seems that people's personal experiences are not the epistemic source of stereotypical knowledge.

To summarize this preliminary analysis, three epistemic questions arise regarding women stereotypes. One, what are the epistemic mechanisms that enable stubbornness of stereotypical knowledge in light of contrary evidence? Two, what are the epistemic mechanisms that enable conflict between the stereotype and the evidence, and between the stereotype and other knowledges, respectively? Three, what is the epistemic source of stereotypical knowledge, if it is not empirical evidence? This paper will explicate the epistemic paradox of stubbornness. In so doing, it aims to answer the above questions, showing the epistemic mechanisms and characteristics that enable such stub-

---

[7] I use the term "knowledges" as the plural for "knowledge" so as to retain the use of the latter for individual units of knowledge, seeing as such distinction proves central in this paper.

bornness of stereotypes regarding women in light of contrary evidence. Specifically, it will highlight the centrality of epistemic heritage passed down to individuals throughout history by their societies, shaped both collectively and individually. For this purpose, it will concentrate on Quine's theory of knowledge.

Quine's Theory of Knowledge

As an empiricist, Quine deems experience the solitary source of knowledge. The novelty in his account, though, is that despite his foundation in empiricism and reliance on evidence for the constitution of knowledge, Quine transfers the judgment of knowledges' truth to a new realm. Traditional empiricists examine the adequacy of knowledges' correlation with empirical evidence to determine their truth value. Quine, though, turns his gaze from the connection between knowledge and evidence to that between the different knowledges themselves. He demands coherence among one's various knowledges, so that there is no conflict between them. To do so, Quine broadens his scope of validation by converting the unit of epistemic significance. Previously, the standard for validation of truth was individual knowledges, judged independently according to the correlation of each knowledge to empirical evidence external to the body of knowledge. Quine replaces this standard with the entirety of the body of knowledge; a corporate whole to be verified in light of its internal coherence.

Quine's endorsement of coherence as validation ensues from his refutation of the analytic-synthetic distinction,[8] negating the possibility of verifying knowledges either as true by virtue of meaning alone or as entirely dependent on personal experience. He contends that every form of knowledge, even the most rudimentary observation statements, inherently entails previous knowledge.[9] It is therefore impossible to judge the truth of

---

[8] Due to the scope of this paper, I will not delve here into this analysis, see Quine, "Main Trends in Recent Philosophy: Two Dogmas of Empiricism". *The Philosophical Review* 60(1), (1951).

[9] Willard Van Orman Quine, "Epistemology Naturalized", Reprinted from Willard Van

knowledges solely in accordance with their empirical adequacy. For, people do not have direct access to viewing knowledge in its rudimentary foundation of empirical evidence. Instead, the criterion of coherency shifts the focal point of epistemic inquiry to the intra-knowledge relationships themselves, examining their interactions and the overarching coherence of the body of knowledge as a holistic unit.

Quine's theory is thus utile in my analysis of stereotypes regarding women. For, what renders stereotypes epistemically puzzling is the very relationship between stereotypical knowledge regarding women as a group and one's experience-founded knowledges of particular women conflicting with the said stereotype. Such prevalent incoherence in people's corporate knowledge begs an inquiry into the mechanisms enabling it.

Additionally, according to Quine's theory of knowledge, the connection between empirical evidence and knowledge is such that they are considered mutually relevant yet not directly correlated. The loose ties between knowledges and empirical evidence makes way for the influence of other mechanisms on epistemic processes. Such mechanisms, for which Quine creates place in his account, may provide for the epistemic incongruences of stubbornness and the conflict found between stereotypical knowledges and empirical evidence.

Furthermore, not all knowledges are equally close to empirical evidence. Quine describes a typology of the body of knowledge in which the knowledges are scaled according to their proximity or distance from experience. The further away knowledge is from experience, the less exposed it is to revision in light of contrary evidence. Yet, these distances and the organization of the knowledges within the corporate body which dictate the knowledges' sensitivity to experience, are not inherent to the knowledges themselves. There is no logical necessity for certain knowledges to be of closer proximity to empirical evidence and

Orman Quine, *Ontological Relativity and Other Essays* (New York: Columbia University Press, 1969) in Kornblith, Hilary (Ed.), *Naturalizing Epistemology* (Cambridge: MIT Press, 1994), pp. 27–28.

others farther away. Rather, Quine describes this typology of knowledges within the body of knowledge as a "conceptual scheme".[10]

A conceptual scheme, according to Quine, is an arrangement into which are fitted "disordered fragments of raw experience",[11] empirical evidence prior to its coming into relation with the social element of previous knowledge entailed in the conceptual scheme. This arrangement of knowledges is that which determines one's "ontology",[12] the perception through which one interprets experience.[13] Therefore, a conceptual scheme is the manner in which empirical evidence is formed into knowledges and positioned relative one to another. This typology is a tool, a framework, which prescribes the perspective through which people view and interpret sensory input.[14] The conceptual scheme, thus, dictates the connections and interactions between knowledges.

Quine describes the conceptual scheme as a "fabric".[15] This fabric is composed of numerous knowledges, the peripheral of which touch upon experience. Though no specific knowledge is correlated to any specific experience, the peripheral knowledges are those more prone to revision in light of new evidence for they are the knowledges of greatest proximity to experience.[16] Quine depicts a causal link between experience and a knowledge, which makes the knowledge susceptible to empirical evidence. Thus, the experience of contrary evidence operates the causal link so that the relevant knowledge can be revised. Quine, therefore, describes the mechanism of revision as a readjustment

---

[10] Quine, "Main Trends in Recent Philosophy: Two Dogmas of Empiricism", pp. 41, 43; Willard Van Orman Quine, "On What There Is", *From a Logical Point of View* (New York: Harper and Row, 1963), p. 11.

[11] Quine, "On What There Is", p. 16.

[12] Quine, "On What There Is", pp. 16–17.

[13] Quine, "On What There Is", p. 10.

[14] Quine, "Main Trends in Recent Philosophy: Two Dogmas of Empiricism", pp. 41, 43.

[15] Quine, "Main Trends in Recent Philosophy: Two Dogmas of Empiricism", p. 39.

[16] Quine, "Epistemology Naturalized", p. 26.

of the fabric of knowledge.[17] When new evidence arises, the knowledges in the fabric are rearranged to incorporate the evidence, the newly formed knowledge, into the body of knowledge. The objective of this readjustment is to maintain maximum coherence within the fabric, thus validating the truth of the corporate body. It first entails the revision of a knowledge in the periphery of the fabric. The process of revision then spreads in a causal chain to certain additional knowledges connected to that knowledge originally revised to prevent conflict and thus incoherence among knowledges.[18]

Quine furthers his explication of the revision of the corporate body of knowledge in light of new evidence. He maintains that not only the knowledges themselves are subject to revision, but so are the connections between them. These connections are the epistemic rules of the conceptual scheme that dictate the relationships between the knowledges. The connections may be those ordained by the rules of logic or affiliations between knowledges deemed associable in the perception implemented by the conceptual scheme.[19] Therefore, the very organization of the knowledges within the corporate body may be altered in light of contrary evidence, the connections between knowledges shifted or morphed into different forms of connections.

The various forms of connections between knowledges produce alternative conceptual schemes. As the framework which prescribes the relationships between the knowledges and the interactions between them, conceptual schemes are undetermined. The fabric which organizes knowledge is not confined in its optional typologies of knowledges but for its internal necessitation of coherence. Not only in processes of revision, but also from the onset conceptual schemes are alternatives chosen between by social groups.[20]

---

[17] Quine, "Main Trends in Recent Philosophy: Two Dogmas of Empiricism", p. 39.

[18] Quine, "Main Trends in Recent Philosophy: Two Dogmas of Empiricism", pp. 39–41.

[19] Quine, "Main Trends in Recent Philosophy: Two Dogmas of Empiricism", p. 39.

[20] Quine, "On What There Is", p. 1, 17; Quine, "Epistemology Naturalized", p. 28.

Quine contends that multiple conceptual schemes may be equally coherent in their formation and arrangement of the same knowledges. Consequently, criteria are needed for choosing between different yet equally coherent conceptual schemes. Such criteria, though, are offered by Quine in point form alone. He notes that the scheme to be implemented is the one most "simple", "conservative", "convenient", "pragmatic", and "elegant".[21] Quine himself admits that these criteria are ambiguous and capable of entailing multiple standards,[22] with no "realistic standard of correspondence to reality".[23] Yet, the details entailed in these qualities of conceptual schemes and processes of revision, and the justification as to the reason they are ascribed such status as epistemic criteria, are not provided by Quine. Neither does he found his claims that these criteria are inherent human tendencies regarding conceptual schemes.[24] In this manner, Quine relinquishes the criteria of conceptual schemes, and thus the question of choice between them remains unclarified. These unelucidated criteria, though constituting a theoretical obstacle in Quine's account, expedite the epistemic analysis of stereotypes regarding women. It is rather through this patchwork in Quine's theory of knowledge that a window may be opened to explicate the paradox of stubbornness.

Quine's Theory of Knowledge and "Recalcitrant" Stereotypes

Stereotypes, being the stubborn form of knowledge they are, may be explained as such due to their location far from the periphery of Quine's fabric of knowledge. For, as situated distant

---

[21] Respectively: Quine, "Main Trends in Recent Philosophy: Two Dogmas of Empiricism", pp. 42–43; Quine, "Main Trends in Recent Philosophy: Two Dogmas of Empiricism", pp. 42–43 and Quine, "On What There Is", p. 16; Quine, "On What There Is", p. 16; Quine, "Main Trends in Recent Philosophy: Two Dogmas of Empiricism", p. 43; Willard Van Orman Quine, "Identity, Ostension, and Hypostasis", *From a Logical Point of View* (New York: Harper and Row, 1963), p. 79; Quine, "Identity, Ostension, and Hypostasis", p. 79.

[22] Quine, "On What There Is", p. 17.

[23] Quine, "Identity, Ostension, and Hypostasis", p. 79.

[24] Quine, "Main Trends in Recent Philosophy: Two Dogmas of Empiricism", p. 44.

from the periphery, stereotypes may be hard to reach by the causal chain of revision. The dictation of the location of stereotypes – as that of all knowledges – is decreed by the conceptual scheme in employment. It may thus seem that stereotypical knowledges regarding social groups are located within the far interior of conceptual schemes. According to this explanation, the stubbornness of stereotypes does not differ from those of other knowledges which share the same distance from the periphery of the fabric of knowledge.

Yet, the intriguing quality of stereotypes regarding women is not only that they are stubborn knowledges in conceptual schemes, but moreover that this is the case in dissimilar conceptual schemes pertaining to different societies. Therefore, perhaps there is an additional mechanism at work which perpetuates stubbornness among stereotypes. A mechanism that ascribes – or reveals – additional characteristics to stereotypical knowledges, differentiating them from simply 'distant knowledges' and accounting for their specific stubbornness. The question to be posed in this regard is whether the distance of stereotypes from the knowledge fabric's periphery is the sole cause of the great difficulty in revising them despite contrary evidence. Or, whether additional mechanisms are at work. The implications of the former may be that stereotypes are not, in actuality, a stubborn form of knowledge. Rather, if distance is the only cause, perhaps all that is needed to change stereotypes is sufficiently strong and sufficiently numerous contrary evidence. Alternatively, a change in conceptual scheme may bring these stereotypical knowledges closer to the periphery for greater ease of revision. If, on the other hand, an additional internal mechanism of the conceptual scheme is at work, it may provide insight about what form of knowledge stereotypes of women truly are and what deems this particular form of knowledge so stubborn and epistemically paradoxical.

In order to explicate the paradox of stubbornness, the following chapter will investigate the mechanisms that enforce the implementation of a certain conceptual scheme over another, as well as the mechanisms of the inner workings of the conceptual scheme. For the former, a significant focus will be the criteria which Quine lists for the championing of one conceptual scheme over another but upon which he does not expound nor offer justification. As to the inner workings of the conceptual scheme, to be explored is what, besides distance, constitutes the specific mechanism within the conceptual schemes that accounts for the stubbornness of stereotypes of women.

This examination of conceptual schemes and the typology of stereotypical knowledge aims to illuminate the paradox of stubbornness. Required here is to answer the two additional epistemic questions raised earlier in this paper regarding: one, the epistemic mechanisms which enable conflicts between the stereotype and contrary evidence and between the stereotype and other knowledges; and two, the epistemic source of stereotypical knowledge.

2. Quine's Conceptual Schemes and Other Myths

Conceptual schemes, Quine contends, are human-made.[25] There exists no empirical necessity for the construction of the fabric of knowledges in any particular arrangement. Rather, conceptual schemes are a tool created by people to organize and simplify the large quantities of sensory data input to which we are exposed.[26] This pragmatic element is inseparable from knowledge itself due to Quine's refutation of the analytic-synthetic distinction. The conceptual scheme is a pragmatic tool among various alternative schemes, chosen for its convenience in working with knowledge.[27] The pragmatism that Quine thus espouses enables him to account for the indeterminism of knowledge in relation to empirical evidence.

Conceptual schemes are both social and individual. They are constructed by and pertain to a community,[28] alongside entailing

---

[25] Quine, "Identity, Ostension, and Hypostasis", pp. 77–79; Quine, "Main Trends in Recent Philosophy: Two Dogmas of Empiricism", p. 41.

[26] Quine, "Main Trends in Recent Philosophy: Two Dogmas of Empiricism", p. 41.

[27] Quine, "Main Trends in Recent Philosophy: Two Dogmas of Empiricism", p. 43.

[28] Quine, "On What There Is", pp. 1, 17; Quine, "Epistemology Naturalized", p. 27.

internal individual variations.[29] There are diverse manners in which people can perceive the world – alternative formulations of the fabric of knowledge, the placement of knowledges within the fabric, and the construction of the logical connectors between them. Yet, these separate and conflicting individual conceptual schemes must be accommodated together into a broader, overarching communal conceptual scheme.[30] For, the body of knowledge that each person holds is part of the collective knowledge of the community at large.

Given such a wide array of equally coherent conceptual schemes, what are the criteria surrounding which scheme is implemented by respective communities? Quine describes the guiding principle as the convenience entailed by people's "pragmatic inclination" toward conservatism and simplicity.[31] Such pragmatism overtakes any standard of correspondence with reality,[32] consistent with Quine's appraisal of coherence within a body of knowledge rather than the adequacy of individual knowledges to particular empirical evidence. For, as knowledge is irreducible to experience, so too is the framework of knowledge. In lieu of correspondence with reality, the objective of conceptual schemes is the simplicity of their laws[33] by which they sort experiences and the ongoing input of empirical evidence.[34] Furthermore, that people prefer to minimize the changes made in the fabric in the process. The pragmatic inclination toward conservatism aims to adjust the existing fabric, the conceptual scheme, as slightly as possible in light of new evidence, including that which is contrary to previous knowledge.[35]

Minor adjustments to the knowledge fabric, therefore, are maintained to those peripheral knowledges deemed by the conceptual scheme most relevant to the particular experience. Yet,

---

[29] Quine, "On What There Is", p. 10.
[30] Quine, "On What There Is", pp. 16–17.
[31] Quine, "On What There Is" pp. 16–17.
[32] Quine, "Identity, Ostension, and Hypostasis", p. 79.
[33] Quine, "Main Trends in Recent Philosophy: Two Dogmas of Empiricism", p. 42.
[34] Quine, "On What There Is", p. 16.
[35] Quine, "Main Trends in Recent Philosophy: Two Dogmas of Empiricism", p. 42.

even conservatism must allow for a 'ripple effect' of readjustments to ensue. No particular knowledge is determined to partake in this causal chain of revision, for none is reducible to any particular empirical evidence. Rather, though any and all variations of readjustments are possible within the conceptual scheme, it is the propensity to simplicity and conservatism that dictates which path of knowledges and connectors the revision will take.[36] This propensity maintains the changes wrought upon the fabric of knowledge at a pragmatic minimum.

As aforementioned, it may be contended that stereotypes are located in the interior of the field of knowledge, distant from the periphery. In such a manner, they would necessitate a great tidal wave of revision for the causal chain to reach and revise them. However, if the paradox of stubbornness is derived solely from the location of stereotypical knowledges within the conceptual scheme, then in accordance with Quine, numerous alternative conceptual schemes could just as well have placed the stereotypes peripherally. Alternatively, the vast extent of contrary evidence would seem sufficient to reach the distant interior of the field of knowledge where stereotypes are situated. Moreover, so much contrary evidence relevant to stereotypical knowledge might appear to indicate stereotypes' peripheral, rather than internal, location. For, Quine's own definition of peripheral knowledges are those deemed most relevant to certain experiences.[37]

That stereotypes conflict with experience is because they do not originate from it; people's personal experiences are not the epistemic source of stereotypical knowledge. Furthermore, stereotypes are generalizations and simplifications of social groups as a whole rather than knowledge respective of a particular experience. And, as Quine contends, it is the conceptual scheme and not raw empirical evidence that associates various experiences into a generalized whole, a convenient simplicity.[38]

---

[36] Quine, "Main Trends in Recent Philosophy: Two Dogmas of Empiricism", p. 40.

[37] Quine, "Epistemology Naturalized", p. 27.

[38] Quine, "On What There Is", p. 17; Quine, "Identity, Ostension, and Hypostasis", p. 70.

The irreducibility of stereotypes to empirical evidence gives the impression of greater severity than 'regular' knowledge; both due to stereotypes' conflict-causing stubbornness, as well as to the question of their origination. This leads to the understanding that stereotypes did not receive their paradoxical characteristics due to placement, rather their placement might be caused by their very stubbornness. Stereotypes themselves are perhaps not a knowledge but rather a mechanism of the inner workings of the conceptual scheme.

Posits

The mechanism within the conceptual scheme that may help to explicate the paradox of stubbornness is what Quine terms "posits". Posits are human-made tools incorporated into conceptual schemes as "convenient intermediaries".[39] They are implemented for the organization of empirical evidence derived from experience. Thus, posits are condensed, locally applied, 'mini' conceptual schemes operating within the broader framework of the conceptual scheme itself. As human-made, posits do not originate from, nor are they reducible to experience.[40] Rather, they are "myths"[41] that are used within the conceptual scheme as convenient tools for conceptually managing the empirical evidence arising from a situation.

These fictitious entities may differ in degree as to their efficiency in ordering extents of empirical evidence. This pragmatic value of posits as a conceptual, epistemically irreducible mechanism, is exemplified by Quine by the variance in degree, though not in kind, between the posit of the existence of physical objects and the existence of the gods of antiquity.[42] Quine contends that empirically there is no knowledge regarding any such complete object that retains identity over time and space, nor in being

---

[39] Quine, "Main Trends in Recent Philosophy: Two Dogmas of Empiricism", p. 41.

[40] Quine, "Main Trends in Recent Philosophy: Two Dogmas of Empiricism", pp. 41–42.

[41] Quine, "Main Trends in Recent Philosophy: Two Dogmas of Empiricism", p. 41.

[42] Quine, "Main Trends in Recent Philosophy: Two Dogmas of Empiricism", p. 41; Quine, "On What There Is", p. 19.

distinguishable in terms of borders separating it from other objects. Rather, human perception of the existence of such physical objects is but the pragmatic typology of the vast empirical evidence into categorized beings, for our more convenient use of the knowledge and conduct in the world. Quine thus categorizes physical objects as the same form of epistemic mechanism as ancient gods. Both are empirically-irreducible myths which are implemented pragmatically by conceptual schemes to organize and process experience.[43]

Not only do posits serve as devices for the simplification of the input of empirical evidence, they simplify epistemic operations too. They do so by simplifying the movement between knowledges, creating jumps that, for the sake of convenience, skip over the logical connectors of the conceptual scheme itself.[44] While logical connectors detail every single relationship between the empirical knowledges, posits exist as a mechanism within the conceptual scheme which is manually "imported"[45] and executed upon knowledge to conveniently sort between the mass of empirical evidence – categorize, organize, and thus utilize the knowledge.

Posits are integral to the understanding and analysis of experience and empirical evidence. Additionally, they appear to provide an adequate candidate to explain the stubborn form of knowledge that stereotypes comprise. In viewing stereotypes as posits, they are understood as internal mechanisms of the conceptual scheme that simplify empirical evidence through generalization and facilitate the conceptual movement between knowledges in manners that pass over the fabric's logical connectors. Indeed, stereotypical knowledge about women causes conceptual leaps between the various knowledges of women in manners not consistent with the logical connectors between them. As posits, stereotypes are undetermined and irreducible

---

[43] Quine, "Main Trends in Recent Philosophy: Two Dogmas of Empiricism", p. 41.
[44] Quine, "Main Trends in Recent Philosophy: Two Dogmas of Empiricism", pp. 41–42.
[45] Quine, "Main Trends in Recent Philosophy: Two Dogmas of Empiricism", pp. 41–42.

to experience. Their relationship to experience is how they act upon the evidence and not in originating from it.

This irreducibility has further significance for stereotypes regarding women and the paradox of stubbornness. Lacking empiric origin renders stereotypes, like all posits, distinct from other forms of knowledge. Whereas other knowledges stem from empirical evidence, differing only in degree of proximity and thus propensity to revision, stereotypes are not situated on that scale. Posits are fictitious myths[46] that are not positioned in line with the empirical knowledges in the conceptual scheme. Stereotypes, as posits, are not woven into the fabric of knowledge as empirical knowledges are. Instead, stereotypes are a mechanism of the very organization of the body of knowledge.

Stereotypes, as posits, are not connected with the other knowledges of the fabric but rather are epistemic mechanisms that act upon it. This explains their absence from causal chains of revision and their invisibility in verifications of coherence. The causal chain of revision operates along the connecting relations within the fabric, revising those knowledges and logical connectors associated with the initially revised knowledge. The verification of coherence, as well, runs along those same pathways to validate the coherence of the fabric. Stereotypes, hence, go unnoticed in both epistemic processes. In this manner, stereotypes regarding women remain stubbornly unrevised in light of contrary evidence, nor does this stubbornness raise a flag of incoherence despite the stereotype's conflict with the newly formed knowledge.

Heritage

Having explicated the paradox of stubbornness and the difficulty of epistemic conflict, the question remains as to the epistemic source of stereotypes regarding women. It may be asked, then, what is the epistemic source of posits in general? Quine

---

[46] Quine, "Main Trends in Recent Philosophy: Two Dogmas of Empiricism", pp. 44–45.

dubs this irreducible, simplifying mechanism of posits as "cultural",[47] explicitly revealing their collective, social trait. Similar to the conceptual schemes themselves, of which posits are in a sense a 'condensed' form, the latter too are collective entities formed and held socially. If so, what are the cultural roots of posits and of conceptual schemes themselves?

Quine briefly mentions the source of conceptual schemes and of their entailed posits – "heritage".[48] According to Quine, people are bestowed with an eclectic framework of knowledge with which they pragmatically work to merge between the inherited conceptual scheme and the personally experienced empirical evidence.[49] The socially shared body of knowledge is passed down generation to generation, *a priori* framing individuals' experiences and formulation of knowledge throughout life. This epistemic heritage, though not expounded upon by Quine, is helpful in examining stereotypes regarding women.

The conceptual scheme rests upon aggregated shared experiences and empirical knowledge held collectively in a social body of knowledge.[50] The shared knowledges structure the conceptual scheme through which empirical knowledge is perceived by individuals. Thus, every individual receives previous knowledge shared by their community as a heritage that entails within it the communal conceptual scheme and posits.

Among the posits held collectively and inherited by individuals are stereotypes regarding women. These stereotypes do not stem from personal experience, for one's experience would in most cases found a more complex and non-stereotypical knowledge about women. Rather, such stereotypical knowledge is entrenched as a posit in one's heritage. An individual knows

[47] Quine, "Main Trends in Recent Philosophy: Two Dogmas of Empiricism", p. 41.

[48] Quine, "Identity, Ostension, and Hypostasis", p. 77; Quine, "Main Trends in Recent Philosophy: Two Dogmas of Empiricism", p. 43.

[49] Quine, "Identity, Ostension, and Hypostasis", p. 77; Quine, "Main Trends in Recent Philosophy: Two Dogmas of Empiricism", p. 43.

[50] It is the community's use of language that deems as true those knowledges not susceptible to differences of experience within the speech community – a foundation of Quine's theory which is beyond the scope of this article and therefore not incorporated in my writing here. See Quine, "Epistemology Naturalized", p. 28.

the stereotype before meeting women to the extent necessitated for the formulation of such a generalized knowledge. People empirically experience women once preconditioned with the stereotype inherited as a posit of the respective society's historical conceptual scheme.

To summarize, posits are integral to the shared body of knowledge of the community; being a socially shared, historic, intersubjective reference aimed at simplifying knowledge at the expense of reality.[51] As posits, stereotypes regarding women partake in this collectivity and irreducibility to personal experience. Quine's theory of knowledge thus provides an epistemic source for stereotypes in the form of social heritage.

3. The Recalcitrance of Stereotypes

Quine's theory of knowledge, with its holistic empirical approach endorsing conceptual schemes, provided fertile ground for this paper's analysis. The conceptual scheme and its internal mechanism of posits accounted for the stubbornness of stereotypical knowledge. This was done by revealing stereotypes as fictitious human-made posits implemented as a mechanism of simplification within conceptual schemes. As posits, stereotypes are not woven into the fabric of knowledge nor connected to empirical knowledge by logical connectors. Thereby, they are not subject to any causal chain of revision, nor are they scrutinized for validation of coherence within the body of knowledge. Thus, the paradox of stubbornness and its entailed epistemic conflicts have been explicated.

Lastly, the epistemic source of stereotypes has been provided for in Quine's conceptualisation of epistemic heritage. Quine claims that conceptual schemes and their entailed posits are held collectively as shared, social knowledge which is inherited by individuals. Thus, knowledge that precedes personal experience is accounted for within Quine's empirical theory. Stereotypes of women are found to originate not in personal experience, but

---

[51] Quine, "Main Trends in Recent Philosophy: Two Dogmas of Empiricism", p. 42.

rather to be hereditary components of conceptual schemes pertaining to society over time.

Having explicated the paradox of stubbornness, the conflicts between stereotypical knowledge regarding women and both empirical evidence and other knowledge, and their epistemic source; one final question remains. As the closing thought to this paper, the question begged relates to the ability to change stereotypes about women. As previously detailed, extensive contrary evidence does not appear to cause revision of these posits, that is, stereotypes, to which empirical knowledges are subject. Perhaps, then, they may only be revised by the changing of the conceptual scheme itself, i.e. a paradigm shift.

Quine describes the changing of conceptual schemes as slow, conscious, and voluntary processes.[52] It is a simultaneous act of reconstruction amidst dependence on the evolving conceptual scheme itself as the body of knowledge, like "a mariner who must rebuild his ship on the open sea".[53] It is unclear whether the "we"[54] that Quine alleges capable of changing the conceptual scheme denotes a multiplicity of individuals or a community as a whole. This question is particularly consequential for the paradox of stubbornness entailed in stereotypes. The conservatism and the pragmatism that Quine invokes in his theory inhibit a socially instigated change to the community's own convenient conceptual scheme. Therefore, it would rather seem, also if not Quine's intentional denotation, that the catalysts of such a voluntary change in the conceptual scheme would rather need to be individuals whose own personal conceptual schemes have, in that respect, differed substantially enough from the community's.

However, Quine does hint at the volatility of the collective conceptual scheme despite its reiterating inheritance as pre-existing knowledge for every individual member of the community throughout history. He writes: "The conceptual

---

[52] Quine, "Identity, Ostension, and Hypostasis", pp. 78–79.
[53] Quine, "Identity, Ostension, and Hypostasis", p. 79.
[54] Quine, "Identity, Ostension, and Hypostasis", pp. 78–79.

scheme in which we grew up is an eclectic heritage, and the forces which conditioned its evolution from the days of Java man onward are a matter of conjecture."[55] The existence of individually varied conceptual schemes within the collective body of knowledge opens the opportunity for such epistemic evolution. This offers an alternative idea as to the ways in which stereotypes regarding women may indeed be dismantled. Perhaps, a sufficient number of voluntary, conscious changes in individual conceptual schemes can cause the build-up of ample pressure on the socially held fabric of knowledge. This pressure will then seep into the interior of enough ruptures may form in the epistemic mechanisms framing the knowledges. If a critical mass of pressure is attained, enough ruptures may form in the epistemic mechanisms framing the knowledges, so that the existing posits will not be able to hold out any longer against the amounting readjustment.

The crumbling of the fabric may eventually lead to a crash, a tipping point in which the individually volunteered changes succeed the ontology of the inherited social conceptual scheme. Such a succession may readjust the very construct of the fabric and thus let loose the existing posits from among its epistemic mechanisms. At such a point, stereotypes regarding women will be revealed as the posits they are: fictitious myths lacking empiric foundation. This stereotypical knowledge of women will then be cast away from the utilized posits of the conceptual scheme, allowed to be recognized as the myth it is, as is the case with the gods of antiquity.

---

[55] Quine, "Identity, Ostension, and Hypostasis", p. 77.

Chapter 12
The Child as the Other
– Some Epistemological Considerations

Zlatana Knezevic

Critical childhood studies has drawn attention to and critically examined common conceptualizations of childhood in a wide range of scholarly works.[1] These works discuss how in various fields and theoretical outlets, childhood is often described as a stage of formation and children as becoming-adults, and how this, in turn, produces a generic and a largely ahistorical, de-politicized and decontextualized child figure. The pre-subjectal generic infant has been pivotal in representations of human ontology yet is usually dehumanized. As a prefix to subjectivity, the child figure stands for the pre-modern, that which is per-ceived as beyond history, yet paradoxically, prior to, and in the process of becoming civilized.[2] A universal childhood biography

---

[1] Some common subfields go under the name of *new sociology of childhood* and *anthro-pology of childhood*. See, for example, Chris Jenks, *Childhood* (London & New York: Routledge, 2005); Alan Prout & Allison James (Eds.) *Constructing and Reconstructing Childhood* (London: Falmer Press, 1990); Jens Qvortrup, William A. Corsaro & Michael-Sebastian Honig (Eds.), *The Palgrave Handbook of Childhood Studies* (Houndmills & New York: Palgrave Macmillan, 2011); Andrea Szulc & Clarice Cohn, "Anthropology and Childhood in South America: Perspectives from Brazil and Argentina." *AnthropoChildren*, Vol. 1, 2012, ff. 1–17; David F. Lancy, *The Anthropology of Childhood: Cherubs, Chattel, Changelings* (Cambridge: Cambridge University Press, 2022).

[2] Erica Burman, *Developments: Child, Image, Nation* (London & New York: Routledge, 2008); *Deconstructing Developmental Psychology* (London & New York: Routledge, 2017); Claudia Castañeda, "The Child as a Feminist Figuration: Toward a Politics of Privilege", *Feminist Theory*, Vol. 2, No. 1, 2001, ff. 29–53; *Figurations: Child, Bodies, Worlds* (Durham & London: Duke University Press, 2002); Jenks, *Childhood*; Nick Lee, *Childhood and Society: Growing up in an Age of Uncertainty* (Buckingham: Open University Press, 2001); Alan Prout & Allison James, "A New Paradigm for the Sociology of Childhood? Provenance, Promise and Problems" in Alan Prout & Allison James (Eds.) *Constructing and Reconstructing Childhood* (London: Falmer Press, 1990); Jens Qvortrup, William A. Corsaro, & Michael-Sebastian Honig, "Why Social Studies of

has therefore come to stand for more than the core and formation of the individual under development and becoming. It has come to stand for that very process of becoming a civilized human being in general. In myriad scholarly attempts to show how these meanings are ascribed to childhood, other generic concepts have emerged. Common terms of reference for the symbolic figure of 'the child' is the child as a figuration, idea, category, metaphor, temporality, and the Other.

Similar concerns and critiques once directed at philosophy, developmental theory, anthropology and social theory, to name a few, have been addressed in relation to feminism. While some feminist works address children and childhoods,[3] and more recently girlhood,[4] children and childhoods have remained on the margins. A vast majority of feminist works are oriented toward adults, privileging the perspectives of adults and, at best, providing adult-centric objectifications of childhoods. This is how the debate about the child as the adult Other becomes inevitable also in relation to feminist theorizing.[5]

In this chapter, I present some *epistemological advantages* and *dangers* of conceptualizing Otherness in relation to children and childhoods. The chapter distinguishes between *the child as the Other* – a figure mirroring the dominant image of children

Childhood? An Introduction to the Handbook" in Jens Qvortrup, William A. Corsaro & Michael-Sebastian Honig (Eds.), *The Palgrave Handbook of Childhood Studies* (Houndmills & New York: Palgrave Macmillan, 2011) Jo-Ann Wallace, "Technologies of the Child: Towards a Theory of the Child Subject", *Textual Practice*, Vol. 9, 1995, ff. 283–302.

[3] de Beauvoir, *The second sex*, Vol. II, Part I; Shulamit Firestone, *The Dialectic of Sex: The case for feminist revolution* (New York: Bantam Books, 1972); Barrie Thorne, "Re-Visioning Women and Social Change: Where Are the Children?" *Gender and Society*, Vol. 1, No. 1, 1987, ff. 85–109; Valerie Walkerdine, *Daddy's Girl: Young Girls and Popular Culture* (London: Macmillan Press, 1997); Wallace, "Technologies of the Child"; See also Burman, *Developments*; *Deconstructing Developmental Psychology*; Castañeda, "The Child as a Feminist Figuration"; *Figurations*.

[4] In more recent girlhood studies, the at times gender-neutral childhood and youth have been replaced with the notion of girlhood. See the journal *Girlhood Studies – An Interdisciplinary Journal*, published by Berghahn Journals; Claudia Mitchell & Carrie Rentschler (Eds.) *Girlhood and the Politics of Place* (New York & Oxford: Berghahn Books, 2016). See also *FlickForsk! Nordic Network for Girlhood Studies*.

[5] Castañeda, "The Child as a Feminist Figuration"; *Figurations*.

as incomplete unfinished projections of adults – and *the child-hood Other* as those children's childhoods that are othered by dominant ideas about childhood. I use this distinction to critically discuss a simplified analogy between the child and the (adult) Other and, in turn, the epistemological danger of using the notion of the Other in relation to the child as a figuration. Using this distinction, I argue that inscriptions of Otherness come with a risk of limiting the theorizing of multiple relations of power and, thus, fail to account for the pluralistic character of childhoods. At the same time, I discuss the epistemological advantage of opening up for inscriptions and contestations of the notion of Otherness in relation to childhoods.

I briefly introduce the chapter by discussing the notion of the Other in different critical schools of thought. Then, drawing on perspectives from intersectional, postcolonial feminist and critical childhood studies, I discuss how the debates surrounding the child as the Other share parallels with feminist scholarly debates. Such a debate concerns the attempts to de-centre the normative image of Woman. This includes the issues that come with the problematic use of this figuration as if it applies to all women while considering only a few.[6] Furthermore, I argue how the tools offered by postcolonial feminism *and* critical childhood studies are necessary to deconstruct the idea of a universal childhood and simplistic notions of Otherness. Such a bridging poses critical questions about why childhoods should be the subject of feminism and why postcolonial feminism should be relevant for studying childhoods.

The Other and Othering in Postcolonial Feminist Thought

In philosophy, the first introduction to the concept of the Other is perhaps mostly associated with the philosopher Georg Wilhelm Friedrich Hegel, who, in the early 19th century, used

---

[6] Avtar Brah & Ann Phoenix, "Ain't I a Woman? Revisiting Intersectionality", *Journal of International Women's Studies*, Vol. 5, 2004, ff. 75–86.

the Other in contrastive manners in relation to the Self.[7] From thereon, Edmund Husserl and Jean-Paul Sartre provided their own approaches to the Other.[8] Finally, a well-known point of reference for feminists is the work of Simone de Beauvoir. In *The Second Sex*, de Beauvoir used the notion of the Other to articulate dominant views of women's inferiority to men.[9]

Postcolonial scholars have introduced additional notions: the colonial Other and the subaltern.[10] Scholars discuss how race is central for the conception of humanity in modernity. Consequently, those who fall outside these narrow definitions of humanity are also constituted by race but racially othered.[11] However, the Other and othering also link to axes of power other than race. Processes of othering may be applied broadly to denote anyone oppressed, discriminated, dehumanised, and deprived of subjectivity, which historically has been ascribed to the White enlightened heterosexual bourgeois European male subject. In this vein, othering could also apply to white heterosexual women in the colonial settler communities who had been in the shadows of the White colonizer. Yet, the status of these women differed from the subaltern in the so-called Third World. The postcolonial feminist Gayatri Chakravorty Spivak

[7] Georg Wilhelm Friedrich Hegel, *The Phenomenology of Spirit*, transl. Peter Fuss & John Dobbins. (Notre Dame: University of Notre Dame, 2019).

[8] Edmund Husserl, *Cartesian meditations: an introduction to phenomenology*, transl. Dorion Cairns (The Hague: Martinus Nijhoff, 1960); Jean-Paul Sartre, *Being and Nothingness: An Essay on Phenomenological Ontology*, transl. Hazel Barnes (London: Routledge, 1969[1958]).

[9] Simone de Beauvoir, *The second sex [Le deuxième sexe]*, transl. Constance Borde & Sheila Malovany-Chevallier (New York: Vintage Books, 2011[1949]).

[10] Frantz Fanon, *The Wretched of the Earth*, transl. Richard Philcox (New York: Grove Press, 2004[1961]) Edward W Said, *Orientalism* (New York: Vintage Books, 1978); Gayatri Chakravorty Spivak, "Can the Subaltern Speak?" in Lawrence Grossberg & Cary Nelson (Eds.), *Marxism and the Interpretation of Culture* (Urbana: University of Illinois Press, 1988).

[11] Anne McClintock, *Imperial Leather: Race, Gender and Sexuality in the Colonial Contest* (New York, London: Routledge, 1995); María Lugones, "Heterosexualism and the Colonial / Modern Gender System", *Hypatia*, Vol. 22, No. 1, 2007, ff. 186–209; Toby Rollo, "The Color of Childhood: The Role of the Child/Human Binary in the Production of Anti-Black Racism", *Journal of Black Studies*, Vol. 49, No. 4, 2018, ff. 307–329.

(re)used the notion of the subaltern to describe what it means to be located outside hegemonic discourse, subjectivity, lacking voice and representation altogether.[12]

Where in all this are childhoods to be located? Analogically, a line of continuity has often been drawn between children as the adult Others and colonial Others, and vice versa.[13] As I will discuss below, the child as the adult Other has been useful in discussions about the asymmetric power relations between children and adults. In this broader conception, children are acknowledged as having lower status than adults because of the dominant conceptualizations of children as different or simply a lesser and not fully accomplished adult version. Some scholars instead turn their attention to constructions of the childlike, childish and processes of infantilization when reflecting on the logic of power and domination in contexts that are not necessarily or primarily linked to child subjects but address processes of othering in general. However, the childhood Other I discuss in this chapter is also the subaltern of childhood itself.

Childhood as Temporality, Power and Otherness

In 1962, in *Centuries of Childhood: A Social History of Family Life*, Philippe Ariès argued that childhood, as 'we' know it in modern times and as a distinct phase of human existence, was not accessible to our understanding until the seventeenth century.[14] This modern and European conception of childhood shifted from the child as a smaller version of the adult to childhood as distinctively different from our conception of adulthood. For instance, childhood today is thought of as a temporary life phase that transitions into adulthood. In social theory, childhood as temporality appears in relation to what is often referred to as socialization. Socialization is represented as a temporality during which individuals undergo practices and rituals that

---

[12] Spivak, "Can the Subaltern Speak?".

[13] McClintock, *Imperial Leather*; Rollo, "The Color of Childhood".

[14] Philippe Ariès, *Centuries of Childhood: A Social History of Family Life,* transl. Robert Baldick. (New York: Knopf, 1962).

introduce the young person to normative adulthood but also to that which constitutes manhood and womanhood in different contexts.[15] In developmental psychology, the temporality of childhood is more intelligible as a phase consisting of specific life stages or 'timings' against which development can be measured. What transpires during these stages determines how and if the individual will develop.[16]

As Ashis Nandy notes, the modern conception of childhood implied a distinctiveness in terms of inferiority. Children are the origin of adulthood and simultaneously

> a blank slate on which adults must write their moral codes – an inferior version of maturity, less productive and ethical, and badly contaminated by the playful, irresponsible and spontaneous aspects of human nature'[17]

The idea of children as inferior to and more formative than adults has been a central object of critique in critical childhood studies. Critical childhood studies summarize long-standing critical scholarly debates and historical analyses of the emergence of childhood. While childhoods and children have been the object of research in many disciplines and bodies of knowledge, such as developmental psychology and anthropology, critical studies of childhood provide new approaches to childhood as a historically contingent and social construction.

Childhood, on the other hand, has biological and cognitive connotations in theories of socialization and development, as Erica Burman points out. References to chronological age are harder to interpret as social constructions and point more readily to essentialism. Therefore, biological age and cognitive

[15] See Danny Hoffman, "Like Beasts in the Bush: Synonyms of Childhood and Youth in Sierra Leone", *Postcolonial Studies*, Vol. 6, No. 3, 2003, ff. 295–308; Walkerdine, *Daddy's Girl*.

[16] Burman, *Developments; Deconstructing Developmental Psychology*; Castañeda, *Figurations*.

[17] Ashis Nandy, *The Intimate Enemy. Loss and Recovery of Self under Colonialism* (Delhi: Oxford University Press, 1983), f. 15.

development are used to deprive children of voice rather than to address age-related power relations. For instance, within the framework of children's rights, biological age and maturity serve as benchmarks in assessing a child's right to be heard. Put differently, age may be depicted as a ground for discrimination and at the same time can be stated as the very ground which legitimately allows adults to exclude children from participation, if children are assessed as not old and mature enough.[18]

Yet, unlike gender, sexuality and race, age as an axis of power is sometimes viewed as a more flexible category that can be more easily transgressed, of course, in due time.[19] To be more precise, the meaning of age on a power axis shifts throughout a person's life-course. For instance, age helps to raise issues about adultism, that is, adult-centrism, adult power and misopaedic attitudes at a certain point in time.[20] Yet, at another point in an individual's life, age may help in identifying the consequences of ageist societies and disadvantages for older people, or gerontocratic societies that privilege the elderly. Both children and old people are frequently associated with their 'deviant' category in contexts where the 'productive' life phase is associated with adult work life as the norm. However, being granted a socially lower rank due to young age does not apply to all children, at all times and circumstances.[21] Therefore, being a child of young age does not necessarily entail Otherness nor subalternity if used alone. Thus, age in interplay with other axes of power needs to be considered.

However, I argue that while older people are also associated with a (temporary) life phase that can only be inhabited at a specific point in the life cycle, this temporality cannot be revisited. Yet, the very idea that childhood is a phase that can be re-appropriated is what makes it distinct as a temporality, seem-

---

[18] Burman, *Developments*; Lee, "The Challenge of Childhood"; Karen Wells, "The Politics of Life: Governing Childhood", *Global Studies of Childhood*, Vol. 1, No. 1, 2011, ff. 15–25.

[19] Burman, *Developments*.

[20] Rollo, "The Color of Childhood".

[21] Spivak, "Can the Subaltern Speak?".

ingly timeless and susceptible to colonization. There are multiple ways of appropriating childhood, one among which is, according to Claudia Castañeda:

> the turn back to one's childhood to repair the adult or to reclaim "the child within" (as in many psychotherapeutic regimes and in wider popular discourse. Once the adult's temporal distance from childhood has been secured, the adult draws on the past as a resource for the present. The adult returns to childhood to reappropriate the child he or she once was in order to establish a more stable adult self. Here, the child is primarily valuable insofar as the condition of childhood can be revisited in order to be left behind once again.[22]

The ideas of a decontextualized childhood and disembodied child contribute to the colonizing of childhoods, i.e., *a posteriori* knowledge claims to children's lives make it possible to have *epistemic access* to (others') childhood retrospectively in the sense that 'I have been there, thus I know'.[23] In addition, colonizing practices include the forming and predicting of futures by making claims on *a priori* knowledge about children's (future) best.[24] From an epistemic perspective, the decontextualized childhood never entirely belongs to children themselves. The idea of the disembodied 'inner child' or 'the child within' is very telling. So is the idea of childhood trauma as shaping adult life, and in more drastic ways than it 'otherwise' would have done. There is, in fact, in these medicalized and psychologized approaches to childhoods and adulthoods a distinct understanding of time as something concealing issues rather than healing them. Childhood, in this sense, stands for the wound. And yet, if therapy enables a 'traveling' in time, it seems less effective on those bound to their childhoods instead of mastering the time that has a hold on them. For those who are considered chronically fixed

---

[22] Castañeda, *Figurations*, f. 5.

[23] Castañeda, "The Child as a Feminist Figuration"; *Figurations*.

[24] Zlatana Knezevic, *Child (Bio)Welfare and Beyond: Intersecting Injustices in Childhoods and Swedish Child Welfare* (Västerås, Mälardalen University Press, 2020).

in a deteriorated maturity level, childhoods are non-reclaimable, yet colonisable (i.e. knowable). Epistemic access to childhood as a temporality does not necessarily imply othering in purely negative terms. These accounts nonetheless highlight how adults and adulthood serve as the backdrop in theorizing and imagining children and childhoods. 'The child' and a generic childhood become theoretical resources in both mainstream and critical theories, as I will discuss below.

The Child as the Adult Other

The feminist critical childhood scholar Claudia Castañeda has insightfully analyzed how 'the child' figures in poststructuralist- and feminist philosophical scholarship. Castañeda shows how children, as figurations, lack subjectivity in some central post-structuralist and feminist works and theories on the subject.[25] According to Castañeda, the presumed subject in the works of Gilles Deleuze and Félix Guattari, Michel Foucault, Jean-François Lyotard, Judith Butler, Valerie Walkerdine, and Teresa de Laurentis is the adult, according to which the child figures as the Other. She discusses how the child in some of these philo-sophical works stand for other ways of being and becoming and alternative spaces for the possibility of thought and for the dis-ruption of normative orders that are open to the male philo-sopher to occupy. Otherness, in these accounts, is not automa-tically linked to inferiority *per se*. It is rather associated with desired spaces, times and states, albeit devoid of subjectivity. Castañeda writes how

> the desire for possibility – or what might otherwise be called 'resistance' or 'agency' – is not in itself problematic. Rather, it is the embodiment of possibility in and through an Other that is the problem. So, too, to identify with and think through one's own childhood [...][26]

---

[25] Castañeda, "The Child as a Feminist Figuration"; *Figurations.*
[26] Castañeda, "The Child as a Feminist Figuration", f. 60.

As creative and analytical feminist uses of Woman, the Black subject, the Cyborg, etc. demonstrate, figurations play an important role in whose stories are heard and what kind of yearnings for transformation are expressed. Thus, despite not being used to primarily or directly depict actual people, figurations as 'conceptual personae' nevertheless imply some material embeddedness in the sense that they emerge from 'embodied accounts of one's power relations'.[27] However, as Castañeda shows, the figuration of the child lacks material embeddedness and the accounts that inscribe the child into theories of subjectivity are accounts by which the scholar's power is reproduced. For instance, she explicates how the feminist Valerie Walkerdine, in her analysis of young working-class girls, does not reflexively position herself as an adult researcher. Instead, Walkerdine draws on her own childhood experiences that are not even *in situ* but are retrospectively merged with those of the child subjects under analysis.

> Psychoanalysis, even in its feminist guises, emerges as a technology of childhood that figures the child as the adult's ontological origin, and as such an origin that the adult theorist can claim to know by way of psychoanalysis itself.[28]

Castañeda's answer to her own question 'Who or what counts as a feminist subject?' points thus to adult subjectivity, and hence foregrounds age. Her analysis prompts me to ask: If the child-figure is the subject's Other, what conceptualisations of Otherness does this leave us with? Theories of subjectivity and subjugation, apart from being adultist, are also racialized and gendered, as postcolonial theorists have demonstrated.[29] Such an

---

[27] Brah & Phoenix, "Ain't I a Woman?"; Rosi Braidotti, "Dympna and the Figuration of the Woman Warrior" in Rosemarie Buikema & Iris van der Tuin, (Eds.), *Doing Gender in Media, Art, and Culture* (London & New York: Routledge, 2009), ff. 243–244; Spivak, "Can the Subaltern Speak?".
Braidotti, "Dympna and the Figuration of the Woman Warrior", ff. 243–244.
[28] Castañeda, "The Child as a Feminist Figuration", f. 29.
[29] Rollo, "The Color of Childhood"; Spivak, "Can the Subaltern Speak?".

analysis is central in theorizations on Otherness in childhoods, and consequently also in acknowledging how the child as the adult Other renders other processes of othering invisible.

While what it means to be a child is vastly different across the world, children inhabit a world in which specific geopolitical ideals shape what can be claimed as their rights, what is regarded to be in their best interest, and what it means to be a normal child. In addition, children's own views of their childhoods interlink with the various meanings associated with childhood in the public discourse.[30] For example, children may stand for that which is desired, such as purity and innocence, as well as the undesired, such as danger, irrationality and disobedience.[31] Furthermore, children may be linked to other time-spaces, philosophically, as discussed above, to otherworldly spirit worlds in regions of the world where spirit belief is widespread, or in terms of better and progressive futures.[32] Because of the multiple and contradictory meanings ascribed to children, they evoke identifications but also disidentifications. I argue that the ambivalences and contradictions that permeate portrayals of children help to analytically distinguish the child as the adult Other from other 'Others' in, and beyond childhood.

For instance, the figuration of the child frequently appears in critical studies as representing the future.[33] However, as José Esteban Muñoz has pointed out, this figuration does not seem to apply to all children. Queer and Black kids are left out of these

---

[30] Tatek Abebe & Yaw Ofosu-Kusi, "Beyond Pluralizing African Childhoods: Introduction", *Childhood*, Vol. 23, No. 3, 2016, ff. 303–316; Lucia Rabello de Castro, "Why Global? Children and Childhood from a Decolonial Perspective", *Childhood*, Vol. 27, No. 1, 2020, ff. 48–62; Hoffman, "Like Beasts in the Bush:"; Walter Omar Kohan, "A conversation with children about children …", *Journal of Philosophy in Schools*, Vol. 5, No. 2, 2018.

[31] Steven Angelides, *The Fear of Child Sexuality. Young People, Sex and Agency* (Chicago & London: University of Chicago Press, 2019); Hoffman, "Like Beasts in the Bush"; Lancy, *The Anthropology of Childhood*; Anneke Meyer, "The Moral Rhetoric of Childhood", *Childhood*, Vol. 14, No. 1, 2007, ff. 85–104.

[32] Lee Edelman, *No Future. Queer Theory and the Death Drive* (Durham & London: Duke University Press, 2004); Hoffman, "Like Beasts in the Bush".

[33] Edelman, *No Future.*

futuristic imaginaries, according to Muñoz.[34] Following Muñoz's lines of thought, racialized, queer and class-situated childhoods that do not fit into the normative script of what childhood should be, are disregarded. For instance, the lifestyles of child (sex) workers, the child soldiers, street children or a child living in what is considered to be a dysfunctional family do not seem to qualify as *the* childhood with a capital C.[35] What can be learned from intersectionality is that figurations, including the notion of the Other, are adult re-inscriptions of some childhoods, while others are left out. A lesson from incorporating the gendered and queer Others into mainstream politics suggests that 'some versions' of Otherness become normalized, mainstreamed, and finally used for Euro-American nationalist and imperialist ends.[36] The child as the adult Other seems predominately to be associated with the asexual and seemingly genderless child who inhabits a world without racialization and classism.

[34] José Esteban Muñoz, *Cruising Utopia. The Then and There of Queer Futurity* (New York: New York University Press, 2009).

[35] Sarada Balagopalan, "Constructing Indigenous Childhoods: Colonialism, Vocational Education and the Working Child", *Childhood*, Vol. 9, No. 1, 2002, ff. 19–34; Elisabeth Chin, "Ethnically Correct Dolls: Toying with the Race Industry", *American Anthropologist*, Vol. 101, No. 2, 1999, ff. 305–321; *Purchasing Power: Black Kids and American Consumer Culture* (Minneapolis: University of Minnesota Press, 2001); Hoffman, "Like Beasts in the Bush"; Knezevic, *Child (Bio)Welfare and Beyond*; Lee, *Childhood and Society*; Conrad John Masabo, "Should Children Work? Dilemmas of Children's Educational Rights in the Global South", *Southern African Journal of Policy and Development*, Vol. 3, No. 1, 2016, Article 5; Muñoz, *Cruising Utopia*; Oishik Sircar & Debolina Dutta, "Beyond Compassion: Children of Sex Workers in Kolkata's Sonagachi", *Childhood*, Vol. 18, No. 3, 2011, ff. 333–349.

[36] Jasbir K. Puar, *Terrorist assemblages. Homonationalism in queer times* (Durham: Duke University Press, 2007); Leticia Sabsay, "The Emergence of the Other Sexual Citizen: Orientalism and the Modernisation of Sexuality", *Citizenship Studies*, Vol. 16, No. 5–6, 2012, ff. 605–623, f. 605.

The Child as the Other or the Othered Childhoods? Bridging Postcolonial Feminism and Critical Childhood Studies

In this chapter, I argue that the conceptual tools postcolonial theory and theory of intersectionality have to offer to childhoods are invaluable, although, as some commentators claim, postcolonial readings of childhoods are downplayed compared to other schools of thought.[37] Axes of power such as race, migration status and gender in intersection with age emphasize childhoods, not as singular but plural.[38] From such a perspective, childhoods are a great concern for feminist scholarship, and it is equally important to stress that postcolonial feminism is fruitful for studies of childhoods.

The idea of the colonial Other has not only had negative effects on the lives of colonized adults and adults facing the effects of colonial legacies but also on children.[39] Some scholars actually highlight that the conceptualization of the Other, while predominantly being linked to the Oriental, the Barbarian, and the Foreign (adult) in postcolonial school of thought, fails to be adequately addressed without an analysis of how children and childhoods figure in processes of othering.[40] To understand the child from a postcolonial feminist perspective, it is necessary to consider the interplay between the naturalization of colonialism, the nuclear family, and patriarchy. They all imply exclusions and

[37] Viruru, Radhika, "The impact of postcolonial theory on early childhood education." *Journal of Education*, Vol. 35, 2005, ff. 7–29.

[38] Abebe & Ofosu-Kusi, "Beyond Pluralizing African Childhoods"; Hoffman, "Like Beasts in the Bush"; Knezevic, *Child (Bio)Welfare and Beyond*; Olga Nieuwenhuys, "Theorizing Childhood(s): Why We Need Postcolonial Perspectives", *Childhood*, Vol. 20, No. 1, 2013, ff. 3–8; Prout & James "A New Paradigm for the Sociology of Childhood?"; Qvortrup, Corsaro & Honig, "Why Social Studies of Childhood?; Sircar & Dutta, "Beyond Compassion"; Szulc & Cohn, "Anthropology and Childhood in South America"; Viruru, "The impact of postcolonial theory on early childhood education".

[39] Balagopalan, "Constructing Indigenous Childhoods"; Liz Conor, "The 'Piccaninny': Racialized Childhood, Disinheritance, Acquisition and Child Beauty", *Postcolonial Studies*, Vol. 15, No. 1, 2012, ff. 45–68; Hoffman, "Like Beasts in the Bush"; Nieuwenhuys, "Theorizing Childhood(s)"; Rollo, "The Color of Childhood".

[40] McClintock, *Imperial Leather*; Rollo, "The Color of Childhood".

oppositional logics, and they all have created and made hierarchies seem natural.[41] Children have been central in this process of the naturalization of power. As Anne McClintock points out, the White 'family man' occupied the dominant image of the 'civilized' colonizer to whom women, children, and the colonized were inferior. The colonial hierarchy is clearly heteronormative and patriarchal. Power is exercised over the unruly and immature sub-human children and adults whose path toward maturity and progress were to be accomplished only by guidance by "superior White male Europeans".[42]

McClintock's work, as well as the work by Ashis Nandy, suggests parallels between the child and the savage. Nandy distinguishes between the 'childlike Indian' and the 'childish Indian'. While the former was reformed, the latter was repressed. The 'corrigible' but childlike, loyal, masculine, innocent and ignorant, yet willing to learn, differed from the childish, who instead was unable to learn, was savage, disloyal, ignorant and unpredictably violent – the incorrigible.[43] Both the childlike and the childish were ascribed to the colonized, albeit in different geopolitical contexts and in relation to the level of a perceived threat of the people's resistance toward colonial 'civilizing' missions.

This helps to understand complex processes of infantilization of the colonized and othered adults. At the center of this polemic is an image of the European bourgeois boy-child while the savage stands for the childlike or childish unaccomplished adult. Unlike the developing white boy, the savage is fixed in terms of underdevelopment and permanent childishness. In addition, the white male child is closer to civilization than the white female child.[44] And yet, nowhere in the polemic that shaped and still shapes the modern notion of childhood as a stage of

[41] Braidotti, "Dympna and the Figuration of the Woman Warrior"; Lugones, "Heterosexualism and the Colonial/Modern Gender System"; McClintock, *Imperial Leather*.

[42] Lugones, "Heterosexualism and the Colonial/Modern Gender System"; McClintock, *Imperial Leather*; Rollo, "The Color of Childhood".

[43] Nandy, *The Intimate Enemy*, f. 16.

[44] Castañeda, *Figurations*; McClintock, *Imperial Leather*; Rollo, "The Color of Childhood"; Nandy, *The Intimate Enemy*.

development, irrationality, unruly passions, and problematic resistance is the *child of the colonial Other* – the Other of childhood *per se* – represented. In this context, the child as the Other is not merely othered but can be viewed as a subaltern, the figure lacking a figuration altogether.[45] Sandrina de Finney makes a similar remark concerning an absent indigenous analysis in girlhood studies.[46] Similarly, Sarada Balagopalan notes how 'indigenous' childhoods, which are often displayed as 'discrete categories', are rendered invisible in a univocal and hegemonic ideal of a western model of childhood.[47] (Girl)children who do not display or are assumed as unable to display the 'right' sense of agency and knowledge – which in western societies are those children who are in schools and part of peer cultures – become the very pre-modern childhoods. Such differentiations of childhoods, according to Balagopalan,

> continues to serve the project of modernity as constructed in the European imaginary, that we will be able to invoke both the premodern and the history of the modern in the Third World, to critique the global circulation of a modern western childhood as the hegemonic ideal.[48]

The *childhood Other*, then, is not to be conflated with a common conceptualization of the child as the (adult) Other. The childhood Other is not adulthood but marginalized, othered childhoods themselves that remain absent in critical discussions about the child as the adult Other or infantilized adults.

Only in the encounter between postcolonial feminist scholarship and critical childhood studies is such an analysis of otherness possible. In this vein, using the Other to say something

---

[45] For example, see Spivak, "Can the Subaltern Speak?".

[46] de Finney, "Under the Shadow of Empire".

[47] Balagopalan, "Constructing Indigenous Childhoods"; See also Sandrina de Finney, "Under the Shadow of Empire: Indigenous Girls' Presencing as Decolonizing Force", in Claudia Mitchell & Carrie Rentschler (Eds.), *Girlhood and the Politics of Place* (New York & Oxford: Berghahn Books, 2016), ff. 19–37.

[48] Balagopalan, "Constructing Indigenous Childhoods", ff. 32–33.

about the child as a figuration or actual children and childhoods becomes, to paraphrase Keith Pringle, both an *epistemological advantage* and an *epistemological danger*.[49] The epistemological advantage, as discussed above, lies in highlighting children as a socially disadvantaged group in adult-centric societies and knowledge production, including critical schools of thought.[50] Feminist and postcolonial school of thought reminds us of the myriad of epistemological disadvantages resulting from simplistic conceptualizations of power. Besides including only some childhoods, non-normative childhoods are thought of in rather static ways and without acknowledging how colonialism and modernity have transformative power over them too.[51]

Discussion: Analogy in Dissonance?

This chapter has discussed some epistemological advantages and dangers of using the notion of Otherness in relation to the child as a figure (the child Other) and childhoods that are excluded from dominant ideas about childhood (childhood Other). I have argued that the child, as the Other, occupies a central place in some postcolonial and critical analyses. Yet, even with this centrality of the child in analyses of power, the generic conceptualization of children it reproduces renders many relations of power invisible. By deconstructing the colonial imaginary, not only is White supremacy disturbed as natural, but also the subordinate position of children. However, elaborations on the latter leave many chapters yet to be written. As discussed, critical childhood studies have challenged the idea of childhoods representing the ontological origin of the adult human or the path toward civilization and maturity. Yet, childhoods still figure as theoretical resources in philosophical, feminist and

---

[49] Keith Pringle, "Epilogue: On Developing Empowering Child Welfare Systems and the Welfare Research Needed to Create them" in Hannele Forsberg & Teppo Kröger (Eds.), *Social Work and Child Welfare Politics: Through Nordic Lenses.* (Bristol: The Policy Press, 2011).

[50] Castañeda, "The Child as a Feminist Figuration"; *Figurations*; Rollo, "The Color of Childhood".

[51] Balagopalan, "Constructing Indigenous Childhoods".

poststructuralist conceptualizations of the pre-subjectal, the alternative and modern power itself.[52] Moreover, using words such as 'infantilized', 'childish', or 'childlike' imply epistemological dangers. These words and the ways in which they are used not only describe processes of othering and degradation of adults but also of anything related to children and childhoods. Consequently, the childlike continues to be viewed as something less vis-à-vis the adultlike. As pointed out by Toby Rollo, to address childhoods without reproducing the idea of children as inferior, postcolonial feminists are forced to abandon the modernist project of imagining equality for whatever and whoever fulfils the status of the rational, mature adult *Human*.[53] Thus, while contesting adult power, the child as the Other still portrays a generic and decontextualized childhood. The issue of why axes of power other than age become invisible even in many feminist analyses, I argue, has to do just as much with conceptualizations of children and childhoods as much as it does with feminism and, to paraphrase Castañeda, the subject of feminism.[54] The child as the Other of feminism gives the impression of feminism as adult-centric but also as white.

In contemporary feminist theory, the analogy of the Other is heavily inspired by postcolonial scholarship and other scholarship of the margin, which have decentered dominant ideas of Woman, and which yet looms largely absent in discussions about childhoods. This may be because critical theory lacks interest and insight into children's lives and the tools for analysis that are not easily applied to child subjects. Thus, it is worth considering how conceptual tools such as gender, sexuality, race and class, which are used to analyze power have historically enabled conceptualizations of certain forms of othering over others. The question is less which analytic tools we use, but rather which associations they evoke or how we use them. The

---

[52] Castañeda, "The Child as a Feminist Figuration"; *Figurations*; Rollo, "The Color of Childhood".

[53] Rollo, "The Color of Childhood".

[54] Castañeda, "The Child as a Feminist Figuration".

notion of the Other seems to bear the tendency of ending up with, to borrow Sara Ahmed's[55] term, 'sticky' biases and categories like those encountered in other intersectional theorizing. Queer theory has made visible stereotypes of othering where 'the homosexual other is White, the racial other is straight'.[56] In a similar manner, I have argued that the racialized Other is assumed to be adult and the child as the adult Other is assumed to be white, middle-class and as feminists and girlhood studies scholars have noted, possibly a boy-child. In this chapter, I have argued that the analogies, both when considered separately and in relation to each other, fail to give justice to othered adults and children alike. Instead, they imply the vanishing of certain subjectivities, paradoxically even in advanced analyses of the Other of the subject. This chapter adds racialized children and their 'disappearance [...] from theoretical and political considerations'.[57] As I have tried to show, childhoods bring new contexts into this picture, opening up for alternative combinations of tools other than age for analyses of power. They also show these tools being unstable, albeit 'sticky'. Axes of power such as gender, sexuality, class and race are heavily interconnected with adult worlds. An epistemological advantage of bridging feminist scholarship with critical childhood studies lies in their possibility to transform these categories to understand what sexuality means in a 5-year-old child's life or what class and livelihood is for a 10-year-old, beyond mere analyses of parents' educational backgrounds and statuses.[58]

Children and Otherness, moreover, are constituted through representations of agency or lack thereof.[59] Children resist not

---

[55] Sara Ahmed, *The Cultural Politics of Emotion* (New York: Routledge, 2004).

[56] Puar, *Terrorist assemblages*, f. 32; see also Sabsay, "The Emergence of the Other Sexual Citizen".

[57] Gurminder K. Bhambra, "Postcolonial and Decolonial Dialogues", *Postcolonial Studies*, Vol. 17, No. 2, 2014, ff. 115–121, f. 119; see also Lugones, "Heterosexualism and the Colonial / Modern Gender System"; Spivak, "Can the Subaltern Speak?".

[58] For example, see Abebe & Ofosu-Kusi, "Beyond Pluralizing African Childhoods"; Angelides, *The Fear of Child Sexuality*.

[59] Angelides, *The Fear of Child Sexuality*; see also McClintock, *Imperial Leather*; Meyer, "The Moral Rhetoric of Childhood"; Rollo, "The Color of Childhood".

only the adult world but also ideas about childhood, peer cultures and gender, sexuality and class stereotypes. In these resistances or the threat of these resistances, othered childhoods become visible. From such a perspective, childhoods should be of great concern for feminist scholarship dedicated to analyses of multiple and intersecting axes of power, including resistance.

Critical childhood studies, girlhood- and boyhood studies have made significant contributions in this regard, including to the world of theories that influence views on children and childhoods.[60] Despite these contributions, developmental psychology still holds a very important place in the theoretical landscape of childhood. Following this, it becomes an epistemological *obligation* to ask how postcolonial feminism can *contribute to* childhoods after having excluded them for decades and how to reclaim childhoods from developmental psychology and life sciences or age-based universalist rights discourses. The disciplinary distinctions produce theoretical divisions between what appears to be the societal world of adults and the psychologized de-politicized child world, even though the concerns they face are the same.[61] From this point of view, epistemological advantages and dangers relate to the location of childhood in certain disciplines and the epistemological limitations of certain knowledge production that continue to naturalize relations of power in childhoods while addressing the same as "inequalities" in adulthoods. The proposed bridging urges a prompt answer as to whether feminism is invested in women – however, multiple and contradictory constructed – or if the subject of inquiry is more acutely related to intersecting power relations. If the latter is the case, how come feminism remains adult centered?

Critical childhood studies and postcolonial feminist studies share the same interdisciplinary faith that requires bridging with

[60] Balagopalan, "Constructing Indigenous Childhoods"; Mitchell & Rentschler (Eds.) *Girlhood and the Politics of Place.*

[61] Burman, *Developments*; *Deconstructing Developmental Psychology*; Firestone, *The Dialectic of Sex*; Knezevic, *Child (Bio)Welfare and Beyond*; Eve Kosofsky Sedgwick, "How to Bring Your Kids up Gay", *Social Text*, Vol. 29, 1991, ff. 18–27; Thorne, "Re-Visioning Women and Social Change".

other schools of thought.[62] Only by bridging critical childhood studies and postcolonial feminism can 'undutiful daughters'[63] become a designation in the full sense of the phrase.

[62] Joanne Faulkner & Magdalena Zolkos, *Critical Childhood Studies, and the Practice of Interdisciplinarity: Disciplining the Child (Children and Youth in Popular Culture)* (Lanham, Boulder & London: Lexington Books, 2016); Viruru, "The impact of post-colonial theory on early childhood education"; Gloria Wekker, "The Arena of Disciplines: Gloria Anzaldúa and Interdisciplinarity" in Rosemarie Buikema & Iris van der Tuin (Eds.), *Doing Gender in Media, Art, and Culture* (London & New York: Routledge, 2009).
[63] Braidotti, "Dympna and the Figuration of the Woman Warrior", f. 244.

Chapter 13
The Emotionalization of Burnout in the Health Care Sector

Ylva Gustafsson

During the last forty years, the healthcare sector has gone through several major changes. An important positive change has been the introduction of patient-centered care. The increasing interest in the patient's perspective was part of a significant societal shift toward acknowledging structural patterns of injustice and oppression in society. However, it was also a specific reaction against the strongly authoritative and cold attitude toward patients, which was still influential among medical professionals in the 1950s. At that time, doctors and nurses were supposed not to get too emotionally involved in their patient's suffering. In the 1970s, this approach was beginning to be questioned. There was widespread public discussion concerning injustice, cruelty, and callousness in health care, and there was a growing awareness of the importance of understanding and respecting the individual patient's perspective and opinions concerning medical treatments. As a result, patient-centered care is today a central feature of nursing ethics.

However, in the 1990s, many countries were struck by a deep economic depression and consequently, there were large-scale cutbacks in staffing numbers. So-called New Public Management was also implemented in the healthcare sector. The main feature of New Public Management was that it adopted perspectives from the private business world and implemented these in the public sector. New Public Management is often described as a rationalization of institutions with cutbacks on staff, tighter working schedules, and stricter control of the production of service. However, New Public Management did not only lead to a rationalization but also a new kind of *emotionalization* of health care. While nurse work had previously primarily been described in ethical terms, nurse work was increasingly described in emotional terms.

Because of the large-scale rationalizations in the healthcare sector, an increasing number of nurses suffer from stress and burnout. Though it is generally acknowledged that structural cutbacks cause these syndromes, burnout is today often described as an emotional reaction. It is also suggested that nurses should be trained in resilience to tackle the increasingly stressful working conditions in the healthcare sector. My aim in this paper is to discuss the meaning of burnout in the healthcare sector and what I will call an emotionalization of both nurse work and burnout.

The chapter proceeds in the following order: I begin by questioning the tendency to describe burnout among nurses as an emotional reaction. I argue that the stress that nurses describe often is ethical. Furthermore, I argue that one can see a tendency to "emotionalize" ethical situations in care work, which reflects the influence of emotional intelligence theory. Furthermore, I argue that the stress nurses experience, specifically in Nordic elderly care, deeply reflects structural changes due to New Public Management. These structural changes have led to a disintegration of the whole meaning of patient-centered care. The experience of stress and burnout among workers in Nordic elderly care is then not a mere emotional reaction but ought to be understood as an experience of the disintegration of ethical space in their work.

In the second part of the paper, I argue that one can see a gendered pattern in how nurses' stress and burnout are described as emotional. I compare how nurses working in the healthcare sector were affected by New Public Management in the 1990s with Sari Charpentier's[1] (2007) description of how middle-aged women in the banking sector were affected by New Public Management in the 1990s. In both cases, one can see a

---

[1] Sari Charpentier, "Ilska som klimakteriesymtom i arbetslivet" ["Anger as a symptom of menopause in working life"] in *Kvinnor, kropp och hälsa,* Elina Oinas and Jutta Ahlbeck-Rehn (Eds.) (Lund: Studentlitteratur, 2007).

tendency to emotionalize women's experiences of stress and exhaustion.

In the last part of the paper, I discuss Elianne Riska's[2] research on the historical development of stress research on male business executives. Riska suggests that one can today see a shift toward a neoliberal conception of "hardiness" that normalizes a certain male type that should be able to handle stress. I compare this normalizing of a male ability to cope with stress with the claim that nurses should be trained to be resilient and to be able to handle stress. I argue that one can see a gender and class pattern in how the ability to handle stress is described. The neoliberal concepts of hardiness and stress uphold a gendered division of labor where women are expected to endure stress in working conditions that lead neither to a career nor a well-paid job, while middle-class men are expected to endure stress in order to achieve both a career and a secure income.

Burnout – An Occupational Problem or an Emotional Reaction?

The concept of burnout was originally coined by Christina Maslach in the 1980s. According to Maslach, people-work with customers, clients, and patients puts workers at greater risk of burnout. Maslach interviewed people working in various customer or patient occupations. Based on these interviews, Maslach wrote the book *Burnout, the Cost of Caring.*[3] She describes how people working in the social sector tend to suffer from a certain kind of exhaustion caused by too much intensive work with customers, clients, and patients. Maslach argues that a major reason people become burned out is due to problematic structural patterns at work, such as a too high workload and reductions in staff numbers. Maslach also defined burnout as consisting of three syndromes: emotional exhaustion, depersonalization and de-professionalization. These syndromes are,

[2] Elianne Riska, "From Type A man to the hardy man: masculinity and health", in *Sociology of Health and Illness*, Vol. 24, No. 3, 2002, pp. 347–358.

[3] Christina Maslach, *Burnout, The Cost of Caring* (Los Altos: Malor, 1982).

according to Maslach, not expressive of personality traits but are caused by structural problems at work. In a later book, Maslach and Michael P. Leiter[4] conclude: "Burnout does not result from a genetic predisposition to grumpiness, a depressive personality, or general weakness. It is not caused by a failure of character or a lack of ambition. It is not a personality defect or a clinical syndrome. It is an occupational problem."[5]

However, even though Maslach emphasized structural problems at work as the major causes for burnout, burnout is today often described as an emotional problem expressive of personal weakness indicating a lack of emotional intelligence. For instance, Dorota Daniela Szczygiel and Moïra Mikolajczak[6] write: "Importantly, our findings show that NE [negative emotions] do not always lead to burnout, but that they particularly do for nurses who lack EI [Emotional Intelligence]."[7] According to Szczygiel and Mikolajczak, burnout in health care is caused by "negative emotions", "emotional exhaustion", and "emotional dissonance". Furthermore, they write: "…experiencing NE enhances one's level of physiological and psychological arousal, which, if long-drawn, can have a deleterious effect on affective and cognitive functioning. […]"[8] As a solution to this problem, Szczygiel and Mikolajczak argue that nurses should become more resilient and be trained in emotional intelligence.

This description may sound fine. One may assume that nurses who feel "negative emotions" or "emotional exhaustion" may also become burnout. However, if one looks at how nurses themselves describe situations that are difficult to bear, it is not

---

[4] Christina Maslach and Michael P. Leiter, The Truth about Burnout: How organizations cause personal stress and what to do about it (San Francisco: Jossey Bass. 1997).

[5] Maslach and Leiter, *The Truth about Burnout*, p. 34

[6] Dorota Daniela Szczygiel and Moïra Mikolajczak, "Emotional intelligence buffers the effects of negative emotions on job burnout in nursing" in *Frontiers in Psychology*, 9, Article 2649, 2018, pp. 1–10.

[7] Szczygiel and Mikolajczak, "Emotional intelligence buffers the effects of negative emotions on job burnout in nursing", p. 6.

[8] Szczygiel and Mikolajczak, "Emotional intelligence buffers the effects of negative emotions on job burnout in nursing", p. 6.

clear that they can be defined generally as experiences of "negative emotions" or "emotional exhaustion". For example, consider the following description by Ericson-Lidman et al.,[9] where a nurse working in municipal elderly care tells of situations that she finds especially difficult to bear.

> It is about pain relief at the end of life//I failed to persuade the doctor to give the large amounts of pain relief that the resident needed// It is our job. At the end of life, they should not have to sit in bed and scream out of pain, fear, and anxiety. We are obliged to provide relief. It is the law.[10]

In the case above, the nurse describes how a dying patient was mistreated by not being administered enough pain relief. This was a situation the nurse experienced as very difficult. From the perspective of EI, this might be defined as a "negative emotion" that eventually causes "emotional exhaustion". However, I think it would be problematic to describe this case in emotional terms. The nurse is not talking about emotions but describing a situation of *injustice* in health care. By talking about "negative emotions" or "emotional exhaustion", the ethical criticism in the nurse's words is ignored.

One thing I am trying to suggest so far is that there is a tendency to *emotionalize* ethical situations in nurse work. This tendency does not originate from nurses' own descriptions but from how researchers on emotional intelligence tend to describe nurse work. This tendency also obscures the essentially ethical meaning of care work, turning it into any kind of customer work. Instead of assuming that burnout among nurses essentially is an emotional problem, it would be important to acknowledge that nurses describe various *ethical* situations as exhaust-

---

[9] Eva Ericson-Lidman, Astrid Nordberg, Birgitta Persson, Gunilla Strandberg, "Healthcare personnel's experiences of situations in municipal elderly care that generate troubled conscience", in *Scandinavian Journal of Caring Science,* June; 27(2), 2013, pp. 215–23.

[10] Ericson-Lidman et al., "Healthcare personnel's experiences of situations in municipal elderly care that generate troubled conscience", p. 220.

ing. These kinds of experiences seem to be on the increase. Ann-Louise Glasberg writes about an increasing number of cases of what she calls "stress of conscience" among nurses, explaining that, due to New Public Management, this has to do with a shift in responsibility: "People are burdened by having to make *difficult prioritizations*, sometimes in conflict with integrated principles.[11] The responsibility for prioritization has been transferred from the organizational level onto the individual staff member."[12] My suggestion so far is that when Szczygiel and Mikolajczak tend to claim that burnout is centrally an *emotional* problem, they tend to disregard that what nurses often describe as exhausting are *ethical* experiences. By defining nurses' responses as emotional, they are assumed to be irrational over-reactions rather than critical ethical appraisals. The concept of stress of conscience differs from the concept of emotional exhaustion in that the ethical aspect of the experience is acknowledged.

Emotional Dissonance or Emotional Labor?

Another emotional syndrome that, according to researchers on emotional intelligence, causes burnout among nurses is that nurses are often forced to hide their true feelings from patients and colleagues. Nurses are then often forced to be kind and calm in situations where they might be upset, feel grief or anger etc. These kinds of situations are described as causing "emotional dissonance". Szczygiel and Mikolajczak write:

> [...] experiencing NE (negative emotions) creates a specific burden upon nurses who, despite their true feelings, must maintain professional and supportive demeanours. [...] Thus, in many job situations nurses must conceal their true emotional reactions and express emotions that they do not feel.

[11] Ann-Louise Glasberg, *Stress of Conscience and Burnout in Healthcare* (Umeå: Umeå University, 2007.)

[12] Glasberg, Stress of Conscience and Burnout in Healthcare, p. 12.

> Which leads to emotional dissonance and feelings of inauthenticity [...][13]

Szczygiel and Mikolajczak suggest that the problem of emotional dissonance is similar to what Arlie Russell Hochschild, in her book *The Managed Heart,*[14] calls *emotional labour.*[15] Hochschild interviewed flight attendants who described how they constantly had to keep a polite and kind appearance even though the mainly male customers were often rude and drunk. Hochschild describes how the demand for a certain kind of emotional behavior for flight attendants creates a system where people must accept being treated in unfair and suppressive ways. These repertoire of emotions upon which flight attendants must draw are classical "female" emotions such as kindness, warmth, empathy, and tolerance. Classically "male" emotions such as anger, courage or pride are not allowed. Emotional labor expresses a standardizing of classical female behavior at work. An emotional behavior that implies a constant acceptance of unequal and suppressive relationships prevails. This demand for a certain kind of emotional appearance is also often an integral part of low-status jobs, jobs that may be part-time and that are often poorly paid, i.e., in dominantly female working sectors.

Even though the concepts of emotional dissonance and emotional labor may seem similar, there are, I think, important differences between them. When Hochschild talks about emotional labor, her point is not to describe an inner psychological conflict where flight attendants are not able to express their innermost feelings to customers or passengers. Instead, she describes how the demand for a certain emotional appearance of constant politeness simultaneously means that flight attendants must accept demeaning and sexist working conditions. According to Hochschild, this is a gendered problem. When

---

[13] Szczygiel and Mikolajczak, "Emotional intelligence buffers the effects of negative emotions on job burnout in nursing", p. 6.

[14] Arlie Russell Hochschild, *The Managed Heart, Commercialization of Human Feeling* (California: University of California Press, 1985).

[15] Arlie Russell Hochschild, *The Managed Heart.*

researchers on emotional intelligence suggest that Hochschild's concept of emotional labor is similar to the concept of emotional dissonance, they misunderstand Hochschild's point. Hochschild is not arguing that flight attendants ought or want to be able to express their innermost feelings all the time. Rather, her point is that there is a systemic requirement for the use of certain emotional behavior that is integral to patterns of gender discrimination and injustice at work. The EI researchers use Hochschild's concept in a way that does not acknowledge sexism or oppression at work. Neither does their concept of emotional dissonance acknowledge how the experience of emotional labor may be an experience of injustice towards patients. Sharon Bolton[16] quotes a nurse who describes the situation in the following way:

> On fraught days when the ward or clinic is really busy and we get the 'complainers' going at it hammer and tongs I walk around with this stupid grin plastered on my face. This is what we have to do now, smile at customers and try not to let them go home unsatisfied. Well, if I was them I'd be unsatisfied. They are getting less than they used to. They used to get my time and attention. Even if we were a bit stern with the 'complainers' at least they knew where they stood and were made to understand that health service can only do so much. But now? We go around smiling at them like everything is alright when it isn't. And what is that smile worth? Nothing. I'm seething inside and can't wait to finish my shift.[17]

What the nurses are critical of here is *not* the need for care and attention toward patients. Neither are they saying that the problem is that they cannot reveal their negative emotions to the patients. Nor, for that matter, are they critical of the need to behave kindly and politely toward patients. Rather, they are criticizing a conception of patient-centered care that is being

---

[16] Sharon Bolton, "Changing faces: nurses as emotional jugglers", in *Sociology of Health and Illness,* Vol. 23, No. 1, 2001, pp. 85–100.

[17] Bolton, "Changing faces: nurses as emotional jugglers", p. 94.

hollowed out, where there is an increasing demand for *superficial* politeness, with less time to really talk with, listen to and care for patients.

Bolton's description reveals how there has been a systematic reduction of the meaning of patient-centered care since the 1990s, with less time to seriously attend to patients while a surface impression of good care is still being kept up. The problem that the nurses describe is not that they experience emotional dissonance. Rather they describe how they must be dishonest toward the patients about the bad quality of the care. Again, this is *not* essentially a personal emotional problem but an *ethical* problem reflecting how the fragmentation of work leads to a loss of space for honesty.

The Corrosion of Elderly Care

In his book *The Corrosion of Character*,[18] Richard Sennett describes how working life has changed during the late 20th century because of the tightening of neoliberalism's grip. According to Sennett, one great change concerns the meaning of time and an increasingly "flexible" working life. Today's working life has become more "flexible", meaning that people often are employed on short-term contracts and are also expected to be open to many job changes throughout their lives. However, according to Sennett, this increasingly flexible working life also profoundly affects who we are: "Perhaps the most confusing aspect of flexibility is its impact on personal character".[19] According to Sennett, character entails a capacity to see life, including work and personal relationships, as long-term commitments. The concept of character is thereby connected with trust and reliability. I think one can see a fragmentation of trust and reliability in the nurses' description in the quote from Bolton above. With today's working life emphasizing adaptability to a fast pace and constant change, there is no room for long-term commitments

---

[18] Richard Sennett, The Corrosion of Character, the Personal Consequences of Work in the New Capitalism (New York: W. W. Norton & Company, 1998.)
[19] Sennett, The Corrosion of Character, p. 10.

and trustful relationships. In this sense, the fragmentation of time in today's working life leads to a fragmentation character.

Sennett further argues that the concept of character gains its meaning through certain kinds of concrete patterns of living where time is itself narratively significant. When working life is cut up into pieces, our life narratives become fragmented. "The conditions of time in the new capitalism have created a conflict between character and experience, the experience of disjointed time threatening the ability of people to form their characters into sustained narratives."[20] Sennett describes this fragmentation of narrative as mainly affecting an individual's conception of life. However, I think a fragmentation of narrative also can be seen on an interpersonal level in elderly care provisions in the Nordic countries. A big change here is that the time to work with individual patients has been cut up into tiny parcels. These structural changes in the healthcare sector have been studied by Marta Szebehely,[21] professor in social work at Stockholm university, with specific focus on elderly care in the Nordic countries. She describes how work in elderly care has changed with respect to time. The change has not only to do with large-scale reductions of staff numbers, but also with the fragmentation of working time. The structure of care has changed so that care work has been cut up into small pockets of time. This means that care workers have to take care of more elderly persons per day, meaning they have less time for each visit. Szebehely describes this as "an assembly line mentality" influenced by work at hospitals that has now been introduced into elderly care. While care workers in what Szebehely calls the 'traditional home care district' cared for three elderly people per day, care workers at the more modern 'service house' cared for nine each day. While care workers in the traditional district had about 1.37 hours per patient, the care workers in the 'service house' generally had six

---

[20] Sennett, The Corrosion of Character, p. 31.

[21] Marta Szebehely, "Vårdbiträdets vardags vid traditionell hemtjänst och vid service-hus", in Rosmari Eliasson (Ed.), *Egenheter och allmänheter, en antologi om omsorg och omsorgens villkor* (Lund: Studentlitteratur, 1992.)

minutes per elderly client. This fragmentation in working time per client affects both the practical work as well as the relationship between the care worker and the elderly client. In a Finnish report on elderly care by Teppo Kröger et al.,[22] the authors note that between 2005 and 2015, the number of home care workers who go to the shop for their clients decreased from 20% to 4%, while the number of home care workers who cook food for their clients has decreased from 17% to 12%. What is more, the number of home care workers having time to drink a cup of coffee with their elderly clients has decreased from 25% in 2005 to 5% in 2015. That is, when time has been cut up into tiny parcels, there is no more time to do things in a way that creates room for social ways of being together. There is a big difference between cooking food for a person and bringing them a ready-made meal. When you cook food, there is room for talking with the client about daily matters. Likewise, the fact that there is no time to drink coffee with their elderly clients means less room for having a conversation with them. This is a fragmentation of narrative time in an interpersonal sense, in that there is no time to create personal bonds between client and care worker.

Some of the erosion of the caring profession also shows in the introduction of new forms of control. Today, home care workers are obliged to register the times of visits on their mobile phones once they have made their house call. Here one could assume that the increased control is a way of protecting the client's rights. However, strict control seems to be more about cost savings than safeguarding the rights of the client. As the Norwegian researcher Mia Vabö points out, this system results in the care worker not being able to stay and chat for a few minutes at the door with the elderly when leaving.[23] An important gesture of ordinary respect and concern is thus undermined. At the same time, as control is increasing, the care workers say they have

---

[22] Teppo Kröger, Lina van Aerschot, Jiby Mathew Puthemparambil, *Hoivatyö muutoksessa, Suomalainen vanhustyö pohjoismaisessa vertailussa* (Jyväskylän Yliopisto, YFI julkaisuja 6, 2018.)

[23] Mia Vabø. "Mellan traditioner och trender", in Marta Szebehely (Ed.), *Hemhjälp i Norden -illustrationer och reflektioner* (Lund: Studentlitteratur, 2003).

fewer possibilities for contact and communication with colleagues and foremen.

It is evident that homecare workers have ever diminishing time for social support and interpersonal relationships with the elderly. These changes in working time and increased control can be described, in Sennett's terms, as a corrosion of character, consisting of a loss of time for personal contact with the patients and a loss of narrative space. From the description above, one can also see that it is not "too much emotion" or too close contact with suffering patients that is the main problem here. The problem is rather that, there is no room left for any kind of personal relationship with clients in elderly care, nor is there any room left for treating elderly clients with respect and dignity.

De-professionalization of Women's Labor and Emotionalization of Women's Tiredness

In her article "Ilska som klimakteriesymtom i arbetslivet"[24] ["Anger as a symptom of menopause in working life"] Sari Charpentier discusses how middle-aged women working in the Finnish bank sector in the 1990s were affected by substantial cutbacks and structural changes. According to Charpentier, these women were subjected to increased pressure, stress, and insecure working conditions. While the women working in the banking sector before the 1990s had stable working conditions, many now had been placed on one-year contracts that were up for periodic renewal. This meant that the workers always felt pressured to work as effectively as possible. It also became increasingly difficult for the women to advance in their careers, with many experiencing a de-professionalization of their jobs, by having to work with tasks that were below their education. Charpentier notes that while also men working in the banking sector were placed under more insecure conditions, they still often tended to get an opportunity to advance in their careers. In this sense, there was a difference between how increased insecurity affected men and women.

---

[24] Charpentier, "Ilska som klimakteriesymtom i arbetslivet".

Despite women's working conditions becoming less secure, with a concomitant de-professionalization of their jobs, women's experiences of being tired and angry were explained away as emotional reactions related to the menopause. According to Charpentier, explaining tiredness as emotional and as having to do with the women's ageing and menopause individualized their experiences and ignored the fact that their working conditions had changed.

One can see a similarity between Charpentier's description of how women in the banking sector were described as emotional and how nurses who become tired at work are described as emotional. When women working in the banking sector became tired and angry because of increasingly insecure and stressful working conditions, their tiredness and anger were attributed to the onset of menopause. Somewhat similarly, when nurses are tired and angry because of significant cutbacks in staffing and due to a fragmentation in the available time to care for patients, these responses are defined as "emotional exhaustion", "negative emotions", or "emotional dissonance". Both in Charpentier's description of the banking sector and today's nurse work, one can also see a de-professionalization of their work. Charpentier describes a pattern of de-professionalization in the banking sector where the middle-aged women were put to work with fewer qualifying tasks than before. Similarly, nurses working in the elderly care in Finland describe how they now must work with tasks that are below their professional education. Since basic staffing has been reduced to a minimum at elderly care facilities, nurses now take care of cleaning, cooking, and laundry alongside caring for the elderly. A systematic degradation of the caring profession is ongoing. In both cases, one can see a pattern where tiredness and stress are defined as emotional reactions and thus as mere personal problems. Structural changes in workplaces are left unacknowledged.

Resilience and the Emotional Blurring
of the Ethical Meaning of Care Work

At the beginning of this paper, I noted that researchers on emotional intelligence, such as Szczygiel and Moïra Mikolajczak, argue that nurses ought to be trained in emotional intelligence in order to become more resilient and cope better with stress. I have also suggested that there is a tendency to emotionalize the meaning of patient-centered care and to reduce and ignore the ethical meaning of nurse work. Talk about the need for resilience is part of this tendency to emotionalize ethical problems at work. For instance, one of the major figures in Emotional Intelligence research, Peter Salovey, writes:

> What distinguishes the resilient person from the person who seldom copes effectively? The answer, we believe, has to do with emotional competencies – individuals differ in how well they perceive, express, understand, and manage emotional phenomena. These emotional competencies are components of a broader construct we have termed *emotional intelligence.* [...] emotional intelligence influences responses to emotional arousal and, as a result, plays a significant role in the coping process.[25]

Coping or being resilient is, according to Salovey, a matter of being able to handle one's own or other people's emotions. Also, consider the following description by Mary Harper and Jon Schenk[26]:

> Given the overall positive correlations established between EI and performance in nurses, knowledge of the EI of successful staff nurses may have widespread potential. First of all, establishing an EI profile of successful staff nurses provides a

---

[25] Peter Salovey, Brian T. Bedell, Jerusha B. Detweiler, John D. Mayer (1999). "Coping intelligently, emotional intelligence and the coping process", in *Coping, the psychology of what works* (New York: Oxford University Press, 1999.) p. 141.

[26] Mary G. Harper and Jan Jones Schenk (2012). "The Emotional Intelligence Profile of Successful Staff Nurses" in *The Journal of Continuing Education in Nursing,* Aug 43 (8), 2012, p. 354–362.

descriptive profile that may support the creation of a predictive model of characteristics that are essential for success in nursing practice. This EI profile may form an organizing framework for employment selection and professional development throughout a nurse's career. In addition to employee selection, an EI profile of successful staff nurses may provide a basis for comparison that can be useful for nursing school selection.[27]

The above descriptions by Salovey and by Harper et al. may sound reasonable. Of course, one may assume it would be good if staff nurses were resilient and emotionally intelligent. But what does this mean? The problem is that by suggesting that nurses need to be emotionally intelligent and resilient, the systematic dismantling of the healthcare sector, which has been going on since the 1990s, is ignored. Ignored is also how the dismantling of the healthcare sector has seriously affected the meaning and possibilities of providing good care. When Harper et al. suggest that staff nurses should be trained in emotional intelligence and resilience in order to handle the increasing exhaustion and burnout among staff, they ignore that staff's experiences of exhaustion reflect serious ethical reactions such as, for instance, having to mistreat patients because of cutbacks in staffing. Instead, these experiences are seen as "emotional".

The Hardy Man and the Resilient Nurse

However, the problem is not only that the concept of resilience blurs an essentially ethical meaning of care work. There is also a problematic gendered dimension in the meaning of resilience. In her paper "From Type A man to the hardy man: masculinity and health,"[28] Elianne Riska discusses research on stress among middle-class male executives, from the 1950s up to the 1990s. According to Riska, during the 1950s, there existed a description of a certain type of stressed middle-class man working in the

---

[27] Harper et al., "The Emotional Intelligence Profile of Successful Staff Nurses", p. 355.
[28] Riska, "From Type A man to the hardy man: masculinity and health".

business sector described as the *type A man.* While the *type A man* was described as someone constantly working, they were also prone to having serious heart conditions. *The type A man* was considered as having a seriously problematic personality, running the risk of a premature death.

However, in the 1970s, a new, more positive description of the middle-class business executive appeared, namely *the hardy man,* a concept coined by Suzanne Kobasa[29] in 1979. Riska writes:

> A new generation of middle-class men can look forward to a new relation between their social position and health: men can be real men, succeed and still be healthy. In contrast to Type A man, who was driven by a seemingly irrational passion to reach extrinsic goals and rewards, the hardy man is constructed as one who is driven by intrinsic motivation.[30]

According to Kobasa, hardiness reflected a new healthy male personality trait that could endure stress better than before and that differed from the Type A man who tended to become ill from stress. Riska quotes Kobasa: "persons who experience high degrees of stress without falling ill have a personality structure differentiating them from persons who become sick under stress."[31]

However, Riska questions this rosy picture of the new hardy man. She points out that the fact that heart attacks are currently not as common among men than in the 1950s is on account of their healthier lifestyles. Middle-class men are today much more aware of the importance of eating well and exercising than middle-class men were in the 1950s, with the consequence that today's business executives do not die as much of heart attacks when compared to the 1950s. Furthermore, Riska argues that the concept of the hardy man normalizes a modern male ideal

---

[29] Suzanne Kobasa, "Stressful life events, personality, and health: an inquiry into hardiness", *Journal of Personality and social Psychology*, 37, 1979, pp. 1–11.

[30] Riska, "From Type A man to the hardy man: masculinity and health", p. 350.

[31] Kobasa, "Stressful life events, personality, and health: an inquiry into hardiness", p. 3.

type of neoliberal manhood where it is expected that men should see the constant pressure at work as a positive challenge and as a possible career move while they should also exercise and think about their health. Riska writes:

> The constitution of hardiness not only demedicalizes male behaviour but, more importantly, legitimizes traditional masculinity. Men can now have a comfortable sense of mastery of their stress level, or may reason that stress might even be good for them. Yet what the new construct of hardiness also did was to confirm that hard work, competitiveness, and self-control were core values of heterosexual masculinity. [...] The concept of hardiness diffuses the social character of masculinity: masculine behaviour is captured as an individual characteristic and personality disposition rather than as an institution and a set of structures that privilege a certain type of white middle-class male behaviour.[32]

There are similarities between the research on hardiness and the research on emotional intelligence. Both research fields originally focused on a dominantly male, middle-class working sector. In a similar way, just as hardiness was described as defining especially modern male business executives and leading to a good career and healthy life, emotional intelligence was described in positive terms as leading to a good career and a happy life for businessmen. Central figures in the research on emotional intelligence were Daniel Goleman, Peter Salovey and John D. Mayer. Emotional intelligence was claimed to offer a fresh perspective on intelligence that contrasted with classical conceptions, such as IQ. In contrast to IQ, which was considered too rationalistic and racist, emotional intelligence was claimed to offer a more socially aware and democratic perspective on emotions. It was claimed that everyone could learn to be emotionally intelligent. However, even if researchers on emotional intelligence tended to claim that it was a democratic field of research, they primarily focused on business leadership in the private

---

[32] Riska, "From Type A man to the hardy man: masculinity and health", p. 355.

sector. Like hardiness, a central aspect of the definition of emotional intelligence was an emphasis on emotions as a personal strength connected with personal virtues in combination with health and getting rich. Peter Salovey[33] writes: "[…] the appropriate regulation of emotions is an important predictor of good health and a key to investing money wisely."[34]

However, as New Public Management began to affect healthcare in the 1990s, researchers on emotional intelligence shifted their focus from the business world to the public sector, specifically health care. Even though the concept remained the same, researchers shifted tone in how they described the connection between emotional intelligence and personality. The business vocabulary of 'emotions leading to success and wealth', which had been a central part of the theory of emotional intelligence when directed to business leadership, did not fit so well with working life at hospitals. Suggesting that nurses will become rich and healthy if they are emotionally intelligent would not persuade those in the public health sector of the importance of the theory of emotional intelligence. Instead, the most important words connected with emotional intelligence were not "wealth", "success", or "personal health" but "resilience". Thus, one can see a shift in the meaning of emotional intelligence when researchers on emotional intelligence shift their focus from the business world to health care. When emotional intelligence researchers shift their focus to health care, EI is no longer defined as having to do with one's capacity to live an economically secure life or to strive for promotion and eventually become a business leader because such aspects are generally non-existent for women working in the health care sector.

The concept of hardiness and the concepts of emotional intelligence, and resilience normalize a picture of the good worker as someone open for a modern working life that is fast-

---

[33] Peter Salovey, "Applied emotional intelligence: regulating emotions to become healthy, wealthy and wise" in J. Ciarrochi, J. P. Forgas & J. D. Mayer (Eds.), *Emotional intelligence in everyday life* (New York: Psychology Press, 2006.)
[34] Salovey, "Applied emotional intelligence: regulating emotions to become healthy, wealthy and wise", p. 229.

paced and shifting; a working life where one is constantly open for "challenges" at work. That these "challenges" for some mean opportunities for promotion while for others they are a product of continuously poorly paid short-term contracts is not acknowledged. From the 1990s onwards, with neoliberalism increasing its influence over society, these concepts have become increasingly popular. One can see a gender and class pattern in how these concepts are used to describe the personality of the good worker. The hardy man is a middle-class business executive, while the emotionally intelligent, resilient nurse has a low-paid job. The concepts of resilience, emotional intelligence and hardiness normalize a gendered division of labor, according to which women are expected to endure stress and uncertain working conditions that do not lead to a career or a well-paid job, while men are expected to endure stress in order to achieve both a career, a secure job and a good income.

Conclusion

In this chapter, I have critically discussed the tendency to describe burnout and exhaustion among care workers in the healthcare sector as an emotional reaction. One can see such a tendency, especially among researchers on emotional intelligence, where ethical situations in care work are described by emotionalized scientific concepts such as "emotional exhaustion", "negative emotions", and "emotional dissonance". In contrast, I have claimed that the stress and exhaustion nurses describe is often an ethical response. By coining these experiences as emotional, the ethical criticism expressed by the nurses is ignored. Furthermore, by discussing Sennett's notion of corrosion of character and Szebehely's description of the disintegration of time in Nordic elderly care, I have suggested that the stress and burnout among care workers reflect a disintegration of ethical and narrative space in care work.

The emotionalization of stress and burnout in the healthcare sector reflects a broader pattern of gendered fragmentation of work and tendencies to describe women's experiences of stress and exhaustion in emotional terms. This can be seen if one compares how care work in Nordic elderly care has been restructured and fragmented from the 1990s until the present with Charpentier's description of the restructuring and fragmentation of the working conditions for middle-aged women working in the Finnish banking sector in the 1990s. By describing women's experiences of stress as emotional, the structural disintegration, uncertainty and de-professionalization of women's work are ignored.

As Charpentier suggests, even though neoliberal policies have affected both male and female working sectors through increasingly insecure working conditions, one can see differences in what this insecurity means for women and men. Furthermore, stress research individualizes stress differently depending on whether it is directed toward female or male working sectors. As Riska notes, stress research connected with the development of concepts like the *A type man* and the *hardy man* tended to focus on male business leadership, connecting stress with economic stability and positive career development. A similar male focus can be seen in how researchers on emotional intelligence have focused on business leadership. Furthermore, I have suggested that when researchers on EI in the 1990s started to take an interest in the female healthcare sector, the tone in how EI was described shifted. Health and wealth disappeared from the descriptions of EI, and instead, EI became a psychological strength connected with "resilience", implying an acceptance of working conditions that will not provide career opportunities or economic stability. In this sense, the neoliberal concepts of hardiness, emotional intelligence and resilience maintain a gendered division of labor where women are expected to endure stress under insecure working conditions that do not lead to a career or a well-paid job, while male business leaders are expected to endure stress in order to achieve a career and a secure income.[35]

[35] This article is a result of two projects: "Critical perspectives on empathy in medicine: the rise of cognitive science and the loss of narrative medicine" funded by the Kone

foundation, and the project "On justice and the shifting meaning of person-centered care" funded by the Ella and Georg Ehrnrooth foundation. I want to thank the external reviewers for valuable comments. I also want to thank the editors for their helpful comments.

Chapter 14
Emancipatory Engagement with Oppression
– The Perils of Identity in Feminist and Anti-Racist Politics

Oda K. S. Davanger

> You never change anything by fighting the existing.
>
> To change something, build a new model and make the existing obsolete!
>
> – Buckminster Fuller

> Am I that name?
>
> – Denise Riley

bell hooks has written extensively about feminism in the U.S. and its lip service inclusion of black women and non-white women in both classist and racist ways. hooks has also criticized the black power movement for a non-revolutionary vision of emancipation that imitates the power structure of white patriarchy.[1] She articulates the interplay of axes of oppression with her concept *imperialist white supremacist capitalist patriarchy*. Here, axes of oppression follow identity category lines such as gender or race. In this chapter, I will engage with and evaluate arguments for and against basing emancipatory politics on identity qualifiers such as race and gender. I will argue that thinking about oppression as operating along the axes of identity signifiers makes it difficult to overcome racism and sexism – even within emancipatory movements themselves. The difficulty arises when emancipatory movements attempt to change society while tacitly accepting so much of its structure, even as part of its emancipatory endeavor, and by reproducing oppressive

---

[1] bell hooks, *Yearning: Race, Gender, and Cultural Politics* (Boston: South End Press, 1990), pp. 15–16.

mechanisms (sexist anti-racism and racist feminism). Why rely on identity categories for emancipatory politics at all? Can reinforcing the identity given to you in society liberate you from the oppression you experience as a consequence of that identity?

I will provide a reading of bell hooks that both invokes and challenges the axis theory of oppression. I engage hooks post-structurally, where the production of a subject norm necessitates the production of peripheral deviants to uphold it and where language plays a vital role in cognition and, by extension, emancipatory politics. This reading justifies a solidarity that does not base itself on identity signifiers. Next, I respond to objections to my stance against founding a politics of emancipation on identity. Lastly, I look toward a post-structurally inspired *politics of alienated desire* beyond well-established identity-based solidarity. I conclude that to radically dismantle feminist and racist systems of oppression, any emancipatory politics must go beyond mechanisms of resistance that engage with the very conceptual premises that uphold the same systems of oppression they oppose.

Differentiated and Devalued Identities

We tend to think of oppression as restrictive social structures that unjustly inhibit people's freedom.[2] However, we also separate forms of oppression conceptually into different *axes* of oppression, such as sexism, racism, imperialism, capitalism and class struggle, and even ageism, discrimination against disability, sexuality, and so forth. Judith Butler denoted the embarrassing "etc." at the end of the list.[3] But this conceptual separation is helpful to see how oppression takes many forms and affects people differently (see Figure 1).

---

[2] See: Marilyn Frye, "Oppression" in Ann E. Cudd & Robin O. Andreasen (Eds.), *Feminist Theory: A Philosophical Anthology* (Malden: Blackwell Publishing, 2005), pp. 84–90.

[3] Judith Butler, *Gender Trouble* (New York: Routledge, 2007 [1990]), p. 143.

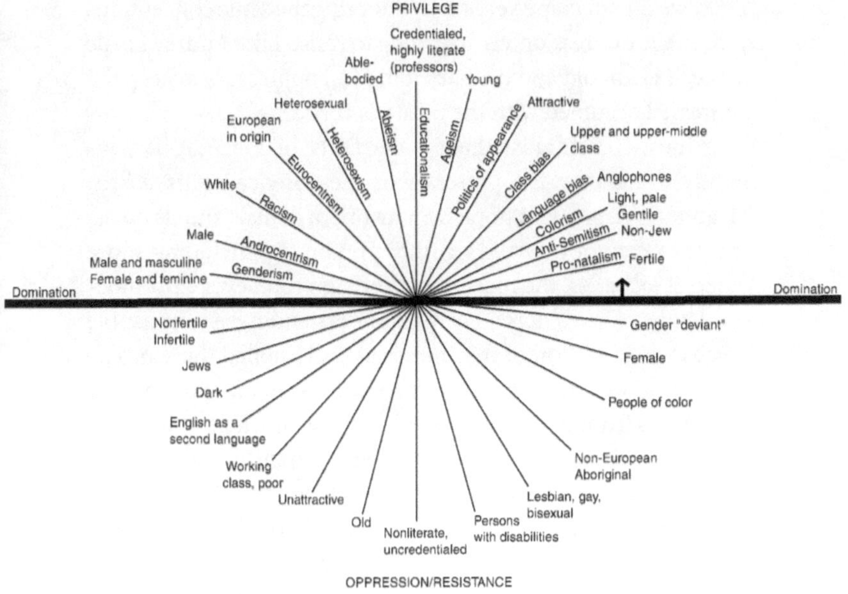

Figure 1: Intersecting Axes of Privilige, Domination, and Oppression.[4]

However, it may also preclude us from seeing the shared origins of oppression. As Butler argues, accepting the premises that have been used to oppress women perpetuates foundational principles of patriarchy:

> If there is a fear that, by no longer being able to take for granted the subject, its gender, its sex, or its materiality, feminism will founder, it might be wise to consider the political consequences of keeping in their place the very premises that have tried to secure our subordination from the start.[5]

---

[4] Kathryn Pauly Morgan, "Describing the Emperor's New Clothes: Three Myths of Educational (In-)Equity" in Ann Diller, et. al. (eds.), The Gender Question in Education: Theory, Pedagogy, And Politics (New York: Routledge; 2018), p. 107.

[5] Judith Butler, "Contingent Foundations" in *Feminist Contentions: A Philosophical Exchange* (New York: Routledge; 1995), p. 54.

Thus, we do not come very far by adopting the same conceptions used in the oppression we are trying to resist. Like Audrey Lorde wrote, it is "an old and primary tool of all oppressors to keep the oppressed occupied with the master's concerns."[6]

In post-structuralist theory, the fixity of meaning is constantly evaded by the presence of the absence of its *others*. Meaning is dependent upon its network of denials and its *others* and thus cannot be fixed or fully present. By including those others it excludes, the meaning of the sign can never exist independently of its *others*.[7] Positive understanding is impossible because the negation of the *other* is always implied therein. The separation of the axes of oppression is made possible by differences from the norm – which is the white male of means – such as woman and non-white. Sabina Lovibond argues that this differentiation is marked in a lower hierarchical relation to sameness and to the male (see Figure 2).[8] Although feminism has long been critical of this devaluation of difference, hooks is not convinced that feminism has managed to overcome this philosophical heritage.[9] Feminism generally opposes the devaluation of feminine difference vis-à-vis the norm. To a lesser degree, it also opposes the devaluation of other forms of identity categories against the norm of the white male or devaluation of difference itself.

---

[6] Audre Lorde, "'The Master's Tools Will Never Dismantle the Master's House'" in Reina Lewis & Sara Mills (Eds.), *Feminist Postcolonial Theory: A Reader* (New York: Routledge, (2003 [1983]), p. 27.

[7] Lena Petrović, "Remembering and Dismembering: Derrida's Reading of Levi-Strauss", *Linguistics and Literature* 3:1 (2004), p. 89.

[8] Sabina Lovibond, "An Ancient Theory of Gender: Plato and the Pythagorean Table" in L. J. Archer, et al. (Eds.) *Women in Ancient Societies* (London: Palgrave Macmillan, 1994), p. 97.

[9] bell hooks, *Feminist Theory, From Margin to Center*, 2nd ed., (London: Pluto Press, 2000 [1984]), p. 33.

Limit (πέρας)	Unlimited (ἄπειρον)
Odd (περιττόν)	Even (ἄρτιον)
Unity (ἕν)	Plurality (πλῆθος)
Right (δεξιόν)	Left (ἀριστερόν)
Male (ἄρρεν)	Female (θῆλυ)
Rest (ἠρεμοῦν)	Motion (κινούμενον)
Straight (εὐθύ)	Crooked (καμπύλον)
Light (φῶς)	Darkness (σκότος)
Good (ἀγαθόν)	Evil (κακόν)
Square (τετράγωνον)	Oblong (ἑτερόμηκες)

Figure 2: Pythagorean Table of Opposites[10]

In my reading of hooks, the conceptual separation into separate axes of oppression is a dangerous master's tool that obscures the interlocking structure of these axes under the "ideology of domination."[11] Each axis of oppression is a devalued difference from the norm, much like in Pythagoras' table of opposites.

One of hooks' main and recurring arguments is that conceptually dividing oppression into axes mistakenly leads to the thought that they can or should be treated separately. She writes, "[…] challenging patriarchy will not bring an end to dominator culture as long as the other interlocking systems remain in place".[12] In my reading of hooks, the metaphysical division of the axes affects how we think of oppression in ways that do not serve the purposes of feminism. For example, although feminism is concerned with sexism as a form of oppression, hooks argues that this understanding of feminism as *primarily* concerned with sexist oppression is ethnocentric. It is ethnocentric because it first and foremost pertains to the experiences of white women,

[10] Aristoteles, *Metaphysics* in Hugh Tredennick (trans.), *Aristotle in 23 Volumes, Vols.17, 18,* (Cambridge, MA: Harvard University Press 1989 [1933]), 1.988a23–27.

[11] bell hooks, *Ain't I a woman, Black Women and Feminism* (London: Pluto Press, 1981), pp. 194–195.

[12] bell hooks, *Writing Beyond Race, Living Theory and Practice* (New York: Routledge, 2013), p. 36.

who can more easily isolate gender as a singular axis of oppression. According to hooks, "ethnocentric white values" have constructed within feminism a "priority of sexism over racism," which does not reflect the reality of lived experience for women suffering from racist and sexist oppression.[13] As such, the language that separates racism from sexism is misleading to most of the women feminism fights for. The uncritical conceptual acceptance of different axes of oppression inhibits an understanding of the overall interlocking oppressive structure, making it more difficult to dismantle, since conception and language precede and inform political and strategic efforts.

Imperialist White Supremacist Capitalist Patriarchy by Divide and Conquer

The 'system of domination' is based on upholding the norm and, by extension, the othering of those who differ from the norm. Therefore, any feminist struggle to eradicate sexism will be limited as long as this basic structure is maintained. Firstly, the norm cannot be dismantled by achieving gender or racial equality alone. Secondly, as long as the ideal of freedom aspired to by feminism is provided by the freedom currently enjoyed by the norm, this freedom will also be built upon the differentiation and devaluation of others, which is inconsistent with feminist values such as 'equality for all'.[14] In this section, I will account for these two aspects in more detail.

For the first point, I want to emphasize hooks' term *imperialist white supremacist capitalist patriarchy* that she coins to describe the 'ideology of domination'. Encompassing multiple axes of oppression in this concept is an attempt to provide "a way to think about the interlocking systems that work together to uphold and maintain cultures of domination".[15] The crux of my argument is the following: Emancipation strategies that conceptually separate the axes will support the status quo of supre-

[13] hooks, *Feminist Theory*, p. 53.
[14] hooks, *Writing Beyond Race*, p. 36.
[15] hooks, *Writing Beyond Race*, p. 4.

macy. These axes of domination – including, but not limited to, imperialism, white supremacy, capitalism, and patriarchy – depend on and sustain one another to uphold the norm. hooks argues that *imperialist white supremacist capitalist patriarchy* benefits from the division of axes of oppression and seeks to obscure the mechanisms of oppression by letting aspects of the system be challenged separately, conceptually and temporally, but never all at once.[16] She writes,

> Since dominator culture relies on interlocking systems [...] to sustain itself, it seeks to cover up the connections between these systems. Or it allows for only one aspect of the system to be challenged at a time: for example, allowing anti-racist critiques while silencing anti-capitalist or anti-sexist voices.[17]

I find it helpful to think of this ideology of domination as a many-legged stool. Imagine a stool with the ability to regrow new legs, each leg represents an axis of oppression, and the stool's seat represents the established norm. If this stool had three legs, attacking one sole leg – say, sexism, would be enough to topple the stool for good. Since the stool has as many legs as there are axes of oppression, the stool will have many other legs to stand on while the one is under siege. Because the language of this epistemological framework takes these axes as given, it shapes our conception and affects the formation of emancipation politics, instead of simply articulating our understanding. This feminism plays by rules of hierarchy and domination, striking only one leg of the many-legged stool. But to think and act differently, we need to speak and conceive differently.

The second point is that feminist ideology looks to the status of the norm for an idea of what liberation is. If feminism takes the norm – white men (of means) – as the standard for freedom or equality, then feminism's vision of emancipation is oppressive. The *difference-identity* dyad upholds one identity as the

---

[16] hooks, *Writing Beyond Race*, p. 24.
[17] hooks, *Writing Beyond Race*, p. 34.

norm over and above others. Therefore, having the norm inform visions of emancipation, freedom, and equality for feminism and anti-racism complicates matters. According to hooks, it is a mistake to think that sexism can be eradicated by a "movement that aims to make women the social equals of men"[18] because men are not equal either. There is no 'liberation' for black women to become the equals of black men because black men are also oppressed. If feminism is about making women equal to (white) men, feminists have made a goal for themselves that involves the domination of *others*. Instead, emancipation without domination requires the production of a new epistemological framework that is not reliant on the master's tools.

Finally, it is important to differentiate between resistance struggle, on the one hand, which may be subversive and destabilizing, and actual substantive change, on the other, which dismantles and supersedes an overarching system. Resistance can be done within the confines of the mechanisms of oppression. In contrast, substantive change entails risking what you have (identity qualifiers of difference) for what you do not (political equality). Therefore, I suggest that political identity signifiers should not be the foundation of emancipation movements. In the next section, I explore and respond to objections to abandoning political strategies *based on* identity qualifiers.[19]

Objections to Discarding Identities

(1) Several feminist theorists argue that coming together around the lived experience of being gendered or racialized is necessary for political agency. This position fears, according to hooks, that without a common, unified notion of identity – blackness for anti-racist struggle or womanhood for feminist struggle – the ground for organized resistance is unstable.[20] For example, Lois

---

[18] hooks, *Feminist Theory*, p. 19.

[19] By 'identity qualifiers,' I am referring to 'forced' political identities of difference that people are immediately categorized as, such as sex or race, rather than personal identities.

[20] hooks, *Yearning*, p. 249.

McNay argues that the phenomenology of gender is central to feminism's ability to analyze oppression, which is necessary for building political consciousness and agency.[21] Phenomenological accounts of similar experiences of oppression lead McNay to hold that the "critique of identity is overstated".[22] Instead, my position risks what McNay calls "social weightlessness"[23], where theory fails to reflect the phenomenological and material reality of the oppressed.

Granted, it is the collective experience of oppression that leads to its coordinated resistance. It does not, however, follow that resistance must tread the path laid out for it by the system of that oppression. One might as well say that oppression is what is necessary for a politics of emancipation. But not all political agency is equally effective. Although consciousness-raising and finding collective oppression along identity lines is useful for understanding mechanisms of oppression, it does not follow that emancipatory politics should be based on those identity axes. As Chandra Mohanty argues, one of the problems with basing an emancipatory politics on political identity qualifiers is that it binds a group together by a "sociological notion of the 'sameness' of their oppression".[24] Shared phenomenology also becomes a way of "characterizing and defining groups in terms of their victim status".[25]

But identity politics as coordinated resistance can also assert forced or oppressive identities. The celebration of difference as a valuable political principle requires categorizing identity into groups that suppress internal differences, reproducing the epistemological models that justified identity-based oppression in the first place. For example, the homogenization of cultures justified colonialism, and the homogenization and dichotomiza-

---

[21] Lois McNay, "Feminism and Post-Identity Politics: The Problem of Agency", *Constellations* 17:4 (2010), pp. 522–523.

[22] McNay, "Feminism and Post-Identity Politics", p. 512.

[23] See: Lois McNay, *The Misguided Search for The Political: Social Weightlessness in Radical Democratic Theory* (Malden: Polity Press, 2014).

[24] Chandra T. Mohanty, "Under Western Eyes: Feminist Scholarship and Colonial Discourses", *Feminist Review* 30 (1988), p. 65.

[25] Mohanty, "Under Western Eyes", p. 67.

tion of gendered identities are similarly used to justify sexism. We also see these mechanisms at work within anti-racism and sexism, where anti-racist movements can be sexist and feminist movements racist because the resistance is centered around one identity axis. Raewyn Connell articulates this homogenization in the following way: "the problem here is that a claim to identity, instead of simply being a liberatory act, may be buying into a system of social control".[26] Whether it is the dominators or the resistors that do so, a homogenizing identity is not without grave risk of oppression. The use of identities inherited from systems of oppression continues to be implicated in those very systems. Writing on racial embodiment, Sekimoto argues that 'racial identity' exists within an ideology that subjectifies and subjectivizes the subject *as* raced (or, I add, as sexed), here exemplified by Louis Althusser's idea of *interpellation*:

> For racialized subjects, there are specific moments that require them to turn around – both literally and figuratively – and acknowledge the ideologies that mark their bodies as illegal, illicit, or inferior. In this case, racialization is not simply about significations of bodies of color, but more fundamentally, it is about how the body is co-opted – or recruited – into a particular ideology.[27]

Assertion by reclaiming one's devalued identity is undoubtedly an important remedy for the racialized subject. But the point is, as Mohanty articulates, that our "analytic strategies and principles carry political implications."[28] When using these identity categories of difference for solidarity in emancipatory politics, one neglects that this subjectivation is the enactment of an oppressive paradigm more so than a shared identity and can,

---

[26] Raewyn Connell, "Identity" in Catharine R. Stimpson & Gilbert Herdt (Eds.), *Critical Terms for the Study of Gender* (Chicago: University of Chicago Press, 2014), p. 167.
[27] Sachi Sekimoto, "A Multimodal Approach to Identity: Theorizing the Self through Embodiment, Spatiality, and Temporality", *Journal of International and Intercultural Communication* 5:3 (2012), p. 234.
[28] Mohanty, "Under Western Eyes", p. 64.

unfortunately, impede political agency because it does not separate from the subjectivizing ideology.

(2) The second objection to dismissing emancipatory politics based on identity qualifiers emphasizes the risk that emancipatory strategies might become irrelevant to those it aims to help. According to this position, political identity frames embodied experiences of oppression. Therefore, a political strategy that prematurely seeks to overcome the identity that frames those experiences is futile.[29] For example, this position holds that the fact of the matter is that women are already divided into groups based on identity qualifiers such as race and visible class markers. Not acknowledging this fact perpetuates the harm these divisions make possible. Ignoring the problem does not make it go away.

Kathryn T. Gines has argued that there is value in "race and ethnic based communities–even in the absence of racism and ethnocentrism", and that it is not necessarily pathological to have a willful attachment to racial identities.[30] Shared identity qualifiers form these communities, and theory should be relevant to these experiences. Critical race theorists like Gines are often skeptical of denouncing subjecthood when it seems integral to justice claims from racial minorities. On this view, eliminating identity qualifiers obscures the analysis of oppression rather than removing it. Gines distinguishes between post-racialism and post-racism to reject the thought that "the long-term goal must be the end of the concept of race" in the struggle against institutional racism.[31] Criticizing what she regards as the racial eliminativism underlying postracialism, she argues,

> Denying that races exist on a physical, metaphysical, and/or ontological level disempowers people who are targets of systematic institutional racism by denying them not only a

---

[29] McNay, "Feminism and Post-Identity Politics", p. 520.

[30] Kathryn T. Gines, "Conserving Race and Complicating Blackness Beyond the Black-white Binary", *Du Bois Review* 11:1 (2014), p. 84.

[31] Gines, "Conserving Race", p. 76.

> framework in which to articulate the experience of oppres-
> sion, but also a means to express solidarity to defend against
> such oppression. […] [Racism is] thriving unchecked because
> many have bought into the false assumption that there can be
> no racism without races.[32]

The same argument can be made for the sexist axis of oppression and other political identity qualifiers. Gines' concern is that the rubric of supposed neutral humanism includes "political structures that continue to disenfranchise under the guise of inclusion," and that the road to post-racism involves "identifying and dismantling systems of racial oppression, especially institutionalised racism."[33] For Gines, politics that seek to overcome identity will not only risk the irrelevance of theory but will also further enable oppression by leaving it unchecked.

My response to this objection is not to dispute that community and shared experiences are empowering, nor that theory should acknowledge these important features. However, although one may find empowerment from willful attachment to one's forced identity, an emancipatory politics should not hinge on the fact that one does. Otherwise, one accepts that these groups are, in Mohanty's words, "somehow socially constituted as a homogenous group identifiable prior to the process of analysis".[34] Organizing emancipatory politics around identity means accepting and not resisting the identities created to uphold an oppressive system. This is so even for 'take-back' initiatives such as affirming and revaluating traditionally feminine qualities or the non-exoticizing aesthetic revaluation of non-white bodies. These initiatives are undoubtedly important measures in resisting racist and sexist values. However, these attempts to counter the devaluation of differentiation are not enough to dismantle *imperialist white supremacist capitalist patriarchy*. A re-valuation of devalued feminized traits and

---

[32] Gines, "Conserving Race", p. 83.
[33] Gines, "Conserving Race", p. 79.
[34] Mohanty, "Under Western Eyes", p. 65.

values, for example, care work or emotional labor, does little to challenge the very gendering of these values. Even the positive acclamation of one's designed identity is still an acceptance of the identity that fortifies the norm. This is so even if accepting and celebrating one's forced identity brings moments of personal relief from oppression and permits one to live a life that is not solely about resistance.

Even when these identities are experienced in empowering ways, basing an emancipatory politics on identity reproduces the very *political logic* it resists. *Political logic* is inherited from the previous political system. For instance, Uma Narayan argues that in India, the colonial discourse has become part of what shapes nationalist agendas:

> The position of 'the Indian woman' as someone to be 'spoken for,' in both British feminist and Indian nationalist discourse, provides a clear example of how challenges to the political status quo often repeat and replicate *aspects* of its political logic.[35]

When Indian nationalism reiterates colonial discourse, it partakes in the system of domination it sets out to resist. Elements of the inherited *political logic* resound in the obsessive focus on homogeneous national identity, which is based on an anti-western attitude that results in a reinforcement of patriarchy. hooks likewise writes that when black liberation is defined by measuring access to opportunities and privileges that many white people enjoy – as it was defined by much of the civil rights movement – this vision of equality conflated black liberation with the imitation of white subject positions. Even the more radical 1960s Black Power movement, which disagreed with this vision of liberation, was not particularly "distinctive or revolutionary" in so far as they connoted authority and power with masculinity.[36]

[35] Uma Narayan, *Dislocating Cultures: Identities, Traditions, And Third World Feminism* (New York: Routledge, 1997), p. 19.
[36] hooks, *Yearning*, pp. 15–16.

Gines' concern about political logic is evident in her skepticism toward universal humanism. In feminist and anti-racist scholarship, the humanist genderless, race-less, ageless, classless, body-less subject is revealed to be a masculinized and white subject under the guise of neutrality. I share Gines' concern about humanism and her aims to "identif[y] and dismantl[e] systems of racial oppression".[37] However, contrary to Gines, I am concerned about the cost of using political identity qualifiers as grounds for solidarity in emancipatory politics. In post-structuralism, the idea is not to assert a neutral subject 'beneath' identity qualifiers, but to seriously question and disturb the identity markers that are imposed upon the subject, in order to lessen their political and societal significance. If the goal of emancipation is dismantling oppression, it is actually in the business of making something new. Suppose the concern is that a politics of emancipation without a focus on identity will commit the same errors as universal humanism. In that case, it is important to note that experiences of oppression are still vital to any emancipatory politics. Different oppressions give rise to different needs, wherein lies the politics. Gines seems either to conflate the idea of eliminating racial categories with ignoring racism or that the former necessitates the latter. It must be acknowledged, however, that identity in emancipatory politics is suitable for measuring and calling out manifestations of oppression. But I maintain that these efforts can only go so far. They express resistance in the form of mitigation to increase the valuation of an identity, but do not dismantle the system of domination that works along axes upholding a norm. Emancipatory movements would do well to recognize this.

(3) The third objection holds that the identity categories used in sexism and racism can serve as tools to improve the life condition of gendered and racialized people. This objection holds that identity can be used to give political rights to marginalized groups. For example, groups resist oppression by

---

[37] Gines, "Conserving Race", p. 79.

embracing their allocated identity qualifiers while asserting dignity, pride, and demanding respect.[38] As such, identity can be at one and the same time emancipatory and empowering, on the one hand, and constraining and oppressive, on the other. Michel Foucault, for instance, argued that power is not only repressive but also available to the marginalized – that the naming of the oppressed, such as black and woman, gave them a place from which to resist.[39] Judith Butler similarly argues that the term 'lesbian' can be *both* oppressive *and* a form of resistance against hegemony due to the plurality of the signifier, which may suggest that although power is oppressive, it can also (perhaps simultaneously) be subversive.[40]

To respond to this third objection, I want to elaborate on an example of identity politics in the legal framework of rights. Although identity may be a place from which to resist and has provided marginalized groups tools with which to claim rights, the politics based on identity are limited in scope. The price to pay, so to speak, for identity-based rights is that the claimant of equality must assert itself *qua* subordinated. Elizabeth Kiss finds that instead of dismantling structures of domination, identity-based rights have simply altered them.[41] She writes, "ours is an age less of rights triumphant than of continuing and massive wrongs".[42] Issues with gaining formal rights are that they leave "underlying social inequalities intact" and "obscure[s] women's continuing subordination by appearing to grant women a dramatic moral victory".[43] The feminist appeals to rights are a way of using the masters' tools to do their own bidding with mixed

---

[38] Connell, "Identity", pp. 162–164.

[39] Michel Foucault, "The Subject and Power", *Critical Inquiry* 8:4 (1982) pp. 777–795.

[40] Judith Butler, "Imitation and Gender Insubordination" in Henry Abelove, et al. (Eds.), *The Lesbian and Gay Studies Reader* (New York: Routledge, 1993), p. 307.

[41] Elizabeth Kiss, "Alchemy or Fool's Gold? Assessing Feminist Doubts About Rights" in Uma Narayan & Mary Lyndon Shanley (Eds.), *Reconstructing Political Theory* (Cambridge, UK: Polity Press, 1997), p. 19 n1.

[42] Kiss, "Alchemy or Fool's Gold?", p. 1.

[43] Kiss, "Alchemy or Fool's Gold?", p. 14.

successes. Feminists have most often succeeded in mitigating rather than dismantling.

Likewise, Wendy Brown argues that identity-specific rights presume *a priori* subordinated identities, paradoxically necessitating a perpetuation of subordination to claim equal rights.[44] The subjectivated may have the same rights as the subject-norm, but far from the same access to those rights. That is not to say that Brown invalidates the importance of rights, but she concludes that rights do not serve as a resolution: They "vanquish neither the regime nor its mechanisms of oppression".[45] The validation of the feminized or the racialized identity is an altogether different project from dismantling entirely these othered and peripheral categories that function to uphold a standard norm. Is it possible to do both at once? Perhaps not – perhaps we are at a crossroads between ideal and non-ideal theory.

(4) The final objection to relying on identity signifiers in emancipatory politics concerns intersectionality as a feminist solution to the essentializing risks of identity politics. Even when identity signifiers such as 'woman' and 'black' are used to end sexist oppression, hooks argues that black women fail to be adequately represented in this language.[46] Feminism can be ethnocentric and anti-racism can be misogynistic. Intersectionality provides feminist analysis a way to recognize how oppression may take different forms along different axes, even simultaneously. Kimberlé Crenshaw, who coined the term, thinks intersectionality as a provisional concept. She admits that her theory employs a model where race and gender are separate categories but hopes that the categories will be destabilized by focusing on the intersections of these axes.[47] By taking issue with homogenizing views on identity, intersectionality has been a

---

[44] Wendy Brown, "Suffering Rights as Paradoxes", *Constellations* 7:2 (2000), pp. 208–229.

[45] Brown, "Suffering Rights", p. 231.

[46] hooks, *Ain't I a woman*, p. 8.

[47] Kimberlé Crenshaw, "Intersectionality and Identity Politics: Learning from Violence Against Women of Color" in Uma Narayan & Mary Lyndon Shanley (Eds.), *Reconstructing Political Theory* (Cambridge, UK: Polity Press, 1997 [1995]), pp. 178–180.

remedy for identity politics by emphasizing that many kinds of oppression are not adequately represented in the false categorization of multifaceted identities.

Despite these improvements, intersectionality does not stray far from identity politics. Rather than seriously challenge the axes of oppression, queer-theorist Jasbir Puar argues that intersectionality's reverse effects revert the focus back onto white women: "Despite the decades of feminist theorising on the question of difference, difference continues to be a 'difference from', that is, the difference from 'white woman.'"[48] The focus on varieties of difference implies a center from which there is a difference and that the center is reinforced as the 'neutral' white woman, similarly to how the *female* may be construed as a variant to the 'neutral' male. Because of this, an *other* is unintentionally (re)produced. Puar argues that this *other* is the woman of color, which is ironic because intersectionality is "meant to alleviate such othering."[49] Unfortunately, intersectional theory does not delve into how these identity categories mutually construct one another. Intersectionality falters as a cure for feminism's racism issues because it is an attempt to include women of color in an epistemological system that is already ethnocentric without serious attempts to change the system that bases itself on exclusions of the *other*. Neither does it replace any emancipatory politics' focus on identity. As such, intersectionality attempts to include women of color in a mechanism that devalues the non-norm (whether the norm is whiteness or maleness), without serious challenges to that system.

These four objections reveal an underlying tension in a politics of emancipation. On the one hand, we can assert our identity as something to be respected and represented on equal par with the norm-identity, i.e., the reevaluation of difference. On the other hand, we can abandon the identity that is tied up in systems of oppression, i.e., rejecting the differential and axio-

---

[48] Jasbir Puar, "'I would rather be a cyborg than a goddess' Intersectionality, Assemblage, and Affective Politics", *Meritum* 8:2 (2013), p. 375.
[49] Puar, "I would rather be a cyborg," p. 388.

matic system of valuation altogether. The former option risks buying into the structure of the hegemonic norm, which may end up perpetuating one's identity as other to the norm. In addition, this option risks subjugating *its others* to an internal norm. The latter risks relinquishing claims to respect and representation in a way that must look elsewhere than the Foucauldian place from where to resist. My point is that resistance can either bring about substantive change or bring about some change without actually dismantling the system of domination. In this way, *imperialist white supremacist capitalist patriarchy* is still intact but comes to fruition in alternative ways that we then work to identify and analyze anew.[50] My argument is not directed against affirmative action, reparations, or movements such as Black Lives Matter or #MeToo, which are justified reactions and counter-initiatives to oppression along identity axes. But what I fear are inverse politics that do not go further in building the society we *do* want but stop at providing a counterforce to oppressions. hooks articulates this aspiration when she writes that it is "one of the most significant forms of power held by the weak" to deny the identity that one receives from the oppressor.[51]

The Risk of Mirroring: "The Pin Game"

Like a pin game, resistance movements risk mirroring and reaffirming the oppressive power they oppose. Gender scholar Jorunn Økland has observed that feminists,

> [...] make ourselves dependent on the same foundation that we criticize. But exactly this shows that women – feminists included – do not have a different language and other thought

---

[50] For the racial axis, Ibram X. Kendi coins the term 'racist progress' to denote this alternative fruition in *Stamped from the Beginning: The Definitive History of Racist Ideas in America* (New York: Bold Type Books, 2017), p. *xi*.

[51] hooks, *Feminist Theory*, p. 92.

structures to speak in and from than those given us by contemporary discourse.[52]

Herein exists an inevitable bind: The discourse that challenges *imperialist white supremacist capitalist patriarchy* depends, in part, on that framework to make the same criticism. The pin game works by pressing your hand or another object into the frame so the pins that are pressed out form an imprint of the object. The force of the hand leaves an inverted imprint of the preceding force. In this case, the hand is anti-oppression resistance, and the pins are the *imperialist white supremacist capitalist patriarchy*. When using identity qualifiers in resistance, emancipation movements change the image, but ultimately remain a mirror-image that does nothing to change the box or the rules of the game. A liberation movement that accepts the terms laid down by the forces of oppression is limited because its counter-force depends on the primary force itself and can only ever do resistance (subversion), not substantial change (dismantling).

The metaphysical presumptions of the division of the axes of oppression into sexism, racism, etc., affect how we think of oppression and, thereby, how feminist political efforts are organized in ways that do not serve feminist purposes. Because the system in its entirety is based on upholding the norm, as long as that basic structure is maintained, any feminist struggle for eradicating sexism will be limited. In the words of Gloria Anzaldúa in *Borderlands/La Frontera*:

> [...] it is not enough to stand on the opposite river bank, shouting questions, challenging patriarchal, white conventions. A counterstance locks one into a duel of oppressor and

[52] Jorunn Økland, "Feminist Reception of the New Testament: A Critical Reception" in Mogens Müller & Henrik Tronier (Eds.), *The New Testament as Reception* (Sheffield: Sheffield Academic Press, 2002), p. 153.

oppressed; locked in mortal combat [...] All reaction is limited by, and dependent on, what it is reaching against.[53]

I have argued that although identity is crucial for phenomenologically understanding one another's lived experiences and analyzing how oppression inherent in *imperialist white supremacist capitalist patriarchy* takes different forms, it does not follow that identity should be the rubric for an emancipatory politics. On the contrary, to avoid the oppositional lockage illustrated by Anzaldúa and to prevent the reproduction of oppression within (typically racist feminism and sexist anti-racism), emancipatory politics should strive to remove the condition – not only the symptoms – of the structure of the axes of oppression. In the next section, I venture 'another route' of the numerous possibilities Anzaldúa promises "once we decide to act and not react."[54]

Alienated Desire

Some may find my caution toward identity-based solidarity an attack on something personal and dear, but it is not. Like hooks, I hold that feminism needs to be "based on a recognition of the need to eradicate the underlying cultural basis and causes of sexism and other forms of group oppression." Otherwise, "no feminist reforms will have long-range impact."[55] My stance is not an insensitivity toward racism or sexism, but rather, in the name of an emancipatory politics, it is an injunction to forge solidaristic ties on shared desires rather than shared identifications.

Although hooks is skeptical about "forgetting identity", she is not particularly loyal to the preconceived notions of identity that exist in the system of domination either.[56] Political solidarity, she finds, cannot be achieved by adhering to the terms set

---

[53] Gloria Anzaldúa, *Borderlands/La Frontera: The New Mestiza* (San Francisco: Spinsters/Aunt Lute, 1987), p. 78.

[54] Anzaldúa, *Borderlands*, p. 78.

[55] hooks, *Feminist Theory*, p. 33.

[56] hooks, *Yearning*, p. 15.

by the ideology of domination.[57] Sara Edenheim has already argued that feminism should shift its focus away from identity and create a politics of desire. Feminist politics of desire asks the question, "what do we *want* rather than who we *are*" and find solidarity on those grounds.[58] A politics of desire does not take self-interest as its objective, but a common desire for a common world without oppression. This desire must be an abstract and alienated desire. By that, I mean firstly a desire abstract enough that no matter one's personal experience with oppression, one can partake in the desire for a world without oppression systematized along the axes of identity signifiers. However, it cannot be so general that feminism can easily be co-opted by other political agendas, whether neo-liberal, capitalist, racist or even sexist.[59] Second, by alienation, I agree with Slavoj Žižek that the right kind of alienation can be a good thing.[60] For feminist solidarity, alienated solidarity is not based on a community of similar experiences of oppression, nor identity or allyship, but rather on the shared idea that we seek to replace the *imperialist white supremacist capitalist patriarchy* and its axis model. This desire should be alienated because we do not rely on a feeling of shared identity or experience, but a recognition of a common desire. Remember: "Eyes on the Prize". When Ibram X. Kendi argues that altruism, exceptionalism, and education will not resolve racism,[61] he articulates something like my vision of alienated desire: We need policies as a basis for emancipatory solidarity.

What is, then, the role of identity? I propose to use identity as a tool to measure whether emancipatory politics have been substantially impactful enough to dismantle or thoroughly change structures of domination, but not as what unites or pro-

---

[57] bell hooks, "Sisterhood: Political Solidarity between Women", *Feminist Review* 23 (1986), p. 129.

[58] Sara Edenheim, "Performativity as a Symptom, The Trembling Body in the Works of Butler", *lambda nordica* 2:3 (2015), p. 143.

[59] hooks, *Feminist Theory*, p. 25.

[60] Slavoj Žižek, *Holberg Lecture* 2019, University of Bergen.

[61] Kendi, "Epilogue" in *Stamped*, pp. 497–511.

vides the foundation for an emancipatory project. A unifying factor here is a general desire to eliminate not just one's own oppression, but also the possibility of one's oppression. What we relinquish are identities given to us by an oppressive system that has used these identities in our subjugation. For these identities are, we do well to remember, forced upon us. We desire to change that.

Conclusion

In this chapter, I hope to have shown that emancipation movements risk becoming 'mere' counter-movements that mirror oppression inward and become stuck in an inverse counter-force against societal oppression. An emancipatory politics that employs identities of difference as the basis for solidarity risks reaffirming the very *differenced* functions of those identities. Alienated desire as the common basis for solidarity can address two problems for emancipatory politics. First, the problem of the many-legged stool (the external enemy of a politics of emancipation) illustrates the issue of resistance not acquiring substantive change. Second, the problem of the pin game (the internal enemy of an emancipatory politics) illustrates the issue of stalemate that happens when accepting conditions of axis oppression while simultaneously trying to dismantle it. These two issues together often lead to an emancipatory politics that bases the vision of freedom on a norm that oppresses its *others*, resulting in ethnocentric feminism and misogynistic anti-racism.

Therefore, feminism and anti-racism should ask not *who* you are but *what* you desire. This can be a foundation for solidarity that, in lesser terms, risks reproducing the same identity signifiers that uphold an identity norm used in identity-based oppression. Stuart Hall argues that because race must be seen in a Eurocentric context, de-racifying identity is to decolonize thinking.[62] Similarly, I find solidarity not in the personal connection to our imposed political identities, or similarities in experiences,

---

[62] Stuart Hall, et al., *The Fateful Triangle: Race Ethnicity Nation* (Cambridge, MA: Harvard University Press 2017).

but rather by finding freedom in the expression of what we desire, not what we are told that we are. Through politics based on this abstract and alienated desire, we can form solidarity with the potential to dismantle beyond resistance. It is based not on *feeling* solidarity but on a *vision toward the new* around which solidarity can form.

There is, however, cause for caution. My argument does not support post-racial or colorblind approaches to racism, nor a gender equality primarily based on masculinist values. Upholding the phenomenological experiences of those with identity signifiers such as non-white skin, gendered bodies, etc., is vital for resistance movements. But I wish to distinguish between movements of resistance and those that eliminate the historico-political significance of the identity sign. Serene Khader convincingly argues that reaching an ideal situation from non-ideal conditions requires the use of non-ideal tools, even tools that are useful for racist or sexist practices.[63] While I wholeheartedly agree with her analysis on negotiating oppression in life and context, her argument concerns resistance. Dismantling-oriented solidarity, however, must build on premises that do not resist *and* fortify *imperialist white supremacist capitalist patriarchy.* My argument may indicate a more significant contention between phenomenological and post-structuralist philosophies of emancipation.

---

[63] Serene Khader, "Transnational Feminisms, Nonideal Theory, and "Other" Women's Power", *Feminist Philosophy Quarterly* 3:1 (2017), pp. 1–23.

Part 5
Openings of Understanding

Chapter 15
Private, Public, Sacred Space
– Why gender studies in Particular Should Consider Sacred Space a Third Spatial Category[*]

Jorunn Økland

In this chapter I will show how and why it is helpful to triangulate, or supplement, the private-public binary with a third spatial category, the sacred, if we want to understand the space of female speech, agency and activity in the past. In particular, Graeco-Roman Antiquity had more fine-masked categories of gender and space than our modern period. Sacred space was not identical to public space nor any part or subfield of public space, but had its own specific meaning, structure, and position in the socio-cultural order. This argument troubles and undermines the received opposition between public male space and private female space.

I will use 'private-public' as the main designation of the binary in question. In my own work, I have often preferred more pragmatic categories ('domestic' space instead of 'private'), just as Joan Scott does ('familial' instead of 'private'). But the degree of semantic overlap with the much more frequently used terms for these spaces, 'private' and 'public', means that deviating terms are more variations of a theme than genuinely new categories.

Theoretical Approaches to Gender and Spatial Categories in Ancient and Modern History

The feminist thinkers presented in this chapter, mainly Mary Beard (Classics), Doreen Massey (Geography), Yvonne Hird-

---

[*] The chapter was initially the opening lecture of the conference "Rethinking Public Space" 8–10 March 2018 at the University of Oslo, organized by the network Feminist Philosophy: Time, History and the Transformation of Thought.

man and Joan Wallach Scott (both History), all take standard distinctions between public and private as their points of departure for further reflections on gender and space.

For theorists coming out of the radical British geography tradition, such as Doreen Massey (and David Harvey), space and time are not static axes along which things take place, rather, space and time are mutually dependent modes of relation. For Massey, "'place' is formed out of the particular set of social relations which interact at a particular location."[1] The set of social relationships constructs and structures the activities taking place there as male or female gendered, and this way the spaces themselves become perceived as gendered. But the activity is not the only thing that genders a space. Doreen Massey states:

> Space and place, spaces and places, and our senses of them (and such related things as our degrees of mobility) are gendered through and through. Moreover, they are gendered in a myriad different ways, which vary between cultures over time. And this gendering of space and place both reflects *and has effects back on* the ways in which gender is constructed and understood in the societies in which we live.[2]

The Swedish modern historian Yvonne Hirdman has also written on the interrelation between space, activity and gender. She is concerned with how the "gender system", the structure of the relations between different genders, is used as a foundation for other social orders and structures.[3] The gender system operates according to two dynamics. First, the dynamics of dichotomy or *separation*, that is the taboo against gender blending: masculine

[1] Doreen Massey, *Space, Place and Gender* (Minneapolis: University of Minnesota Press, 1994), 168.

[2] Doreen Massey, "17. Space, Place and Gender" in Rendell, Jane, Barbara Penner & Iain Borden (Eds.), *Gender Space Architecture: An Interdisciplinary* Introduction (London: Routledge, 2000: 128–133), p. 129.

[3] B: Yvonne Hirdman, Rapport 23. Genussystemet – teoretiska funderingar kring kvinnors sociala underordning (Uppsala: Maktutredningen, 1988).

and feminine should be kept strictly separated. The second dynamic is *hierarchy*: the masculine is norm. This second dynamic is dependent on and legitimated through the first.[4] Hirdman states: "We know that the "law" of segregation exists everywhere with regard to physical and psychic order. It structures actions, places and characters."[5]

With her background in historical materialism (= Marxism), Hirdman finds that the fundamental expression of the law of segregation is found in the gendered division of *labor* and in notions of masculine and feminine. She shows how character, action and place are intimately linked to one another and "stand in a legitimizing, reinforcing, dialectic relationship with each other: sort 1 performs action 1 on place 1; sort 2 performs action 2 on place 2; since sort 1 performs action 1, sort 1 becomes sort 1. If one is located on place 2, one performs action 2 and is sort 2 etc."[6] In my own work, this insight has been particularly helpful to illuminate how the distribution of ritual patterns of actions (roles) between men and women serves to represent the sacred space in question as gendered in a particular way. But put the other way around, her theory also helps us see how the placing of people in different gendered spaces is an important way of inscribing gender upon them.

Hirdman does not ask where these dynamics of segregation and hierarchy "come from", but she does underscore their unique structuring abilities (Hirdman actually calls them the two *logics* of the gender system). Dichotomies and hierarchies are tools that always nourish and reward logical thought by ordering the world and leaving an impression of understanding or controlling it. They *make* sense. But referring to Simone de Beauvoir who stated that one cannot be an A without suppressing a B, Hirdman also finds that the two logics or dynamics

---

[4] Hirdman, Rapport, pp. 7–9 and 13.

[5] A: Yvonne Hirdman, "Genussystemet – reflexioner kring kvinnors sociala underordning," (*Kvinnovetenskapelig tidsskrift* 1988 3: 49–63), p. 52. my translation.

[6] Hirdman, "Genussystemet – reflexioner," p. 52.

make power structures: what sort 1 does is legitimated by constructing a contrast with sort 2.[7]

While inspired by the scholars just mentioned, the current chapter takes its special cue from *Sex and Secularism* by Joan Wallach Scott.[8] Scott uses historical evidence to do several things with the public-private distinction, which she labels 'politics and economics' (male) and 'familial' (female), respectively: First, Scott presents historical data from the long 19th century when a new, secular realm of society emerged with the separation of church/sacred space from the state. The secular realm was divided further into politico-economic and familial spaces. Thus, secondly, Scott shows (even down to her choice of labels) that what we perceive to be standard in the public-private distinction is in fact historically contingent. Third, she deconstructs the public-private distinction as a clear-cut, spatial distinction relating to historical, material physical spaces (e.g. town halls and market places versus houses people owned or rented, slept and stayed in). Especially when it comes to gender, no such material distinction is stable over time. Instead, she sees the distinction as a sort of spatialized discourse, a classification of concepts and ideas that were associated with each of their material spaces and in turn linked to different forms of (dis-)empowerment. Scott is far from the first to make this argument; Hirdman, mentioned above, argued the same based on social systems theory many years earlier. Fourth, Scott challenges the false notion that secularism is a guarantee of gender equality, arguing instead that this notion has served to divert attention from a persistent set of difficulties related to gender difference. She also suggests that gender equality became a primary feature of the discourse of secularism only in the latter half of the 20th century, with the arrival of Muslim immigrants in Europe.[9]

[7] For a fuller summary of what I see as the significance of Hirdman's theory, see overview in Jorunn Økland, *Women in Their Place: Paul and the Corinthian Discourse of Gender and Sanctuary Space* (London: Bloomsbury, 2004), pp. 59–60.

[8] Joan Wallach Scott, *Sex and Secularism* (Princeton: Princeton University Press, 2018).

[9] Scott, *Sex and Secularism*, p. 10 and 17.

Thus, Scott demonstrates that gender equality, invoked today as a fundamental and enduring principle of modern, secular societies and their public space in particular, was not originally associated with the term "secularism" when it first entered the lexicon in the nineteenth century. *Inequality* of the sexes was presupposed also in the spatial articulation of the separation of church and state that inaugurated Western modernity, or in other words: when religious authority yielded from spaces beyond the walls of churches, religious schools and meeting places, etc., non-sacred spaces were left in a vacuum. In theory, they might have become "neutral" and open to full participation by all people.[10] In historical practice, it was clear that "secular" at the time had little to do with changing religious habits, practices or beliefs among the population, and more to do with changes in arbitration, authorization, and power.

Western nation-states found it necessary to construct a new ground for women's subordination when it could no longer be grounded in the religious authority emanating from 'sacred' spaces (at this time mostly Christian churches). Hence the *secular* sphere was further subdivided into private and public, and women were assigned to the "private", familial sphere meant to complement the rational masculine realms of "public" politics, economics, institutions of learning, etc. While Scott does not pay attention to important details especially regarding historical religion and how Christianity was embedded historically in Europe (as opposed to Christianity's function in the

---

[10] This optimism has never fared well in practice. In his 1999 article "Secularization, R.I.P.", sociologist Rodney Stark argues that the "secularisation theory" is out-dated, old-fashioned and, as the title suggests, the theory is dead and should be left to rest. To Stark the secularization thesis has failed to be an accurate prediction due to six reasons. Firstly, it is a myth that there has been a decline in religious belief and participation because "there has been no demonstrable long-term decline in European religious participation" and in Europe "levels of subjective religiousness remain high." Next, he argues that there has never been an "Age of Faith," as most Europeans did not attend church during the Middle Ages and Renaissance. In fact, Stark highlights that many clergy were incomepetent and often absent from their parishes. Finally, while there were "periodic explosions of mass religious enthusiasm" (cf. below on the Quakers), these offer even stronger evidence against involvement in organized religion. See Rodney Stark, "Secularization, R.I.P." (*Sociology of Religion*, 1999 Autumn: 249–273).

U.S.), she nevertheless constructs a strong argument for an important point.

Secularism – the term itself derives from *saeculum, saeculare*, meaning age, time, generation – as opposed to what is eternal, beyond finite time and space, that is, an order of being associated with the gods. Humans inhabit the finite world, which is often subdivided into further spaces roughly equivalent to Western categories of public, private – and "sacred". While I still believe that in the present, secularism is the best guarantee of gender equality we have (it is much harder to argue with gods or find hearing among their human representatives....), it is important to understand secularism as a contingent *value* of public space in modern Western societies, an ideology excluding gods or their representatives as the final arbiters of matters relating to public space. Secularism is neither a material, objective feature of it, nor a future prediction.[11] Further, the autonomy and authority that women have held historically in what I here and elsewhere have labelled "sacred" space – while being excluded from public space – should warn us further from concluding that female agency and authority is *necessarily* linked to a secular public space. It depends on how the religion in question is construed – and how gender is construed in relation to it. It is this latter point that this article will continue to explore through examples from historical societies we refer to as our heritage. I will make the point that sacred spaces have, to a larger extent than both private and public spaces, accommodated female agency and authority.

---

[11] i.e. my opinion is that Stark, mentioned in the previous footnote, partly misses the point in his otherwise important critique of the secularisation theory. We have to study *value theory*, not sociology, to get a grasp of secularism's relationship to social and material realities. Further, after multiculturalism, pluralism, etc., it has become clearer that state-endorsed and -implemented values cannot be imposed on domestic space without becoming totalitarian.

The Distinction Between Public, Domestic and Sacred Spaces

Gendering the Public/Private/Sacred Distinction in the Ancient World

In scholarship on women's lives in Antiquity, women's ritual roles are often discussed as if they were regular public roles. The rationale is that religion is an inseparable part of culture and society, and such holistic approaches can illuminate e.g., how ancient women's ritual roles were related to their sexual and social status. However, the identification of the ritual/sacred with the public, in the case of women's roles does not explain why, if they could have "public" roles in the cult, women could not have various other public roles. Further, this reductionist identification of religion with public life, render invisible many women's ritual roles.

In ancient public discourse we frequently find gendering definitions of space: the authors state which spaces are "for women", and which spaces are "for men". One example by Philo must suffice:

> Market-places and council-halls and law-courts and gatherings and meetings where a large number of people are assembled, and open-air life with full scope for discussion and action – all these are suitable to men both in war and in peace. The women are best suited to the indoor life which never strays from the house.[12]

Philo's quote should not be taken as objective description of space, or as descriptions of what actually happens in the spaces in question, as if women were not present in marketplaces and

---

[12] Philo, *De specialibus legibus* 3.169 (in F. H. Colson, G. H. Whitaker, et al. [trans.] *Philo in ten volumes* [Loeb Classical library; Cambridge, MA: Harvard University Press, 1927–1953]). Cf. the striking similarities with approximately contemporary Columella, *De re rustica*: 12, Preface 4–5 (in H. B. Ash, E. S. Forster, et al. [trans.] Columella, *On Agriculture: in three volumes* [Loeb Classical Library; Cambridge, MA: Harvard University Press, 1941–1955]).

gatherings and meetings.[13] Different values are attached to different spaces according to what gender they are mostly associated with.

Read within Hirdman's frame of reference, one could say that Philo confers importance and power on one space over the other space. One cannot at the outset just assume that society functioned according to these rules. It is exactly because the distinctions were not so clear that it was continually important to reinforce them through discourse.[14] By representing public space as male space, ancient public men legitimized the exclusion of women from power positions, public discourse and processes of decision-making. Women were never forbidden to enter public space even if it was discursively constructed as male.[15]

While it is not un-common to see the *public* and *domestic* as distinct, binary spatial discourses, it is rare to consider *sacred* space as a third spatial category, equally discursively constructed through speech and ritual action. Is the reason that our cognitive preference is for binary thought, so that we overlook additional, distinct spaces? Ritual constructs and structures space by drawing on a gendered, divine cosmology that can often be different from the rules governing human interaction in public and domestic spaces.[16]

---

[13] Among scholars who discuss working women or women who in other ways are present in public space, see especially Susan Treggiari, "Lower Class Women in the Roman Economy," *Florilegium* 1979 1: 65–86; Mary Lefkowitz, Maureen Fant (Eds.), *Women's Life in Greece & Rome. A Source Book in Translation* (Baltimore: Johns Hopkins University Press, 1992): 208–224.

[14] John J. Winkler, *The Constraints of Desire. The Anthropology of Sex and Gender in Ancient Greece* (New York: Routledge, 1991), p. 6: "to know when any such male law-givers – medical, moral, or marital, whether smart or stupid – are (to put it bluntly) bluffing or spinning fantasies or justifying their 'druthers' is so hard that most historians of ideas – Foucault, for all that he is exceptional, is no exception here." For a more recent, nuanced discussion, see Kate Cooper, "Closely Watched Households: Visiblity, Exposure and Private Power in the Roman *domus*," *Past and Present* 2007, 197: 3–33.

[15] See e.g. Ville Vuolanto, "Public Agency of Women in the Late Roman World, in Jussi Rantala (Ed.), *Gender, Memory, and Identity in the Roman World*. Amsterdam: Amsterdam University Press, 2019: 41–62 (DOI: 10.5117/9789462988057_CH01).

[16] Ritual space is just the space that is constructed through ritual, whether it is conceived of as sacred or not.

An important function of certain sacred/ritual spaces was exactly to *transgress* the boundaries of proper behavior in public and domestic spaces.[17] With regard to women, this difference in gendered expectations between public and sacred spaces is telling. It is particularly evident in material from ancient Greece: while the *deme* (commune) in its political aspect necessarily remained an all-male preserve, the *deme* in its religious aspect operated under a different set of imperatives. As John Gould states:

> In the sacred and ritual activities of the community the active presence of women in the public world (was) not merely tolerated but required. As priestesses in many of the major cults of the *polis* (priestesses of gods as well as of goddesses), … *the participation of women is indispensable to the sacral continuity, the ordering of society.*[18]

In addition to their priesthoods, Gould also lists a range of other official ritual roles for women: in the great religious processions through the *public* spaces of the city, as "temple servants" of the city goddess Athena (tending her statue and weaving her clothes) and of Artemis at Brauron nearby; as raisers of the ritual, sacrificial scream; their "song" in mourning, at funerals, in the rituals of marriage, and much more. Further, the exclusively female festival *Thesmophoria* took place at Pnyx, the location where the council of (male) Athenian citizens usually gathered. This festival was a rite of reversal, in which women did and said many things that could not be expressed by them outside of the sacred space.[19]

We note that among Gould's examples, women's loud uses of their voice dominate: In her recent book *Women and Power*, Classicist Mary Beard expands on how authors in Greek and

---

[17] Winkler, *Constraints,* chapter 7.

[18] John P. Gould, "Law, Custom and Myth: Aspects of the Social Position of Women in Classical Athens," *Journal of Hellenic Studies* 100, 1980: 38–59 (p. 50f).

[19] Cf. Winkler, *Constraints of Desire,* p. 193–196; Gould, "Law, Custom," p. 51.

Roman Antiquity meant that the sound of the female voice disqualifies its owner from opening her mouth in public space.[20] Beard gives several examples of how the female voice is described as equal to the sound of cows, dogs' barking, or other animal sounds. Beard presents these ancient examples of perceptions of women's voices in public to point out that we also find traces of them in modern times, mentioning the habit of female top politicians (e.g. Margaret Thatcher) attending voice education to make her voice stronger, deeper – and more authoritative. But as we have seen, in the ancient world there was another conceptual space (sacred) taking place in the same material environment (e.g. Pnyx) where women could use their different voice, and this was seen as vital to the survival of the community.

Women's Religious Offices

The fact that women could hold sacred offices as priestesses, servants, patronesses etc.,[21] even if public offices were not open to them, has led many scholars to believe that ritual activity constituted the primary exception to the rule of "seclusion and exclusion" of ancient women from the public sphere.[22] Yet, the separation between public and sacred space has functioned differently through history: Compared to ancient Greece, in the Roman period sacred spaces were less liminal with regard to women's place and presence. The female priesthood of Ceres/Demeter at Rome was characterized as a public office. Such a priesthood seems to have represented the greatest public honour

---

[20] Mary Beard, *Women and Power: A Manifesto* (London: Profile Books, 2017), especially pp. 25–34.

[21] For further examples of women's religious offices, see e.g. Lefkowitz and Fant, *Women's Life*, section 10.

[22] Cf. Helene Foley, "The Conception of Women in Athenian Drama," in Helene P. Foley (Ed.), *Reflections of Women in Antiquity* (New York: Routledge, 1981): 127–68, "Women in drama do not confine themselves to the domestic and religious spheres to which they were relegated in reality" (p. 151).

to which a woman could aspire.[23] Even "respectable" matrons[24] had to attend rituals in public space to fulfil their sacred obligations. Respectable wives could participate in the festival *Thesmophoria*, but not go shopping in the marketplace.[25] Ancient authors could therefore mention even women they considered "respectable" in ritual contexts without bringing shame upon these women or their husbands. Taking place both in sanctuaries and in open, public spaces of the city, the cult activities of women are not all about "seclusion and exclusion" since in a way they took place in some kind of sacred "third space" in the same material environment as "public space".[26] We must therefore reformulate the axiom and say that *what* women were thought to represent, was considered vital in sacred space, whether these spaces were constructed as liminal or in direct continuation with other public spaces – or more conventionally, inside dedicated sanctuaries.

Summing up, there are significant differences in the ways gender categories worked in sacred spaces and in the public and domestic spaces of daily life in the ancient world. Therefore, sacred space should be considered as a separate space in the study of gender, and not be conflated with the public – or domestic – spaces. Surely, ritual is *also* a place for (social) value reinforcement, ritual hierarchies can reflect social hierarchies, but neither in Greek, Roman or Judaean religious cultures were

[23] Plutarch, *Bravery of Women*, 262D (in F. C. Babbitt, et al. [trans.] Plutarch, *Moralia: in sixteen volumes* (Loeb Classical Library; Cambridge, MA: Harvard University Press, 1927–1976).

[24] Athenaeus, *Deipnosophists* 13.574B-C (in C. B. Gulick [trans], *Deipnosophists Book 6* [Loeb Classical Library; Cambridge, MA: Harvard University Press, 2009]): "But that the prostitutes also celebrate their own festival of Aphrodite at Corinth is shown by Alexis in 'the girl in love': 'The city celebrated a festival of Aphrodite for the prostitutes, but it is a different one from that held separately for freeborn women'."

[25] E.g., this "rule" applies only to representation of "respectable" women: there must have been lots of women out of doors in Greece before Hellenistic times, too. For a very nuanced presentation, see Gould, "Law, Custom."

[26] I have not drawn further on Soya's influential work to discuss the spatiality of the sacred as a kind of "thirdspace" due to its lack of attention to gender. For other purposes, his "thirdspace" can be illuminating. Edward Soya, *Thirdspace: Journeys to Los Angeles and Other Real-and-Imagined-Places* (Oxford: Blackwell, 1996).

women discursively excluded from sacred space even though they were mostly discursively excluded from public spaces.

In this section I have talked about sanctuary, cultic, ritual, sacred as if they were synonymous. Sacred is the most common term, which I use as the overarching category. Sanctuary, cultic or ritual space, on the other hand, are more precise subcategories. Sacred space can be discursively constructed through either speech, ritual action, or through architecture.

Second Period: Post-Reformation Europe

Although Ancient Greece may be the most pertinent case in point, I will present one more recent example from Europe, in order to show that in spite of constant change, there is still good reason to consider sacred space a separate category when we study the space for women's speech and agency in history.

But first an interlude.

We saw that in the ancient world, women's agency in sacred space often took place within the material environment of public city spaces. In Medieval Europe on the other hand, it was the material provision of a women's *monastery* that provided the infrastructure for women-dominated sacred spaces – although they, too, were ultimately under male-clerical supervision. Running a post-Reformation *vicarage* or *stately home* on behalf of a husband, and with children around one's legs, gave less space and time than the nuns had for reading, visions, letter writing between nuns and between nuns and church authorities, church politics, etc. In other words, the differences in conditions for women's agency in the mentioned three spaces, meant that times changed: It has often been lamented that Protestantism, exemplified by Martin Luther in the 16th century, who married a former nun (Katharina von Bora), practically destroyed the space for female autonomy, power, agency, and literacy when he discursively obliterated the sacred space of the monasteries as a distinct spatial category. Instead, he described society as divided into precisely private and public spheres (and limiting the space of women to the 'private', familial sphere). Aligning the monasteries with the public sphere, was his way of getting rid of the "sacred space" of the monasteries altogether. The side effect was that the realm of the sacred as a more autonomous space for women disappeared, too – for a while.[27]

The post-Reformation period saw an eruption of sects, and women preachers emerged in their "sacred spaces". The early period from 1650 is probably more dynamic in Britain, while as we gradually move toward the French Revolution, other European countries began to take the lead. I have previously presented English Quakerwomen Priscilla Cotton and Mary Cole, who were imprisoned for "prophecy" in 1655 after they extended their preaching activity to public spaces,[28] here I will present Margaret Fell (1614–1702), founder of Quakerism.

The Quaker movement represented the radical end of the Puritan movement. They believed in the "inner light", that the light of/or God resides inside each individual; that therefore every Christian, man *and* woman, can speak prophecy, speak for Christ. George Fox, Margaret Fell's second husband, is often credited as the movement's founder, but in practice his wife Margaret Fell Fox should be considered the movement's founder and George Fox its inspiration and earliest advocate: She was 10 years his senior, but survived him by 11 years. They first met when he visited the stately home Swarthmoor Hall, which Margaret shared with her first husband, the lawyer. She had opened up the home for religious gatherings – in our terms, she created a sacred space within the walls of a domestic space. After her first husband died and Fell married Fox, "it was

---

[27] See Lyndal Roper, *The Holy Household: Women and Morals in Reformation Augsburg* (Oxford: Clarendon, 1991). But see also Katharina Schütz Zell, *Church Mother: The Writings of a Protestant Reformer in Sixteenth-Century Germany*, edited and translated by Elsie McKee. Chicago: The University of Chicago Press, 2006.

[28] See Jorunn Økland, "4. Donne interpreti della Bibbia nella tradizione protestante", in Adriana Valerio and Giuseppe Barbaglio (Eds.), *Donne e Bibbia: Storia ed esegesi* (Bologna: Dehoniane, 2006): 99–116. From prison the two wrote the pamphlet *To the Priests and People of England.*

Margaret who administered the finances, indeed donated her own fortune, kept track of correspondence at her home at Swarthmore, visited meetings, and spoke out publicly in defense of Quakers. Even after the death of George in 1691 she continued with her vigilant activities."[29]

In 1666, Margaret Fell Fox published the tractate *Women's Speaking Justified, Proved and Allowed of by the Scriptures,*[30] which she had written during one of her many imprisonments (for, among other things, using her home as a space for religious meetings). The text was based on what was practiced within the "sacred space" in her home, where also husband George supported women's preaching,[31] and was also based on the preaching practices of other Quaker women during a time when priesthoods were public offices and reserved for men. The argument was built on quotes from Paul's letters. Paul the Apostle took for granted that women prophesy and pray in the ritual gatherings (i.e., sacred space) taking place in private homes, but he also told them to be quiet in some instances. In Fell's own time, the church was a more integrated part of public space. Hence Paul's silencing of women during some parts of the ritual were read as a general silencing of women's speech, by conflating the sacred space of the gathering into which they were spoken with the public space of the 17th century. Fell shows how such a reading is wrong and inconsistent. Quakerism quickly grew into a subversive movement protesting that the authority of both the church and the Bible had been abused and corrupted. The Quaker practice of having women preachers and leaders were considered by the establishment as a "monstrous" practice, "condemned as against nature".[32]

---

[29] Fulltext in e.g. Moira Ferguson (Ed.), *First Feminists: British Women Writers 1578–1799* (Bloomington: Indiana University Press, 1985): 114–127. For more on Fell, see Jacqueline Broad, "Margaret Fell," in Edward N. Zalta (Ed.), *Stanford Encyclopedia of Philosophy* Spring 2020: https://plato.stanford.edu/archives/spr2020/entries/margaret-fell/

[30] Selvidge, *Notorious Voices,* p. 36.

[31] See more on Paul's texts in Økland, *Women Place,* chapter 6.

[32] Barry Reay, *The Quakers, and the English Revolution* (London: Temple Smith, 1985),

This history was repeated several times over the next centuries. It was a recurring post-Reformation phenomenon that sects tended to be more open toward the spiritual equality of men and women than mainstream churches. Such sects gathered in homes or outdoors and often ended up in conflict when they ventured into "public space", its establishment and institutions[33] – until the arrival of universal suffrage and women priests. Other sects were quicker to move in a mainstream direction. As they became more institutionalized, integrated into the general public, their radical gender agenda was often discarded.

Space, History, and the Transformation of Thought

As stated above, the way Scott describes the new, 19th century gendered spheres of the 'familial' on the one hand, vs. the spheres of 'politics and economics' on the other, overlaps largely with the standard designations "private" and "public". In some form, this distinction can be found in pre-modern societies too, but the configuration of it, which much gender research seems to presuppose, is definitely a product of the Enlightenment: In the modern context, the principal focus for Scott, both private and public are in fact located within the new, autonomous *secular* sphere. Within the church's sacred space, gender divisions continued to be based on a divinely sanctioned gender *hierarchy*. Hence Scott's discussion illustrates how the private/public distinction, so fundamental in much gender research, is a historically conditioned distinction, just like male/female. And like the male/female distinction, many historical societies have operated with further categories alongside these two sets of binaries. It is, I propose, as a third category that we should understand sacred space, just like some gender models have operated with a third gender.

When a secular sphere emerged as *independent* of the religious sphere, private and public spaces became subdivisions, but

p. 58, quoting from *Antichrist in Man* by Rev. Joshua Miller (1655).

[33] For a selection, see Andrew Bradstock and Christopher Rowland (Eds.), *Radical Christian Writings* (Oxford: Wiley-Blackwell, 2002).

the religious spheres continued (as many do still) to follow their inherited sacred space configuration. This is important to point out, because the history toward women's equality has often been written as the history of women conquering public roles in public spaces. Thereby it is overlooked how some sacred spaces in earlier times had women exerting relative power and leadership, as illustrated with the examples given above, and further one could add how women's speech, initiative and knowledge production was facilitated in monasteries in the Middle Ages, and how the first recognized professions for women in the early 19th century were within religious hospitals and schools, where women worked as nurses/deaconesses, teachers and missionaries. The oversight is regrettable from the point of view of historical detail, but it also produces a false narrative. The very powerful female abbesses or prioresses of the High Middle Ages (e.g., Hildegard of Bingen), or the earliest post-Reformation founders of new religious communities (e.g., Margaret Fell), put the progress made in the long 19th century regarding women in public space, into a different perspective. In much of this long century, gender equality progress was mostly about catching up with whatever women had been able to do centuries earlier, in sacred space.

I have tried to show through argument and examples that in the modern world, the public/private distinction pertains to the secular realm, and that if we want to understand gender dynamics in historical perspective we also have to take into account sacred/ritually constructed spaces as a third category. This third category also deconstructs the binary as such, something which is not achieved by just changing names (e.g., from private to domestic, familial, etc.). Thus, when feminist thinkers have taken the private/public binary as a point of departure for criticism and reflection – as if it covered the whole of human activity, they have effaced an ancient space of huge importance for women's agency, for ancient societies – and for our understanding of ancient women in particular.

Before the 19th century that is Scott's focus, women found a certain place for their agency, speech, action and initiative in sacred spaces, although it was never unrestricted. Neither should it be denied that even the sacred spaces that functioned according to their own rules, were still sub-divisions of a larger whole of general patriarchal society. In periods when sacred space has been more aligned with public space, sacred spaces have still been gendered, but in other ways: seating men and women in separate aisles, balconies, or separate rooms for worship (or even gender-specific rituals); or putting items on display in the worship space that all allude to only one gender.

Chapter 16
The Inner Landscape of the Body
– Phenomenology of Thinking

Guðbjörg R. Jóhannesdóttir

In many languages, we name specific landscape features after body parts. In Icelandic, for example, we speak about shoulder, neck, forehead, thigh, and nose in a landscape, and this can be seen in many Icelandic place names.[1] This connection between the concepts of landscape and body is interesting, not least in how it can shed light on the role of what Icelandic philosopher Páll Skúlason has called "the feeling of situatedness" in an environment[2], in the creation of knowledge. The feeling of situatedness refers, generally speaking, to our relations to the world; to how the base of our existence always already involves feeling and sensing our situation.[3] The feeling of situatedness, which I discuss here, refers specifically to the embodied experience of environment of situated knowers.[4] Feminist philosophies of situated knowing emphasize primarily the socio-political conditions that shape and determine knowledge. Taking feminist

---

[1] According to Valgarður Egilsson these place names can be found in Icelandic: Head, neck, forehead, eyes, nose, ear, cheek, mouth, tongue, back, shoulder, spine, chest, breast, nipples, fingers, elbows, hips, ass, crouch, testicles, thighs, knees, heel, toe, foot, man. See Valgarður Egilsson, "Örnefni við Eyjafjörð [Place names in Eyjafjörður]", *Nefnir-vefrit Nafnfræðifélagsins [Nefnir – The online journal of the Onomastics Society]*. https://www.arnastofnun.is/is/utgafa-og-gagnasofn/pistlar/ornefni-vid-eyjafjord. This tendency to name landscape features after body parts can be found in many other languages.

[2] Páll Skúlason, *Merking og tilgangur [Meaning and Purpose]*, (Reykjavík: University of Iceland Press, 2015), p. 52.

[3] Simone de Beauvoir, *Le Deuziéme sexe* (Paris: Gallimard, 1949); Maurice Merleau-Ponty, *Phénoménologie de la perception* (Paris: Gallimard, 1945).

[4] Donna Haraway, "Situated Knowledges: The Science Question in Feminism and the Privilege of Partial Perspective," *Feminist Studies* Vol. 14, 1988, pp. 575–599; Sandra Harding, *Whose Science? Whose Knowledge? Thinking from Women's Lives* (Ithaca: Cornell University Press, 1991).

phenomenologies of embodiment on board, I pay attention to how embodiment is part of situatedness and how bodies are always embedded in landscapes and environments.

When examining the body-environment/landscape continuum, I notice a surprising connection between landscape and body in the earliest examples of the Icelandic word for landscape. *Landslag*, for instance, in the Icelandic Sagas, is written *landsleg*. "Leg" in Icelandic refers to a place where something can lie and has been used both to refer to a woman's uterus and to a final resting place (*leg-staður* means resting place). This linguistic resemblance brings to mind a comparison between the fetus' being in the womb and our being in a landscape, as well as between the phenomenology of pregnancy[5] and the phenomenology of landscape.[6] As I will examine further in this paper, this comparison can shed light on a relational understanding of the human being, which, as I will argue, should be the basis of our understanding of knowledge creation. My goal is not to go into a detailed etymological analysis of the connections between the words landscape and body. Instead, I aim to use this interesting use of words as a starting point for examining an understanding of the human being as a relational knowledge-creating being. The basis for this examination is a phenomenological understanding of landscape and body. I aim to deepen this understanding by exploring the connection between these concepts that appear in the aforementioned use of words.

I start by sketching out shortly how these concepts are understood through the lens of phenomenology. Then, I go on to explore the understanding of landscape that appears in the word *landsleg* in the Sagas and its connection to the phenomenology of pregnancy. Finally, I show how connecting these two perspectives allows for a deeper understanding of the role of the aesthetic in our sensing and thinking. The underlying aim of

---

[5] Jonna Bornemark, "Life Beyond Individuality: A-subjective Experience in Pregnancy" in Jonna Bornemark, & Nicholas Smith, (Eds.), *Phenomenology of Pregnancy* (Huddinge: Södertörn Philosophical Studies 18, 2016).

[6] Guðbjörg R. Jóhannesdóttir, *Icelandic Landscapes: Beauty and the Aesthetic in Environmental Decision-making* (Reykjavík: University of Iceland, 2015).

the approach presented here is to re-evaluate some of the qualities of human thinking and being that have been rejected in the past as being feminine. As feminist philosophers have pointed out, the Western philosophical tradition has neglected in understandings of the human being the aesthetic, sensuous, and bodily dimensions of our being and thinking.[7] Shining a new light on these dimensions can thus be seen as an essential part of the feminist epistemological project of challenging limited notions of rationality and knowledge creation.

Landscape and Body: A Phenomenological Perspective

Looking at landscape from a phenomenological perspective and acknowledging the relationship between the concepts of beauty and landscape leads to a relational understanding of landscape. Accordingly, landscape is an environment perceived aesthetically and thus includes the relation between subject and object, human and environment.[8] Landscape refers to our perception of land or space as a whole (whether it is a physical or mental space) and how all its qualities, visible and invisible, come together in one's perception of it. As I have written about elsewhere, this type of perceiving is aesthetic perception – when we perceive only to perceive. We use the word landscape when we are referring to the aesthetic values or qualities of the land; when we are grazing our horses, we call it pasture; when we are building a factory, we call it a construction site, when we perceive only to perceive we call it landscape.[9]

At the core of a phenomenological account of the body is Husserl's differentiation between the body as *Leib* and *Körper*.

---

[7] Richard Shusterman, *Thinking Through the Body: Essays in Somaesthetics* (Cambridge: Cambridge University Press, 2012); Peggy Zeglin Brand & Carolyn Korsmeyer (Eds.), *Feminism and Tradition in Aesthetics* (University Park, Pennsylvania: Pennsylvania State University Press, 2010).

[8] Jóhannesdóttir, *Icelandic Landscapes,* p. 154. See also Joachim Ritter, "Landschaft. Zur Funktion des Ästhetischen in der modernen Gesellschaft", in *Subjektivität,* pp. 141–163 (Frankfurt: Suhrkamp, 1989).

[9] Jóhannesdóttir, *Icelandic Landscapes.*

While *Körper* refers to the objectified body that can be measured and evaluated by scientific methods, *Leib* refers to the lived body, the lived experience of an embodied being.[10] This lived body has often been forgotten in philosophical thought, as many feminist philosophers have emphasized and, for their part, feminist phenomenologists have thus elaborated on embodied and embedded being in their research.[11] From the point of view of feminist phenomenology, the body is central to our understanding and practice of philosophical thought, since the body is precisely what allows us to experience, perceive and think about the world in the first place.[12] My agenda in discussing landscape and the body is, among other things, to direct our attention to the importance of not forgetting that we are bodies; just like plants and other animals, we are living organisms that are constantly interacting with different environments.[13] I aim to bring out and explore why it is vital to speak about the fact that we are always already bodies in landscapes when we try to understand what characterizes human sensing and thinking. To shed light on the interaction between inner and outer landscapes and further examine the connection between the sensing and

[10] See Sigríður Þorgeirsdóttir, "Heimspeki líkamans og heimspeki í líkamanum og hvers vegna hugsun er ekki kynlaus" [Philosophy of the Body and Philosophy in the Body and Why Thought is not Gender-free], *Hugur*, Vol. 27, 2015, pp. 65–80; Gústav Adolf Bergmann Sigurbjörnsson, "Líkamlegar hugverur: Líkaminn og líkamleiki í fyrirbærafræði Edmunds Husserl" [Embodied Mind-Beings: The Body and Embodiment in Edmund Husserl's Phenomenology], *Hugur*, Vol. 27, 2015, pp. 48–64.

[11] Sara Heinämaa, *Toward a Phenomenology of Sexual Difference: Husserl, Merleau-Ponty, Beauvoir* (Lanham: Rowman & Littlefield, 2004).

[12] Sigridur Thorgeirsdóttir, "The Torn Robe of Philosophy: Philosophy as a Woman in The Consolation of Philosophy by Boethius", in Sigridur Thorgeirsdottir and Ruth Hagengruber (Eds.), *Methodological Reflections on Women's Contribution and Influence in the History of Philosophy* (London/New York: Springer, 2020), pp. 83–96; Antonio Damasio, *Descartes' Error: Emotion, Reason and the Human Brain* (New York: G.P. Putnam's sons, 1994); George Lakoff and Mark Johnson, *Philosophy in the Flesh: The Embodied Mind and its Challenges to Western Thought* (Michigan: Basic Books, 1999); Mark Johnson, *The Meaning of the Body: Aesthetics of Human Understanding* (Chicago: University of Chicago Press, 2007).

[13] Eugene Gendlin, "Arakawa and Gins: The Organism-Person-Environment Process" in Donata Schoeller and Edward Casey (Eds.), *Saying What We Mean: Implicit Precision and the Responsive Order* (Evanston: Northwestern University Press, 2017).

thinking involved in this interaction, I start by looking at how the word *landscape/landslag* or *landsleg* was used in early Icelandic manuscripts.

Landslag or Lands*leg*

The earliest examples of the Icelandic word for landscape, *landslag*, appear in the sagas from the 12–13th century, where it is written lands*leg*, i.e., with *leg* instead of *lag*.[14] This ancient way of spelling landscape also occurs in later examples from the 17th–19th century. From this etymological observation, we can conclude that landscape, in Icelandic, refers to how everything "lies" or connects as a whole in a certain place or a certain situation and to how we can, as bodies, "lie" within this whole or connect to it. As can be seen from the following quotes from *Eiríks saga rauða* (Saga of Erik the Red) and *Vatnsdæla saga* (Saga of the people of Lake valley), the landsleg, its beauty, and other qualities are examined in the context of exploring the situation that the land offers the settlers to dwell (or lie) within:

> The Finns' prophecy must be coming true, for I now recognise the **landsleg** from their account of it, hither we are being directed, and things are now getting much better; I see now extensive land and if it is accompanied by resources, then perhaps this is a good site to build. (*Vatnsdæla saga*)

> They called it Straumfjord. They carried their things from the ship and settled. They had all kinds of livestock. There was beautiful **landsleg**; they paid attention to nothing other than exploring the land. (*Eiríks saga*)[15]

A few examples of the word *landsleg* can be found from the 17th–19th century, but after that, landscape is always written *landslag*. In these examples, *landsleg* always seems to refer to

---

[14] Edda R. H. Waage, *The Concept of Landslag: Meaning and Value for Nature Conservation* (Reykjavík: University of Iceland, 2013), p.100.
[15] Waage, *The Concept of Landslag*, p. 113 and 115.

"how things are – how they are arranged".[16] From this, we can see that *landsleg* is something that one can explore and examine; one knows how it is and can compare it with something else. The word *leg* can also be found in examples from the 17th century onwards, where it is always used to refer to a place where something can lie – *leg* is the place where the fetus can lie in the mother's womb, and it is also a place where one can have a final resting place – *legstaður*, as well as a place where for example a boat can lie on the beach or a machine part can lie within the machine. However, it also seems to refer, like *landsleg*, to how things are, how they lie.

By referring to how things lie, *landsleg* refers to how everything lies together and connects as a whole. It also relates to a human's possibilities of connecting to the landscape. In other words: What possibilities do we have to make it our home? In the examples from the Icelandic sagas above, the word *landsleg* is used to describe, for example, what happens when you sail to a new place and sense the land ahead. You see the land in front of you that lies before your feet, and you perceive it as if for the first time because it is the first time. As we saw in the example from *Eiríks saga*, it is suggested that when you are "paying attention to nothing other than exploring the land," you perceive its beauty or its aesthetic qualities: "There was beautiful **landsleg**; they paid attention to nothing other than exploring the land". This is what you do when you experience a place for the first time; you perceive just to perceive, to feel *how you feel* there, whether you find the landscape beautiful, whether you can imagine yourself dwelling there, making it your home. In her writings on the importance of landscape beauty, the German philosopher Angelika Krebs, discusses the German concept of *Heimat*,[17] which is an equivalent to *heima* in Icelandic but has

---

[16] Ritmálssafn Orðabókar HÍ [The University of Iceland Written Language Archive]: https://ritmalssafn.arnastofnun.is/daemi/283716

[17] Roger Scruton uses the Greek word oikos for the same purpose. See Roger Scruton, *Green Philosophy: How to Think Seriously About the Planet* (London: Atlantic Books Ltd, 2014).

no exact match in English.[18] Krebs claims that being able to experience beautiful landscapes is an "essential part of the good human life. We humans cannot fare well without it. The reason for this is that the experience of beautiful landscapes makes us feel at home in the world. Their great and irreplaceable value lies therein".[19] This is the value of landscape beauty, according to Krebs. And why is it so important to be able to feel at home in the world? For her, beautiful landscapes and the feeling of being at home teach us to dwell on the earth with respect and care for it. A beautiful landscape calls for us to put our roots down and feel that we care for the landscape as our special home.[20]

This connection between landscape beauty and feeling at home is interesting in light of how the concept of *landsleg* is used in these early examples from the Icelandic sagas. In these medieval texts, *landsleg* is almost always accompanied by judgments of beauty and judgments of whether one can imagine making the *landsleg* one's home, as is evident in this example from *Vatnsdæla saga*:

> Then the team moved up the valley and saw that there were good resources from the land with regard to grass and wood;

[18] The word *heimat* in German has two meanings according to dictionaries, it can have the historically problematic meaning of home as in hometown, homeland, motherland, native land and it can mean home as in living somewhere/having a home and being at home. The Icelandic word *heima* has only the second meaning of being at home or living somewhere, it does not refer to homeland without adding to it, heima*land*. When I say that *heimat* and the Icelandic *heima* are not exact equivalents of home in English I'm referring to how the words are used in the context of being at home/living somewhere. In Icelandic we can say: *Ég er heima/ég á heima* where *heima* does not have the connotation of only the space/object you are *at* or *have* like it is in English: I am *at* home/I live in/*have a* home in. The only occasion you would say I'm home in English is when you are arriving, as in I'm here. Where home in English seems to refer to an object/a space, *heima* seems to include both the space and the being in the space as one whole contained in one word. To translate home as an object/space into Icelandic we would use the word *heimili*, but *heima* includes more than the objective space *heimili*, it includes the act of being in space as well. As Krebs also points out, *heimat* means "'being at home' or living in a 'place' as opposed to a space", see: Angelika Krebs, "Why Landscape Beauty Matters", *Land*, 3(4), 2014, p. 1257

[19] Angelika Krebs, "Why Landscape Beauty Matters", *Land*, 3(4), 2014, p. 1251.

[20] Krebs, "Why Landscape Beauty Matters", p. 1262.

> there was beautiful to look around; people then felt in a much better mood. ... Ingimundr chose his dwelling in a very beautiful hollow and established a farm. (*Vatnsdœla saga*)

When we speak of a beautiful landscape, we are describing that moment when we perceive just to perceive, which is like asking oneself: "Could I live here? Does this phenomenon pull me towards it? Am I attracted to it? Can I relate to it?" This experience of choosing a *heima* is also going on when we are experiencing art. For example, when we go to concerts or other art events; then we choose to "live in" or "have our home in" this artwork; pay attention to it in the same way as we pay attention to a place we are considering as a future home. When we choose a home, we sense inside ourselves to see how we feel there and ask ourselves: How do I feel in this space/this situation? What possibilities of relating to it can I imagine? Can I lie here within these walls? What qualities does it have that make me attracted to it or not?

What all this reveals is that landscape (or *landsleg*) does not only refer to what is there: it does not only involve listing the objects or phenomena that create the whole of the landscape; mountains, valleys, fjords, buildings – it also refers to how you sense this whole, whether you could see yourself living there; in other words, it relates to how you could lie within this landscape. So perhaps the gap we are used to seeing between beauty and utility is not as big as is often implied. Let us leave that question open for now. The understanding of landscape that can be derived from this examination of word use is the following: Landscape (*landslag/landsleg*) refers to our perception of how everything lies together as a whole within a particular situation or a space that you can perceive as a whole, and how you sense in your body your relation to this situation or space and the processes that create it.

We use the word landscape to describe our being in touch with the world when we sense how we connect to it as a possible home. This is the touching of the world that we sense and direct our attention to in aesthetic perception; when we perceive only to perceive – to receive how that perception makes us feel. As Merleau-Ponty repeats after the painter Paul Klee, he sometimes felt that he was receiving meaning from the forest:

> That is why so many painters have said that things look at them. As André Marchand says after Klee: "In a forest, I have felt many times over that it was not I who looked at the forest. Some days I felt that the trees were looking at me, were speaking to me... I was there, listening... I think the painter must be penetrated by the universe and not want to penetrate it... I expect to be inwardly submerged, buried. Perhaps I paint to break out". We speak of "inspiration", and the word should be taken literally. There really is inspiration and expiration of Being [...] it becomes impossible to distinguish between what sees and what is seen, what paints and what is painted.[21]

This is an excellent example of this type of being in touch with the world, where we receive meaning rather than project it onto the world. It is important to keep this touching of the world in mind when we speak about philosophical thinking and know-ledge creation. Merleau-Ponty used the word flesh (fr. *chair*) to describe this pre-discursive level of being, and it is in my mind no coincidence that he chose to use a word that has such a strong connection to the body as nature.

So, what happens if we move beyond the flesh, further into the body, and use the word *leg* (uterus) or *landsleg* to describe this relation to the world, and which Merleau-Ponty used the word flesh to describe? Can we use the meaning of the word *landsleg* as an encouragement to think about the commonalities between our being as bodies in landscapes and the being of the fetus in the womb? As feminist philosophers have pointed out, pregnancy and birth have been neglected within philosophy, and paying attention to these fundamental aspects of life can

---

[21] Maurice Merleau-Ponty, "Eye and Mind", in Galen A. Johnson (Ed.), *The Merleau-Ponty Aesthetics Reader: Philosophy and Painting* (Evanston: Northwestern University Press, 1961/1993), p. 167.

help us understand our situatedness and relationality more profoundly. The pregnant body, as a body nurturing and sharing life with another one within it, with its own intentionality, has more than anything else challenged traditional, disembodied philosophical conceptions of subjectivity that do not include how the self is always multiple, interdependent, and interrelational.[22] The phenomenologist Jonna Bornemark has written about the phenomenology of pregnancy,[23] and her understanding of our being in the womb and my understanding of our being in landscape share a common core. Björn Þorsteinsson has also discussed how the human condition is, from a phenomenological perspective, like being in water – our movements in the world create currents and waves that influence others at the same time as we are influenced by the currents and waves that others make.[24] What can we learn from this metaphor? To be a sensing and thinking being always involves already being a part of all the others with whom we share the world. Being in the world is like being in water – splashing onto others and being splashed at by others. As mentioned above, Jonna Bornemark has written about a related metaphor in her chapter in the book *Phenomenology of Pregnancy*, where she examines the experience of pregnancy both from the perspective of the mother and the perspective of the fetus to shed light on our being and sensing in the world. What was it like to be in the womb? In just a few weeks, we have already started perceiving. Hearing is the first sense to kick in around the 26th–28th week, but as Bornemark remarks, "perception is of another character in the womb":

---

[22] See for example, Alison Stone, *Being Born: Birth and Philosophy* (Oxford: Oxford University Press, 2019); Johanna Oksala, "The Birth of Man", in Dan Zahavi, Sara Heinamaa and Hans Ruin (Eds.), *Metaphysics, Facticity, Interpretation: Phenomenology in the Nordic Countries* (Dordrecht: Springer, 2003), pp. 139–153; Robin-May Schott (Ed.), *Birth, Death and Femininity: Philosophies of Embodiment* (Indiana: Indiana University Press, 2010).

[23] Bornemark, "Life Beyond Individuality".

[24] Kristján Guðjónsson, "Þurfum meiri hugsun og færri skoðanir" [We need more thought and less opinion], DV, February 26, 2017, https://www.dv.is/fokus/menning/2017/02/26/thurfum-meiri-hugsun-og-faerri-skodanir/

Vision is less important, and hearing takes precedence. There is taste and smell (of the amniotic fluid) – but not connected to feelings of hunger.

There are no objects in the sense of autonomous and thematized "things" that are identified as one and the same in the stream of perceptions. The perceptions are thus not understood as belonging to objects, but flow in a stream, intertwined with other perceptions. These perceptions also linger, in what Husserl calls retention: i.e. non-thematized memories. As retentions they linger and affect the following experiences. The layers of perception are still few, and each moment is more filled by its presence than by earlier perceptions or expected later perceptions. Patterns are formed through what Husserl called passive synthesis, in which layers of experiences through retention are put on top of each other and form patterns. Some of these patterns are continually there: the rhythm of the mother breathing, of her heartbeats, of the foetus's heartbeats, and more sporadically of the mother's intestines. These rhythms are felt and heard in a perception where touching and hearing are not separated. Every sound or pulsation is also magnified through the amniotic fluid. The kinaesthetic feeling of movement is not yet connected to movement in a world, and there are no bodies experienced as entities that would be held together, neither of the self nor of others. Instead there are a lot of motions going on, though these are not yet separated into inner and outer.[25]

So, what can this description of what it is like for the fetus to be in the womb/leg tell me about the concept of *landscape/landsleg*? As our use of the words neck, shoulder, foot to describe features of the landscape suggests, we can perceive the landscape and our bodies as one and the same flesh, just as the fetus perceives the womb and itself as the same flesh. Imagining what it was like to be in the womb gives us a feeling for what is involved in a phenomenological understanding of how we are sensing and thinking beings in the world: we sense the world as whole

---

[25] Bornemark, "Life Beyond Individuality", p. 255.

bodies, not as separated sense organs. The field of perception that is awakened first, where sound and touch are not yet separated, is the field of perception that is the basis of all perception – the field of perception that never stops being there. However, we might forget to pay attention to it. This is the basis for all our more complex perceptions – and that is why it is so important to remember this field of perception and pay attention to it. This field of perception is at play in the aesthetic perception of environment, which is what we are referring to when we use the word landscape. This is the perception of how we take everything in that we are immersed in – whether it makes us feel at home, whether it makes us feel connected.

It is now time to return to the questions with which I started this paper: Why is it important to connect the concepts of landscape and body? How does the meaning of these concepts affect our understanding of philosophical thinking and knowledge creation?

The Body and Landscape as the Zero Point of Sensing and Thinking

As sensing and thinking beings, we are bodies in landscapes; as bodies we are always already in an environment. We are always already as if swimming in water out of which we have no way out. We are always situated; we are always "heima", always in a landscape we are immersed in. As sensing and thinking beings, we are constantly experiencing the world through the field of perception that is first awakened in the womb, which I choose to describe with the word landscape. To examine this relationship between landscape and body further, it is useful to look into what characterizes the body as *Leib*. For Husserl, *Leib* refers to movement and action; it is the site of perceiving the whole of what is around us; the lived body is a kind of "zero point", as Husserl called it, which refers to the fact that the body always has a specific "here".[26] If we try to fit these qualities with the concept of landscape, we see that they are very applicable to what I have

---

[26] Sigurbjörnsson, "Líkamlegar hugverur", p. 56–57.

said so far about *landsleg*. The landscape is characterized by movement and action; when we speak about landscapes, we speak of being in the landscape, moving in it, and letting it move us. The landscape is the site of perceiving the whole of what is around us; when we speak of landscapes, we are speaking of perceiving environments aesthetically, which involves sensing how the landscape as a whole affects our senses and how it moves us and makes us feel. The landscape is a type of "zero point", which refers to the fact that the landscape always has a specific "here". The landscape is always somebody's "heima" – just like there is no "heima" without a body in, there is no landscape without a body – in the same way that there is no body without a landscape.

When we come into the world from the mother's womb or *leg*, we are born into the womb or *leg* of the land – *landsleg*. This characterizes us as embodied beings – the basis for all our perceptions is this synaesthetic field of perception that is always active, though we do not always pay attention to it. We are always already situated, always already swimming around in a landsleg. As Páll Skúlason describes, being has "always-already-felt-itself": "[…] being feels (good or bad) among things, feels its situation […] the feeling of situatedness is […] the background of our existence, it symbolizes one of the basic dimensions of human existence".[27] In my mind, the feeling of situatedness is *the body's inner landscape* – it refers to how the outer landscape we perceive resonates within us in the body's inner landscape. Most of the time, we don't notice this feeling of situatedness or synaesthetic field of perception. Still, in these moments that I refer to as aesthetic moments, we pay attention to this field of perception that is always there – which is why they are so important. These aesthetic moments can, I argue, give us a deeper understanding of the human being (more profound than a dualistic understanding of the human being), which is very much needed.

[27] Skúlason, *Merking og tilgangur*, p. 52.

According to this new understanding of the human being (which is perhaps, after all, an old one), we are relational embodied beings, just like plants and animals. This relational understanding of the human being is fundamental when it comes to understanding how we gain knowledge of the world. We are sensing and thinking bodies; we *feel-know,* as Jonna Bornemark remarked about how the fetus knows the world. We feel-know everything that the landscape/lands*leg* has made into the patterns that are always there – these patterns are the sediments of everything we have sensed and known through our journey in the world. Aesthetic perception allows us to open into these patterns or inner sediments of the body.[28] The following examples of the emergence of an artist's or a scientist's new ideas help to explain this further.

An artist once told me how she got the idea for a new artwork while sitting outside sketching the landscape during her travels around the Icelandic countryside. During the act of drawing, we are tuned into an aesthetic perception of our environment, of our outer and inner landscapes; we are tuned into perceiving only to perceive. When the artist tunes into this type of perception, a new thought is often born, a new idea, or a new connection. In a lecture given by an expert from NASA at a conference on the protection of the Icelandic highlands (where he regularly dwells with his team doing research), he showed us photos of the team of scientists sitting in the middle of a lava field or on top of a mountain in the highlands with their sketchbooks or diaries, seemingly very deep in thought and inspired. While showing these photos, he told us how they always made some discoveries and managed to think so well together during the weeks spent in the highlands doing their research.

These two examples captured my attention owing to their common thread. In my mind, the highland landscapes bring us very easily into aesthetic perception, perceiving only to perceive;

---

[28] Just as the sediments of earth are the geological foundation of the landscape, we could say that the inner sediments/patterns of the body are the biophysical and phenomenological layers of the lived body.

in the highlands, there are so many things that create a strong sense of wonder, so many things that draw our attention to our senses. In such situations, many of us are automatically tuned into this type of perception for which drawing calls and in which artists are trained. When we let all our attention go into our senses, an opening occurs into the body's inner landscape – we automatically tune our focus into the body. When we experience a beautiful or even sublime landscape, we start paying attention to what we are sensing and feeling because the outer landscape brings out such strong reactions. This scanning of the body's inner landscape begins with us focusing on what the outer landscape makes us sense or feel. However, when we stop focusing on the details we are perceiving, we still hold our attention on what we are sensing. Then we start scanning the inner landscape of what we are feeling, what we sense and what we know at this moment, and perhaps what is important to us at this moment. What happens in this scanning is that when the inner landscape opens up (all everyday thoughts disappear, and the mind is emptied for a while), then thoughts, memories, visions, and ideas start popping into mind. We can see all these thoughts, memories, and visions (rooted in the *retentions* of lived experience) as sediment after sediment, layer upon layer, thread upon thread, that are woven together and lie within the body. And what is in these sediments? Everything we have perceived before, even since the very beginning, in our mothers' wombs.[29] When we are given the space to scan the body's inner landscape, we are afforded an opportunity to look separately at each thread and layer and how they are related. Just like when we are walking in a landscape, and we name what we see around us or try to speculate about what it is, what story it tells, we do the same when we examine the inner landscape of the body – perhaps we recognize some things that we find there im-

---

[29] Studies have shown that a trauma that a mother experiences during pregnancy can affect the baby after birth. See for example: Sarah R. Brand, Stephanie M. Engel, Richard L. Canfield, and Rachel Yehuda, "The Effect of Maternal PTSD Following in Utero Trauma Exposure on Behavior and Temperament in the 9-Month Old Infant", *Annals of the New York Academy of Sciences* 1071:1 (2006), pp. 454–458.

mediately, but others we have to examine more closely and listen to their story.

Henry David Thoreau, Ralph Waldo Emerson, and other philosophers have emphasized how dwelling alone in nature, or hiking and walking, supports independent, critical, philosophical thinking. In recent years the philosophy of walking has gained greater attention,[30] where stories are told of how philosophers such as Rousseau, Nietzsche, and Kant often did their philosophizing while walking. In my view, it is not only the walking, the movement itself, that creates this connection between thinking and walking. Instead, it is what happens when we are walking: that we direct our attention to the landscape we are walking in and let our senses be in the foreground rather than our analytical thinking. In other words, we connect to the inner landscape of the body, the wisdom, and knowledge that resides in the sediments and threads of our lived bodily experience, and let our thinking rise freely from there. We need to pay more serious attention to this in the context of thinking in philosophy. We do not think as detached brains but as bodies. We need a phenomenology of thinking, and this is my suggestion: As sensing and thinking beings, we are made in such a way that thoughts, memories, visions, and ideas pop up in our minds when our attention is focused on the inner landscape of the body. These are reactions that we sometimes express when we say out loud how something makes us feel or we write down what we are thinking at such moments, but if not, they just settle in the body and become one of the layers or threads that creates the whole of the being I am and knowing what I know. Just as the sediments and layers of stories, events, and human structures generate the whole of what it is to be the landscape of a specific place, the landscape that is somebody's "heima".

To acknowledge the body as the source of thinking is essential for philosophy because philosophy has the role of thinking what it is to think, and it has the role of helping us get our heads around the emerging new understanding of the human

---

[30] Frédéric A. Gros, *Philosophy of Walking* (New York: Verso Books, 2014).

being. Philosophy's role is to think about the world and to help us think about ourselves in relation to the world. This acknowledgment is also important in the context of education systems based on a dualistic understanding of the human being where reasoning and sensing, reason and emotion, mind and body, and human and nature are seen as separate.[31] Furthermore, these systems have mostly ignored the bodily source of knowledge, emphasizing more what is called rational thinking while neglecting intuitive, sensuous, embodied thinking. This neglect of the dimensions associated with the senses, emotions, the body, and nature is a reflection of how the systems on which our societies are built are based on deeply ingrained gender hierarchies, where the qualities associated with the feminine are seen as inferior to the qualities associated with the masculine.

However, there are some signs of changes on the horizon, not the least because of the advances in cognitive science research. The interplay of body and mind cannot be ignored in education systems for too much longer, for the time has come to direct our attention toward the deep roots of all our knowledge and values in natural sciences, humanities, and the arts. The scientist's body is, as Claire Petitmengin writes, "at the source of meaning."[32] Similarly, Susan Stuart writes that verbalized ideas and notions are just the tip of an iceberg that hides the embodied conditions from which they emerge.[33] This change is, therefore, crucial for research in general because, like elsewhere in our education systems, universities have neglected this kind of sensuous know-

[31] Genevieve Loyd, *The Man of Reason: "Male" and "Female" in Western Philosophy* (Abingdon: Routledge, 2002).

[32] Claire Petitmengin, "The Scientists's Body at the Source of Meaning", in Donata Schoeller & Vera Saller (Eds.), *Thinking thinking: Practicing radical reflection* (Freiburg/ München: Karl Alber, 2016), pp. 28–49. Petitmengin's research illuminates the dimension of creativity at the level of the body, "inter-action between people as well as within oneself, navigating between discursive, pre-discursive, trans-modal and gestural dimensions of experience" as "capacities involved in the maturation of an idea – as well as in its inquiry", p. 18.

[33] Susan A. J. Stuart, "Enkinaesthesia and Reid's natural kind of magic", in Schoeller & Saller (Eds.), *Thinking thinking*, pp. 92–111.

ledge and prioritized the "objective" natural sciences much more than, for example, research in the arts and humanities.

The knowledge that the arts and humanities provide is one of the most important types of knowledge societies create – the knowledge that the arts create, for example, is knowledge to which other areas should pay much more attention, especially in their trans-, inter-, or multidisciplinary projects. In such projects, the arts should not be seen as an add-on or a tool to mediate the knowledge that other fields create but rather as an active participant in creating and mediating knowledge.

In recent years, the crisis of philosophy, or even the crisis of the humanities as such, has been much discussed, suggesting that we have somehow lost sight of the importance of these fields. Among the criticisms of philosophy that feminist philosophers and phenomenologists have emphasized is the lack of attention and acknowledgment of the feeling of situatedness, a lack of acknowledgment that as thinking beings, we are always already situated in time and space as diverse bodies in complex relations. This criticism points to the need to strengthen philosophical thinking as embodied thinking. What does it mean for the practice of philosophical thinking and the teaching of this practice to take this relational understanding of the human being seriously?[34] There are methods available, in the arts, as well as in philosophy and the sciences, for example Petitmengin's microphenomenological interview method[35] and Gendlin and Hendrick's Thinking at the Edge method.[36] These methods allow us to closely examine the body's inner landscape and engage in conversation with and about what we find there. This inner landscape has been shaped by what we have felt and, what we know, what we feel-know. Traveling around this inner land-

---

[34] This is one of the questions asked in the research project *Embodied Critical Thinking*. For further information, see: http//www.ect.hi.is. This chapter was partly written as part of *ECT*.

[35] Claire Petitmengin, "Describing one's Subjective Experience in the Second Person: An Interview Method for the Science of Consciousness", *Phenomenology and the Cognitive Sciences* 5 (2006), pp. 229–269.

[36] Eugene Gendlin, "Introduction to Thinking at the Edge", *The Folio* 19:1 (2004), pp. 1–8.

scape, for example, while walking, is probably familiar to many of us, although we might not be aware of it. But we can also do this consciously by directing our focused and open attention to our thoughts and feelings of situatedness.

Directing our attention toward our feeling of situatedness, how we at each moment sense our situation in a bodily way, is a key aspect of embodied critical thinking. However, this does not mean that practicing such thinking involves unconditionally trusting one's own emotions, sensations, and intuitions. Directing our attention to the bodily dimensions of thinking does not imply that we use the feelings and sensations that occur, for example, while hearing an argument or reading a philosophical text, as a basis for critical thinking without any filters. If, for example, I'm reading a philosophical text and my bodily reactions, the feeling of situatedness that I sense, is characterized by a feeling of agreement, I do not stop there and simply accept the argument in the text. Rather I go further, engage with this feeling of agreement, and ask what it is about this text that creates this particular sense of the situation, then analyze this feeling further and then build my argument about the text on this basis. In this process, I might find out that what creates this initial feeling of agreement is some experience that colors my opinion in an unacceptable way. If I then read another paper that brings out a strong bodily response of resistance, I also do not stop there but instead ask, what is it that creates this resistance, what it is in my experience and perception that causes me to disagree with what I am reading? The answers to these questions then form the basis of my criticism of the paper. In this manner, we can critically reflect on our feelings and bodily responses to what we are working with instead of ignoring them as dimensions of thought. Critical thinking is this movement between embodied sensing and thinking with words, a process of examining and analyzing our responses to the situations we find ourselves in at each moment. The linguistic turn needs to be supported by a turn toward lived experience.[37] Practicing critical thinking is an experience of using words and sensing how they fit our experience of reality.[38] Contemporary cognitive science shows us how close the interaction is between language and feeling and how vital the role of our bodies, sensations, and experiences is in our thinking processes.[39]

In our contemporary technological environment, where it is undoubtedly easy to manipulate our feelings and perceptions of reality, it is even more important than ever that we acknowledge the part that feelings and sensations play in our thinking and build our critical thinking on this fact rather than imagining that we can separate our logical thinking from our sensing of the world, or in some way put our feelings aside and apply some sort of pure rationality that has nothing to do with our feelings, sensations, and experiences. There is no such rationality. On the contrary, rationality is closely connected to sensation, as the Icelandic word for rationality, *skyn*semi, implies, where *skyn*, refers to sensing. Using our rationality or skynsemi means paying attention to one's sensing, examining, and analyzing it. In that way, we can distinguish between those moments where our sensing is shaped by outside forces, in contrast to when it is built on our independent analysis of all sides of the matter in light of the most trustworthy and detailed information we obtain. It is time to direct our attention to the bodily roots of knowledge and values. Doing so enables us to see the potential of feminist philosophy that includes and celebrates the body, the senses, and emotions to transform philosophy.[40] Signs of more balance between logical and intuitive thinking in the future can also be

---

[37] Donata Schoeller & Sigridur Thorgeirsdottir, "Embodied Critical Thinking: The Experiential Turn and its Transformative Aspects", *PhiloSOPHIA* 9:1 (2019), pp. 92–109.

[38] Donata Schoeller, "Somatic-semantic Shifting: Articulating Embodied Cultures", in Schoeller & Saller (Eds.), *Thinking Thinking*; Donata Schoeller, *Close Talking: Erleben zur Sprache bringen* (Berlin/Boston: Walter de Gruyter GmbH, 2019).

[39] Damasio, *Descartes' Error*.

[40] Sigridur Thorgeirsdottir and Ruth Hagengruber (Eds.), *Methodological Reflections on Women's Contribution and Influence in the History of Philosophy* (London/New York: Springer, 2020).

seen in emerging discussions about the value of art education in our education systems in recent years. Many national school curriculums now put more emphasis on the role of creative thinking, and discussions of the implications of the fourth industrial revolution suggest that there is a transformative era ahead, where our education systems may be adjusting to a new way of thinking about their role. Their role is no longer only to pass information, to fill our minds with pregiven ideas that we can learn by heart, but rather to educate us in a way that makes us more human; more able to sense our environment with full attention and respond to it in a responsible and reasonable manner, find our own solutions and find our own voice.

Chapter 17
Philosophical Compassion and Active Hesitation
– A Non-Critical Approach to Understanding

Nicole des Bouvrie[1]

Posing the Question of Truth

Long before we entered the time of post-truth, in which having an opinion is valued above all else, we had already lost the foundation of what it means to be. Truth either no longer existed or was already reduced to simply be a justified belief. Nietzsche's death of God heralded a time in which we understood that a church is empty of meaning except for the one we ourselves put in it. Life is the meaning we create. And although most people are successful imposters, the core of human life has become utterly devoid of meaning. But instead of trying to find one more existentialism, one more method of justifying our existence through a dependency on something that lies outside of ourselves, I will argue that we need to return to truth itself.

The question of truth is fundamentally an ontological question, aiming for a grounding of what is, rather than delineating what we can know. But it is simultaneously an ethical question, as ontology should always be understood ethically[2] – it is me, human, asking for the being of things, and therefore the question of truth is always being asked from within the relationship of the human with the thing. In other words, we will have to take

---

[1] The ideas presented in this essay have been developed over time and alongside fellow thinkers. With special thanks to Peter Tamas and Gabriel Yoran. Part of this research was supported by Fudan University and the Bahá'í Chair for World Peace at the University of Maryland. None of this would have happened without the support, conversations and warmth presented by the people involved in the feminist philosophy study circle at the Nordic Summer University: Synne, Vala, Johanna, Milka, Suzy, Laura, Eret, Anne, Petra, Karolina, Erik, Sara, Helgard, Oda, among others.
[2] Emmanuel Levinas, "Is Ontology Fundamental?" (1951) in *Entre Nous. On Thinking-of-the-Other* (London: Athlone Press, 1998).

up the Heideggerian endeavor of returning to the question of being, without reducing everything to a fundamental thingness.[3] But as always we are already trapped in the Shakespearian illusion of being versus not-being: as if there is such a space from which we can think being that is not already being, we ask the question of truth as if we are an outsider even though we can never be unless we are already within some truth. And so life continues and the dualistic illusion persists in insisting on a dualistic question to which only one answer exists. As we breathe, and even beyond, there is a rudimentary 'always already' – that philosophical nightmare that ends all conversations. (For how can we create, how can we have a convers(at)ion, how can we think one moment different from another, when there is no before and no after?).

Framing this question of truth already brings up enough problems. For who is this 'we' that needs to take up this question? How can I talk about something more than myself, how am I appropriating the other that I don't know, the other that is not-me, in this search for a truth? How is the one I address not rigorously refusing to be included in my thinking?[4] Am I not already making a claim by saying this is a concern of me as a human being – who am I including and who am I excluding in and through this question? Why should I understand this to be an ethical problem, why not leave it as a metaphysical question that can be solved outside of language and human perception? Why not be a speculative realist, and deal with each relationship between things equally, not relying on the assumption of human superiority? Yet performing the Husserlian epoché on myself as a self, bracketing the mouth that speaks, the body that lives, is not possible after Heidegger. We are thrown into life not just as an exercise in boredom, but as the foundation of being. Taking

---

[3] Although it would go too far to go into this here, it must be made clear that reducing the human to one more thing as is proposed by object oriented ontologists, is not possible when understanding Heidegger in this way, in which being is always already from within a human relationship.

[4] Avital Ronell, personal conversation, August 12, 2018.

up this question of being thus muddies the water we call rationality. Pretending reality can be addressed outside of language, as something other than a well-crafted inherited construction of reality, outside of being-alive, is dangerous. For this pretense of a complete objectivity leaves out the lived history that is concurrent with every being.

Yet despite all these problems of even asking the question, there is an urgency to this question of truth. For without taking it up, my own understanding trumps anything else. If there is no road map that establishes the relationship between myself and the other, there are only different versions of me. My past, present and future merge into one. What remains is a continuous rehashing of things and the throwing up of whatever does not fit, relying only on what I already know, which equals that which was always already. It would make everything correct, every opinion just as valid and valuable as the next. This is multiculturalism that has triumphed in its death. This is the danger that contemporary democracy forces upon us, equating equality and justice, thereby foregoing all claims on the singularity of truth. Presenting truth as something that excludes others, that considers vulnerability and not-knowing as a denial of one's self instead of it being its fundamental possibility. This kind of truth-claiming foregoes the possibility of being loyal to a singular truth instead of accepting the constant fragmentation that leaves one groundless. What remains is a reality which consists of (paraphrasing Derrida) being completely inside the text, a reality (with Foucault) that functions only as long as we believe in it. But philosophers are more than chroniclers of the present. What is needed is a philosophy that allows for a future that is as of yet unknown and impossible. A future that is not a mere extraction of past and present, that goes further than a simple linearity of thought. A future that is not a "not-yet" that is reduced to an "always-already".[5] A future that allows for a truth that is defined in- and for-itself, not as a negation or an absence of the past and

[5] See: Luce Irigaray, *The Forgetting of Air in Martin Heidegger* (Austin: University of Texas Press), p. 53.

present that had come before it.[6] A truth that does not impose a violent inclusion upon that which it has itself excluded.

Understanding Understanding

Truth is the moment of openness, the *aletheia*, the not-being-shrouded by knowledge and justified beliefs. That space in the middle of the forest where there is a clearing, an openness that is contained within each tree without exhausting the possibility that is necessarily left as an empty space. Picture Heidegger walking along the path in his beloved *Wald*,[7] but then as if he didn't already know where he was going, where he was and who he was. Because that is the openness that is required, the foundation of any being-toward-truth that is more than a collision with what you already are.

So, what then does it mean to understand anything, when any claim on knowledge would destroy the possibility of truth and is therefore to be avoided? Whenever we say or think or feel, whenever something is, it puts forward a claim of being, ending endless amounts of possibilities. Thus, we are drawing back, performing the ancient epoché on ourselves; a suspension of knowledge that allows for a not-knowing. Yet by searching for a possibility of not-knowing, are we not simply conjuring up an illusion of singularity, of otherness that simply reinstates the status quo? Is the opening in the forest really creating a newness out of the old, or is it an experience that deludes us to think we are clear of the trees? Is the sky not already thought while we walk through the forest? Is the blueness of the sky something we get from the world or project upon the world?[8] And if at least some of our knowledge is, in the Kantian sense, *a priori*,[9] are we

---

[6] See Fanny Söderbäck, *Revolutionary Time: On Time and Difference in Kristeva and Irigaray* (Albany: State University of New York, 2019), p. 46.

[7] Cf. Martin Heidegger, Holzwege, Gesamtausgabe 5 (Frankfurt am Main: Vittorio Klostermann 2003).

[8] Some studies suggest that sky has only been blue since modern times, noting that in ancient Greek texts, no single mention of the blueness of the sky is made. Cf. Guy Deutscher and William Gladstone.

[9] See: Immanuel Kant, *Kritik der reinen Vernunft* (Frankfurt am Main: Suhrkamp, 1974).

then doomed to understand the world as we do, foregoing any possibility of the openness required for truth?

In any crisis we can hear people voicing the longing for change. Whether it is the climate crisis, the Arab spring, or the Covid-19 pandemic; the words people use are the same – but what is it that is asked for in the cries of 'we don't want to go back to the old normal', 'we want things to change'. We see the rupture of the prevailing norms as a possibility for radical change, a possibility to finally work on fighting climate change, on changing the economic system, on re-evaluating the notion of care. And it is not as if everything stays completely the same. The United Nations was formed, universal basic income schemes are being introduced. But, fundamentally, our outlook on life, on order, on how things work, does not change. As Cornel West explains:

> The system cannot reform itself. We've tried black faces in high places. Too often our black politicians, professional class, middle class become too accommodated to the capitalist economy, too accommodated to a militarized nation-state, too accommodated to the market-driven culture of cele-brities, status, power, fame, all that superficial stuff that means so much to so many fellow citizens. And what happens is (…) they really don't know what to do because all they want to do is show more black faces – show more black faces. But often times those black faces are losing legitimacy too…[10]

And while we protest that which puts us down, that which we dismiss as backward, that which systematically undermines our dreams, and while we look forward, the more we look at the world around us, the more our eyes are getting accustomed to the patterns, to the possibilities of which our present system allows us to think. This is what Foucault meant when he intro-duced the panopticon – it is not us who actively decide on what truth is, what reality is, this is decided for us by the space that is

---

[10] CNN live news, hosted by Anderson Cooper, 29 May 2020.

never empty. And if a shift were to happen, we can only observe this from the position of the victors, understanding truth from the power of the present corrupts, and when we want to understand the unknown future, we bring in the past as there is nothing else we can use to make sense of the world around us. So even when we are in the position to think the future anew, we fundamentally sabotage ourselves.

In other words, by living in the world we have internalized its (male) gaze.[11] We ourselves have become the object we must fight. When we understand truth as that radical opening, we must lose our minds. We follow in the footsteps of Nietzsche, whose life project to re-evaluate values after he had eliminated the horizon by which we understand the world around us, made him lose touch with reality. It is no surprise that philosophers and scientists are so much more capable of criticizing the present than presenting a critical alternative of the future. For truth and the future are negated by the present. And it is this dualism, this either/or thinking, that presupposes everything as being-in-being and does not allow for anything that is not already to be thought, that kills all possibility. A system that sets up an order of things can soften the borders but can never take the divisions between things away. Once men and women, mind and body, human and animal, were divided, their division became the backbone of the system itself. It is this dualism, this 'othering' of what is actually connected, that creates the panopticon, the prison of the present.

Non-Critical Approach

The critical approach to understanding posits the subject in opposition to the object, where the subject is a unified whole looking out at something that is essentially foreign to the subject. This means that in a critical approach to understanding there is a directionality to understanding, and an essential distance between subject and the object.

[11] See: Bracha L. Ettinger, *The Matrixial Borderspace* (Minneapolis: University of Minnesota Press 2006).

The relation between the subject and the object in such a critical scenario can be delineated by its two extremes. Critical understanding at its worst is a projection of the subject who posits his own world on that which he seeks to understand, resulting in a knowledge limited to what can be seen and what is already known. The limits of one's own world, the limits of the subject, are the limits of the understanding of the other. Categories of thought, language and previous experience are the kind of projections that the subject takes with him. It is in this sense that philosophers like Derrida and Foucault speak of the impossibility of change[12] and the panopticon[13] – of us being stuck in the present that recreates itself in a continuous loop.

At the other end of the spectrum, critical can be seen as being more in line with Levinas, who realizes that the subject is dependent on the other being looked at. In this case there is a projection of the object upon the subject. Here the subject is dependent upon the object. In this case the subject conforms to the object, and we could say that the subject is being destroyed in favor of the truth of the object. While this movement is in fact a reversal of the destruction happening in the other approach of critical understanding, the result is the same, namely the continuation of the either/or dichotomy between object and subject.

Even the more neutral Hegelian option of sublimation of both subject and object, where each is overcome by a third term, is still tied to this essential dichotomy. It simply substitutes a third reality and continues to allow the object and the subject to exist through their difference. True, the critical relationship of the subject outside of the object is overcome, but it is still a critical approach towards understanding where both self and other are destroyed and the difference between the two remains essential.

In this chapter I propose to look at understanding in a non-critical manner. This entails that subject and object are never in

---

[12] Jacques Derrida, "A Certain Impossible Possibility of Saying the Event", *Critical Inquiry*, Vol. 33, No. 2, pp. 441–461.

[13] Michel Foucault, *The Archaeology of Knowledge* (London: Routledge 2002).

opposition, which is not to say that this approach demands that subject and object are the same, which would be another form of violence to the uniqueness of either one. This also means that neither object nor subject 'wins' in favor of the other. Instead, the non-critical approach to understanding argues for a method in which the idea of winning and destroying is relinquished. This also means that there can be no directionality, there is no looking from the subject to the other, because in this (male) gaze already lies the primal element of destruction. The search for a non-critical approach to understanding therefore aims for an understanding without destruction, an approach which allows for truth without violence.

Presenting the Other

To understand what lies outside of the realm of what can be understood, to understand in a way that does not rely on presupposed knowledge and categories of thought, to understand in a non-critical way, we need to leave behind the dualism inherent in the subject that thinks. We need to find a method of thinking that does not allow difference to divide us, but that lets us work with difference, in line with the project of Luce Irigaray.[14] Irigaray worked to banish the dichotomy that "stands at the heart of a logic incapable of thinking difference (sexual, racial/colonial, and other forms of difference) beyond hierarchical dichotomies."[15] We need a change that does not undo being, that does not force sameness or equality on things that are not the same, and which does not presuppose that the one can be substituted by the other if only we try hard enough. Together with Irigaray this chapter endeavors "to criticize the metaphysical tradition of presence not by escaping presence altogether, but by establishing that said tradition never has been able to think presence other than as absence, and that a proper critique of such tradition therefore depends on our rethinking

---

[14] See for instance: Penelope Deutscher, *A Politics of Impossible Difference: The Later Work of Luce Irigaray* (Ithaca: Cornell University Press 2002).
[15] Söderbäck, *Revolutionary Time*, p. 121.

the relation between presence and absence in non-oppositional terms."[16] To think truth without succumbing to the thinking that is in charge, we need a radical movement that does not present an alternative, that does not consider things in terms of linear progress, nor as something that presents the feminine as taking over or on the side of male logic. What we are looking for is something that does not simply repeat the Hegelian dialectic.

But even language is making this understanding of truth as not-the-other-as-the-same impossible. We talk about rupture, about change, about otherness, but all these terms plot to divide us, to have the one facing the other. Whether it is time or space that stands between the two, we always approach reality from an outer-space, from the future or the past, looking at the one present of which we know only one thing: that it is not us.[17]

Although the initiative of Levinas to ground the subject in the relationship to the Other is worthwhile, laying the foundation of an ethics as preceding ontology,[18] as Bracha Ettinger explains, he continues the logic inherent in the male gaze – thereby perpetuating the linear logic of progress that I will call a critical male approach to difference. By presenting ourselves as starting from the other, we take the removal of ourselves from that which we are not as a starting point for ourselves. Defining something through a lack, the not-being-male, the non-white, non-Western, non-rational. The other is then reduced and limited to being not-me. The o-ther is over-there, and the distance between the I and the other as the beginning of knowledge reinforces the inability to understand truth except through this lack that forms the basis of the critical male approach. The more we think we move closer to what is, the Levinasian self, the more fundamental the difference between the I and the other – which results in a violence either way. By trying to understand the Other/Self we immediately become violent: we either reinstate the duality

---

[16] Söderbäck, *Revolutionary Time*, p. 121.

[17] Cf. The problem that Immanuel Kant outlined in *Kritik der reinen Vernunft* but only solved by enforcing the distinction of a prior and a posteriori knowledge – imposing another division to make up for the inaccessibility of truth as an experience.

[18] Levinas, "Is Ontology Fundamental?".

by Othering the Other, or we reduce the otherness to a sameness and thereby destroy the singularity that is presented in each and every Other. Even by asking the other to tell the subject what is required, what is the right way to behave to allow the otherness to exist, we violate the other – since there remains a 'we' that needs to ask and an 'other' that is burdened with defending itself due to its otherness. As long as there is a 'we', there must be an other. And as long as there is an other, there is a gaze, there is a minority, there is a power structure that prevents understanding.

Instead of the critical approach that violates, let us look for a kind of understanding that is to be open toward all possibilities. If understanding invokes a structure of any kind, truth remains enslaved to the powers that be. Whether it is called the male gaze, or biopower, whether it presents itself as racism, sexism, ableism – the result of a structure of understanding that does not allow for the Other is a totalitarian worldview that encompasses all possibilities and thereby excludes truth.

Are we then to conclude that a non-critical manner of understanding is impossible? When we think of understanding in terms of object–subject relations, when we consider the other always outside of the self, there is no other way than to label the question of an understanding as one that is based on difference – and the question of truth continues to be an impossible question.

The I and the non-I

Instead of presenting the Other as other, invoking the duality that kills any possibility of truth not already drowned in the present, let me accept myself as not part of such a duality. I am not on one side of any equation. I am just as much self as non-self. The border that links me to any perceived other is the border that is within me, that presents myself to myself. When there is a distinction made, this is a distinction that is contained within, not as a limit of the outside-of-me. If there is an-other, then I relate to myself as this other. Which is destructive when I consider everything to be (a) given, when limiting the I to a notion of the self that presupposes a set world and a set understanding of what it means to be human. But the opposite is just as problematic: to consider the self an endless realm of possibilities that has no borders. For without borders there is no self, but with borders there is always an other that lies outside of the self which is excluded. So the way forward is neither a contained understanding of truth/self, nor an empty realm of nothingness/possibility.

The problem lies not in the self, but in the frame that is used, the understanding of duality in the sense of a dichotomy that is an either/or, a with me or against me. By lining up difference as the starting point for the self, as the source of understanding, as the fixation within a struggle for survival in which the weaker one will perish. But duality does not necessarily entail power in the sense of power-over. There is also the possibility of a power-with, a power-to. Presenting a self, an I, is already a power-move, but this power does not need to be understood as a power-over, a power that is based on a degradation of an other.[19] There is a difference between *macht* and *kracht*, the first one being a power-over that creates a hierarchy of the one over the other and fixes positions. The latter, power as *kracht,* is the potential to act, that remains inside even though it needs things outside of it.

This is how we can understand the distinction that Bracha Ettinger raises when she talks about the I and the non-I.[20] It is not a distinction through which a power-over-structure emerges. It provides a framework to help us use the words we have to relocate the essence of what we are after. When searching for understanding there remains the limit of the I that understands, but within the framework of Ettinger this limit is not a line that excludes. This border can be understood as a space, one in which we can dwell, as a borderspace that allows for a blurring of limits without denying or framing the I and/or the non-I.

[19] Cf. Steven Lukes, *Power: A Radical View* (London: Palgrave Macmillan 2005).
[20] Ettinger, *The Matrixial Borderspace.*

The borderspace is matrixial, the place in the womb where the difference between the child and the mother is not clear, where both merge without losing their respective places. They combine and work together, fragilizing themselves as they both allow the other to come so close that it may threaten their own life, yet this matrixial borderspace also gives them life. Without the child, there would be no mother, and without the mother, there would be no child. But we could take this metaphor even further and say that there is not just dependency between the I and the non-I, there is also an instantaneousness that Ettinger indicates with (m)Other. The existence of the mother and the child takes place in an in-between, a non-place that cannot be indicated in a way that understanding in the phallic meaning of the word would require. There is no distance between the I and the non-I, no gaze is possible, no violence against the one without destroying the other.

As a result, there is no language for this in-between space. One is not-yet, not-yet-child and not-yet-mother. This can be seen from the fact that it remains impossible to talk about miscarriage, that there are no words for what is lost that adequately describe what Alison Reiheld speaks of as a 'liminal event'.[21] An event that takes place on a threshold, in a space in which one social status no longer applies but neither does the new one (yet). It is an event that remains outside of understanding, as defining it as anything except for this liminality would destroy the essence of this experience. But this still doesn't explain what understanding in this liminal space means, as without the possibility of an understanding that allows for a not-knowing, a hesitation of being, the liminal space would be "a place of ambiguity and anxiety",[22] as Ronald Carson defines the liminal space. But we need to be careful, as this anxiety only exists because of the need for an understanding that is fixed, that

---

[21] Alison Reiheld, "The Event That Was Nothing: Miscarriage as a Liminal Event", *Journal of Social Philosophy*, Vol. 46, No. 1, Spring 2015, 9–26.

[22] Ronald Carson, "The Hyphenated Space: Liminality in the Doctor-Patient Relationship." In Rita Charon & Martha Montello (Eds.), *Stories Matter: The Role of Narrative in Medical Ethics* (New York: Routledge, 2002), p. 180.

is either/or instead of a place where the I and the non-I can enter a state of borderlinking. This anxiety is not part of the in-betweenness of the liminal event, it is simply due to not being able to let go of the need for the security and definiteness that is associated with a critical approach to understanding.

Compassion as an Active Hesitation

Within the borderspace there is a manner of understanding the possible that does not rely on propositional knowledge. An understanding that is not based on a critical approach. But how to define a type of understanding that defies all defining? How to defend what is defenseless? How to evaluate what is beyond value, what is more fundamental to all values?[23]

What is needed is a kind of understanding which I would like to call a kind of philosophical compassion, or active hesitation. Hesitation is normally understood as a pulling back, a passive attitude. A withholding of something, not engaging with some-thing head-on, but waiting, observing, reflecting. What is meant here is a reluctance to judge, not a reluctance to engage.

Hesitation in this sense is a process, an act. It is not the same as Husserl's epoché, which is a bracketing of everything that makes up the self and thereby reducing the subject to an open object that has no presuppositions. Epoché denies the sources and branches of what one is and one's context and background, history. In this, it is violent as it begins the process of under-standing with a purge of what is individual in order to hold on to the illusion of objectivity. Active hesitation is the opposite. Instead of denying one's problematic past and present that muddies the water and makes it impossible to see anything but with one's own eyes, the process of active hesitation takes in and accepts all those contexts and manners of being all at once. The messiness of life, being all opposites at the same time, being more than any one definition, more than the name you give

---

[23] This is how I understand Nietzsche's fundamental question of the 'Revaluation of All Values' that he posited in his planned publication just before the onset of his madness.

yourself and that is given to you – all of this forms the foundation for a place from which one can start the process of non-critical understanding.

Take for instance the case of racism. Many approaches to the problem of racism are critical in nature, they continue to promote and are based on and act within difference. Because, any course of action that denies the fundamental difference upon which racism is founded, as well as actions that try to overcome these differences by giving out a new paradigm in which the difference simply does not or no longer exists, perform a violence to those suffering from and living with the consequences of racism. Reality cannot be rethought or made anew by changing words, by erasing concepts. And trauma that is repressed in this way only grows in new and more devastating ways.

An act of active hesitation on the other hand would require us to live with these differences, with the fact of all the pain and the troublesome positions that exist whether I want them to or not, both the positions and attitudes that are mine and the ones that can never be mine. Active hesitation is hard work, it is neither a denial nor a sugarcoating,[24] it is a withdrawal in the sense of not allowing the system that one knows as reality to be the only possibility. In the case of injustice there cannot be justice by taking away the root of the experienced trauma. It is being with the history of oppression, being with the color of my own skin and the consequences of that fact, being with the system as it is and being with the responsibility that lies on my own shoulders as a participant in these systems, being with the actions that are necessary. This is what it means to engage within the borderspace... to refuse the definitions that are thrown upon us by means of the world, to take away the verdict of what is the limit, of not having to take a decision between things even if they contradict one another. In the borderspace it is possible to learn to live with and within contradictions.

---

[24] See: Layla F. Saad, *Me, and White Supremacy: How to Recognise Your Privilege, Combat Racism and Change the World* (London: Quercus Editions, 2020).

The hesitation does not mean that we hesitate to call something by its name. The hesitation lies in the fact that we don't limit something to the name we have given something, not limit anything to the judgment I've passed onto it due to my upbringing, experiences, education, etc. We open up those judgments and accept that there are more sides and that my own take, although valid, is not more or less valid than any other judgment. Within the borderspace, what is mine and what is not, fades. I am not becoming other people; the I cannot appropriate the non-I that resides with the I in the borderspace. But this being-with is what is key. Understanding then becomes a slow process of being in conversation within the borderspace, where I become as alien to myself as the non-I that together with the I makes up the borderspace. The limits of the I and the non-I do not disappear or become meaningless, but these limits are no longer the essence of what exists. As Ettinger explains, in the matrixial borderspace there is a transsubjective relationality which is a "relations-without-relating to the other based on re-attuning of distances-in-proximity".[25] As such the human subject is not a subjugation but should be understood as a carrying, as a carried-cared-for being.[26]

In this respect the difference between empathy and compassion as noted by Ettinger is important.[27] Empathy is the capability of someone to feel what another is feeling, which is entirely based on the notions that reside in the empathic person. What is presented in the other somehow relates to something in me, a recognition, which makes it possible for me to feel what the other feels. Yet this is entirely based on my notions, my way of looking at things. I can have empathy without the other being involved. Empathy is thus a selfish mechanism, doubling one's own experience and reliving one's own trauma.

---

[25] Ettinger, *The Matrixial Borderspace*, p. 65.

[26] Birgit M. Kaiser & Kathrin Thiele, "If You Do Well, Carry! The Difference of the Humane: An Interview with Bracha L. Ettinger", *philoSOPHIA*, Vol. 8, No. 1, Winter 2018, p. 114.

[27] Bracha Ettinger, "(M)Other Re-spect: Maternal Subjectivity, the Ready-made mother-monster and The Ethics of Respecting", in *Studies in the Maternal*, 2 (1) 2010.

Compassion is different. Compassion does not require the person to understand the other, in the sense of definite knowing what is going on with the other person. I can show compassion without pretending to know, without presupposing that I can even understand what is going on with the other person, without presupposing that my own experience that relates to what I see in the other person is even somehow related. Compassion leaves the other person as is, and accepts the experience of the other person without imposing (violently) one's own world upon the other. Compassion is thus a hesitation of judgment, a way to not yet say that in order for me to do anything the other needs to fit in a box of my choosing.

While Levinas gives ethical priority to Cain as a subject always having a responsibility toward the guilt one carries with respect to the other, Ettinger invokes the example of Eve as a figure we are much more indebted to as an ethical archetype.

> The difficult path to compassion begins with Eve's com-passion. If the other can never be your total Other, there is an Other of the Other – in the feminine. Transcendence is therefore translucence – in the feminine. The sorrow, shame, and guilt of carrying the living and the dead can be sublimated. The conditions for the ethical attitude do not depend only upon recognizing that you are already a Cain, but also upon recognizing that you are also already an Eve as well as that you are indebted to Eve, to her birthing and her lamentation.[28]

Conclusion: Possible Practices

This type of compassion, this ethics of active hesitation, requires a certain type of madness. It requires a looking toward parts of our self that have been denied due to their incongruence with the world as it is presented to us. And even though we are thrown into the world, as Heidegger puts it, that does not mean that we must be victims to the systems of knowledge that are

---

[28] Kaiser & Thiele, "If You Do Well, Carry! The Difference of the Humane: An Interview with Bracha L. Ettinger", p. 120.

forced upon us. Anne Dufourmantelle notices that this kind of risk-taking is essential to life, the foundation of what it means to be human.[29] Simone Weil referred to it as a conversion, becoming what we cannot behold.[30] This kind of madness can be found in some practices of understanding that are non-critical in its nature. They each contain a durability with the simultaneous inconsistencies of the I and the non-I, the being-with what cannot be known. As Ettinger explains:

> I insist on the duration of dwelling and wit(h)nessing to achieve compassion, on the process of co/in-habit(u)ation and on the awareness to this process. To carry is also to en-dure: to sustain and support. We are here, hence we have been carried. Each one of us.[31]

To conclude I would like to offer some possibilities of engaging with this type of non-critical understanding. These examples serve only as openings for further research.

We could relate to philosophical compassion as a non-critical way of understanding as a kind of circumlocution.[32] The walking around something to understand it – not in order to approach it directly, since it is fundamentally impossible to approach. Circumlocution is the maximal kind of approaching of that which cannot be approached but neither can be left alone. A direct approach would mean a destruction, a decision on what remains at the limit of oneself; it would ask us to impose a decision. Circumlocution is a way of giving it time, of staying with it even though it remains just beyond our definite reach. It gives us understanding in the sense of a relationality, without reducing the non-I to the terms of the self.

---

[29] Anne Dufourmantelle, *In Praise of Risk,* translated by Stephen Miller (New York: Fordham University Press 2019).

[30] Nicole des Bouvrie, *The Necessity of the Impossible* (Nuenen: Exilic Press, 2019) p. 199.

[31] Kaiser & Thiele, "If You Do Well, Carry! The Difference of the Humane: An Interview with Bracha L. Ettinger", p. 106.

[32] Circumlocution can be practiced in writing, see for instance the work of Shoghi Effendi. Personal conversation with Bahiyyih Nakhjavani, Winter 2004.

Another way to make sense of philosophical compassion as a form of active hesitation is to think of it through the body itself. There is a kind of knowing while staying with the body, a knowing that cannot be approached in definite terms. The embodiment practices of dancing for instance, of prayer, of meditation are sources of understanding by staying with a concept, lingering without decision. In these embodied processes there might be a kind of active hesitation present. It is the eating that Simone Weil was referring to, that sustains being which simultaneously is and is not linked to the physicality of the body.

Alain Badiou gives some examples of experiences in which what he calls an event, can take place.[33] An event is a rare thing, it is a radical moment that lies outside of time, where the subject is only loyal to the outcome. Willing to give up every way of relating to the world, we can only recognize the event afterwards, since in that moment there is nothing but the change taking place. A new reality takes root in us, even though afterwards it will be impossible to think back to what the old world was like. Once we know one plus one is two, we can no longer imagine a world or a time in which this was not the case for us. Besides this kind of mathematical understanding, Badiou mentions how love can also be such an event. Love as a moment of connection that cannot be sustained, in which you lose the self without becoming the other. In the practice of love the limit of the other is easily digressed, as love is easily conflated with ownership and sacrifice, yet in essence the moment of love is nothing like that. It is a letting go of the self, regardless of the future, without presupposing what comes after. And it is at such a moment that understanding through compassion and active hesitation can come about.

Truth, then, is not a matter of decision, of claiming a ground for ourselves and defending it. Truth is that moment in which reality presents itself through borderlinking, through an opening toward that which is not me, while fragilizing the concept of what is and what is not part of me. This is the truth that can be

---

[33] Alain Badiou, *Logics of Worlds* (New York: Continuum, 2009).

experienced through circumlocution, through embodiment and through acts of love. It exists outside of language and other power structures, ready to be understood whenever and wherever we are.

Configuring Feminist Philosophy in the Context of the Nordic Summer University

Synne Myrebøe, Valgerður Pálmadóttir & Johanna Sjöstedt

While feminist philosophy has had a place at Western universities for several decades, the question of how to understand the relationship between feminism and philosophy is still a disputed territory. Moreover, the concept of "feminist philosophy" is contested in several camps.1 From the perspective of philosophy, feminist philosophy might seem compromised from its commitment to political change, thereby opening up for the charge of being dogmatic; from the perspective of feminism, the practice of philosophy might seem too far removed from the pressing concerns of injustice in ordinary life. Thus, when outlining the themes and activities of the study circle *Feminist Philosophy: time, history, and the transformation of thought,* our project description was oriented around exploring these tensions. Having backgrounds both in philosophy and the discipline of the history of ideas, we wanted to discuss the bearings of these concerns within the frames of history. Among the circle's aims was to organize a transdisciplinary space to reflect on feminist philosophy while also discussing the abovementioned tensions on their own terms. Initially, however, starting this circle within the framework of the Nordic Summer University (hereafter NSU), we had little knowledge of the institutional history of NSU and its connection to the emergence of women's studies.

This chapter briefly introduces NSU as an institution that has generated both personal and scholarly values for decades and constituted the organizational home for *Feminist Philosophy: Time, History and the Transformation of Thought.* Taking our point of departure from what we perceived as the marginalization of feminist philosophy within the institution of philosophy, on the one hand, and the growth of feminist philosophizing in several fields of research, on the other, we place the scholarly interests of this study circle against the background of previous scholarly engagements with feminist issues at NSU. Lastly, we describe and analyze some significant experiences from the Feminist Philosophy Circle, with the purpose of discerning the forms of knowledge that emanated from our work during these years of relational and educational tours.[1]

The Nordic Summer University
– A Democratic Space for Thought and Practice

NSU is an independent, migratory network for cultivation and research founded in 1950 by a group of scientists and scholars from the Nordic region. The initiative was formed in the image of the *Internationale Hochschulwochen*, which had been active in Austria from the end of the second world war onward, and had close connections to the Vienna circle.[2] Thus, NSU is part of

---

[1] In the fall of 2015, we initiated the sketch for a new study circle within the Nordic Summer University (NSU), which then received support to organize an ad-hoc conference to attract future participants. Thus, what would become the circle *Feminist Philosophy: Time, History, and the Transformation of Thought*, had its first winter symposium in Umeå in Sweden in March 2016. Invited keynote speakers were Kristina Fjelkestam and Claudia Lindén from Stockholm, Sara Edenheim from Umeå, and Tuija Pulkkinen from Helsinki. The same year at NSU's summer session in Orivesi, Finland, the circle was accepted for a three-year program within the framework of NSU's activities. Since then, the circle has attracted more than 200 scholars from more than 20 countries. Invited keynote speakers at the circle's symposiums during the time of its activities (four years) were Kristie Dotson (U.S.), Nancy Bauer (U.S.), Alison Jaggar (U.S./U.K.), Willow Ververk (CA/U.K.), Jorunn Økland (NO), Line Cecilie Engh (NO), Cecilia Rosengren (SWE), Sigríður Thorgeirsdóttir (IS), Naomi Scheman (U.S.), Fanny Söderbäck (SWE/U.S.), Cecilia Sjöholm (SWE) and Ingvild Torsen (NO). In addition to the collaboration with Umeå University, the circle has held a large international conference in collaboration with the University of Iceland and the network Feminist Philosophy: Transforming Philosophy based there in 2017; and symposiums in collaboration with Oslo University in 2018 and lastly with Södertörn University in 2019. After the circle's program had come to an end, a new feminist philosophy circle was formed by members of the former circle and accepted into the study program of the NSU for the following three years. Hence, the work that started in 2015 continues along new paths, and the network prevails, expands and continues to expand.

[2] Karolina Enquist Källgren, "Fristående akademiskt nätverk som har haft story inflytande," *Respons* (no. 5, 2020) available online at http://tidskriftenrespons.se/artikel/fristaende-akademiskt-natverk-som-har-haft-stort-inflytande/

a European tradition of academically independent, international forums for scholars and researchers that started in the interwar and post-war era and aimed at creating academic and intellectual arenas to contribute to the development of international cooperation within the sciences and promote peace. An additional aim was to give researchers and students the possibilities to understand and exchange ideas with actors from civil society and the cultural sector.[3]

The context for the establishment of NSU was, among other things, a felt crisis of the Universities and the sciences in the aftermath of World War II.[4] As explained by Troels Degn Johansson, former chair of NSU, the organization was initially established as an elite "task force" to promote much-needed cooperation between various academic disciplines and different countries. The aim was to increase understanding between the theoretical and applied sciences and to discuss pressing social issues that needed perspectives from various research fields. A democratic organizational form has been a trademark of NSU from the beginning. It is based on several study circles that are active for some time, three years at a minimum – accepted through a democratic process informed by scholarly reviews. Today, each circle organizes one symposium or a workshop during the winter, and then all circles gather for a summer session for at least one week, where each circle has its own program open for all. NSU's activities are held in different places in the Nordic and the Baltic region, often in collaboration with some local academic or artistic institutions or networks. Around 200 people annually gather at the summer sessions to discuss, study and socialize. The summer university facilitates scholarly advancement for researchers and students with children, since even children are invited, with the Children's Circle arranging activities during the daily study program.

[3] Poul Hermansen, "NSU – et kort historisk tilbageblik", *Kritik og Krise*, (NSU Press, 2000).

[4] Troels Degn Johansen, "Af Nordisk Sommaruniversitets nyeste historie", *Kritik og Krise*, (NSU Press, 2000).

The summer session's time frame of one week, where participants interact across study circles and seminars with topics that are followed up during the winter, facilitates unexpected meetings, critical discussions, and a rare opportunity to expand horizons of thought. NSU strives to create a room free of competition, where the formulation of problems are foregrounded and where performance and reflection meet. It has been a source of innovative intellectual interchange for several decades, resulting in many publications and cross-border collaboration between academics and actors in practical and artistic activities. NSU offers a place to present issues and ideas and to work across theoretical and practical experiences, academic disciplines, and hierarchies. These boundary transgressions constitute a very valuable – yet often underrated – aspect of research. The themes dealt with within the different study circles are formulated based on issues presented by the participants. Lecturers from all over the world also provide a basis for the conversation as invited keynote speakers. The freedom of innovative research and collaboration that NSU facilitates have, among other things, created opportunities for the development of research fields in the Nordic and Baltic countries, such as human ecology, peace and conflict research, gender studies, and research into artistic practice.

Participating in NSU is a democratic experience rarely accommodated within today's academic institutional structures. Degn Johansson wrote in 2000 that NSU is, "despite its age as a research organization within the framework of Nordic cooperation, still characterized as an ongoing project and experiment: a dream of an organization [...] in which the work is driven by desire and idealism."[5] As we are writing this chapter twenty years later, Degn Johansson's description seems to be as relevant as ever. The organization proved to be a fitting platform for a transdisciplinary exploration of feminist philosophy. Sadly, as we write this in 2022, NSU now stands at a crossroads and might have reached the end of its history in the form that has

---

[5] Troels Degn Johansson, "Förord," *Kritik og Krise* (NSU Press, 2000), p. 1.

characterized it over the last 70 years since the main sponsor, The Nordic Council of Ministers, has decided to withdraw its funding. Nevertheless, we hope that the organization finds a way to survive. As we will discuss further in this chapter, the organizational structures and the egalitarian ethos of NSU enabled fruitful intellectual exchanges and lasting networks that continue within traditional universities and expand outside academic contexts.

The history of feminist scholarship within NSU

NSU was greatly affected by the expansion of higher education and the accompanying student uproar in the late sixties that, among other things, resulted in more egalitarian organizational structures and the entrance of Marxist perspectives in many circles.[6] Consequently, in the 1970s, the organization became a prominent forum for critical studies, and a number of new interdisciplinary subjects and research fields in the Nordic region had an early start in NSU.[7] It was in this context that the circle "Kvindesituationens specifikke karakter under kapitalismen" [The specific character of women's situation under capitalism] – with close connections to the new radical women's movements in the Nordic countries – was established in 1971 and accepted in NSU's program in 1973.[8] As the circle's name indicates, the analytical perspectives were Marxist feminist. This circle, which soon came to be referred to simply as the 'women's

---

[6] Arne Overrein, "Vitenskap, kritikk og krise. Om Nordisk Sommeruniversitetets utvikling og idegrunnlag i et vitenskaps- og utdanningshistorisk perspektiv" in Johansen, Overrein & Rendtorff (Eds.), *Kritik og Krise – Nordisk Sommeruniversitet i 50 år* (Århus: NSU Press, 2000).

[7] Alexander Ekelund, *Kampen om vetenskapen: Politisk och vetenskaplig formering under den svenska vänsterradikaliseringens era* (Gothenburg: Daidalos, 2017).

[8] Signe Arnfred & Karen Syberg, *Kvindesituation & kvindebevægelse under kapitalismen* (København: Nordisk Sommaruniverstets skriftserie 1974).

circle,[9] marked the beginning of a strong and longstanding presence of feminist scholarly work within NSU.[10]

In historiographical accounts of gender- and feminist research in the Nordic region, international cooperation is typically highlighted and described as essential for the development of the field. In that context, NSU is frequently mentioned as an important context for the early development of Nordic academic feminism.[11] Hence, when the circle *Feminist Philosophy: Time, History and the Transformation of Thought* applied for its first ad-hoc symposia in 2016 in the aspiration to become a study circle within NSU's program, it connected with a tradition where feminist activism was entangled with scholarship and intellectual curiosity.

[9] Signe Arnfred, "Fortrinsvis historisk beretning om 'Kvindekredsen's udvikling i NSU, og herunder om sammenhæng og manglende sammenhæng mellem kvindebevægelse, fagkritisk arbejde og ventrefløjspolitik", *Nordisk Forum: Tidskrift för universitets- och forskningspolitik*, Vol. 4, No. 12 (Nordisk Sommaruniversitet: Roskilde Universitetsforlag: 1976.)

[10] Subsequent 'women's circles' include "Familjen som institution för social reproduktion" [The family as an institution for social reproduction] (1975–1977), "Kvinnorörelse och kvinnoforskning" [Women's movement and women's research] (1979–1891); "Kvinnokultur och kvinnokamp" [Women's culture and women's struggle] (1982–1983), "Æstetik, køn og kultur" [Aestetics, gender, and culture] (1987–1989) and "Feminism och kunskapsutveckling" [Feminism and knowledge development] (1991–1993). Feminist perspectives were also higly present in other circles such as and "Socialisationsteori" [Socialization theory] (1978–1981); "Mellan män och maskuliniteter" [Between men and masculinities] (1995–1997); "Køn i Norden" [Gender and Sex in the Nordic countries] (2010–2012); "Exploring Affect" (2013–2015). See Valgerður Pálmadóttir och Johanna Sjöstedt, "Nordic Feminism Reconsidered: Activism, scholarly endeavours, and women's research networks at the Nordic Summer University 1971–1990" (*Nora: Nordic Journal on Feminist and Gender research*, 30 (1) 2022).

[11] See for example Nina Lykke, "Rethinking socialist and Marxist legacies in feminist imaginaries of protest from postsocialist perspectives," *Social Identities*, Vol. 24, No. 2, 2017, pp. 173–188; Britt-Marie Thurén, *Genusforskning – Frågor, villkor och utmaningar* (Stockholm: Vetenskapsrådet, 2003); Bente Rosenbeck, "Nordic women's studies and gender research," in von de Fehr et al. (Eds.), *Is there a Nordic Feminism?* (UCL Press, 1998); Drude Dahlerup, *Rødstrømperne. Den danske Rødstrømpebevægelses udvikling, nytænkning og gennemslag 1970–1985*, Lindhardt og Ringhof, 1998; Ulla Manns, "En ros är en ros är en ros. Konstruktionen av Nordisk kvinno- och genusforskning," (*Lychnos*, 2009).

An important document from the early engagements with feminist questions within NSU is *Kvindesituation & kvindebevægelse under kapitalismen* [Women's Situation and Women's Movement under Capitalism], a collection of essays reflecting the activities of the first 'women's circle' edited by the coordinators Karen Syberg and Signe Arnfred and published in 1974. In the introduction to the anthology, Syberg and Arnfred write about the potential risks involved when feminist activities and initiatives take shape in academic settings:

> The pitfalls with the connections to the university is [...] that the need for theoretical insights does not spring from political problems but on the contrary from that which is socially sanctioned in a narrow university environment.[12]

The risk with this, the authors further write, is that "the theory that is not created in an attempt to understand and further develop a practice" will lead to "depoliticization as an effect in the final instance."[13] What is suggested, and which also reappears in today's feminist discussions, is whether a theoretical academization tends to be alienated from the everyday life that takes place in homes and workplaces, where higher education is no exception. Rather than underlining arbitrary gaps between practice and theory, the circle Feminist Philosophy has strived to understand the implications of theory as practice and practice as theory.

Regarding the practices demanded by the authors of the anthology from 1974, there is reason to ask whether this still constitutes an underdeveloped and neglected area of higher education. Much indicates that current academic structures and cultures do not mirror the vast knowledge produced by feminist

---

[12] "Det farlige ved universitetsanknytningen er [...] at behovet for teoretisk indsigt ikke udspringer af politiske problemstillinger, men at det derimod bliver hvad der er socialt sanctioneret i et snævert universitetsmiljø der kommer til at styre arbejdet." Arnfred & Syberg, *Kvindesituation & kvindebevægelse under kapitalismen*, p. 7.

[13] Arnfred & Syberg, *Kvindesituation & kvindebevægelse under kapitalismen* (København: Nordisk Sommaruniverstets skriftserie 1974).

scholarly work in the last decades. Instead, at times it seems that the academic world has developed more in accordance with the last words of the anthology's title, "Women's Situation and Women's Movements under Capitalism", i.e., along with market rationality. For instance, the current meritocratic apparatus does not acknowledge so-called 'academic housework' that is more often in the hands of women, resulting, e.g., in unequal possibilities for employment, which is based on publications and citations. An early study of the effects of pandemics also showed that women's research production internationally decreased radically compared to their male colleagues when schools closed and children were made to stay at home.[14] Furthermore, sexism thrives within universities, just as within other social institutions. Signs of that are found in the countless examples of sexual violation, harassment, belittlement, and exclusion based on gender expressed in stories that were publicly voiced during #metoo.[15] Intertwined with this pervasive inequality are the racist and ableist structures maintained through educational institutions' hierarchization of knowledge and bodies.

At the same time as discriminating structures prevail, new conservatives claim that the rise of feminism has meant a politicization of universities.[16] In countries governed by nationalist and conservative parties, this claim is advanced at the same that governments seek to ban knowledge on sexuality and gender. Hence, if the interest in feminist theory was described as a danger of depoliticization half a century ago, this is now turned

---

[14] Eunji Kim and Shawn Patterson, "The Pandemic and Gender Inequality in Academia," (July 20, 2020) Available at SSRN: https://papers.ssrn.com/sol3/papers.cfm?abstract_id=3666587

[15] Thamar Melanie Heijstra, Finnborg Salome Steinthorsdóttir, & Thorgerdur Einarsdóttir, "Academic career making and the double-edged role of academic housework", *Gender and Education*, (Vol 29, No 6, 2017), pp. 764–780.; "Gender Bias in Academe: An Annotated Bibliography of Important Recent Studies, Danica Svavonick & Cathy N. Davidson, https://blogs.lse.ac.uk/impactofsocialsciences/2016/03/08/gender-bias-in-academe-an-annotated-bibliography/#new

[16] Ivar Arpi & Anna-Karin Wyndhamn, *Genusdoktrinen* (Stockholm: Fri tanke, 2020); Mikko Lagerspetz, "'The Grievance studies affair'" Project: Reconstructing and Assessing the Experimental Design", Science, Technology, & Human Values, (Vol. 46, No 2, 2021), 402–424.

upside down. Feminist theory, in the understanding of theory as practice – as different ways of reading, writing, speaking, and perceiving the world, is indeed political in the understanding that it strives to dissolve oppressive structures.

During the early 1970s, when the aforementioned anthology *Kvindesituation & kvinnbevægelse* was published, far fewer people could pursue academic education than today. Furthermore, the women who wrote and read the anthology in reading circles in Iceland, Norway, Denmark, and Sweden were part of the first generation to combine caretaking of young children with higher education, i.e., family life and academic life. Today, questions on who gets access to and influence higher education are still pressing, and feminist networks engage internationally in multiple ways to gather and transform higher education into more democratic institutions. Despite the differences in scope and scholarly interests between the initial feminist study early circles of feminists at NSU and our circle on feminist philosophy, our shared goal is to try to understand and further develop a practice. Yet, putting emphasis on historical analysis, the circle Feminist Philosophy wanted to restrain from moralizing in favor of a broader and contextual understanding of contemporary practice.

Outlining the Circle

In the aptly named text "Is feminist philosophy a contradiction in terms?" the philosopher Nancy Bauer discusses the relationship between the two enterprises in detail and notes the "curious lack of serious work on the question of how philosophy and feminism are supposed to go together.[17] Rather than assembling arguments "in favor" of feminist philosophy – however that notion is defined – Bauer wants to open up a space for doing scholarly work regarding the possible tensions in the project of combining feminism and philosophy. Such a project does not subscribe to the patriarchal notion that feminism and philo-

---

[17] Nancy Bauer, *Simone de Beauvoir, Philosophy, and Feminism* (New York: Columbia University Press, 2001), pp. 20–21.

sophy mix as oil and water; instead, it is the starting point for serious work on thinking about these tensions. However, Bauer does not discuss questions about the institutional norms of philosophy or the role of history in conceptualizing the relationship between feminism and philosophy.

As a matter of fact, women compose a smaller portion of the student body and faculty in philosophy compared to other disciplines.[18] This lack of women (including trans and non-binary people) in philosophy can be viewed from a larger historical perspective: Already in the early 15th century, Christine de Pizan noted that the path for women to philosophize was through literature.[19] There seems to be much truth in Pizan's remarks. According to Mary Ellen Waithe, a precursor for research on women philosophers, women's philosophical works throughout history have been classified as belonging to disciplines other than philosophy, and they have thus been omitted from what we understand as the Western philosophical tradition, i.e., the philosophical canon.[20] Hence, as literary scholar Claudia Lindén has argued, philosophers have discussed gender since the birth of philosophy, but the modern construction of philosophy does not allow for the inclusion of questions of gender and/or feminism.[21] In this analysis, feminist philosophy would appear to be a contradiction in terms because gender and feminism do not count as subjects of philosophy.[22] This exclu-

[18] Inga Bostad & Tove Pettersen, "Kjønn og feminisme i norsk filosofi – Noen betraktninger", Norsk filosofisk tidsskrift, No. 03–04 / 2015; Martina Reuter, "Varför så få kvinnor? Könsfördelningen inom den akademiska filosofin", *Tidskrift för politisk filosofi*, No. 3, 2015; Thompson, Morgan et al. "Why Do Women Leave Philosophy? Surveying Students at the Introductory Level", Vol. 16, No. 6, pp. 1–36.

[19] Christine de Pisan, *The book of the city of ladies* (New York: Persea Books, 1998).

[20] Mary Ellen Waithe, "Sex, Lies, and Bigotry: The Canon of Philosophy" in Sigridur Thorgeirsdottir & Ruth E. Hagengruber (eds.), Methodological Reflections on Women's Contribution and Influence in the History of Philosophy (Springer, 2020).

[21] Claudia Lindén, "Mary Wollstonecraft och filosofin som feminism", *Glänta* 2001, (Vol. 9, No. 1–2), pp. 130–140.

[22] Lindén, 2001: Mary Wollstonecraft and Jean-Jacques Rousseau are cases in point. While Rousseau, with his *Emile, or on education*, is counted among the philosophers, Wollstonecraft's critique of his treatment of Sophie in the same text is classified as literature.

sion highlights how the genre is a gendered practice and how certain topics are excluded from philosophy proper.

It's important to stress that the processes of definition that have eliminated women philosophers from the history of philosophy, either by relegating them to other disciplines or by forgetting about them altogether, still operate today. In the past two decades, several prominent feminist philosophers have reflected on the relationship between philosophy, feminism, and their position as women in philosophy.[23] In the essay "Can the other of philosophy speak?", Judith Butler tells the story of her way into philosophy and how she, propelled by her writing on feminist philosophy, came to occupy a place outside the institutions of philosophy.[24] She also notes how she shares this destiny with several feminist philosophers in the United States. Her discussion of the place of philosophy on the border of social critique is both institutional and methodological. Describing the work of French philosopher and psychoanalyst Luce Irigaray, Butler writes: "This work cannot be read without philosophy, for that is its text, and yet including it in the canon is not possible for most philosophy departments".[25]

Butler's remark also has implications for how to read feminist theory. As noted in the introduction, feminist theory has a somewhat paradoxical relationship to time and history. While, on the one hand, emphasizing the situatedness of both the knowing subject and of the claims of knowledge, there has been less interest in the historicity of the philosophical concepts used to make these claims. Hence, Ingeborg Owesen argues that

---

[23] Rosi Braidotti, *La philosophie là où on ne l'attend pas* (Paris: Larousse, 2009); Michèle le Dœuff, *Hipparchia's Choice: An essay concerning women, philosophy,* trans. Trista Selous, (Oxford: Blackwell, 1991); Catherine Malabou, *Changing difference: The Feminine and the Question of Philosophy*, trans. Carolyn Shread, (Cambridge: Polity Press, 2011); Naomi Scheman, "Vad är en kvinna? Från fakta till erkännande", trans. Ellen Söderblom Saarela, in (eds.). Evelina Johansson Wilén & Johanna Sjöstedt, *Vad är en kvinna Språk, materialitet, situation,* (Gothenburg: Daidalos, 2021).

[24] Judith Butler, "Can the other of philosophy speak", *Undoing gender* (New York: Routledge, 2004).

[25] Butler, 2004, p. 245.

"contemporary feminist theory is largely oriented towards the present" and that the philosophical history of modern feminism has received insufficient scholarly attention.[26] This is noticeable not least in gender studies as a discipline, which increasingly has turned toward the social sciences. Intertwined with the epistemological and ontological framework of social sciences, the philosophical knowledge of diverse peoples is marginalized and thus withdrawn from both philosophy and the social sciences. Currently, the practice of such pervasive epistemological violence is one of the central concerns within higher education. In her article "How is this Paper Philosophy", Kristie Dotson recounts her younger sister Alexis' conversation with her Guidance Counselor when she was a college student:

> Counselor: Why don't you major in Social Work?
>
> Alexis: Social Work sounds good, but I am interested in Philosophy.
>
> Counselor: (Snorts) Philosophy is not for black women. That's a white man's game.
>
> Alexis: My older sister is a philosophy professor.
>
> Counselor: Well, she's probably the only one, and that should tell you something. (2009)[27]

Dotson's article does not only point to the practices of injustice but also to the need for philosophical work that can transgress a moralizing demand for homogeneity. Furthermore, Dotson suggests engaging in a culture of practice that values "contribution, multiple canons, and multiple forms of disciplinary validation".[28] This definition of a curious and inclusive culture of practices is aligned with the scrutiny of epistemological and peda-

---

[26] Owesen, 2021, p. 1.

[27] Kristie Dotson, "How is this Paper Philosophy?", *Comparative Philosophy* (Vol. 3, No. 1, 2012), p. 3.

[28] Dotson, "How is this Paper Philosophy?", p. 26.

gogical norms within higher education that have been important for the community of Feminist Philosophy.

Reading Together – Or: Philosophy Embodied

Starting the interdisciplinary feminist philosophy circle, we did not know who would apply. Over the years, the circle has gathered over 200 scholars from more than 20 countries and five continents. Many participants have chosen to return year after year, and we have been able to follow each other's work and interests. Although the circle has had a historical-philosophical focus, it has been an interdisciplinary meeting place. The participants have been students, artists, doctoral students, and senior academics from philosophy, history of ideas, literary studies, gender studies, sociology, law, and the educational sciences. This heterogeneity in age, career, and academic culture has placed great demands on the individual participants and the pedagogical approaches adopted. A question that arose quite quickly was what it would mean also to explore feminist philosophy in pedagogical practice, that is, in a relational learning context of which we were all part. Although pedagogical practice was not manifestly a part of our focus when we started the circle, it proved to be highly important at our individual meetings and during the entire period the circle ran. Four aspects of our experience that could, with advantage, be developed as an asset to higher education pedagogy, and gender equality issues in higher education will here be exposed. We call the four aspects *time, history, dissonance,* and *voice.* Together, these aspects point to a practice of embodied philosophy.

Time

We enter the pedagogical space in time, but also with different expectations and experiences of time. This became clear at our very first seminar in Orivesi, Finland. On a beautiful but very hot day in July, we gathered in one of the smaller seminar rooms. The topic for the seminar was "Empowerment and vulnerability".[29] What became apparent during the seminar was how the theme itself went beyond the texts read and could also be registered in our own practice. The participants' respective pre-understandings of the overarching project of Feminist Philosophy were clearly asymmetrical. Some of us had earlier experience and knowledge of feminist activism where questions of space for speech were highly important. Others were trained in philosophy but were new to feminist thought. For some, the historical perspective was elemental, while for others, it was something to be left behind. Hence, setting out on a collective journey of thought is inevitably also a vulnerable practice. The pedagogical challenge is thus to navigate between different orientations in the unknown territories with a direction of individual and common empowerment in sight.[30]

History

As mentioned in the introduction to this anthology, feminist history can be translated in different ways: as lamenting the violence and suppression in the past, as a women's history that presents the neglected voices, or as a critical re-writing of a canon of white-male-supremacy. The circle "Feminist Philosophy" has engaged with all these perspectives. The most prominent pedagogical challenge has been the translation of ideas, where so-called canonical texts have been read next to feminist philosophy and theory. Rather than an orientation toward injustice, our pursuit has been to open history as a poetic practice. Philosophy understood as the love of wisdom, cannot be

---

[29] The texts we discussed in this seminar were Claire Colebrook, "Norm Wars" in *Revisiting Normativity with Deleuze*, Braidotti and Patricia Pisters (eds.) (Bloomsbury, 2012) Rosi Braidotti "The ethics of becoming imperceptible" in Constantin Boundas (ed.), *Deleuze and Philosophy* (Edinburgh: Edinburgh university press 2006); Carolyn Culbertson, "The ethics of relationality: Judith Butler and social critique" (Continental Philosophy Review 2013); Judith Butler and William E. Connolly, "Politics, Power and Ethics: A Discussion Between Judith Butler and William Connolly", *Theory & Event* (Vol. 4, no. 2, 2000).

[30] Throughout her academic work, Sarah Ahmed has conceptualized feminist practice in academic settings: Sara Ahmed, *Queer Phenomenology: Orientations, Objects, Others* (Durham: Duke University Press, 2006); Sara Ahmed, *Living a feminist life* (Durham: Duke University Press, 2017).

reduced to the institutional practice of a few in modern European universities. As Claudia Lindén emphasizes in her chapter in this anthology, literature is not only the path intellectual women have chosen or assigned throughout history. What feminist critique has exposed is also how the disciplines of History and Philosophy are inevitably gendered narratives. Reading history and philosophy as literary narratives, and literary narratives as history and philosophy, became a central consideration for understanding the temporal rhythms constituted by and through the circle. Besides reading canonized texts by Sophocles, Plato, Aristotle, Hegel, and Nietzsche in dialogue with now more recognized texts by women philosophers like Arendt, Butler, Cavarero, Irigaray, and Lorde, the participants have presented their own work.

Dissonance

Driven by passions to transform thought and practice, feminist philosophy is inevitably political and thereby also pluralistic. In contrast to feminist theory as a way of seeing, feminist philosophy can be understood as questions of what we see, including what is not immediately visible. In a seminar with participants from different academic cultures, our ways of seeing, reading, and sensing are not the same. When reading the same texts, the asymmetry mentioned above results in dissonances. Conceptions we take for granted are suddenly put at risk in a seminar room where the participants' voices are equal but different. Although this dissonance might be one of the core conditions for critical work, it is not without friction. Nevertheless, we have appreciated the space for disagreement upheld by the study circle. A prominent example of this dissonance was a seminar announced as

> How do we read concepts in context? Departing from our reading of Aristophanes *Lysistrata*, Aristotle, Irigaray, and

> Burke, we will discuss how ideas on sex, passivity, and activity
> can be read and formulated.[31]

The sore point of the seminar turned out to be Irigaray's text "When our Lips Speak Together".[32] From the ensuing discussion, the difficulties recognizable as central to feminist work were unveiled. For some of the participants, Irigaray's philosophy of difference had been a game-changer in their academic life, giving them access to philosophy. For others, her purported essentialism symbolized the threat of alienation from a common ground that has been central for post-colonial theory to overcome. A challenge for everyone, and in particular for us as moderators, was to draw out and embrace these tensions.

From this experience, several questions can be discerned that put philosophy to the test: are we supposed to keep up a supposedly rational and disinterested attitude when conflicting emotions play out in the room, i.e., reject emotional and bodily engagement as misplaced and alienated from rationality? How can we discern the difference between text and bodies, between theories and the persons theorizing (what is there to be seen and how is this affected by the persons seeing)? And what are the implications of exposing vulnerability – what does it mean for how voices are distributed and heard? The reflection to which many women and persons identifying themselves within LGBT+ return is whether experiences from life are welcome within institutional philosophy. However, a relevant concern is also where the limits and restrictions begin and end for personal and bodily experiences. For what is the moral and epistemological position of oppressed groups? What is the role – ethically and epistemologically – of the intellectual who wants to produce critical knowledge? The precarious balancing act is to maintain a space for bodily and emotional engagement and presence to

---

[31] From the invitation sent out to the participants before the summer session at Fårö, Sweden, 2019.

[32] Luce Irigaray & Carolyn Burke, "When Our Lips Speak Together" *Signs* (Vol. 6, No. 1, 1980), pp. 69–79.

the texts we read while at the same time keeping an awareness of the tipping point of emotional stickiness and vacuity. Obviously, no general didactics can be drawn from this experience except for the fact that every time a seminar room gathers, mood and atmosphere will play an important role. Without reaching a final conclusion about the specific difficulties that appeared during this seminar (among others), the risk of being together on unstable ground can also be seen as important food for thought for those who are in love with wisdom.

Voice

The interaction and shared interest, understood as *inter-est* – being together – has been possible only through the patience and hard work of the participants. With feminist philosophical texts at our disposal, we have had the possibility to discuss important feminist philosophers who, throughout history, have sought to make the unspeakable speak and the absent present. Just to mention a few, Judith Butler has described the common experience of alienation with the concept of disidentification: "this experience of misrecognition, this uneasy sense of standing under a sign to which one does and does not belong".[33] Drawing on Lauren Berlant she writes that "indeed, it may be precisely through practices which underscore disidentification with those regulatory norms by which sexual difference is materialized that both feminist and queer politics are mobilized".[34] However, the politics mobilized can also generate new regulatory norms. Thus, another approach to the phenomenon of disidentification can be found in a philosophical gesture that resigns from identifications and seizes the nonidentical as "an open existence".[35] Joan Scott and Joan Copjec have both written about how

[33] Judith Butler, *Bodies that matter: On the Discursive Limits of "Sex"* (Abingdon: Routledge, Oxon, 2011[1993]), p. 219.

[34] Butler, *Bodies that matter*, p. 4 and Lauren Berlant, "The Female Complaint," *Social Text* (No. 19 Vol. 20, Fall, 1988), pp. 237–59.

[35] Marcia Sá Cavalcante Schuback, "Exilens språk", *Exilens språk. Texter.* (Gothenburg: GFFP, 2016), p. 48. Bracha Ettinger, *The matrixial borderspace* (Minneapolis: University of Minnesota Press, 2006).

the non-sense or nonknowledge has been a condition for western epistemology and philosophy.[36] Further, Adriana Cavarero has emphasized how inclinations have been regarded as a pervasive threat to a philosophical and political tradition that has been characterized by desires for rectitude.[37] The feminine voice has thus been regarded as a threat to the progress of rationality.[38] This politics of interpretation has facilitated the male-coded philosophy to maintain its sovereignty by ignoring the voice in the understanding of logos: "from the perspective of language as a system [...] what is not heard is, paradoxically, the uniqueness of the sound", Cavarero writes.[39] Against this background, Feminist Philosophy has created a space for philosophical polyphony. In this spirit, we have read classical plays together. During our four years, Plato's *Symposium*, Sophocles' *Antigone*, Aristophanes' *Lysistrata* and Euripides' *Hippolytos*, were all discussed. These sessions were opportunities to converse at night in the company with other circles of the Nordic Summer University. The seminar room was also exchanged for the beach with wine, snacks, and blankets. Passing the text between participants, we read aloud the whole plays as the sun set. This way of sharing voices has also been important for thinking about the practice of feminist philosophy, and thereby actualizing the poetic tradition of philosophy, subordinate to the 19th century historiographical construction of institutional philosophy. In the end, as we pose the question on how to understand feminist philosophy, what appears is first and foremost what can be characterized as philosophy's Other.

*

[36] Joan Copjec, *Read my desire – Lacan Against the* Historicists (Verso Books, 2015), p. 17; Joan Scott, *The Fantasy of Feminist History* (Durham: Duke University Press, 2011).
[37] Adriana Cavarero, *Inclinations: A Critique of Rectitude,* trans. Amanda Minervini and Adam Sitze (Stanford, California: Stanford University Press, 2016).
[38] Martha Nussbaum, *Political Emotions: Why Love Matters for Justice* (Cambridge, M.A: Belknap Press of Harvard University Press, 2013); Adriana Cavarero, *For More than One Voice: Toward a Philosophy of Vocal Expression,* translation Paul Kottman Stanford (California: Stanford University Press, 2005).
[39] Cavarero, *For More than One Voice,* p. 9.

If the discipline of philosophy has been greatly influenced by the analytical tradition after WWII, both internationally and in Sweden, the history of ideas in Sweden has come to occupy a disciplinary space where the history of philosophy has been scrutinized from critical perspectives, for example, feminism and postcolonial theory. In starting the project "Feminist Philosophy: Time, history, and the transformation of thought," we wanted to create a platform where philosophy and feminism appear dialogically, both in historical as well as contemporary perspectives, and where tensions between the different terms are interrogated and used as a starting point for productive academic work.

As already mentioned, working with feminist history of philosophy requires a move toward literature. Our point of departure and our way of approaching philosophy thus arises in a situation where philosophy is already and historically outside itself. Still, we wanted to maintain a relationship with the word "philosophy," since the love of wisdom does not fit unproblematically with any disciplinary borders. In retrospect, this also turned out to be important in terms of the response to our call for papers. We discovered that the word philosophy bore a special attraction not only for philosophers in a narrow sense but also for scholars outside of philosophy departments.

The relevance of the discourse of philosophy and the history of ideas for feminist interdisciplinary work should not be underestimated. What was exposed throughout the work of "Feminist Philosophy: Time, History, and the Transformation of Thought", was an international and transdisciplinary desire to be given a space for thought, wonder, and discussion that transgress feminism as theory and practice. Our hope is that feminist philosophy as a productive culture of practice can carve out further spaces within more academic institutions and thus contribute to critical inquiry and transgression of the contemporary logic of profit, self-assertion, and competition.

The Authors

Nicole des Bouvrie freelance philosopher, epistemologist, art/ACT therapist, teacher, and fiction writer. She holds a PhD in Philosophy, Art and Critical Thought from the European Graduate School. Her dissertation on 'The Necessity of the Impossible' was supervised by Anne Dufourmantelle. Des Bouvrie is interested in art, theater, books and life, as well as the concepts of feminism, motherhood, democracy and equality and their meaning in the 21st century.

Marta-Laura Cenedese works as a researcher at the University of Turku and at the Centre Marc Bloch Berlin. She holds a PhD in French and Comparative Literature from the University of Cambridge. She is an interdisciplinary scholar whose research focuses on 20th- and 21st-century postcolonial literatures, the interlacing of literature, history and politics, cultural memory studies, critical theory, critical medical humanities, death studies, and feminist writing methodologies. She edited the volume *Written on the Body: Narrative (Re)constructions of Violence(s)* (2023) and is the author of *Irène Némirovsky's Russian Influences: Tolstoy, Dostoevsky and Chekhov* (2021).

Oda K. S. Davanger is a PhD candidate in Philosophy at the Norwegian University of Science and Technology (NTNU). She has a BA from Earlham College and an MPhil from the University of Oslo. Her research interests include phenomenology, political philosophy, continental philosophy and feminist epistemology. The working title of her doctoral thesis is "The Politics of Being Seen", a phenomenological critique of democratic citizenship. Liberal democracy both presumes and promises freedom and equality, which she argues is a paradox that comes to the fore in feminist and woke political philosophy.

Sara Edenheim is Docent in History and senior lecturer at Umeå Centre for Gender Studies at Umeå University. She conducts research at the intersection between feminist theory and philosophy of history with a focus on Swedish 20th century history. She has previously analyzed how normative and deviant gendered and sexual identities are constructed in Swedish legislation and public reports and is currently focused on questions about how ideas about the family are reproduced within contemporary feminist politics and research.

Kristina Fjelkestam is a Professor in Gender Studies at Stockholm University and has a PhD in Comparative Literature. Her research profile is based in feminist cultural theory with a historical focus. She is currently interested in the research field of queer temporality studies, which combines queer theory with critical historiography and theory of history.

Ylva Gustafsson is a Postdoctoral Researcher and teacher in Philosophy at Åbo Academy university. Her research focuses on philosophical questions related to healthcare, psychology, emotions and interpersonal understanding. She is currently working on the project "On justice and the shifting meaning of person-centered care", funded by the Ella and Georg Ehrnrooth foundation.

Guðbjörg Rannveig Jóhannesdóttir is an Associate Professor at the Iceland University of the Arts. She holds a PhD in philosophy from the University of Iceland. Her thesis *Icelandic Landscapes: Beauty and the Aesthetic in Environmental Decision-making* discusses the meaning and values that are derived from aesthetic experiences of landscapes and the role of such values in environmental decision-making. Her research centers on environmental ethics, phenomenology and aesthetics. Her current research focuses on human-environment/body-landscape relations and processes, and their role in human thinking and understanding.

Zlatana Knezevic is an Assistant Professor at Dalarna University in Sweden. Her background is in Gender Studies and she holds a PhD in social work. Her research interests link to child welfare and intersecting injustices in childhoods as well as young people's health activism. Her research crosses disciplinary boundaries in the social sciences and humanities, typically by using postcolonial feminist theory, critical childhood studies and anthropology as inspiration.

Helgard Mahrdt holds a PhD. in German Literature from the University of Tromsø and a cand.philol. in Philosophy from the University of Oslo. Currently she is a guest researcher at the Centre of Gender Research at the University of Oslo. Hannah Arendt is in the center of her research, publications and lectures. She co-edited several books on Hannah Arendt, among the latest are "The Indispensability of Complete Openness for the Future of Humanitas: Hannah Arendt & Karl Jaspers in and on Free Communication, Conversation and Correspondence" (2018), "Hannah Arendt and the Notion of Plurality" (2018), "Responding to wrong doing" (2022) and "Hannah Arendt om kjærlighet, vennskap og politikk" (2022).

Synne Myrebøe works as a postdoctoral researcher at the Center for Foundations of Education at the University of Vienna with a project on the configurations of Intellectual History and History of Ideas in the UK, Norway and Sweden since 1989. She holds a PhD in History and Education from Umeå University and her research interest concerns philosophy of education, political/feminist philosophy and the intellectual history of higher education.

Cecilia Rosengren is Associate Professor in History of Ideas and Science at the University of Gothenburg. Her research comprises Early Modern intellectual and cultural history, with a special interest in women philosophers. She has written on Anne Conway, Margaret Cavendish and Emelie du Châtelet. Among her latest publications are "The wilderness of Allaert van Everdingen – experience and representation of the north in the age of the baroque" (2020) and the anthology *Changing Satire. Transformation and Continuities in Europe, 1600–1830* (2022).

Claudia Lindén is Professor in Comparative Literature at Södertörn University in Stockholm, Sweden. Her research interests include 19th-century Scandinavian literature, Gothic literature, animal studies, gender studies, queer theory, theory of history. Lindén is currently working on the animal studies-project "Bear traces: A study of the bear in national romantic literature around the Baltic Sea."

Tuija Pulkkinen is a Professor of Gender Studies at the University of Helsinki. Her research is in the area of feminist theory and philosophy, political theory, and the history of concepts including work on German idealism, on the 20th-century French thought (Derrida, Foucault), and on the politics of philosophy in contemporary feminist theory. She is the author of several books, among the latest is the special issue 'Vulnerability' within Contemporary Feminist Politics and Theory (2020), and the Palgrave Handbook on German Idealism and Feminist Philosophy (2022). She is also the editor-in-chief of the journal Redescriptions. Political Thought, Conceptual History and Feminist Theory.

Valgerður Pálmadóttir holds a PhD in History of Ideas from Umeå University. She is currently a Postdoctoral Researcher at the Institute of History at the University of Iceland. Her research interests include the relationship between political activism and ideas about power, identities and liberation in a historical context, and the relationship between social movements and historical change. Pálmadóttir's current research project is about women's strikes as a political strategy.

Erik Poulsen holds an MA in Aesthetics from Södertörn University. He is currently an independent researcher and literary critic and specialises in German literature. For several years, he has been working as an editor for *tydningen,* a Swedish literary journal on Scandinavian poetry and art criticism. He is currently writing a book about psychoanalysis and queer theory.

Naomi Scheman is a Professor Emerita of Philosophy and Gender, Women, and Sexuality Studies at the University of Minnesota. She has held visiting positions at the University of Gothenburg and Umeå University. She has published work in feminist epistemology, among the co-edited *Feminist Interpretations of Wittgenstein.* Her more recent work brings feminist and relational epistemology and metaphysics into conversation with issues of political concern, including police and prison abolition, and with efforts to fundamentally rethink research universities to be focused less on generic "excellence" and more on the problems and challenges that arise from the particular local and global relationships in which they are embedded.

Johanna Sjöstedt holds double MA-degrees in History of Ideas and Gender Studies from the University of Gothenburg. Specializing in the history of feminist philosophy and theory, she is interested in how notions of gender, time, and history intersect in feminist theory and how feminist theory transforms modern notions of temporality and change. Her work has appeared in *NORA, Slagmark,* and *Ideas in history.* She is also the editor of the anthology *Vad är en kvinna? Språk, materialitet, situation* (Daidalos, 2021).

Fanny Söderbäck is an Associate Professor of Philosophy at Södertörn University and the co-founder and co-director of the Kristeva Circle. She holds a PhD in Philosophy from the New School for Social Research and has held positions at Siena College and DePaul University. She is the author of *Revolutionary Time: On Time and Difference in Kristeva and Irigaray* (SUNY Press, 2019). She has edited *Feminist Readings of Antigone* (SUNY Press, 2010) and is a co-editor of the volume *Undutiful Daughters: New Directions in Feminist Thought and Practice* (Palgrave Macmillan, 2012). She is currently working on a book project on Italian feminist philosopher Adriana Cavarero (forthcoming with SUNY Press).

Sagy Watemberg Izraeli is a cotutelle Doctoral Researcher in the Faculty of Law at Bar-Ilan University and in the Study of Religions at Åbo Akademi University, having received her BA in Philosophy, Politics, and Economics from the Hebrew University of Jerusalem. Her doctoral research asks what defines membership in religious communities in multicultural legislation, from the internal perspective of the communities themselves? Her additional interests include social epistemology, socio-legal studies, theories of gender, Jewish law, religious hermeneutics, and inter-religious feminism.

Jorunn Økland is a Professor of Gender Studies at the Humanities, and a Professor II, Faculty of Theology, U. of Oslo (2016–2021). Director at the Norwegian Institute at Athens (2000–2008); Director, Centre for Gender Research, U. of Oslo; Senior Lecturer, Faculty of Arts, U. of Sheffield. Author/editor of 9 books, among them Marxist Feminist Criticism of the Bible (2008). Latest publication: "Women's Bravery: Jane Dieulafoy, Queen Parysatis, and the Reception of the Persian Empire in 19th Century France," in The Hunt for Ancient Israel: Essays in Honour of Diana V. Edelman Ed.C. Shafer-Elliott et al.

SÖDERTÖRN STUDIES IN INTELLECTUAL
AND CULTURAL HISTORY

2. Anders Burman & Shamal Kaveh (eds.),
*Demokratin och det politiska. Essäer om samtidens
politiska tillstånd*, 2020.

3. Anders Burman & Tore Lund (eds.), *Efter
Viktor Rydberg. Receptions historiska studier*,
2020.

4. Anders Burman & Joakim Landahl (eds.), *1968
och pedagogiken*, 2020.

5. Anders Burman, Marcia Sá Cavalcante
Schuback & Synne Myrebøe (eds.), *En plats för
tänkande. Essäer om universitetet och filosofin*,
2020.

6. Crister Skoglund, *Kreativitet, fantasi och
bildning. Idéhistoriska essäer*, 2021.

7. Anders Burman & Sven-Olov Wallenstein
(eds.), *Benjamin Höijer. Metafysik, estetik,
historia*, 2021.

8. Anders Burman, Joakim Landahl & Daniel
Lövheim (eds.), *Moderna pedagogiska utopier*,
2021.

9. Hjalmar Falk, My Klockar Linder & Petter
Tistedt (eds.), *Perspektiv på politisk idéhistoria*,
2023.

10. Synne Myrebøe, Valgerður Pálmadóttir &
Johanna Sjöstedt (eds.) *Feminist Philosophy – Time,
History and the Transformation of Thought*, 2023.

Series editors are Anders Burman and Leif
Runefelt.

Södertörns högskola | publications@sh.se

www.ingramcontent.com/pod-product-compliance
Lightning Source LLC
LaVergne TN
LVHW042345190726
843493LV00005B/927